Law, Society, and Culture in the M

Focusing on the Maghrib in the perio ılyzes the application of Islamic law through the role of the *muftī*. To unravel the subtlety and sophistication of the law, he considers six actual cases which took place in the Marīnid period on subjects as diverse as paternity, fornication, water rights, family endowments, the slander of the Prophet and disinheritance. The source for these disputes are *fatwā*s issued by the *muftī*s, which the author uses to situate each case in its precise historical context and to interpret the principles, rules and norms of Islamic law. In so doing he demonstrates that, contrary to popular images and stereotypes, *qāḍī*s and *muftī*s were in fact dedicated to reasoned thought and argument, and highly sensitive to the manner in which law, society and culture interacted with, and shaped, one another. The book represents a groundbreaking approach to a complex field. It is certain to be read by students of Islamic law and by anyone with an interest in traditional Muslim societies.

DAVID S. POWERS is Professor of Arabic and Islamic Studies at Cornell University. He is the author of *Studies in Qur'an and Hadith: The Formation of the Islamic Law of Inheritance* (1986), co-editor of *Islamic Legal Interpretation: Muftis and their Fatwas* (1996), and editor of the journal *Islamic Law and Society*.

CAMBRIDGE STUDIES IN ISLAMIC CIVILIZATION

In memory of my nephew
Benjamin Louis Powers
12 December 2000 – 27 January 2001

Law, Society, and Culture in the Maghrib, 1300–1500

DAVID S. POWERS
Cornell University

CAMBRIDGE
UNIVERSITY PRESS

CAMBRIDGE UNIVERSITY PRESS
Cambridge, New York, Melbourne, Madrid, Cape Town, Singapore, São Paulo, Delhi

Cambridge University Press
The Edinburgh Building, Cambridge CB2 8RU, UK

Published in the United States of America by Cambridge University Press, New York

www.cambridge.org
Information on this title: www.cambridge.org/9780521120593

First published 2002
This digitally printed version 2009

A catalogue record for this publication is available from the British Library

National Library of Australia Cataloguing in Publication data

Powers, David Stephan.
Law, society and culture in the Maghrib, 1300–1500.
Bibliography.
Includes index.
ISBN 0 521 81691 2.
1. Islamic law – Africa, North – History – To 1500.
2. Fatwas. 3. Africa, North – History – 647–1517. I. Title.
(Series: Cambridge studies in Islamic civilization).
340.590961

ISBN 978-0-521-81691-5 hardback
ISBN 978-0-521-12059-3 paperback

Contents

Figures and Tables

Preface

Work on this book began in the academic year 1991–92 when a grant from the National Endowment for the Humanities provided me with release time from teaching to conduct a survey of the *Kitāb al-Miʿyār* of Aḥmad al-Wansharīsī. During that year, I prepared draft translations of *fatwā*s that contain transcriptions of legal documents. These translations became the basis of courses on Islamic law that I have taught at Cornell in subsequent years, both in the College of Arts and Sciences and the Law School. I thank the students who participated in these courses for their questions, comments, criticisms, and insights, many of which have helped to shape the final form of the book.

While on sabbatical leave at the Hebrew University in the academic year 1996–97, I taught a graduate-level seminar on Islamic law in which we read several *fatwā*s in their Arabic originals. Participants in the seminar included Haim Gerber, Aharon Layish, Oded Peri, and Ron Shaham. I could not have asked for a more stimulating intellectual environment in which to work out the meaning and interpretation of the texts that we read together.

A grant from the American Institute for Maghribi Studies made it possible for me to visit Morocco from December 1996 to January 1997, to examine manuscripts of the *Miʿyār* in the Bibliothèque Générale, and to visit the village of Zgane in the Middle Atlas Mountains, near Sefrou.

I thank my friend and colleague Baber Johansen for nominating me as *Directeur d'études-associé* at the Ecole des Hautes Etudes en Sciences Sociales for the period between 25 December 1998 and 21 January 1999, during which I presented several of the cases to his seminar on Islamic law.

I have presented earlier versions of individual chapters at workshops, seminars, and conferences both in the United States and abroad. Chapter one was presented at the workshop on Gender, Family and the Courts, co-organized by Leslie Peirce and myself, Cornell University, 15–17 October 1993. Chapter two was presented at the seminar, The Public Sphere in Muslim Society, organized by Shmuel Eisenstadt and Nehemia Lev Zion, Van Leer Institute, 17 April 1997; at the workshop on Family and the Social Order, organized by Ted Fram and Nimrod Hurvitz, Ben-Gurion University, Israel, 9 June 1998; at the Mellon Seminar on *Fatwas* in Islam: Text, Subtext, Hidden Agenda, organized by John R. Willis,

Princeton University, 13 March 1998; and at the conference on Law and the State, organized by Yohannan Friedman and Nurit Tsafrir, Institute for Advanced Study, Jerusalem, 12 January 2000. Chapter three was presented at the workshop on The Dynamics of Legal Change in Muslim Societies, organized by Aharon Layish and Ron Shaham, The Hebrew University, 19 March 1997; at the Workshop on Evidence in Islamic Law, organized by Bernard Haykel, New York University, 2–3 April 1999; and at the Summer Academy of the Berlin Working Group on Modernity and Islam, Notions of Law and Order in Muslim Societies, organized by Güdrün Kraemer, Casablanca, Morocco, 13–25 September 1999. Chapter four was presented at the annual meeting of the American Oriental Society, Boston, March, 1992; at the Conference on Law and Praxis, organized by Engin Akarli and Cornell Fleischer, Washington University, May 1992; and at the XXII Medieval Workshop, University of British Columbia, 13–14 November 1992. Chapter five was presented at the workshop on Approaches to Islamic Law, organized by Petra Sijpesteijn and Orit Bashkin, Princeton University, 7–8 May 2000. Chapter six was presented at the Symposium on Islamic Law, organized by Gerhard Bowering, Yale University, September 1993; and at the Forum in Memory of Professor Baneth, Hebrew University, 26 February 1997. I thank the organizers of these events for their generosity and hospitality and the participants for their valuable comments on work in progress.

I am grateful to friends and colleagues who read draft versions of individual chapters and offered valuable comments and criticisms: Senwan Akhtar, Richard Antoun, Omar Benmira, John Bowen, Patricia Crone, Maribel Fierro, Peter Hennigan, Baber Johansen, Jonathan Katz, Timur Kuran, Aharon Layish, Paul Milliman, Martha Mundy, Aḥmad Nāṭūr, Richard Polenberg, Buni Rehav, Lawrence Rosen, Everett Rowson, Ron Shaham, Susan Spectorsky, Justin Stearns, Dan Varisco, and Francisco Vidal Castro. I thank Wael Hallaq, Munther Yunis, and Qadi Aḥmad Nāṭūr for their assistance with difficult Arabic texts.

Special thanks to my friend and colleague Brinkley Messick, who read the entire book in manuscript and offered detailed suggestions for improvement; to the two anonymous readers of the manuscript who offered important suggestions for improving the book; and to my friend and long-time editor Penny Beebe, who has read nearly every word that I have ever written and helped me to sharpen my thinking and polish my prose.

An earlier version of chapter one appeared in *Islamic Law and Society*, 1:3 (1995). Chapter six draws on a book chapter and an article: "The Art of the Legal Opinion: al-Wansharisi on *Tawlīj*," in *Islamic Legal Interpretation: Muftis and their Fatwas*, ed. Muhammad Khalid Masud, Brinkley Messick, and David S. Powers (Cambridge, MA.: Harvard University Press, 1996), 98–115; and "The Art of the Judicial Opinion: On *Tawlīj* in Fifteenth-Century Tunis," *Islamic Law and Society*, 5:3 (1998), 359–81. This material is reproduced here with the permission of the publishers.

Finally, I thank my wife, Jane, and my children, Kate, Sarah, and Andrew, for their love, support, encouragement, and understanding.

Introduction

Drawing upon the legal rules and principles either stated in the Qur'ān and the prophetic *sunna* or capable of being derived from these two sources by analogical reasoning (*qiyās*) or juristic consensus (*ijmā*ʿ), Muslim jurists have constructed the large and impressive corpus of legal rules and principles known as *fiqh*.[1]

Since the last quarter of the nineteenth century, western scholars have devoted considerable attention to the study of *fiqh* and its relevance to everyday life. An important pioneer in this enterprise was the Dutch Orientalist Snouck Hurgronje, who argued that the *fiqh* was not a system of law, strictly speaking, but a system of religious norms that seeks to promote an ideal society of believers by regulating the moral and ethical behavior of Muslims. The practical relevance of *fiqh*, Snouck Hurgronje said, was applied only to the areas of ritual law, personal status, inheritance and endowments.[2] A generation later the French Orientalist G.H. Bousquet characterized the *fiqh* as a system of religious duties in which human acts are classified as either obligatory, recommended, neutral, disapproved of, or forbidden.[3] These views dominated western scholarship on Islamic law for much of the twentieth century.

Writing at about the same time as Snouck Hurgronje, the Hungarian scholar Ignaz Goldziher advanced the idea that the *fiqh* was a system of law, albeit a "religious" law. Another scholar, the German sociologist Max Weber, characterized the *fiqh* as a "sacred law" that was irrational in two important respects. It was *procedurally* irrational because the tools employed to determine its legal norms (that is, oaths, curses, and the appeal to divine authority) were not subject to human reason; and it was *substantively* irrational because *qāḍī*s, or judges, decided cases according to ethical, political, personal or utilitarian considerations, rather than an established body of legal doctrine. This combination of procedural

1 Bernard Weiss, *The Search for God's Law: Islamic Jurisprudence in the Writings of Sayf al-Dīn al-Āmidī* (Salt Lake City: University of Utah Press, 1992). On the sources of Islamic law (*uṣūl al-fiqh*), see also Mohammad Hashim Kamali, *Principles of Islamic Jurisprudence* (Cambridge: Islamic Texts Society, 1991); Wael B. Hallaq, *A History of Islamic Legal Theories: An introduction to Sunnī* uṣūl al-fiqh (London: Cambridge University Press, 1997).

2 C. Snouck Hurgronje, "De la Nature du droit Musulman," in *Selected Works of C. Snouck Hurgronje*, ed. G.H. Bousquet and J. Schacht (Leiden: E.J. Brill, 1957), 256–63.

3 *EI*², s.v. ʿIbādāt.

and substantive irrationality gave rise to the term "*kadijustiz*" and to the image that has dominated the popular perceptions of Islamic law to this day.[4]

Our current understanding of the nature of Islamic law owes much to the work of another German scholar, Joseph Schacht. Like Snouck Hurgronje and Bousquet, Schacht regarded the *fiqh* as "an all-embracing body of religious duties."[5] At the same time, however, he argued that the *fiqh* is a rational and coherent legal system in which individuals possess rights that make it possible for them to pursue claims against one another in the world of social relations.[6] It was Schacht who placed the study of Islamic law into an historical perspective, constructing a rigorous methodology for tracing its development from the time of the Prophet until the ʿAbbāsid period.[7] The year 287/900 was, for Schacht, a major watershed that marks the boundary between the dynamism of the formative period and the increasing rigidity of the classical and post-classical periods. He associated this watershed with the "closing of the door of *ijtihād*," or independent reasoning.

> By the beginning of the fourth century of the hijra (about AD 900) ... the point had been reached when the scholars of all schools felt that all essential questions had been thoroughly discussed and finally settled, and a consensus gradually established itself to the effect that from that time onwards no one might be deemed to have the necessary qualifications for independent reasoning in law, and that all future activity would have to be confined to the explanation, application, and, at the most, interpretation of the doctrine as it had been laid down once and for all. This 'closing of the door of *ijtihād*', as it was called, amounted to the demand for *taḳlīd*, a term ... which ... came to mean the unquestioning acceptance of the doctrines of the established schools and authorities.[8]

For Schacht, it was the transition from a regime of *ijtihād* to a regime of *taqlīd* that explains the "essential rigidity" of Islamic law since the fourth/tenth century and the fact that Islamic law purportedly "lost touch" with subsequent political, social, economic and technological developments.[9] Schacht also knew that Muslim civilization flourished for centuries after the "closing of the door of *ijtihād*." How was it possible for this civilization to retain its dynamism when the legal system according to which it operated suffered from "*ankylose*"?[10] Schacht acknowledged that Muslim scholars living under a regime of *taqlīd* might be as creative as their predecessors who lived under a regime of *ijtihād*, although he qualified this assertion with the caveat that the creativity of scholars living under a regime of

[4] See Max Weber, *Wirtschaft und Gesellschaft* (2nd edn 1925), translated by Edward Shils as *Max Weber on Law in Economy and Society* (Cambridge: Harvard University Press, 1959), xlviii–xlix, lv; Bryan S. Turner, *Weber and Islam: A critical study* (London: Routledge and Kegan Paul, 1974), 107–21, at 109; Baber Johansen, *Contingency in a Sacred Law: Legal and Ethical Norms in the Muslim* Fiqh (Leiden: E.J. Brill, 1999), 42 ff.

[5] Joseph Schacht, *An Introduction to Islamic Law* (Oxford: The Clarendon Press, 1964), 1.

[6] Johansen, *Contingency in a Sacred Law*, 51 ff.

[7] *The Origins of Muhammadan Jurisprudence* (Oxford: The Clarendon Press, 1950).

[8] Schacht, *An Introduction to Islamic Law*, 71.

[9] Ibid., 75.

[10] Joseph Schacht, "Classicisme, traditionalisme et ankylose dans la loi religieuse de l'Islam," in *Classicisme et déclin culturel dans l'histoire de l'Islam*, ed. R. Brunschvig and G. von Grunebaum (Paris: Maisonneuve et Larose, 1977), 141–61, at 141.

taqlīd would have been constrained by the "limits" established by the "nature" of the *sharīʿa*.[11] But this begs the question: what are these limits and how is it possible for jurists operating within the constraints of a rigid and unchanging system of law to express legal creativity?

To the best of my knowledge, Schacht never directly and fully addressed the tension between his views of the rigidity of classical Islamic law and the creativity of Muslim jurists living after the year 900. But he was clear about the mechanism by which this tension might be resolved. He wrote, "New sets of facts constantly arose in life, and they had to be mastered and moulded with the traditional tools provided by legal science."[12] These tools, and the methods by which they might be employed to deal with new facts and social change, were the cultural capital of the *muftī*, a specialist in the law who is qualified to issue an expert legal opinion, or *fatwā*, on points of legal doctrine. The fatwās issued by individual muftīs were often put into collections; if the decision of a muftī came to be regarded as correct by subsequent scholars, it would be incorporated into the doctrinal lawbooks of the school to which he belonged. Thus, the doctrinal development of Islamic law in the period following the closing of the door of *ijtihād* owed much to the work of the muftī.[13]

If we want to understand how Islamic law functioned in practice after the fourth/tenth century, we would do well to examine the activity of the muftī, a task that is still in its scholarly infancy.[14] In the present study, I seek to make a small contribution to our understanding of the work of the muftī and its relation to the application of Islamic law in a particular time and place: the Mālikī muftī in the Islamic West in the period 1300 to 1500 CE. On the following pages, I will undertake a close reading of a series of fatwās that were issued in the Islamic West during this period in an attempt to answer the following questions: Was the application of Islamic law limited to the areas of ritual law, personal status, inheritance, and endowments, or did it extend to other areas? What was the nature of the work of the qāḍī and the muftī, and how did the work of one complement that of the other? Did qāḍīs issue their judgments on the basis of ethics, politics, personal expediency, or utility or on the basis of Islamic legal doctrine? Or did they perhaps issue their judgments on the basis of a combination of extra-legal and legal considerations? Is there any evidence of creativity in the opinions of the muftīs? If so, what is the nature of that creativity? How was the office of the muftī regulated? How effective a mechanism was Mālikī legal doctrine in resolving disputes and regulating society? What was the relationship between the legal system and the state?

[11] Schacht, *An Introduction to Islamic Law*, 71–3.

[12] Ibid., 73.

[13] Ibid., 74–5; see now Wael B. Hallaq, "From *Fatwās* to *Furūʿ*: Growth and Change in Islamic Substantive Law," *Islamic Law and Society*, 1:1 (1995), 29–65.

[14] See now *Islamic Legal Interpretation: Muftis and Their Fatwas*, ed. Muhammad Khalid Masud, Brinkley Messick and David S. Powers (Cambridge, MA.: Harvard University Press, 1996). For the Ottoman period, see Judith E. Tucker, *In the House of the Law: Gender and Islamic Law in Ottoman Syria and Palestine* (Berkeley: University of California Press, 1998); Haim Gerber, *Islamic Law and Culture, 1600–1840* (Leiden: E.J. Brill, 1999).

al-Wansharīsī and the *Miʿyār*

The fatwās to be analyzed in this book are all found in the *Kitāb al-Miʿyār* of Aḥmad al-Wansharīsī, who was born in 834/1430–31 in Jabal Wansharīs (Ouarsenis), a range of high mountains in today's western Algeria.[15] Political instability forced his family to move to Tlemcen, the capital of the Zayyānid dynasty, in all likelihood when Aḥmad was five or six years old. In Tlemcen al-Wansharīsī studied the Qur'ān, Arabic grammar, and, eventually, Islamic law with distinguished scholars. After completing his studies, he began to teach, issue fatwās, and write juridical treatises – at least five treatises by 871/1466–67. A key turning point in al-Wansharīsī's life occurred in 874/1469, when he was forty years old. For reasons that are obscure, he incurred the wrath of the Sulṭān of the Banū ʿAbd al-Wād, Muḥammad IV, who ordered the plundering of his house. Leaving everything behind, including his books, al-Wansharīsī fled to Fez, where the Waṭṭāsids recently had taken over as regents for the Marīnids. Adopting Fez as his permanent residence, al-Wansharīsī continued his activities as a muftī, teacher, and writer. During his first decade in Fez he wrote four additional legal treatises and by 890/1485 was one of the city's most distinguished jurists.[16]

As a refugee scholar, al-Wansharīsī was dependent on the excellent private libraries of Fez, one of which belonged to his former student, Muḥammad b. al-Gardīs, scion of a family that had been involved in Fāsī scholarship and politics since the time of the Idrīsids (172–314/789–926).[17] Over the course of several centuries, the al-Gardīs family had assembled a magnificent collection of precious Andalusian and Maghribī manuscripts that was especially strong in Mālikī substantive law and jurisprudence. Ibn al-Gardīs opened the doors of the library to his master, giving him unrestricted access to the manuscripts. As al-Wansharīsī moved through the library, he came across thousands of fatwās that had been issued in the Islamic West in the period between approximately 391/1000 and

15 His full name is Abū al-ʿAbbās Aḥmad b. Yaḥyā b. Muḥammad b. ʿAbd al-Wāḥid b. ʿAlī al-Wansharīsī. On his life and work, see the indispensable articles of Francisco Vidal Castro, "Aḥmad al-Wanšarīsī (m. 914/1508). Principales Aspectos de su Vida," *al-Qanṭara*, XII (1991), 315–52; idem, "Las obras de Aḥmad al-Wanšarīsī (m. 914/1508). Inventario analítico," *Anaquel de Estudios Árabes*, III (1992), 73–112; idem, "El *Miʿyār* de al-Wanšarīsī (m. 914/1508). I: Fuentes, manuscritos, ediciones, traducciones," *Miscelánea de Estudio Árabes y Hebráicos*, XLII–XLIII (1993–94), 317–61; idem, "El *Miʿyār* de al-Wanšarīsī (m. 914/1508). II: Contenido," *Miscelánea de Estudio Árabes y Hebráicos*, 44 (1995), 213–46. Cf. Mohamed b. A. Benchekroun, *La vie intellectuelle marocaine sous les Mérinides et les Waṭṭāsides (XIIIe XIVe XVe XVIe siècles* (Rabat, 1974), 395–401. For a convenient summary of the contents of the *Miʿyār*, see Vincent Lagardère, *Histoire et Société en Occident Musulman au Moyen Age: Analyse du Miʿyār d'al-Wanṣarīsī* (Madrid, 1995); on the problematic and disturbing genesis of this book, see the review of Francisco Vidal Castro in *Al-Qanṭara*, 17 (1996), 246–54.

16 Vidal Castro, "Aḥmad al-Wanšarīsī (m. 914/1508). Principales Aspectos de su Vida," 320–9. For a detailed discussion of al-Wansharīsī's literary *oeuvre*, see idem, "Las obras de Aḥmad al-Wanšarīsī," 73 ff.; cf. Benchekroun, *La vie intellectuelle marocaine*, 398–400.

17 Abū ʿAbdallāh Muḥammad b. Muḥammad b. al-Gardīs al-Taghlibī (d. 897 or 899/1491–92 or 1493–94). For biographical details, see *Miʿyār*, introduction, iv; Vidal Castro, "Aḥmad al-Wanšarīsī (m. 914/1508). Principales Aspectos de su Vida," 333.

890/1495. These fatwās represented nearly half a millennium of Mālikī legal activity, which, with regard to the Andalusian material, was drawing to a fast and dramatic close.

I imagine that it was on one of al-Wansharīsī's visits to the library that he conceived the idea of compiling a single, integrated collection of fatwās. Perhaps this decision was motivated by his awareness of the impending defeat of the Naṣrids of Granada (which would occur in 897/1492) and by a desire to preserve an important aspect of the Andalusian cultural heritage. Perhaps he was following a new trend in Mālikī legal scholarship; at least two other collections of fatwās issued by various muftīs had appeared during the middle third of the ninth/fifteenth century.[18] Certainly, he was inspired by his awareness of the potential usefulness of such a collection for contemporary judges and jurists and, perhaps, for posterity.

Some time around 890/1485, al-Wansharīsī began his project. With the permission of Ibn al-Gardīs, he removed from the library several manuscripts, or fascicles thereof, and loaded his cargo on a donkey. He then made his way through the narrow and winding streets of Fez to his house, where he guided the donkey through the entrance and into the courtyard, unloaded his cargo, and arranged the materials into two piles. Once inside the house, the scholar would remove his outer cloak, exposing a wool garment (*qashshāba*) fastened with a leather belt that left his bald pate uncovered. With an inkwell hanging from his belt, a writing instrument in one hand, and a piece of paper in the other, he would walk back and forth between the two piles, selecting individual fatwās for transcription.[19] One imagines that the toils of transcription were eased by his interest in the texts, which gave access to the litigants' lives and to the jurists' wisdom, against which he tested and honed his own legal skills. In this manner he toiled, at what pace we do not know, for eleven years.[20] In the colophon to the finished work, al-Wansharīsī indicates that he completed the text on Sunday, 28 Shawwāl 901 (10 July 1496).[21] But he continued to make corrections and revisions and to add new material until his death in 914/1508, nearly a quarter of a century after beginning the project.[22] The preface to the *Miʿyār* contains the following brief statement of purpose:

18 See al-Burzūlī (d. 841/1438), *Jāmiʿ al-masāʾil mimmā nazala min al-qaḍāyā bi'l-muftīn wa'l-ḥukkām*, and Abū Zakariyāʾ Yaḥyā b. Mūsā b. ʿĪsā al-Maghīlī (d. 883/1478), *al-Durar al-maknūnā fī nawāzil Māzūna.*

19 The use of "Rūmī" paper was itself the subject of a fatwā issued by Abū ʿAbdallāh Ibn Marzūq (d. 842/1439). See al-Wansharīsī, *Miʿyār*, vol. 1, 75–104. I hope to analyze this fatwā in a subsequent publication.

20 Upon the death of Ibn al-Gardīs in either 897/1491–92 or 899/1493–94, al-Wansharīsī presumably secured permission for the continued use of the library from his former student's heirs.

21 Ibid., vol. 12, 395.

22 Although the private library of Ibn al-Gardīs was al-Wansharīsī's primary source for the fatwās of al-Andalus and the far Maghrib, it was not his only source. Other texts, in other libraries, provided him with fatwās from the Near and Middle Maghrib, Ifrīqiya, and Tlemcen. Especially important in this regard were the *Masāʾil* of al-Burzūlī and *al-Durar al-maknūnā fī nawāzil Māzūna* by al-Maghīlī (see above, note 18). On the sources of the *Miʿyār*, see Vidal Castro, "El *Miʿyār* de al-Wanšarīsī (m. 914/1508). I: Fuentes, manuscritos, ediciones, traducciones," 323–36.

> ... This is a book that I have entitled *al-Miʿyār al-Muʿrib wa'l-jāmiʿ al-mughrib ʿan fatāwī ʿulamāʾ Ifrīqiyā wa'l-Andalus wa'l-Maghrib* [The Clear Measure and the Extraordinary Collection of the Judicial Opinions of the Scholars of Ifrīqiya, al-Andalus, and the Maghrib].[23] In it I have assembled responses [issued by] modern and ancient [scholars], those which are the most difficult to find in their sources and to extract from their hiding places on account of their being scattered and dispersed and because their locations and the access to them are obscure. [I have assembled the book] in the hope that [it] will be of general utility and that the [heavenly] reward that results from it will be augmented. I have organized it in accordance with the categories of the law in order to facilitate its use by whoever examines it, and I have specified the names of the muftīs – except on rare occasions. I hope that God – praised be He – will designate it as one of the means for obtaining happiness and as a road leading to a happy outcome and increase. For He – may He be magnified and exalted – is the one from whom one inquires with regard to the most abundant reward and guidance towards the truth.

The voices that dominate the remainder of the text are those of hundreds of muftīs who lived in the Islamic West between 1000 and 1500 CE. Only on rare occasions does the reader discern the presence of the compiler and copyist, as, for instance, when al-Wansharīsī makes certain editorial remarks relating to the identification of documents that he has transcribed, offers a brief comment on a fatwā with which he disagrees, or inserts one of his own fatwās into the text (as he does twenty-seven times, by my count). In terms of modern notions of authorship, al-Wansharīsī's subordination of his own voice is striking when one considers the enormous labor – both mental and physical – involved in the compilation of the *Miʿyār*.[24]

The size, geographical range, and chronological parameters of the *Miʿyār* set it apart from most other fatwā collections. Although the individual responses in the lithograph and printed edition of the *Miʿyār* are not numbered, I estimate that there are approximately 6,000 fatwās in the text.[25] Muḥammad Ḥajjī, the modern editor of the *Miʿyār*, has compared the collection to a bottomless ocean that easily swallows anyone who penetrates its depths, observing that it was the legal text that he feared most as a student.[26] Further, whereas fatwā collections compiled prior to the ninth/fifteenth century generally incorporate the relatively limited output of a single muftī living in a particular time and place, the *Miʿyār* contains fatwās issued

[23] Note the minor discrepancy between the title that al-Wansharīsī gives to his book and its modern title (*ahl* versus *ʿulamāʾ*). For a discussion of variants in the title, see ibid., 321.

[24] Lithograph, 12 vols, Fez, 1314–15 [1897–98]; new edition, 13 vols, Rabat, Ministry of Culture and Religious Affairs, 1401–03 [1981–83]. The lithograph was produced on the basis of five manuscripts by a committee of eight jurists under the supervision of Ibn al-ʿAbbās al-Būʿazzāwī. The Rabat edition is essentially a transcription of the lithograph produced by a committee of seven scholars under the supervision of Muḥammad Ḥajjī. It contains many typographical errors and should be used with caution. All references to the *Miʿyār* in this book are to the Rabat edition. For further details on the publication history of the *Miʿyār*, see Vidal Castro, "El *Miʿyār* de al-Wanšarīsī (m. 914/1508). I: Fuentes, manuscritos, ediciones, traducciones," 344–7.

[25] I arrived at this figure by muliplying the number of fatwās that I have determined to be included in volume seven (480) by the total number of volumes in the collection (twelve).

[26] Wansharīsī, *Miʿyār*, vol. 1, 7:D.

by hundreds of muftīs who lived in the major towns and cities of Ifrīqiya, the Maghrib, and al-Andalus over nearly half a millennium.[27]

As al-Wansharīsī indicates in his preface, one of the underlying motivations of his project was to create a collection of judicial opinions that would be of practical use to judges. A judge who was confronted with a difficult case might want to consult a fatwā issued previously in a similar case; this judge would have been interested in the underlying legal issues of the earlier case, not its specific human details. It was for this reason that fatwās such as those included in the *Miʿyār* generally underwent a process of editing and abridgement. W. Hallaq, describing this process, distinguishes between primary fatwās and secondary fatwās. A primary fatwā is one that mentions the names of the litigants, the location of the dispute, and the date of specific events; it may also include a transcription of one or more legal documents relating to the case. These details were eliminated when the primary fatwā was transformed into a secondary fatwā. This process involved two steps: (1) the stripping away (*tajrīd*) of concrete historical details such as the names of people and places, the omission of words and phrases that were not of direct legal relevance, and the omission of documents attached to or embedded in a primary fatwā; (2) the reduction of the length of the fatwā through summary (*talkhīṣ*). As a result of this two-step process, a narrative dealing with a specific and historically contextualized situation was transformed into an abstract case that refers to one or more nameless individuals living in an unspecified place at an undetermined time.[28]

The following *istiftāʾ*, or request for a fatwā, addressed to Sīdī Miṣbāḥ al-Yāliṣūtī (d. 750/1349), is an example of a fatwā that has undergone the process of editing and abridgement:

> He was asked about a man who died leaving a specific number of heirs, according to the witnesses who testified on their behalf. Then, some time after [the man's] death, a ruddy-face youth claimed that he was a child (*walad*) of the aforementioned deceased by a concubine named So-and-So who [had served] in his presence; and that [the deceased] had acknowledged this [fact] during his lifetime. However, no testimonial evidence was given with respect to the [alleged] acknowledgement, except that witnesses testified on behalf [of the youth], on the basis of hearsay knowledge (*samāʿ*) – the duration of which was not specified as being long-standing – that the claimant was a son of the deceased, although [the identity of the mother] was not known; nor were they eyewitnesses [to the alleged acknowledgement]. This was established in the presence of the local qāḍī.
>
> One of the deceased's heirs countered that it had never been reported (*lam yusmaʿ min*) about his father that he had impregnated a concubine; that [such an assertion] was

[27] For mention of other fatwā collections, see Ḥajjī Khalīfa, *Kashf al-ẓunūn ʿan asāmī al-kutub wa'l-funūn*, 2 vols (Istanbul: Maarif Matbaasi, 1941–43), vol. 2, 1218–31; C. Brockelmann, *Geschichte der arabischen Litteratur* (Leiden: E.J. Brill, 1937–49), supplement III, index, s.v., *fatāwā(ī)*; Fuat Sezgin, *Geschichte des arabischen Schrifttums*, 9 vols (Leiden: E.J. Brill, 1967–), vol. 1, 393–596, passim.

[28] Hallaq, "From *Fatwās* to *Furūʿ*, 43–8.

> not widespread among the neighbors; [that his father was not known to have] affiliated the claimant to himself in terms of paternity; that [the deceased] was not known to have had a concubine with whom he had sexual intercourse [at any point in his lifetime]; and that the affiliation of the ... [claimant to the deceased] after his death was merely a result of the fact that [the claimant] was subject to his guardianship (*tawliyatihi*), together with his [true] sons. This was established on the basis of [the testimony] of witnesses.
>
> [It was also established] that ... [the female slave] who allegedly gave birth to the claimant had remained the private property of the deceased's daughter, So-and-So, who had reached puberty and attained mental discernment; and that when [the female slave] died, [she was] still the private property of [the daughter of the deceased, although in the meantime the daughter] had married [the female slave] to a man; and that she had given birth to the claimant, and that there was no knowledge of [the daughter's] having sold the two of them [viz., the mother or the child] until the time of ... [the mother's death]; [nor was there any knowledge regarding the alienation] of her child after [his mother's death] until the moment when he brought the testimony [on his behalf] ...[29]

Because the muftī to whom the *istiftāʾ* was addressed is well known, we can establish the year 750/1349 as the *terminus ad quem* of the events mentioned in the summary narrative. But we do not know the identity of the female slave, her master, her son, indeed of anyone mentioned in the *istiftāʾ*. Nor do we know the identity or status of the person who solicited the fatwā, the location of the dispute, or its chronological parameters. If this secondary fatwā were the only available evidence, we would have no contact with the lives that gave rise to this case. Many facts that would be of interest to the historian have been eliminated so as to focus on the underlying legal issues: must a widespread rumor be of long-standing duration in order to serve as probative evidence in a lawsuit; is the testimony of large numbers of non-professional witnesses acceptable; and must the witnesses have been present at the event about which they are testifying?

Fortunately, however, this secondary fatwā is not the only available evidence. One feature of the *Miʿyār* that sets it apart from other fatwā collections is that it includes a small number of primary fatwās that have escaped editing and abridgement. Some of these primary fatwās contain transcriptions of documents giving the names of the parties, the locations of transactions, and the dates of legal events. These transcriptions – precious artifacts of Islamic court practice of which little evidence has survived for the period prior to the Ottomans – include bequests, endowment deeds, gifts, oaths, acknowledgements, marriage contracts, dower agreements, deposits, appointments of agency, and judicial certifications. Al-Wansharīsī's inclusion of these documents in the *Miʿyār* demonstrates that the fatwās contained in the collection, although generally formulated in abstract and hypothetical terms, are in fact responses to real-life situations; they are not hypothetical answers to hypothetical questions, as some scholars believe to be true of this and other collections.

[29] *Miʿyār*, vol. 10, 360. Note: I have modified the text slightly for heuristic purposes.

The above-mentioned paternity dispute was the subject of a second fatwā preserved in the *Miʿyār* that, for whatever reason, was not subjected to editing and abridgement. The *istiftāʾ* mentions the name of the *mustaftī*, and it includes a transcription of several legal documents in which the names of the protagonists in the dispute are preserved, the location of the dispute is identified (albeit in general terms), and exact dates are specified. In this particular instance, the "deceased man", to whom the plaintiff sought to affiliate himself as a son, was a well-known person about whom additional information is available in other sources. The presence in the *Miʿyār* of primary fatwās such as this one opens up new avenues of investigation into the history of Islamic law in the Maghrib, making it possible to observe how the law was applied and to analyze the complex interplay between legal doctrine and social practice.

The Scope of The Book: Six Case Studies

For the greater part of the twentieth century, western students of Islamic law focused their scholarly energy and attention on *uṣūl al-fiqh* (Islamic jurisprudence) and *fiqh*.[30] It was only during the last quarter of the century that historians devoted increasing attention to fatwās in general and to the *Miʿyār* in particular, in large part because of their conviction that these texts bring us closer to social practice than other sources do – a conviction which I share. A pioneer in the study of fatwās was Hady R. Idris, who, using the *Miʿyār* as his primary source, produced a series of important studies on family law,[31] maritime commerce,[32] and the status of non-Muslims.[33] V. Lagardère has written several studies on judicial administration[34] and water law.[35] Others have written about women and property, child marriage,

[30] Schacht, *An Introduction to Islamic Law*, 209.

[31] Hady R. Idris, "Le mariage en occident musulman d'après un choix de *fatwās* médiévales extraites du *Miʿyār* d'al-Wanšarīsī," *Studia Islamica* 32 (1970), 157–67; idem, "Le mariage en occident musulman: analyse de *fatwās* médiévales extraites du "*Miʿyār*" d'al Wancharīchī," *Revue de l'Occident Musulman et de la Méditerranée*, 12 (1972), 45–62; 17 (1974), 71–105; and 25 (1978), 119–38.

[32] Idem, "Commerce maritime et *qirāḍ* en Berbérie orientale d'après un recueil de *fatwās* médiévales," *Journal of the Economic and Social History of the Orient*, 4 (1961), 225–39.

[33] Idem, "Les tributaires en Occident musulman médiéval d'après le 'Miyār' d'al Wanşarīsī," *Mélanges d'Islamologie. Volume dédié à la mémoire de Armand Abel*, 3 vols (Leiden, 1974), vol. 1, 172–96.

[34] Vincent Lagardère, "La haute judicature à l'époque almoravide en al-Andalus," *Al-Qanṭara* 7 (1986), 135–228; cf. David S. Powers, "On Judicial Review in Islamic Law," *Law & Society Review*, 26:2 (1992), 315–41.

[35] V. Lagardère, "Droit des eaux et des installations hydrauliques au Maghreb et en al-Andalus au XIe et XIIe dans le *Miʿyār* d'al-Wanşarīsī," *Les Cahiers de Tunisie*, 37–8 (1988–89), 83–122; idem, "Moulins d'occident musulman au Moyen Âge" (IXe au XVe siècles): al-Andalus," *Al-Qanṭara*, 12:1 (1991), 59–118; idem, "Agriculture et irrigation dans le district (*iqlīm*) de Vélez-Málaga. Droits des eaux et appareils hydrauliques," *Cahiers de Civilisation Médiévale*, 35:3 (1992), 213–25.

endowments (*aḥbās*), and even Christian festivals.[36] As a group, these scholars generally treat the *Miʿyār* as a source from which they "extract" information – usually from the *istiftāʾ*; this information is then processed according to the conventions and methods of historical investigation. In this manner, the *Miʿyār* has served as a useful auxiliary to one or another type of investigation.

However, these scholars have based their research largely on secondary fatwās; primary fatwās have not been the object of concentrated study. It is important to recall that the *Miʿyār* was compiled by al-Wansharīsī so that it might serve as a collection of *legal opinions*, and we must ask ourselves what approach to this corpus will be most faithful to its essential nature. The present study seeks to shift the scope and scale of the scholarly investigation of Islamic law to the scrutiny of individual cases. To this end, I have chosen for analysis seven primary fatwās (I will analyze two fatwās in chapter six). In each instance I shall attempt to treat the fatwā in its entirety, both the *istiftāʾ* and the *jawāb*, as a cultural artifact that reflects the often complex and dynamic interplay between the legal and social values of the society in which it was produced.

The six cases to be analyzed here unfolded at different times during the Marīnid period (614–869/1217–1465) and deal with a broad range of legal issues. These cases will be presented in roughly chronological order. In chapter one I will analyze the above-mentioned paternity dispute in which the son of a female slave struggled to establish his filiation to the man whom he regarded as his biological and legal father. In chapter two I examine the case of a well-known and popular jurist whose unorthodox views and un-Islamic behavior resulted in his being flogged, imprisoned, and eventually exiled. Chapter three presents a dispute over the allocation of water rights between the inhabitants of two villages in the Middle Atlas mountains, a dispute that lasted a century and a half. Chapter four focuses on wealthy proprietors who sought to ensure familial continuity when faced with the ravages of the Black Death. In chapter five I explore the character of a muftī who endeavored to restore communal harmony after it had been sundered by an ugly verbal altercation between two jurists, one a distinguished *sharīf*, the other a Berber. Finally, in chapter six I compare two cases in which a father allegedly sought to disinherit one or more of his children.

I have chosen these six cases because it is possible to situate them in their historical context and because the surviving documentation permits a case-method

[36] Maya Shatzmiller, "Women and Property Rights in al-Andalus and the Maghrib: Social Patterns and Legal Discourse," *Islamic Law and Society* (1995), 219–57; Harald Motzki, "Child Marriage in Seventeenth-Century Palestine," in *Islamic Legal Interpretation: Muftis and Their Fatwas*, 129–40; David S. Powers, "The Mālikī Family Endowment: Legal Norms and Social Practice," *International Journal of Middle East Studies*, 25:3 (1993), 379–406; idem, "A Court Case from Fourteenth-Century North Africa," *Journal of the American Oriental Society*, 110.2 (1990), 229–54; idem, "*Fatwās* as Sources for Legal and Social History: A Dispute over Endowment Revenues from Fourteenth-Century Fez," *al-Qanṭara*, 11 (1990), 295–341, esp. 332–8; F. de la Granja, "Fiestas cristianas en al-Andalus (Materiales para su estudio). II: Textos de Ṭurṭūšī, el cadí ʿIyāḍ y Wanšarīšī," *al-Andalus*, 35 (1970), 119–42.

approach. Each chapter begins with a reconstruction of the facts of the case, moves to a discussion of the relevant legal doctrine, and then turns to an analysis of one or more legal opinions issued in connection with the dispute. In each instance, I seek to analyze the muftī's use of authoritative legal texts to define what it means for a particular society to be Islamic in a particular place and at a particular time; the underlying normative contexts of these disputes and the interplay between different rule complexes and legal norms; the manner in which men and women used the law as an instrument to negotiate their status in society; the mechanisms available for the resolution of disputes; and the role played by different legal actors in the dispute process. The issues raised in each case and the answers put forward by the muftīs reveal the manner in which society and legal thought shaped each other. It is also noteworthy that in almost every case that we will examine, two or more muftīs disagreed about the proper outcome of the dispute, thereby demonstrating that the norms and values of Maghribī society in the Marīnid period were highly contestable.

The Historical Setting

The cases to be analyzed in this book are best seen against the background of three inter-related historical forces that shaped the character of the Maghrib in the Marīnid period: the expansion of Mālikism, the rise of Sharīfism, and the growth of institutional Sufism.

The Expansion of Mālikism

Mālikism was introduced into North Africa by Asad b. al-Furāt (d. 213/828) and was established as a formal school of law by Saḥnūn (d. 240/854). Mālikism dominated the Maghrib under the Aghlabids (184–296/800–909) but suffered a setback with the arrival of the Fāṭimids in Ifrīqiya in 298/910. When the Fāṭimids were expelled from Ifrīqiya in 440/1048, Mālikism was adopted by the Almoravids (448–541/1056–1147) as the official *madhhab*, or law school, of the dynasty. Under the Almoravid sovereigns, and with their encouragement, Mālikī jurists accorded supreme importance to the study of *fiqh* manuals, at the expense of direct interpretation (*ijtihād*) of Qur'ān and *ḥadīth*.[37]

[37] My discussion of Mālikism draws on *EI*², s.v.v. Mālikiyya, al-Muwaḥḥidūn, Marīnids; Robert Brunschvig, *La Berbérie Orientale sous les Hafsides*, 2 vols (Paris: Adrien Maisonneuve, 1940–47), vol. 2, 286 ff.; Roger Le Tourneau, *Fez in the Age of the Marinides*, tr. Besse Alberta Clement (Norman: University of Oklahoma Press, 1961); Benchekroun, *La vie intellectuelle marocaine*, 450 ff.; Abdallah Laroui, *The History of the Maghrib: An Interpretive Essay*, tr. Ralph Mannheim (Princeton: Princeton University Press, 1977); Jamil M. Abun-Nasr, *A History of the Maghrib in the Islamic Period* (Cambridge: Cambridge University Press, 1987). See also Mansour H. Mansour, *The Maliki School of Law: Spread and Domination in North and West Africa 8th to 14th Centuries* CE. (San Francisco and London: Austin & Winfield, 1995).

In reaction to this policy, Ibn Tūmart (d. 525/1130), the founder of the Almohad dynasty (524–667/1130–1269), sought to return to the pristine form of Islam practiced during the lifetime of the Prophet. Ibn Tumart claimed to be the *mahdī*, that is, "the rightly guided one" who would restore religion and justice, and a descendant of the Prophet. He was a religious reformer who banned works of substantive law (*furūʿ*) and sought to recreate the atmosphere of the early Islamic community by treating the Qurʾān, the *sunna* of the Prophet, and the practice of Muḥammad's companions as the exclusive sources of the law. Regarding himself as the founder of a new *madhhab*, Ibn Tūmart engaged in the direct interpretation of the Qurʾān and *sunna*; that is, he exercised *ijtihād*. Under Abū Yūsuf Yaʿqūb (r. 580–95/1184–99), the Mālikī *madhhab* was formally banned and the works of important Mālikī jurists burned in public. Abū Yūsuf also ordered religious scholars to prepare collections of Prophetic traditions and to classify them according to legal subject, for the convenience of judges and jurists. Experts in the *sunna* of the Prophet gained a prominent position during his reign.

The Marīnids came to power at the end of the sixth/twelfth century. Like the Almohads, they were Berbers. However, whereas the Almohads were Maṣmūda, the Marīnids were Zanāta; and whereas the Almohads had been religious reformers, the Marīnids showed little interest in religious reform per se. The early Marīnids encountered stiff opposition from the urban populations of Fez, Sijilmasa and Marrakesh and from a powerful religious and intellectual élite, part of which had been trained by the Almohads. A series of popular revolts against the new rulers resulted in the execution of several famous jurists. In an effort to deal with the hostility of the urban population and to secure their position in the Maghrib, the first Marīnid sulṭāns undertook a number of actions that were designed to neutralize the opposition, secure their hold on power, and create a stronger basis for political and religious legitimacy. They constructed a new military and administrative center that came to be known as Fez Jedid, staffed with an administrative élite that was recruited from a large pool of Andalusian émigrés. The sulṭāns assumed control over the appointment of the imāms and preachers serving in mosques. And, perhaps most important for our purposes, they recognized the potential of Islamic law as an instrument of political control: thus, they re-instituted Mālikism as the official *madhhab* of the Maghrib and introduced the *madrasa*, or law school (for the first time in the Islamic West), skillfully using this institution to train local élites who were loyal to the regime (see chapter two).[38]

[38] See Mohamed Kably, *Société, pouvoir et religion au Maroc à la fin du Moyen-Age* (Paris: Maisonneuve et Larose, 1986), 271–84; Maribel Fierro, "The Legal Policies of the Almohad Caliphs and Ibn Rushd's *Bidāyat al-Mujtahid*," *Journal of Islamic Studies*, 10:3 (1999), 226–48; Maya Shatzmiller, "Les premiers Mérinides et le milieu religieuse de Fès: l'introduction des médrasas," *Studia Islamica*, 43 (1976), 109–19; idem, *The Berbers and the Islamic State* (Princeton: Markus Wiener, 1999), 60–3, 85–94.

Sharīfism

A second important force in the Maghrib was Sharīfism. Membership in the "House of Muḥammad" (*ahl al-bayt*) was then, as now, a mark of special distinction in Muslim societies. The ability to trace one's descent back to this "House" through Hāshim, ʿAlī, or Ḥasan conferred upon the descendant an important social and religious status, signified in Arabic by the term *sharīf* (pl. *ashrāf, shurafāʾ*), which literally means "noble," "exalted," or "eminent." Over time, the title came to be associated especially with the ʿAlids. As a mark of their status, *sharīfs* often wore green turbans, received pensions from the ruling dynasty, and were the beneficiaries of endowments created expressly for them. The special status of *sharīfs* extended to their relations with non-*sharīfs*, who were expected to love them, refrain from criticizing them, and bear with patience – indeed, gratitude – any wrong inflicted by them.[39]

In certain Muslim societies, *sharīfs* developed into an influential local and regional élite that wielded considerable social and political power – what Bulliet has called "a blood aristocracy without peer".[40] This was especially true in the Maghrib, where, after the arrival of Idrīs I in 170/786–87, families of *shurafāʾ* played an important role in society and politics.[41] Beginning in the eleventh century, leaders of the three Berber dynasties that came to power in the Maghrib sought to buttress their religio-political authority by promoting and supporting families of those *sharīfs* who traced their descent back to Idrīs I and, through him, to al-Ḥasan, the son of ʿAlī b. Abī Ṭālib and Fāṭima.[42] When the Marīnid prince Abū Yūsuf Yaʿqūb defeated the Almohads, he acknowledged the political importance of the *shurafāʾ* by marrying a *sharīfa*, who gave birth to his son and successor, Abū Yaʿqūb Yūsuf (r. 685–706/1286–1307). This son established contacts with the *shurafāʾ* of Mecca and, in 691/1292, designated the *mawlid*, or birthday of the Prophet, as an official holiday that was to be celebrated throughout the realm.[43] Following a revolt in Walīla in 718/1318, Abū Saʿīd ʿUthmān II (r. 710–32/1310–31) conferred special favor and privileges on another branch of the *shurafāʾ*, the Jūṭīs.

Interest in, and support for, the *shurafāʾ* increased during the reigns of subsequent Marīnid sulṭāns, who conferred many presents and marks of honor upon members of this group. Accordingly, the status of *sharīf* became highly desirable, and many began to claim membership in the family of the Prophet. Since the

[39] *EI*², s.v. Sharīf; on *sharīfs* in seventeenth-century Morocco, see Jacques Berque, *Ulémas, fondateurs, insurgés du Maghreb, xvii*ᵉ *siècle* (Paris: Sindbad, 1982), 31, 36–37, 113, 233, 251, 261.

[40] R.W. Bulliet, *The Patricians of Nishapur: A Study in Medieval Islamic Social History* (Cambridge, MA: Harvard University Press, 1972), 234; cited in *EI*², s.v. Sharīf.

[41] See *EI*², s.v. Idrīs I.

[42] On the Berbers in the Islamic West, see Shatzmiller, *The Berbers and the Islamic State*.

[43] See N.J.G. Kaptein, *Muhammad's Birthday Festival* (Leiden: E.J. Brill, 1993); *EI*², s.v. Mawlid; Kably, *Société, pouvoir et religion au Maroc*, 285–7, 297. See also Brunschvig, *La Berbérie Orientale*, vol. 2, 166–7.

resources of the Public Treasury were limited, it was critical to exercise control over membership in the group. For this reason, the office of *naqīb al-ashrāf* (supervisor of the *sharīfs*) was introduced, probably during the reign of Abū al-Ḥasan ʿAlī (r. 732–49/1331–48), to preserve the sacred genealogy of the Prophet. In an effort to prevent false claimants from adding their names to the list of legitimate *sharīfs*, the *naqīb* kept a register in which he recorded the births and deaths of all *sharīfs*. He was also charged with the responsibility of preventing female members of the group from marrying men who were not *sharīfs*. Henceforth, claimants to the status of *sharīf* were called upon to present convincing documentation on their behalf. The award of a fixed allocation from the sulṭān was limited to those who were duly registered and certified. Over time, the *sharīfs* became a community apart, separate and superior.[44]

Many individuals and groups regarded the descendants of the Prophet as opportunists who were using – or abusing – their privileged status to acquire fortune, rank, and influence. At the beginning of the ninth/fifteenth century, the Marīnids suffered a series of military defeats, including the fall of Ceuta to the Portuguese in 818/1415. An ensuing economic crisis forced Abū Saʿīd ʿUthmān III (800–23/1398–1420) to ban the official festivities associated with the celebration of the *mawlid*, reduce the level of material support for *sharīfs*, and downgrade their importance in matters of state protocol. Although the reduction of sharīfian privileges continued during the first part of the reign of ʿAbd al-Ḥaqq (823–69/1420–65), this trend was reversed in Rabīʿ II 841/October 1437, when the Portuguese siege of Tangier was repelled, in large part due to the actions of a family of *sharīfs* who played a key role in the defense of the city. By demonstrating their ability to defend Islam and to serve as able military and political leaders, the *sharīfs* not only raised the morale of the Moroccans but also increased their own prestige.[45] It is perhaps no coincidence that three months later, in Rajab 841/January 1438, the tomb of Idrīs II, founder of Fez, was "discovered" during excavations at the Mosque of the Shurafāʾ in that city; or that the tomb was transformed into a *zāwiya*, or sufi convent, that became an important pilgrimage site. These two events of 841/1437 gave a powerful impetus to Sharīfism and prepared the ground for the eventual rise to power of a sharīfian dynasty, the Saʿdīs (see chapter five).[46]

[44] On these developments, see Herman L. Beck, *L'Image d'Idrīs II, ses descendants de Fās et la politique sharīfienne des sultans Marīnides (656–869/1258–1465)* (Leiden: E.J. Brill, 1989); Kably, *Société, pouvoir et religion au Maroc*, 261–2, 296–300; Brunschvig, *La Berbérie Orientale*, vol. 2, 167; *EI*², s.v.v. Marīnids, Naḳīb al-As̲h̲rāf.

[45] Beck, *L'Image d'Idrīs II*, 225–8; Kably, *Société, pouvoir et religion au Maroc*, 326; Vincent J. Cornell, *Realm of the Saint: Power and Authority in Moroccan Sufism* (Austin: University of Texas Press, 1998), 162–3.

[46] Kably, *Société, pouvoir et religion au Maroc*, 320 ff. The "discovery" of the tomb in 841/1437 may be an historical fiction, as no author mentions it until 1098/1687. See Beck, *L'Image d'Idrīs II*, 228–39.

Sufism

A third key historical factor in the Maghrib was Sufism, which became an important force in the middle of the sixth/twelfth century. Under the Almohads, several sufi groups emerged whose masters traced their spiritual genealogy to Abū Madyan (d. 594/1197), who was the "spiritual grandfather" of al-Shādhilī (d. 656/1258), the founder of an important sufi order.[47]

After a degree of decay, Sufism in the Maghrib underwent a renewal during the seventh/thirteenth century. Based initially in small villages, it took the form of an intensely personal piety. The Sufism of this period encouraged the pursuit of a vigorous interior life while allowing its members to participate in ordinary daily affairs. Sufis were integrated into the life of normative Islam: they participated in traditional religious studies and in the functions and occupations of community life. Moroccan Sufism was heavily influenced by al-Ghazālī (d. 505/1111), who had endeavored to reconcile the traditional religious sciences with mysticism. The Marīnid sulṭāns studied Sufism so as to better exploit it as a source of political legitimacy; they expressed a deep interest in the spiritual masters of the day and were known to read works devoted to mysticism.[48]

The rise of Sufism in the Maghrib was inextricably linked to the spread of Sharīfism.[49] The Shādhilī order emphasized the veneration of the Prophet and his descendants, who served as vehicles through whom the sufi mystic might experience union with the Divinity, either mystically in this world or physically in the next. Sufi shaykhs commonly claimed to be descendants of the Prophet. Al-Shādhilī himself referred to the Prophet as his "ancestor" (*jadd*) and made excellent use of his status as a *sharīf* in his struggles with opponents.[50] In the middle of the ninth/fifteenth century, another important sufi, al-Jazūlī (d. 869/1465), declared, "One is great because of the greatness of nobility (*sharaf*) and lineage (*nasab*). I am noble in lineage (*anā sharīfun fi' l-nasab*). My ancestor is the Messenger of

[47] Alfred Bel, *La Religion musulmane en Berbérie: Esquisse d'histoire et de sociologie religieuses* (Paris: Librairie Orientaliste Paul Geuthner, 1938), vol. 1, 341 ff.; Benchekroun, *La vie intellectuelle marocaine*, 485 ff.; Kably, *Société, pouvoir et religion au Maroc*, 306–7; Brunschvig, *La Berbérie Orientale*, vol. 2, 317 ff.; *EI*[2], s.v.v. Abū Madyan, al-Shādhilī, Shādhiliyya. On Sufism in the Maghrib in the seventeenth century, see Berque, *Ulémas, fondateurs, insurgés*, 125 ff.

[48] *Ibn ʿAbbād of Ronda: Letters on the Sūfī Path*, trans. and intro. by John Renard, S.J. (New York: Paulist Press, 1986), 46; Kably, *Société, pouvoir et religion au Maroc*, 303.

[49] I am simplifying what is in fact a complicated relationship. For details see Kably, *Société, pouvoir et religion au Maroc*, 285, 303, 315. On the relationship between Sufism and Sharīfism in a later period, see M. Garcia-Arenal, "La Conjonction du soufisme et du sharifisme au Maroc: le mahdi comme sauveur," *Revue d'études du monde méditerranéen*, 55–6 (1990), 233–56; idem, "Mahdī, murābiṭ, sharīf: l'avènement de la dynastie saʿdienne," *Studia Islamica*, 70 (1990), 77–114; Houari Touati, *Entre Dieu et les hommes: Lettrés saints et sorciers au Maghreb (17e siècle)* (Paris: L'école des hautes études en sciences sociales, 1994); Henry Munson, Jr, *Religion and Power in Morocco* (New Haven: Yale University Press, 1993).

[50] Cornell, *Realm of the Saint*, 149; Kably, *Société, pouvoir et religion au Maroc*, 329; Munson, *Religion and Power*, 14–16.

God – may God bless him and grant him peace – and I am nearer to him than all of God's creation."[51] Sufi orders (*ṭuruq*) proliferated in the Maghrib and Ifrīqiya in the ninth/fifteenth century, and sufi saints (*awliyāʾ*) acquired tremendous social prestige and power.

The relationship between Sufism and Mālikism in the Marīnid period is equally important, although less well understood. Whereas French scholars of the colonial period have posited a sharp divide between orthodox and heterodox Islam, between the *ʿulamāʾ* of the urban centers and sufi *awliyāʾ* of the countryside, contemporary scholars have argued that the relationship between these two groups should be regarded as "points along a continuum, not independent spheres of behavior."[52] In fact, the sources indicate that Sufism and Mālikism have gone hand-in-hand in the Maghrib since the fourth/tenth century. Many of the most important saints of early Moroccan Sufism were legal specialists. In Fez the earliest saints were a group of ascetics trained in the law who were known as "anchors of the earth" (*awtād al-arḍ*).[53] The spread of Mālikism throughout the Maghrib was in large part the work of men such as Ibn al-ʿArīf (d. 536/1141) and ʿAlī b. Ḥirzihim (d. 559/1164), who were both sufis and accomplished legists. According to one estimate, one out of every five jurists living at the end of the Marīnid period was a sufi.[54]

Under the Marīnids, members of the Shādhilī order living in the urban centers of the north sought to harmonize sufi beliefs with Mālikī doctrine and entered into a political alliance with Marīnid leaders. The *madrasa*s established by the Marīnid sulṭāns promoted an "orthodox" version of Islam that worked against the heterodox popular practices prevailing in the countryside. Young men were attracted to Fez and trained in the new law schools, where they studied Mālikī religious doctrine and were subjected to a measure of political discipline. As moderate Sufism became reconciled with Mālikī orthodoxy, the institutional boundaries between these two religio-political forces were blurred; it was not uncommon to find Mālikī jurists teaching law in sufi *zāwiya*s and sufi masters teaching mysticism in *madrasa*s. Similarly, the social boundaries between mystics and jurists dissolved: circles of sufis and legists overlapped either entirely or in part.[55]

There emerged in the Maghrib a particular brand of Sufism that was heavily influenced by the law. This juridical Sufism, which regarded itself as subordinate

[51] Muḥammad al-Mahdī al-Fāsī, *Kitāb mumtiʿ al-asmāʾ fī dhikr al-Jazūlī wa'l-tabbāʿ wa-mā lahumā min al-atbāʿ* (Fez: lithograph, 1316/1898–99), 3; cited and translated in Cornell, *Realm of the Saint*, 186; see also Kably, *Société, pouvoir et religion au Maroc*, 329.

[52] Jonathan G. Katz, *Dreams, Sufism and Sainthood: The Visionary Career of Muḥammad al-Zawâwî* (Leiden: E.J. Brill, 1996), 17–19.

[53] Ibid., 17.

[54] Cornell, *Realm of the Saint*, 106–7 (68 out of 316 saints).

[55] See Bel, *La Religion musulmane en Berbérie*, vol. 1, 321; Brunschvig, *La Berbérie Orientale*, vol. 2, 317 ff., esp. 330, 336; Benchekroun, *La vie intellectuelle marocaine*, 487–88; Kably, *Société, pouvoir et religion au Maroc*, 315; Katz, *Dreams, Sufism and Sainthood*, 15; *EI*², s.v., Shādhiliyya. On the relationship between Sufism and "orthodoxy" in the East, see Jonathan Berkey, *The Transmission of Knowledge in Medieval Cairo: A Social History of Islamic Education* (Princeton: Princeton University Press, 1992), 56–60, 84–5.

to the law rather than above it, was oriented toward daily practice and was based upon careful attention to what V. Cornell has called "a jurisprudence of inter-personal behavior."[56] One sufi master taught, "Be a legist first and a sufi second, not a sufi first and a legist second."[57] The intimate link between law and intellectual Sufism was a characteristic feature of the Marīnid period, when Mālikism triumphed as the law of the land. Many of the muftīs whom we will encounter in this book were practitioners of this juridical sufism (see chapter five).[58]

The Qāḍī Court System Under the Marīnids

The cases that have been chosen for analysis all involve individuals or groups who brought their grievances to the Marīnid court system; together they are evidence of the manner in which Mālikī qāḍīs and muftīs engaged in the work of dispute resolution. Before turning to the cases themselves, it will be helpful to present a brief summary of the structure, function, and mode of operation of the qāḍī court system under the Marīnids and to identify the primary legal agents who manned the system: the sulṭāns, qāḍīs, and muftīs.[59]

The Sulṭān

The early Marīnids used the title *amīr al-muslimīn*, "Commander of the Muslims". Beginning with Abū ʿInān (r. 1348–58), they added the epithet *amīr al-muʾminīn*, "Commander of the Believers," which suggested general leadership of the Muslim community at large. The sulṭān was the supreme political and religious authority in the far Maghrib; some regarded him as the *khalīfa* of the Prophet Muḥammad (see chapter two). In practice he regularly delegated his authority to judicial agents who exercised that authority on his behalf, although he was responsible *inter alia* for the proper functioning of the judicial system and the proper behavior of his agents. To this end, the sulṭān held a weekly *majlis*, or council, at which he and the leading jurists of the capital heard complaints (*shakāwā*, sg. *shakwa*) from subjects who maintained that their affairs and interests had been improperly handled by agents

[56] Cornell, *Realm of the Saint*, 67; cf. Kably, *Société, pouvoir et religion au Maroc*, 316.

[57] Aḥmad al-Zarrūq (d. 899/1493), *Qawāʿid al-taṣawwuf*, ed. Muḥammad Zuhrī al-Najjār and ʿAlī Muʿbid Firghalī (Beirut, 1992), cited and translated in Cornell, *Realm of the Saint*, 197; cf. Kably, *Société, pouvoir et religion au Maroc*, 304–5, 314–5.

[58] Benchekroun, *La vie intellectuelle marocaine*, 488–9.

[59] See Brunschvig, *La Berbérie Orientale*, vol. 2, 113–23; Emile Tyan, "Judicial Organization," in *Law in the Middle East*, ed. Majid Khadduri and Herbert J. Liebesny (Washington DC: The Middle East Institute, 1955), 236–78; Kably, *Société, pouvoir et religion au Maroc*, 260–1, 265.

of the legal system. One or another of the Marīnid sulṭāns was involved in three of the six cases to be studied here (see chapters one, two, and four).

The Qāḍī al-Jamāʿa *and other qāḍīs*

The sulṭān appointed the *qāḍī al-jamāʿa*, or chief qāḍī of the capital city, and charged him with the task of resolving disputes among Muslims. The chief qāḍī was an important member of the political bureaucracy.[60] Outside of the capital, provincial qāḍīs sat in each town or locality that was subject to the sulṭān's authority. These judges were appointed by the sulṭān, who might also dismiss them, usually after consultation with the chief judge and other important religious functionaries of the capital city. The activities of provincial judges appear to have been supervised by the *qāḍī al-jamāʿa*, who instructed them in their duties, exercised disciplinary powers over them, supervised their conduct, and made inquiries regarding their character. In both theory and practice every judge constituted a single court and was competent to deal with all matters envisioned by the *sharīʿa* except those specifically delegated to special judges.[61]

The qāḍī normally held court either in the Friday mosque or in his home. One function of his court was to serve as a kind of public record office to which residents of the town came in order to certify legal transactions, authenticate witness testimony, and confirm the authenticity of previously issued fatwās. Copies of the resulting documents were kept in the qāḍī's register, known as the *dīwān al-qāḍī*. Unfortunately, no qāḍī registers are extant from the period prior to the rise of the Ottomans, and the surviving documentary record is small and uneven. Lacking first-hand evidence relating to the work of the *qāḍī* in his court, we have derived our knowledge of his work largely from the evidence of doctrinal lawbooks, historical chronicles, and biographical dictionaries. As we shall see, the evidence of the fatwās is a partial remedy to this gap in our knowledge (see chapter one).

The primary function of the qāḍī was to settle disputes. In this regard his role was reactive. Claimants brought their disputes to him, and it was his task to determine if there were sufficient grounds to issue a judgment. If so, he tried to distinguish the "truth" in a case by adhering to the procedural norms of Mālikī law. Disputes typically were decided on the basis of an acknowledgement (*iqrār*), testimonial evidence (*bayyina*), or the imposition of an oath (*yamīn*). The value of a witness's testimony corresponded to the qāḍī's assessment of his personal integrity (*ʿadāla*). It was the qāḍī's responsibility to guarantee the rights of both parties. He could not pass judgment without first summoning the defendant to his court so that

[60] The chief qāḍī reportedly would express his subordination to the sulṭān by prostrating himself in front of the ruler and kissing his feet. See Kably, *Société, pouvoir et religion au Maroc*, 261, 265.

[61] Brunschvig, *La Berbérie Orientale*, vol. 2, 113 ff.

he might present evidence on his behalf, a process known as *iʿdhār*. The defendant might defend himself either by challenging the integrity of the witnesses who testified on behalf of the plaintiff or by presenting counter-evidence, often in the form of documents attested by witnesses. In cases in which the defendant presented counter-evidence, the litigation might stretch over several court sessions and a considerable length of time. All legally relevant facts established by the parties to a dispute were recorded in the qāḍī's minutes (*maḥḍar*). Before issuing his judgment (*ḥukm*, pl. *aḥkām*), he customarily consulted with the jurists who were members of his *shūra*, or council; qāḍīs appear to have been reluctant to issue a judgment without having first secured the support of their judicial advisors.[62] Both the final judgment and, in many instances, any fatwā issued in connection with the case, were recorded in the *dīwān al-qāḍī*.[63]

The judgment of a qāḍī was binding, although it might subsequently be reversed if it were demonstrated either (1) that the issuing judge had lacked proper jurisdictional authority or (2) that the original judgment violated a provision of the Qurʾān or *ḥadīth* or was based on a false or inappropriate analogy (*qiyās*).[64]

Mālikī procedural law sometimes made it difficult or impossible for a qāḍī to issue a judgment, usually because of the absence of reliable witness testimony. In such cases the qāḍī nevertheless might play a key role in the resolution of a dispute by offering his services as a mediator. He listened to the litigants' arguments, translated those arguments into the language of the law, authorized his agents to gather additional "facts" relating to the case, and attempted to guide the parties to an amicable settlement (*ṣulḥ*). If the parties agreed, the terms of the settlement would be recorded in the qāḍī's *sijill*, or register. If they refused, the qāḍī might nevertheless request a fatwā from a distinguished muftī, whose response would then serve as the basis of an imposed resolution of the case (see chapter three).

The Marīnid qāḍī was a well-trained and highly skilled legal technician and, in many instances, a distinguished jurist. The work of the qāḍī required extensive familiarity with the details of Mālikī substantive and procedural law. He sought to base his judgment on certain knowledge (*ʿilm*) and on the authority of Islamic legal doctrine. He was not only familiar with legal doctrine but also capable of manipulating that doctrine, for example, by identifying factual similarities and

[62] See, for example, Abū Bakr Aḥmad al-Khaṣṣāf, *Kitāb adab al-qāḍī*, ed. Farhat Ziadeh (Cairo: American University Press, 1978), 105; Brunschvig, *La Berbérie Orientale*, vol. 2, 129.

[63] On Mālikī judicial procedure, see, for example, Ibn Rushd, *The Distinguished Jurist's Primer*, trans. Imran Ahsan Khan Nyazee and Muhammad Abdul Rauf, 2 vols (Reading, UK: Garnet Publishing, 1996), vol. II, 553 ff.; Peter Scholz, *Malikitisches Verfahrensrecht: Eine Studie zu Inhalt und Methodik der Scharia mit rechtshistorischen und rechtsvergleichenden Anmerkungen am Beispiel des malikitischen Verfahrensrechts bis zum 12. Jahrhundert* (Frankfurt: Peter Lang, 1997); Christian Müller, *Gerichtspraxis im Stadtstaat Córdoba: Zum Recht der Gesellschaft in einer mālikitisch-islamischen Rechtstradition des 5./11. Jahrhunderts* (Leiden: E.J. Brill, 1999); idem, "Judging with God's Law on Earth: Judicial Powers of the *Qāḍī al-jamāʿa* of Cordoba in the Fifth/Eleventh Century," *Islamic Law and Society*, 7:2 (2000), 159–86.

[64] See Brunschvig, *La Berbérie Orientale*, vol. 2, 129–30; Powers, "On Judicial Review in Islamic Law."

differences with prior cases. At the same time, he was keenly aware of his position in society and, when passing judgment on cases that came before him, his sense of *realpolitik* may have been as important as his understanding of the legal issues involved in a particular case.

The Muftī

As the cases to be examined in this book demonstrate, muftīs were an integral part of the Marīnid judicial system. They regularly received requests for fatwās from qāḍīs, acting in their capacity as *mustaftī*s. And the qāḍīs used these fatwās as the authoritative basis for their judgments. Although the qāḍī usually did not formulate a written explanation of the grounds for his decision, to the extent that his judgment was informed by a fatwā, it would have been based upon rational, legal considerations. In my view, most of the fatwās preserved in the *Miʿyār* have survived precisely because they were issued in connection with qāḍī court litigation. The *istiftāʾ*, especially when it contains a transcription of one or more legal documents, is an important trace or echo of the work of the qāḍī. Thus, the muftī's role in the judicial process cannot be over-estimated.

The issuing of fatwās has been a pervasive feature of Muslim societies since the first/seventh century.[65] Fatwās came into existence in several ways. In principle a request for a fatwā might emanate from a layman. Certainly, private individuals frequently solicited legal opinions on the many issues of daily life that were governed by Islamic law. Some of the resulting fatwās have been preserved; most have not.

Most of the fatwās preserved in the *Miʿyār* were issued in response to requests by qāḍīs. Among the Mālikīs in al-Andalus and the Maghrib, two or more muftīs typically were attached to each qāḍī court as advisors (*mushāwar*s), although in difficult, unusual, or politically sensitive cases, a qāḍī might supplement the authority of his personal advisors by soliciting a fatwā from another distinguished local muftī or one living elsewhere.[66] In such cases the qāḍī was required to provide the muftī with a written summary of the litigation, formulated in the abstract, impersonal, and ostensibly objective language of the law.[67] In his summary, the qāḍī cum *mustaftī* rendered the utterances of the litigants and witnesses into the language of legal discourse as he set down in writing their representations of the facts of the case. (This process may account for the uniform traits of many

[65] For an historical survey of the institution of *futyā*, see Muhammad Khalid Masud, Brinkley Messick and David S. Powers, "Muftis, Fatwas and Islamic Legal Interpretation," in *Islamic Legal Interpretation: Muftis and their Fatwas*, 3–32.

[66] See Brunschvig, *La Berbérie Orientale*, vol. 2, 138–43; Tyan, "Judicial Organization," 251–3; Manuela Marín, "*Šūrā* et *ahl al-Šūrā* dans al-Andalus," *Studia Islamica*, 62 (1985), 25–51; Müller, *Gerichtspraxis im Stadtstaat Córdoba*, index, s.v. *mušāwar*; idem, "Judging with God's Law on Earth," 163–4.

[67] On the conventions of *futyā*, see, for example, Abū Zakariyāʾ Yaḥyā al-Nawawī (d. 676/1277), *Adab al-fatwā wa'l-muftī wa'l-mustaftī* (Damascus: Dār al-Fikr, 1988).

surviving fatwās.) Upon receiving the *istiftā'*, the muftī scrutinized the case, issued a written response (*jawāb*), and returned to the qāḍī both the *istiftā'* and the *jawāb* (which, together, constitute the fatwā). Although the fatwā was not binding, in those cases in which the qāḍī did rely on it in issuing his judgment, it often became part of the documentary record associated with the case; indeed, the qāḍī sometimes entered the fatwā into his *sijill.*

Whereas qāḍīs were situated within a legal hierarchy that extended from the sulṭān to the provinces, muftīs were situated within a hierarchy of *ʿilm*-knowledge composed of three levels: at the top of the hierarchy were those muftīs whose mastery of jurisprudence qualified them to derive solutions to new cases from the recognized sources of the law; a middle category included those jurists who were capable of distinguishing between opinions that were in conformity with Mālikī legal doctrine and those that were not; and the bottom level was occupied by jurists who were mere memorizers of legal doctrine.[68] Most of the jurists whom we will encounter in this book were no doubt second-level muftīs.

In addition to being knowledgeable, a muftī was expected to be a moral and ethical individual whose behavior embodied and exemplified the values that he sought to transmit to others, values such as magnanimity, humility, independence, generosity, and avoidance of forbidden actions. In short he was expected to be a model of the "legal man", and a jurist who violated the norms of his profession might suffer severe consequences (see chapter two).

The *jawāb*, or response, of the muftī is a text in which he explains the general legal issues raised by a particular case, how he proposes to resolve those issues, and why he resolves them as he does. The opinion of the muftī is what James Boyd White has called – with reference to judicial opinions written by justices of the American Supreme Court – "a form of language and of life". Like an American justice, the muftī is expected to explain his opinions and to provide a reasoned justification for them. A response issued in the eighth/fourteenth century might serve as an authoritative source text for subsequent generations of jurists. Taken as a whole, a series of responses issued over time represents a collective effort to come to terms with a problem of legal judgment in varying contexts.[69]

As we proceed with our investigation, the reader should keep in mind that fatwās are not transparent documents but complex literary constructions that collapse, and mediate among, several levels of "reality": (1) the events as they happened, to which we have no direct access; (2) the same events as related to a local authority, frequently a qāḍī, either directly or with the assistance of a legal agent (*wakīl*) who translated the litigants' oral accounts of what happened into the language of the law; (3) the summary re-presentation of these narratives by the qāḍī, acting in his capacity as a *mustaftī* – the *istiftā'* might include a transcription, more or less complete, of any documents and testimonial evidence presented by the litigants;

[68] This typology is outlined in a fatwā issued by Ibn Rushd. See *Miʿyār*, vol. 10, 30–5.

[69] James Boyd White, *Justice as Translation: An Essay in Cultural and Legal Criticism* (Chicago: University of Chicago Press, 1990), 215 ff.

and (4) the muftī's response to the *istiftā'*, which on occasion introduces facts not mentioned by the *mustaftī*. With careful attention to the literary composition of a fatwā and to its multiple levels of "reality," the historian attempts to unpack the narrative representation of the case and to engage in yet another round of translation, this one having as its goal a reconstruction of the case in a manner that is as faithful as possible to its actual development.

ONE

Kadijustiz or Qāḍī-Justice? A Paternity Dispute from Fourteenth-Century Morocco

The United States Supreme Court does not sit like a kadi under a tree dispensing justice according to considerations of individual expediency.
(Justice Felix Frankfurter)

The image of the Muslim qāḍī comfortably dispensing justice without reference to any body of legal principles or rules is shared by many laymen and not a small number of specialists. Weber defined *kadijustiz* as a system of law in which judges are empowered to decide each case according to what they see as its individual merits, without referring to a settled and coherent body of norms or rules and without employing a rational set of judicial procedures. In Weber's view, the qāḍī's judgments were driven by considerations relating to politics, ethics, personal expediency, and/or general utility.

Based on his study of judges serving in the town of Sefrou, Morocco, in the 1960s and 1970s, Rosen has attempted to refine and qualify Weber's thesis by detaching the notion of doctrine from that of consistency. Like Weber, he argues that Muslim judges do not focus on substantive legal doctrines or on the similarities to, and differences from, the facts of prior cases; do not emphasize antecedent concepts; and do not employ a mode of judicial reasoning that would result in increasingly refined modes of legal analysis. Unlike Weber, however, Rosen contends that Islamic law is rational and consistent, although dependent in these respects on the skill with which the qāḍī interprets the testimony of reliable witnesses, analyzes oral testimony, assesses competing social interests, and relies upon local experts. Rosen concludes that the qāḍī's primary goal in deciding a case is to determine the consequences of his judgment on the social relationships of the litigants. The judge's central aim, Rosen asserts, is to return people to a position in which they can negotiate their own permissible relationships outside of the legal realm. Only secondarily and incidentally does the qāḍī seek to enforce individual rights or impose a resolution to a dispute.[1]

In this chapter, I will analyze the work of a qāḍī who was called upon to resolve a paternity dispute in the vicinity of Fez, not far from Rosen's Sefrou, at the

[1] Lawrence Rosen, *The Anthropology of Justice: Law as Culture in Islamic Society* (Cambridge: Cambridge University Press, 1989).

beginning of the eighth/fourteenth century. Our documentation is of special importance because, exceptionally, it includes a long, detailed and carefully formulated narrative, written by the qāḍī, in which he describes the claims of the litigants, transcribes the written evidence submitted to his court, and explains how he went about assessing that evidence in his effort to resolve the dispute. Our source does not indicate that the qāḍī tried to position the litigants so that they might negotiate the terms of their relationship. Indeed, the qāḍī's judgment was a clear victory for the plaintiff and a bitter defeat for the defendant. As he went about his work, the qāḍī referred to established legal doctrine, cited earlier cases, and used sophisticated hermeneutic and rhetorical tools to analyze the facts of the case and to weigh conflicting evidence. Certainly, a close reading of this case suggests that he also was influenced by palpable but unidentified extra-legal considerations, but these, whatever they may have been, served only as a catalyst for the qāḍī's attempt to establish the facts of the case, to weigh the evidence submitted to his court on the scales of justice, and to ground his judgment in a correct interpretation of the relevant Islamic legal doctrine. In this respect, I submit, he was typical of other qāḍīs in the Marīnid period.

The Facts of the Case in their Historical Context

Toward the end of the seventh/thirteenth century, ʿAlī b. Abī al-ʿUlāʾ, a leading figure in a Moroccan town of undetermined location, probably in the north of the country, arranged to marry his virgin daughter, Tāwatarā, to a man whose name is nowhere mentioned in the *Miʿyār*.[2] The dower presented by the bridegroom to his bride included the female slave, Maymūna.[3] Our source specifies that ʿAlī accepted the female slave on behalf of his daughter, presumably because she was a minor. Subsequently, Maymūna became pregnant and gave birth to a son, Sālim, who was raised in ʿAlī's house together with his children – the aforementioned Tāwatarā (who seems not to have left the family's residence) and her two brothers, Muḥammad and ʿAbd al-Raḥmān (alternatively, Raḥḥū).

Sālim's childhood coincided with a tumultuous period in the history of the Marīnid dynasty, then headed by the Sulṭān Abū Yaʿqūb Yūsuf (r. 685–706/1286–1307).[4] The "House of Abū al-ʿUlāʾ" was related to the royal family, and

[2] The fatwā analyzed in this chapter may be found in al-Wansharīsī, *Kitāb al-Miʿyār*, vol. 10, 361–7; a second, related fatwā, issued in connection with the same case, is recorded at ibid., vol. 10, 360–1.

[3] On concubines, see *EI*[2], s.v.v. ʿAbd, Umm al-walad; *Dictionary of the Middle Ages* (New York: Charles Scribner's Sons, 1982–89), s.v.v. "Concubinage, Islamic," "Slavery, Islamic World."

[4] On the Marīnids, see Mohammad Kably, *Société, pouvoir, et réligion au Maroc à la fin du Moyen-Age* (Paris: Maisonneuve et Larose, 1986); Maya Shatzmiller, *The Berbers and the Islamic State: The Marīnid Experience in Pre-Protectorate Morocco* (Princeton: Markus Wiener Publishers, 2000); Roger Le Tourneau, *Fez in the Age of the Marinides* (Norman: University of Oklahoma, 1961); *EI*[2], s.v. Marīnids; Jamil M. Abun-Nasr, *A History of the Maghrib in the Islamic Period* (2nd edn, Cambridge: Cambridge University Press, 1987).

many of its members served in the administration of the country.[5] Our source specifies that ʿAlī b. Abī al-ʿUlā''s brother, Yaḥyā, was a governor (*wālin*) of the sulṭān, in which capacity he no doubt was responsible for the collection of taxes.[6] But many members of the House of Abū al-ʿUla' were restless, and, over the two decades of Abū Yaʿqūb's rule, several of them rose in revolt against their kinsman. The most famous of these rebels was the capable and notorious ʿUthmān b. Abī al-ʿUlā'. After crossing the Straits, this dissident Marīnid prince came under the influence of the Naṣrid sovereign, Muḥammad III Ibn al-Aḥmar, who put him in charge of a detachment of "warriors for the faith" (*ghuzāt*) responsible for defending Malaga and its environs from the Christians of Castile. In 705/1306, while the Marīnid Abū Yaʿqūb was engaged in the siege of Zayānid Tlemcen, then in its eighth year, ʿUthmān b. Abī al-ʿUlā' returned to the Maghrib, landing in the port-city of Ceuta, where, with Naṣrid support, he proclaimed himself sovereign of the Marīnids and took control of Arzila, Larache, and the mountainous region in the north of the country. Disregarding this challenge, Abū Yaʿqūb persisted in the siege of Tlemcen but was assassinated by one of his eunuchs on 7 Dhū al-Qaʿda 706/10 May 1307, just as the city was about to surrender. Abū Yaʿqūb was succeeded by his 23-year-old grandson, Abū Thābit, who died of natural causes on 8 Ṣafar 708/28 July 1308, after having devoted much of his short reign to the threat posed by ʿUthmān b. Abī al-ʿUlā' in the north. Abū Thābit was succeeded by his 19-year-old brother, Abū al-Rabīʿ, who managed to recover possession of Ceuta on 10 Ṣafar 709/20 July 1309. Slightly more than one year later, on 29 Jumāda II 710/23 November 1310, Abū al-Rabīʿ died after a brief illness. He was succeeded by Abū Saʿīd ʿUthmān, during whose long reign (710–32/1310–31) the dispute that is the subject of the present investigation unfolded.[7]

The oppositional role of the House of Abū al-ʿUlā' in Marīnid politics may explain the tribulations suffered by some of its members. Some time prior to his death in 706/1307, Abū Yaʿqūb Yūsuf seized and imprisoned both Yaḥyā b. Abī al-ʿUlā' and his brother, ʿAlī, simultaneously confiscating certain familial properties. Our source does not mention the reason for their incarceration, except for a brief allusion to financial malfeasance.[8] While the two men remained incarcerated, Sālim lived in ʿAlī's house until he reached the age of maturity, at which time, our

[5] See Ibn Khaldūn, *Kitāb al-ʿIbar*, 7 vols (Beirut: Dār al-Kitāb al-Lubnānī, 1959), vol. 7, 770 ff.; French trans. de Slane, *Histoire des Berbères et des dynasties musulmanes de l'Afrique Septentrionale*, 4 vols (Paris: P. Geuthner, 1925–56), vol. 4, 468 ff. I would like to thank my colleague, Maya Shatzmiller, for her assistance in identifying the House of Abū al-ʿUlā'.

[6] *Miʿyār*, vol. 10, 362, l. 4.

[7] Ibn Khaldūn, *ʿIbar*, vol. 7, 770 ff.; de Slane, *Histoire*, vol. 4, 468 ff.; Ibn Abī Zarʿ, *Rawḍ al-Qirṭās*, trans. Ambrosio Huici Miranda, 2 vols (2nd edn, Valencia, n.p., 1964), vol. 2, 685 ff.; Kably, *Société, pouvoir, et réligion*, 113–14; Rachel Arié, *L'Espagne musulmane au temps des Naṣrides (1232–1492)* (Paris: Editions E. de Boccard, 1973), 86–8; Charles-Emmanuel Dufourcq, *L'Espagne Catalane et le Maghrib aux XIIIe et XIVe siècles* (Paris: Presses Universitaires de France, 1966), 384; *EI*[2], s.v. Naṣrids.

[8] *Miʿyār*, vol. 10, 361–2. On the issue of public accountability of governors, see Kably, *Société, pouvoir, et réligion*, 268–71.

source informs us, he "set off on a journey."[9] But he, too, incurred the displeasure of the political authorities – again, for reasons not mentioned – and was imprisoned in Fez for ten years. At an unspecified time following the death of Abū Yaʿqūb Yūsuf in 706/1307, Yaḥyā and ʿAlī (but not Sālim) were released from prison and their properties were attached to the State Treasury (*makhzan*) so that the revenues might be used against certain outstanding debts (*istighrāq al-dhimma*). ʿAlī died several years later, before 712/1312–13, early in the reign of Abū Saʿīd ʿUthmān. Because ʿAlī's estate had been attached to the State Treasury, his children did not inherit the properties themselves but were awarded shares of the revenues (*ghalla*) generated by those properties. Sālim, who was either in prison or absent, was not included in this arrangement.

Abū Saʿīd ʿUthmān reportedly began his reign by releasing political prisoners,[10] and it must have been shortly after he came to power that Sālim regained his freedom and returned home, whereupon he learned of the special arrangements that had been made for the division of ʿAlī's estate. At the time of Sālim's return, two of ʿAlī b. Abī al-ʿUlā''s children, ʿAbd al-Raḥmān and Tāwatarā (Maymūna's mistress), were still alive, although Muḥammad had died. Maymūna, too, was dead. Upon his arrival, Sālim asserted that he was one of ʿAlī's children and heirs and that he therefore was entitled to a pension.[11] Sālim's claim, which no doubt posed a threat to ʿAbd al-Raḥmān's status as ʿAlī's sole surviving son,[12] apparently was rejected by the family, whereupon Sālim proceeded to the court of the local qāḍī, ʿĪsā b. Muḥammad al-Tirjālī,[13] before whom he claimed that Alī had acknowledged him as his son during his lifetime,[14] thereby setting in motion a lawsuit that lasted for several months and attracted the attention of many local residents. Al-Tirjālī listened to the respective claims and counterclaims, interrogated the witnesses who were summoned to testify, assessed the legal value of their testimonies, and consulted with his local judicial advisors. Strongly inclined to hold in favor of Sālim, al-Tirjālī nevertheless was unsure about certain aspects of the case.

Prior to issuing his judgment, the qāḍī consulted with a distinguished muftī in the capital city of Fez, Ibrāhīm b. ʿAbdallāh al-Yaznāsinī (d. > 740/1339–40).[15] In a long, detailed, and carefully formulated *istiftāʾ*, al-Tirjālī summarized the facts of the case, presented a summary transcription of the testimonial evidence, and asked the muftī to issue a fatwā corroborating the validity of his impending

[9] *Miʿyār*, vol. 10, 362, l. 6.

[10] Ibn Abī Zarʿ, *Rawḍ*, vol. 2, 722–3.

[11] *Miʿyār*, vol. 10, 362, ll. 1–11.

[12] The underlying social dynamic of the dispute might be more readily apparent if we knew if Sālim was older than ʿAbd al-Raḥmān, in which case the relationship between the two men would have been structurally similar to that between the Biblical Ishmael and Isaac.

[13] My inability to identify this qāḍī in the biographical dictionaries suggests that he was an undistinguished jurist.

[14] *Miʿyār*, vol. 10, 360, l. 7.

[15] Abū Mūsā Ibrāhīm b. ʿAbdallāh al-Yaznāsinī. For biographical details, see Muḥammad b. Muḥammad Makhlūf, *Shajarat al-nūr al-zakiyya fī ṭabaqāt al-mālikiyya*, 2 vols in 1 (2nd edn, Beirut: Dār al-Kitāb al-ʿArabī, 1975), vol. 1, 218, no. 77.

judgment. Exceptionally, the *istiftā'* is signed by the qāḍī and preserves the names of the litigants, thereby making it possible to situate the case in its historical context. In this chapter, I shall analyze the *istiftā'*, paying special attention to the work of the qāḍī and his understanding of justice, for example, his familiarity with legal doctrine, ability to manipulate legal discourse, and handling of witness-testimony; to the local, cultural assumptions embedded in judicial activity; and to what I call "the art of Islamic judicial narrative."[16] At the same time, I seek to shed light on the institution of concubinage, the regulation of human sexuality, and the relationship between social practice and the law in fourteenth-century Morocco.

From the perspective of Mālikī legal doctrine, Sālim's claim raised three, interrelated questions: Are sexual relations between a man and a female slave who belongs to his daughter licit or illicit? If they are illicit, what is the appropriate punishment? And is a child born of such a union slave or free? As the present case suggests, there apparently was considerable confusion in the minds of many Muslims with regard to these questions, despite the fact that Mālikī legal doctrine provides explicit answers to both, answers that were known to judges and jurists such as al-Tirjālī and al-Yaznāsinī. Indeed, as we shall see, ignorance of the law on the part of both the litigants and their witnesses played a central role in the case.

Mālikī Legal Doctrine

Because al-Tirjālī could assume knowledge of the law on the part of al-Yaznāsinī, he made only cursory reference to the underlying doctrinal issue and focused his attention on the legal value of the testimonial evidence submitted by the litigants. The modern reader, however, cannot appreciate al-Tirjālī's handling of the case without first examining Mālikī legal doctrine on the subject of sexual relations, especially those between masters and slaves.

Islamic law considers sexual relations not only between a man and his wife but also between a man and his female slave to be lawful (*ḥalāl*). Any other type of sexual relationship is forbidden (*ḥarām*), and anyone who engages in unlawful intercourse commits fornication (*zinā*), one of the crimes for which the Qur'ān specifies a punishment known as *ḥadd* (pl. *ḥudūd*). In the case of men or women who have not experienced lawful intercourse at the time of their fornication, the *ḥadd* punishment is 100 lashes; for lawfully married individuals who have engaged in intercourse with their spouses prior to the crime, it is stoning to death.[17]

At the same time that Islamic law imposes harsh punishments for illict sexual activity, it establishes broad parameters for licit sexual activity that make it possible

[16] For an interpretation of qāḍī-justice at variance with the view advanced in this essay, see Rosen, *The Anthropology of Justice*; idem, *The Justice of Islam* (Oxford: Oxford University Press, 2000).

[17] See *EI*[1], s.v. Zinā; *EI*[2], s.v. Ḥadd; cf. Peter Scholz, *Malikitisches Verfahrensrecht* (Frankfurt: Peter Lang, 1997), 508 ff.

for a man to engage in sexual intercourse with several different women. Not only may a man marry up to four wives at a time, but he also may own and have intercourse with as many concubines as he can afford to maintain. With regard to concubinage, the law holds that if a man impregnates his female slave, she acquires the status of *umm al-walad* (mother of the child). Henceforth, she may not be sold, pledged, or given away as a gift, and upon the death of her master she becomes free. Her child by her master is born free and is affiliated to its father, on the condition that the father admits to having had sexual relations with his female slave or that he formally acknowledges the child as his own. A man may deny the paternity of a child born to his female slave if he can prove that it was impossible for him to have had sexual relations with her or that she already was married to a third party; alternatively, in the absence of such proof, he may swear an oath that he had abstained from sexual intercourse with his concubine for at least six months prior to the date of the child's birth and that he had not had sexual relations with her at any time subsequent to the child's birth (a procedure known as *istibrāʾ*).[18] Thus, had Maymūna belonged to ʿAlī, and had ʿAlī acknowledged impregnating her, she would have become an *umm walad*, and Sālim would have been ʿAlī's freeborn son. But Maymūna was the property of ʿAlī's daughter, Tāwatarā, on whose behalf ʿAlī merely had taken legal possession of the female slave.

Because a sexual union between a man and a female slave belonging to his daughter does not fall within the category of either marriage or lawful concubinage, one might conclude that it constitutes fornication and, further, that ʿAlī's sexual relations with Maymūna constituted unlawful use (*taʿaddī*) or usurpation (*ghaṣb*) of property.[19] The Mālikī jurists teach that if a man seizes (*ightaṣaba*) a female slave belonging to a third party and has intercourse with her, he commits fornication and is subject to the appropriate *ḥadd* punishment. If the female slave becomes pregnant, the child is affiliated to its mother and is considered to be the slave of her master. In the event that the mother had been a virgin, the fornicator must compensate her master for the decrease in her value caused by the loss of virginity (the technical term for such compensation is *ʿuqr*).[20] Thus, if one were to apply the notion of unlawful use to the present case – as many of the litigants and witnesses involved appear to have done – ʿAlī would have been subject to the *ḥadd* punishment of stoning, while Sālim would have been affiliated to his mother and considered Tāwatarā's slave. The stakes for both men were high, indeed.

[18] See Ibn Juzayy al-Gharnāṭī (d. 741/1340–41), *Qawānīn al-aḥkām al-sharʿiyya wa-masāʾil al-furūʿ al-fiqhiyya* (Cairo: ʿAlam al-Fikr, 1985), 328–9; *EI*², s.v. Umm al-walad. Note: The specification of *six* months thus made it possible for a man who had in fact impregnated his female slave to nevertheless swear an oath denying paternity of the child without perjuring himself before God.

[19] On the distinction between *taʿaddī* and *ghaṣb*, which is specific to the Mālikīs, see Ibrāhīm b. ʿAlī Ibn Farḥūn (d. 799/1396), *Tabṣirat al-ḥukkām fī uṣūl al-aqḍiya wa-manāhij al-aḥkām*, 2 vols (n.p.: n.p, 1986), vol. 2, 168; David Santillana, *Istituzioni di Diritto Musulmano Malichita con riguardo anche al sistema sciafiita* (Roma: Istituto per l'Oriente, 1925–38), vol. 2, 455–63. On *ghaṣb*, see also Yūsuf b. ʿAbdallāh Ibn ʿAbd al-Barr al-Qurṭubī (d. 1070–71), *al-Kāfī fī fiqh ahl al-madīna al-Mālikī* (Beirut: Dār al-Kutub al-ʿIlmiyya, 1407/1987), 428–30; Ibn Juzayy, *Qawānīn*, 284.

[20] Ibn ʿAbd al-Barr, *Kāfī*, 430. Ibn Juzayy (*Qawānīn*, 285) specifies that the fornicator must compensate the master for the decrease in the market value of the female slave.

But the notion of unlawful use was not applicable in this case, because sexual intercourse between a man and a female slave belonging to his child falls into a category of exceptional circumstances in which the *ḥadd* punishment for fornication is not applied. These exceptions have their origin in the Prophetic dictum, "Avoid the *ḥadd* punishments in cases of *shubuhāt*."[21] The term *shubuhāt* is the plural of *shubha*, a verbal noun that signifies, generally, a "likeness" or "resemblance."[22] As a technical, legal term, *shubha* signifies uncertainty or doubt resulting from a resemblance between an unlawful action and a lawful one. Because of the resemblance between the two actions, the jurists exempt the wrongdoer from the normal punishment, while continuing to view the action in question as unlawful.[23] With regard to fornication, Muslim jurists identified a dozen or so instances of sexual intercourse to which the notion of *shubha* applies – for example, a man who has intercourse with a woman whom he mistakenly believes to be his wife; a man who has intercourse with a slave whose master has given him permission to have intercourse with her; and a man who has intercourse with a female slave whom he owns jointly with another individual.[24] In the course of enumerating these examples, the jurists invariably mention a man who has intercourse with a female slave (*ama* or *jāriya*) belonging to his son or daughter. Such a union was classified as an example of *shubha* by Mālik b. Anas (d. 179/795), to whom is attributed the statement, "If a man cohabits with his son's or his daughter's female slave, the *ḥadd* punishment is averted from him, but he must pay the female slave's [price], whether or not she is pregnant."[25] A similar view is attributed to Ibn ʿAbd al-Barr (d. 463/1070–71),[26] Ibn Rushd (d. 520/1126),[27] and Ibn Juzayy (d. 741/1340–41).[28] The point is routinely reiterated in later Mālikī lawbooks (and it is the unanimous position of the four Sunnī *madhhabs*), in the chapter devoted to *zinā*;[29] further, in

[21] See A.J. Wensinck, *Concordance et indices de la tradition musulmane*, 8 vols (Leiden: E.J. Brill, 1936–88), vol. 3, 63–4. We will encounter this prophetic dictum in chapter two, again in connection with an accusation relating to fornication.

[22] See Edward W. Lane, *Arabic-English Lexicon*, 2 vols (reprint Cambridge, Eng.: The Islamic Texts Society, 1984), vol. 2, 1500.

[23] *EI²*, s.v. Shubha.

[24] Ibn ʿAbd al-Barr, *Kāfī*, 574–5; Muḥammad b. Aḥmad b. Rushd al-Qurṭubī (d. 520/1126), *Bidāyat al-mujtahid wa-nihāyat al-muqtaṣid*, 2 vols (Cairo: Maktabat al-Kulliyāt al-Azhariyya, 1389/1969), vol. 2, 468 [= *The Distinguished Jurist's Primer*, tr. Imran Ahsan Khan Nyazee and Muhammad Abdul Rauf, 2 vols (Reading, UK: Garnet Publishing, 1996), vol. 2, 522; Ibn Juzayy, *Qawānīn*, 303.

[25] Mālik b. Anas, *al-Muwaṭṭaʾ*, ed. Muḥammad Fuʾād ʿAbd al-Bāqī (Cairo: ʿĪsā al-Bābī al-Ḥalabī 1370/1951), vol. 2, 830. The existence of uncertainty or doubt in this instance is sometimes justified with reference to the prophetic dictum, "You and your wealth belong to your father." See, for example, Ibn Rushd, *Bidāya*, vol. 2, 468 [= *The Distinguished Jurist's Primer*, vol. 2, 522].

[26] Ibn ʿAbd al-Barr, *Kāfī*, 575.

[27] Ibn Rushd, *Bidāya*, vol. 2, 468 [= *The Distinguished Jurist's Primer*, vol. 2, 522].

[28] Ibn Juzayy, *Qawānīn*, 303.

[29] On the Mālikīs, see Muḥammad b. Aḥmad al-Dāh al-Shinqīṭī, *al-Fatḥ al-rabbānī: sharḥ ʿalā naẓm risālat Ibn Abī Zayd al-Qayrawānī*, 3 vols in 1 (Cairo: Maktabat al-Qāhira, 1969), vol. 3, 118; Khalîl Ibn-Ish'âk', *Précis de jurisprudence musulmane; ou, Principes de législation musulmane civile et religieuse selon le rite mâlékite*, tr. M. Perron, 6 vols (Paris: Imprimerie Nationale, 1848–52), vol. 6, 226; al-Mawwāq (d. 897/1492), *al-Tāj wa'l-iklīl li-mukhtaṣar Khalīl*, on the margin of al-Ḥaṭṭāb (d. 954/1547–48), *Mawāhib al-jalīl li-sharḥ mukhtaṣar Khalīl*, 6 vols (Ṭarābulus, Libya: Maktabat al-Najāḥ), vol. 6, 356; Ṣāliḥ ʿAbd al-Samīʿ al-Ābī al-Azharī, *Jawāhir al-iklīl: sharḥ mukhtaṣar al-ʿallāma al-shaykh Khalīl*, 2 vols (Cairo: ʿĪsā al-Bābī al-Ḥalabī, 1913 or 1914), vol. 2, 313.

these same texts, in the chapter devoted to the *umm walad*, one finds, for example, that "if a man has intercourse with a female slave belonging to his minor or major son [or daughter], the *ḥadd* punishment is averted from him, he owes [his child] the market value of the [female slave] on the day intercourse occurred, and she becomes his *umm walad*."[30] It goes without saying that any child born of such a union is free and is affiliated to its father.

Having established what the law says, we turn now to al-Tirjālī's application of legal doctrine to the "facts" of the present case.

In the Qāḍī's Court (1)

Shortly after his release from prison and return to the home in which he had been raised, Sālim approached the jurist and qāḍī, ʿĪsā b. Muḥammad al-Tirjālī, demanding inclusion in the group of ʿAlī's heirs on the ground that ʿAlī had acknowledged him as his son. In accordance with the requirements of Mālikī judicial procedure, al-Tirjālī summoned ʿAbd al-Raḥmān and Tāwatarā so that they might respond to Sālim's claim. Although Tāwatarā was perhaps best situated among the children of Abū al-ʿUlā' to testify regarding Sālim's status in the family, she did not appear personally before the qāḍī because her brother, ʿAbd al-Raḥmān, secured an appointment of agency from her (perhaps in return for a promise of protection or some other consideration).[31] After presenting himself to the qāḍī and speaking on behalf of himself and his sister, ʿAbd al-Raḥmān derisively rejected Sālim's claim on the ground that the man "was nothing more than the son of a female slave by the name of Maymūna who was the property of his ... sister, Tāwatarā, who had received her as part of her dower (*ṣadāq*)"; he further specified that "Sālim had been born to Maymūna while she was owned" by Tāwatarā; and he concluded his statement by indicating that Maymūna and her son had served the family as slaves until Maymūna's death, following which Sālim had continued to serve Tāwatarā as a slave.[32] From this statement, it would appear that ʿAbd al-Raḥmān was unfamiliar with the doctrine of *shubha* and was operating on the assumption that a female slave acquired the status of *umm al-walad* only if she was impregnated by *her* master.

In the *istiftā'*, al-Tirjālī included only one feature of Sālim's response to ʿAbd al-Raḥmān's statement: Sālim agreed that his mother had been a woman by the name of Maymūna, but said that she was someone other than the female slave by

[30] Al-Mawwāq, *al-Tāj*, vol. 6, 356 (citing the *Mudawwana*); cf. Khalîl Ibn-Ish'âk', *Précis de jurisprudence*, vol. 6, 226; al-Azharī, *Jawāhir al-iklīl*, vol. 2, 313; Abū al-Barakāt Aḥmad al-Dardīr (d. 1786), *al-Sharḥ al-ṣaghīr ʿalā aqrab al-masālik ilā madhhab al-Imām Mālik*, ed. Muṣṭafā Kamāl Waṣfī, 4 vols (Cairo: Dār al-Maʿārif, 1972–74), vol. 4, 562; Aḥmad b. Muḥammad al-Ṣāwī al-Mālikī (d. 1825–26), *Bulghat al-sālik li-aqrab al-masālik ilā madhhab al-Imām Mālik*, 3 vols (Cairo: ʿĪsā al-Bābī al-Ḥalabī, 1978), vol. 3, 537. See also *al-Mudawwana al-kubrā li-Mālik b. Anas al-Aṣbaḥī. Riwāyat Saḥnūn b. Saʿīd al-Tunūkhī*, 6 vols (Cairo: Maṭbaʿat al-Saʿāda, 1323/1905; repr. Beirut: Dār Ṣādir), vol. 3, 320–2.

[31] *Miʿyār*, vol. 10, 362, ll. 11–12. [32] Ibid., vol. 10, 362, ll. 12–15.

the name of Maymūna who belonged to Tāwatarā.[33] This curious statement subsequently played a key role in the qāḍī's deliberations.

Sālim's claim raised a question, not of law, but of fact: Was he or was he not the biological son of ʿAlī b. Abī al-ʿUlāʾ? Had ʿAlī been alive, his acknowledgment or denial of Sālim as his son would have been decisive. But ʿAlī apparently had died without having formally acknowledged Sālim as his son. In the absence of the requisite acknowledgement, how could anyone *prove* his or her biological identity? And what level of proof was considered sufficient to establish one's filiation to a putative father? The distinctive manner in which Mālikī law dealt with such a dilemma is one of the more interesting features of the present case.

Confronted with two contradictory assertions about an event that was as indeterminate as an event possibly could be, al-Tirjālī charged the litigants to produce testimonial evidence that might support their respective claims; that is, he instructed them to find reliable, trustworthy witnesses (*ʿudūl*, sg., *ʿādil*).[34] Although it is not expressly mentioned in the *istiftāʾ*, the initial burden of proof lay upon Sālim, whose claim contradicted the existing state of affairs. In anticipation of this burden Sālim had previously canvassed his neighborhood soliciting the testimony of (alleged) relatives, friends, neighbors, and acquaintances, including an unspecified number of professional witnesses who were attached to the qāḍī's court. No less than ninety individuals responded to the call, and it was at this point that the process of "translation" from the language of everyday discourse to that of legal discourse began. A notary familiar with the law no doubt played an instrumental role in the collection of their testimony by asking them legally relevant questions, for example, whether they had any knowledge of ʿAlī's having acknowledged Sālim as his son, or of ʿAlī's children having acknowledged Sālim as their sibling. The witnesses' answers to these questions were inscribed by the notary in a document known in Arabic as a *rasm istirʿāʾ*, that is, a document that contains the testimony of witnesses regarding a certain fact or facts that might be produced in an hour of need.[35] This

[33] Ibid., vol. 10, 362, ll. 15–16. For another claim of mistaken identity involving a female, see chapter four (= ibid., vol. 7, 312–13).

[34] On witnesses, see Emile Tyan, *Histoire de l'organisation judiciaire en pays d'Islam*, (2nd rev. edn, Leiden: E.J. Brill, 1960), 236 ff.; Jeanette Wakin, *The Function of Documents in Islamic Law* (Albany: State University of New York Press, 1972), 65 ff.; Scholze, *Malikitisches Verfahrensrecht*, 239 ff.; Clifford Geertz, *Local Knowledge: Further Essays in Interpretive Anthropology* (New York: Basic Books, 1983), 190–3; *EI*², s.v. Shāhid.

[35] *Istirʿāʾ* testimony appears to have been specific to the Mālikīs. See *Miʿyār*, vol. 10, 199–200; Ibn Farḥūn, *Tabṣira*, vol. 1, 314, 452–7; Santillana, *Istituzioni*, vol. 1, 348; vol. 2, 219, 222 ("atto segreto con cui l'attore protesta mediante notari, facendo prendere atto della causa che gli impedisce di agire"); Christian Müller, "*ṣahāda* und *kitāb al-istirʿāʾ* in der Rechtspraxis: Zur Rolle von Zeugen und Notaren in Gerichtsprozessen des 5./11. Jahrhunderts," in *Tagungsband des XXVII. Deutschen Orientalistentag, Bonn (1998)*, (Würzburg: Ergon-Verlag, 2001); Leon Buskens, *Islamitisch Recht en familiebetrekkingen in Marokko* (Amsterdam Bulaaq, 1999), 208–10. For models of *istirʿāʾ* documents, see Ibn al-ʿAṭṭār, *Formulario Notarial Hispano-Árabe por el alfaquí y notario cordobés Ibn al-ʿAṭṭār (s. X)*, ed. P. Chalmeta and F. Corriente (Madrid: Instituto Hispano-Árabe de Cultura, 1983), 230, 234–5, 281, 319–28, 336, 342, 355, 361, 364–8, 371, 376, 378–9, 438. For additional examples, see *Miʿyār*, vol. 13, index, 35–6. This type of document is also frequently attested for seventeenth-century Morocco. See Jacques Berque, *Ulémas, fondateurs, insurgés du Maghreb, xviiᵉ siècle* (Paris: Sindbad, 1982), 210, 217, 222. In certain respects the *rasm istirʿāʾ* is similar in function to the testimony of secondary witnesses (*shahāda ʿalā shahāda*). On the latter, see Wakin, *The Function of Documents*, 68–71.

document, dated "Jumādā of last year," was submitted by Sālim to the qāḍī, who, in turn, produced a summary transcription of it in his *istiftāʾ*.[36] The legal value of the testimony contained in this document was the central issue on which the determination of the case hinged.

According to al-Tirjālī's summary transcription of the *rasm istirʿāʾ*, the ninety witnesses testified as follows: some testified to having heard ʿAlī acknowledge (*yuqirru*) Sālim as his son; to having heard ʿAlī's late son, Muḥammad, acknowledge Sālim as his brother; or to having heard Tāwatarā acknowledge Sālim as her brother.[37] Others testified to the existence of a rumor that was "widespread and detailed on the tongues of professional witnesses and others" to the effect that Sālim was the son of ʿAlī and Maymūna.[38] Others testified that as a youth, Sālim had held an apprenticeship in the silk market, where he had been known exclusively as "Ibn Abī al-ʿUlāʾ", or that the townspeople, without exception, had referred to him as "Ibn Abī al-ʿUlāʾ" from the time of his birth until he reached puberty. Others testifed that whenever ʿAlī had summoned "his children," he had included Sālim in the summons, adding that ʿAlī would assign tasks to Sālim in the same manner as he did to his other children. Others testified to the special, sibling-like relationship between Sālim and Tāwatarā, who apparently had been responsible for dressing young Sālim and for purchasing his clothes and certain other necessities; in this regard, she reportedly had expressed concern that Sālim receive an allotment equal to that of her brothers and her.

The *mustaftī* was careful to include at the very end of his summary transcription of the *rasm istirʿāʾ* the testimony of an unnamed nephew of ʿAlī, whom the *mustaftī* had rejected as unreliable (*ghayr maqbūl*) for reasons not specified. This testimony nevertheless was important to al-Tirjālī because it suggested a possible explanation for ʿAlī's behavior. The nephew reported having heard his father, Ṭalḥa, imploring ʿAlī, when the latter was on his deathbed, saying, "O my brother, Sālim is your son, so attach him [to your other children]."[39] To this plea, the dying man reportedly responded in apparent fear and, perhaps, indignation, "Do you mean that I should suffer the *ḥadd* punishment when my body is about to be washed for burial?"[40] The statement attributed to ʿAlī was important to al-Tirjālī – notwithstanding the unacceptability of the witness – for it suggested a motive for ʿAlī's refusal. At this point in the summary, the *mustaftī* interjected that ʿAlī mistakenly had believed that a "person who had impregnated his daughter's female slave would be subject to the *ḥadd* punishment [for fornication, that is, stoning]."[41]

[36] *Miʿyār*, vol. 10, 362, ll. 17–18.
[37] On acknowledgement of paternity and filiation, see *EI²*, s.v. Iḳrār; Scholze, *Malikitisches Verfahrensrecht*, 132 ff.
[38] On hearsay testimony in connection with paternity, see Ibn ʿAbd al-Barr, *Kāfī*, 467–9; Ibn Farḥūn, *Tabṣira*, vol. 1, 432–3.
[39] Text: *yā akhī Sālim ibnuka fa-alḥiqhu*. On *istilḥāq*, see Ibrāhīm b. Ḥasan Ibn ʿAbd al-Rafīʿ (d. 733/1332), *Muʿīn al-ḥukkām ʿalā al-qaḍāyā wa'l-aḥkām*, 2 vols (Beirut: Dār al-Gharb al-Islāmī, 1989), vol. 2, 857–60.
[40] *Miʿyār*, vol. 10, 362 (l. 19)–3 (l. 7). Text: *a-turīdu an uḥadda ʿalā al-maghsil*. I am grateful to my colleague, Ron Shaham, for his assistance in clarifying the meaning of this phrase.
[41] Ibid., vol. 10, 363, l. 6.

It was only this erroneous assumption based upon ignorance of the law, the *mustaftī* hinted, that prompted ʿAlī to deny paternity of Sālim.

Although Sālim's document contained compelling and seemingly overwhelming evidence of his social identity, the evidence for his legal identity – the issue that was of concern to al-Tirjālī – was less weighty although still significant. In this regard, the only legally relevant information were the second-hand testimonies purporting that ʿAlī had acknowledged Sālim as his son and that Tāwatarā and Muḥammad had acknowledged Sālim as their brother, and the widespread rumor to the effect that Sālim was the son of ʿAlī and Maymūna.[42] Whatever effect the other testimonies may have had on the qāḍī, he focused his attention on the legally relevant items, which he examined carefully and divided into three categories: (1) The most important item in the document was the assertion of an unspecified number of witnesses who testified to having heard ʿAlī's acknowledgement (*iʿtirāf*) of Sālim as his son on several different occasions when ʿAlī had been sound of mind and body and therefore legally competent to make such an acknowledgement. This testimony was accepted by the qāḍī on the ground that it had been given by reliable witnesses, including one "outstanding" professional witness (*ʿādil*) who lived in Tāwatarā's neighborhood and who was the son of a distinguished jurist. This witness, a certain Ibn ʿAbd al-Salām al-Ṣanhājī,[43] specified that on one occasion Tāwatarā had summoned him to attest to her purchase of clothes on behalf of Sālim, at which time he heard her refer to ʿAlī's acknowledgement of Sālim as his son. (2) Also relevant was the testimony of nine of Tāwatarā's paternal cousins who reported having heard Tāwatarā refer to Sālim as "her brother" on at least one occasion when they had assembled in order to settle their accounts in connection with the purchase of merchandise for their minor children. Here, al-Tirjālī intervened, explaining that he did so in order to dispel a possible ambiguity with regard to this testimony; Tāwatarā, he said, may have used the word "brother" to indicate either that Sālim was related to her by common descent (*nasab*) from ʿAlī or merely to indicate their common humanity, as in the expression, "All men are brothers." In the latter event, the testimony was irrelevant. In an effort to close this linguistic loophole, al-Tirjālī asked each of the nine witnesses to specify his understanding of Tāwatarā's use of the word "brother". All nine concurred that she had used the word in the sense of common descent from the same father. Their clarification was added to their original testimony as a supplementary statement.[44] (3) The third legally relevant item in the document was the widespread rumor circulated by professional witnesses and others in the markets and on the streets to the effect that Sālim was the son of ʿAlī b. Abī al-ʿUlāʾ; one of these witnesses added by way of supplement to his testimony that ʿAlī "had fathered [Sālim] together with his [*sic*] female slave, Maymūna." Disregarding the erroneous attribution of ownership, al-Tirjālī accepted this testimony on the

[42] On the distinction between direct and indirect paternity, see EI^2, s.v., Iḳrār.

[43] His father's name was Abū Muḥammad ʿAbd al-Salām al-Ṣanhājī. I have not succeeded in identifying either the father or the son.

[44] On supplementary testimony, see Wakin, *Documents*, 69–70.

ground that it had been given by a large number of prominent individuals (shaykhs) and professional witnesses.[45]

By summoning witnesses who testified to ʿAlī's utterances and actions, Sālim succeeded in persuading the qāḍī that there was a direct link between those reported utterances and actions and the "fact" that he was ʿAlī's son. On the strength of the testimonial evidence contained in the *rasm istirʿāʾ*, al-Tirjālī apparently was prepared to issue a judgment in favor of Sālim. At this point in the litigation, the burden of proof shifted to ʿAbd al-Raḥmān, who was now offered the opportunity to refute the legally relevant evidence presented by Sālim (the technical term for this procedure is *iʿdhār*), for which purpose the qāḍī stipulated a deadline.[46] In an act of resistance, ʿAbd al-Raḥmān ignored the initial deadline, either to signal his contempt for the judicial proceedings or to buy time. Only after receiving several extensions did ʿAbd al-Raḥmān make any attempt to refute the evidence, arguing, the *mustaftī* explained, that Sālim was not entitled to anything because the wealth in question belonged to the sulṭān and because Sālim had not been a partner to the arrangement devised by the sovereign for the provisioning of ʿAlī's children.[47]

Interlude: In the *Majlis* of the Sulṭān

ʿAbd al-Raḥmān's reference to the sulṭān in his "explanation" may have suggested to Sālim (or to his legal agent) an alternative means to resolve the dispute. From Sālim's perspective, his omission from the previous sulṭān's arrangement was a mistake that might be rectified by the current sulṭān, Abū Saʿīd. Accordingly, Sālim proceeded to the Royal Palace, where he submitted a complaint (*shakwā*) to the sovereign (*mawlā*), presumably at one of the weekly sessions of his Council (*majlis*).[48] This "interlude" takes up less then two lines in our source, which does not convey any details relating to the complaint. Sālim no doubt asked the sulṭān to add his name to the list of ʿAlī's children who were entitled to a pension. The sulṭān, however, refused to intervene directly in the dispute. Instead, he issued a directive, returning the case to the qāḍī's court and instructing al-Tirjālī to decide between the two men.[49]

[45] *Miʿyār*, vol. 10, 363, ll. 7–20.
[46] On *iʿdhār*, see Ibn Farḥūn, *Tabṣira*, vol. 1, 97, 194.
[47] *Miʿyār*, vol. 10, 363, ll. 20–3.
[48] On the Marīnid *majlis*, see Muḥammad al-Manūnī, *Waraqāt ʿan al-ḥaḍāra al-Maghribiyya fī ʿaṣr Banī Marīn* (Rabat: Kulliyyāt al-Ādāb wa'l-ʿUlūm al-Insāniyya, 1979).
[49] *Miʿyār*, vol. 10, 363, ll. 23–4. For additional cases in which a sulṭān became involved in a property dispute, see chapters four and five.

In the Qāḍī's Court (2)

ʿAbd al-Raḥmān, no doubt realizing that he was likely to lose the case unless he refuted the evidence presented by Sālim with evidence of equal or greater import, now sought testimonial evidence that would support the existing state of affairs. The witnesses that he summoned for this purpose, members of the local community, probably were familiar with Sālim's position in the family of ʿAlī b. Abī al-ʿUlāʾ, and ʿAbd al-Raḥmān surely informed them of the contents of Sālim's *rasm istirʿāʾ* so as to facilitate their formulation of credible statements that would neutralize the impact of the statements made by Sālim's witnesses. After securing this testimony, ʿAbd al-Raḥmān submitted four documents to al-Tirjālī.

First document

The first document (another *rasm istirʿāʾ*) is dated "Ramaḍān of last year" (that is, three or four months subsequent to the date of Sālim's document) and contains the testimony of (only) thirteen witnesses. After noting their familiarity with ʿAlī, these witnesses asserted that "he did not have a child by the name of Sālim, he did not treat [Sālim] as a blood-relative, and he did not affiliate himself to him by way of descent during his lifetime."[50] Acknowledging their familiarity with the rumor regarding Sālim's status as ʿAlī's son, the witnesses offered a chronological specification: it was only subsequent to ʿAlī's death that certain people began to refer to Sālim as ʿAlī's "son" because the boy had been raised subject to ʿAlī's interdiction and tutelage.[51]

Al-Tirjālī sought to undermine the evidentiary value of this testimony. Based upon his interrogation of the witnesses, he rejected the testimony of ten (including three scholars), accepting that of only three.[52] Then, exercising his powers of judicial discretion, the qāḍī elicited supplementary statements from the three acceptable witnesses in which they reformulated their original testimony. Two of the three witnesses qualified their initial testimony, stating that "ʿAlī was not known to have any child except for Raḥḥū, Muḥammad, and Tāwatarā" and conceding that "Sālim was raised in their midst." The third witness – described by al-Tirjālī as "the best of them with respect to status" – added that "Maymūna, Sālim's mother, was the property of the daughter, the aforementioned Tāwatarā; she sometimes served in the presence of (*ʿinda*) ʿAlī and at other times in the

[50] Ibid., vol. 10, 363 (l. 25)–4 (l. 1).

[51] Ibid., vol. 10, 364, l. 1. Text: *fī ḥajrihi wa-kafālatihi.*

[52] Although al-Tirjālī does not specify the grounds for his rejection of these ten witnesses, he does mention that two of the three scholars testified merely to the contents of the document, apparently without any direct personal knowledge of the facts. Al-Tirjālī may have rejected the testimony of the third scholar, who testified that "ʿAlī was not known to have any child (*walad*) except for Muḥammad and Raḥḥū," on the grounds of the witness's apparent disregard for Tāwatarā.

presence of his daughter"; this witness also testified that he had never heard ʿAlī acknowledge Sālim as his son or affiliate the boy to him by way of descent.[53]

These reformulations were important because they made it possible for al-Tirjālī to undermine the force of the testimony presented on behalf of ʿAbd al-Raḥmān. Invoking an underlying assumption about the truth-value of competing statements, he explained that the testimony of ʿAbd al-Raḥmān's three acceptable witnesses did not *necessarily* contradict the evidence presented by Sālim because their testimony did not produce epistemological certainty (*ʿilm*) regarding the *non*-existence of a child of ʿAlī's about whom they may have been unaware. Indeed, al-Tirjālī observed, these same three witnesses conceded that some people currently regarded Sālim as ʿAlī's son precisely because the boy had been raised under ʿAlī's guardianship and protection. Finally, the *mustaftī* noted that the supplementary statement by the third, and most reliable, witness – the witness who asserted that Maymūna sometimes served as a slave in ʿAlī's house – constituted *prima facie* evidence of ʿAlī's having had the opportunity to engage in sexual relations with, and to impregnate, his daughter's female slave.[54]

Second document

Undeterred, ʿAbd al-Raḥmān produced another *istirʿāʾ* document, dated 712/1312–13, in which an unspecified number of witnesses testified to the fact of ʿAlī's death and to the identity of his heirs – without making any reference whatsoever to Sālim. This testimony, according to ʿAbd al-Raḥmān, demonstrated that Sālim could not have been ʿAlī's son. Again invoking an *a priori* assumption about the truth-value of competing statements, al-Tirjālī countered that these witnesses' unfamiliarity with Sālim did not necessarily prevail over the positive assertions of Sālim's witnesses.[55] Drawing upon his familiarity with the events of Sālim's life, the *mustaftī* added another reason for rejecting the testimony included in the second document – that the omission of Sālim's name from the list of ʿAlī's heirs may be explained by Sālim's absence from his "family" when the death-and-inheritance certificate was inscribed.[56]

Third document

It had now become clear to ʿAbd al-Raḥmān that the testimony contained in Sālim's *istirʿāʾ* document constituted a major obstacle to his interests. Shifting from a defensive to an offensive strategy, he now attempted to set a trap for the

[53] Ibid., vol. 10, 364, ll. 1–8.
[54] Ibid., vol. 10, 364, ll. 8–14.
[55] Ibid., vol. 10, 364, ll. 14–17.
[56] Ibid., vol. 10, 364, ll. 23–4.

qāḍī by impugning the credibility of a witness who had testified on behalf of Sālim. ʿAbd al-Raḥmān produced a third document, in which, after asserting their familiarity with Tāwatarā, witnesses testified that the latter's ownership of Maymūna had been legally valid; that Sālim had been born to Maymūna while she was owned by Tāwatarā; and that they had no knowledge of Tāwatarā's having sold or alienated Maymūna at any time prior to the female slave's death.[57] After the qāḍī had accepted the testimony of these witnesses, ʿAbd al-Raḥmān drew attention to the fact that one of them had also testified in Sālim's *istirʿāʾ* document, where he had stated that both Tāwatarā and her brother, Muḥammad, had acknowledged Sālim as their brother. But how could Sālim be their brother when he was the product of a sexual union between ʿAlī and a female slave belonging to his daughter? Clearly unfamiliar with the doctrine of *shubha*, ʿAbd al-Raḥmān argued that this "contradiction" impugned the reliability of this witness and rendered his testimony inadmissible, and, ʿAbd al-Raḥmān continued, since the testimony of this "tainted" witness had served as the basis for the testimony of other witnesses in Sālim's *istirʿāʾ* document, the testimony of the latter also should be rejected.[58]

Al-Tirjālī first refuted this argument on its own merits. Drawing upon his training as a jurist, he argued that there was no necessary contradiction between the two statements of the witness in question, who could have given his testimony at two different times, as follows: After initially testifying on the basis of his personal knowledge that Maymūna was a slave who was the property of Tāwatarā (as recorded in ʿAbd al-Raḥmān's third document), the witness subsequently may have learned that both Tāwatarā and Muḥammad had acknowledged Sālim as their brother, testifying to this effect in Sālim's *istirʿāʾ* document.[59] But even so, the point was moot, the *mustaftī* continued, because the argument advanced by ʿAbd al-Raḥmān was specious. In a critical statement, the *mustaftī* succinctly summarized the underlying legal basis of his impending judgment, asserting that ʿAbd al-Raḥmān's third document established two legal facts: Tāwatarā was Maymūna's legal owner, and Sālim was Maymūna's son. If it were further established that ʿAlī had impregnated Maymūna, the legal consequences of that determination, the *mustaftī* explained, would be as follows: the *ḥadd* punishment for fornication would be averted from ʿAlī (because of *shubha*); the child would be affiliated to ʿAlī (on the basis of the evidence establishing impregnation); and ʿAlī would be indebted to Tāwatarā (that is, she would have a claim against his estate) for an amount equal to Maymūna's *qīma*, or market value (so that the female slave would acquire the status of an *umm walad*).[60]

[57] Ibid., vol. 10, 365, ll. 9–11.
[58] Ibid., vol. 10, 364, ll. 17–21. Note: For the purpose of clarity I have reversed the order of the third and fourth documents, as recorded in the *istiftāʾ*.
[59] Ibid., vol. 10, 364, ll. 21–3.
[60] Ibid., vol. 10, 365, ll. 15–17.

Fourth document

ʿAbd al-Raḥmān now presented as evidence a fourth and final document, a testamentary instrument in which ʿAlī b. Abī al-ʿUlāʾ had specified that in the event of his death, his son, ʿAbd al-Raḥmān, was to serve as the guardian of "his minor children." ʿAbd al-Raḥmān drew the qāḍī's attention to the fact that although Sālim had been a minor at the time that this instrument was drafted, he had not been mentioned in the document. Had Sālim in fact been ʿAlī's son, ʿAbd al-Raḥman contended, ʿAlī surely would have included him.[61]

Al-Tirjālī rejected this argument on the strength of customary social practice and law: drawing upon his knowledge of social practice, he first explained that it was customary for a father to appoint a different guardian for each set of consanguine siblings (if Sālim were in fact ʿAlī's son, he had a different mother to that of ʿAlī's other children). Second, it reportedly was customary for a prominent individual – such as ʿAlī – to acknowledge the impregnation of a female slave, especially a slave who belonged to his daughter. ʿAlī's failure to make any such formal acknowledgement prior to the moment at which he drafted the testamentary instrument presumably made him reluctant to acknowledge Sālim as his son at that time, for, "as one of the leaders of the people of the town," he would have suffered "disgrace" (*ʿār*) in the eyes of his siblings and other relatives. Asserting his ability to understand ʿAlī's state of mind, al-Tirjālī explained that fear of this consequence accounts for ʿAlī's silence. Third, this fear may have been compounded by ʿAlī's erroneous assumption that by acknowledging his impregnation of a female slave belonging to his daughter, he would have become subject to the stoning penalty for unlawful intercourse.[62] ʿAlī apparently did not realize, al-Tirjālī observed, that the impregnation of a female slave belonging to one's daughter does not result in any punishment; that is, he was unaware of the doctrine of *shubha*. Finally, al-Tirjālī explained, the present argument was analogous to that of a man who left a last will and testament in which he designated a guardian for his minor sons, whom he specified by name. Following the testator's death, it was discovered that a minor child of his had not been mentioned in the testamentary instrument. According to Mālikī school doctrine, al-Tirjālī explained, that child is included within the scope of the instrument.[63]

Having exhausted his testimonial resources, ʿAbd al-Raḥmān now placed one last card on the table, reminding al-Tirjālī of the statement uttered by Sālim at the very outset of the litigation, when the two men had been summoned by the qāḍī to present their respective sides of the dispute. At that time, Sālim had stated that his mother, whose name was Maymūna, should not be confused with the female slave by the name of Maymūna who belonged to Tāwatarā. But in ʿAbd al-Raḥman's

[61] Ibid., vol. 10, 364, ll. 24–6. Note again: For the purpose of clarity I have reversed the order of the third and fourth documents, as recorded in the *istiftāʾ*.

[62] Ibid., vol. 10, 365, ll. 2–6.

[63] Ibid., vol. 10, 364 (l. 26)–5 (l. 9).

third document, witnesses had testified that "Sālim was born to [Maymūna the slave] while she was owned by [Tāwatarā]." Further, the qāḍī himself had gone on record as accepting this statement as a legal fact (see above). In ʿAbd al-Raḥmān's view, this legal fact flatly contradicted Sālim's earlier statement, thereby undermining Sālim's credibility as a witness.[64]

This argument placed al-Tirjālī on the horns of a dilemma: if he accepted it, then all of the legal work that he had performed to this point would come unraveled; if he rejected it, then any judgment he might issue in favor of Sālim would be open to challenge on the ground that it was based on the testimony of a demonstrated liar. Of all the arguments advanced by ʿAbd al-Raḥmān, this is the only one that seems to have troubled and distressed the qāḍī, presumably because it threatened to undermine his professional reputation as a judge. Trapped in a web of his own making, al-Tirjālī conceded that Sālim's statement was false and indicated that there might be some validity to ʿAbd al-Raḥman's argument. Be that as it may, he declared, Sālim's statement about his mother was nonetheless legally irrelevant and should be disregarded, for four reasons: first, again invoking an epistemological consideration, al-Tirjālī explained that Sālim had been under no legal obligation to respond to a question regarding his mother's legal status, for he could not have had any knowledge regarding her legal status prior to his birth (note: in his formulation of the *istiftāʾ*, al-Tirjālī skillfully obscured the fact that it must have been he himself who posed the question). And although Sālim subsequently may have acquired information regarding his mother's legal status at the time of his birth, any testimony that he gave on this subject would constitute merely his recollection of his developing awareness – not reliable knowledge. Second, claiming knowledge of Sālim's state of mind, al-Tirjālī argued that if Sālim did know that his mother had been a slave at the time of his birth, he would have been reluctant to acknowledge that fact for fear that he, too, would be classified as a slave. Third, Sālim's denial of the fact that the slave by the name of Maymūna was his mother does not undermine the force of Tāwatarā's acknowledgement of Sālim as her brother – again, on the ground that a positive assertion prevails over a negative one. Finally, pushing judicial logic to its limits by assuming the opposite of his desired conclusion, al-Tirjālī argued that so long as Sālim was considered a slave, no acknowledgement he made was binding.[65]

The Case is "Appealed"

At this point, a potentially significant shift of venue occurred. Rebuffed at every turn and realizing that a judgment in favor of Sālim was imminent, ʿAbd al-Raḥmān sought to thwart that outcome by taking his claim to another judicial authority. This turn of events is described by al-Tirjālī in his *istiftāʾ*, where he relates that

[64] Ibid., vol. 10, 365, ll. 17–20. [65] Ibid., vol. 10, 365, ll. 20–5.

ʿAbd al-Raḥmān "set out for the city of Fez"[66] and asked a muftī (whose name he does not specify) to examine the case. If the muftī determined some irregularity in the qāḍī's handling of the case, it was in his power to instruct the qāḍī to reconsider his impending judgment.[67] But, al-Tirjālī added, it was necessary for such a request to be accompanied by a letter written by the initial, presiding qāḍī and containing an authoritative summary of the legal facts pertaining to the case. Ignorant of this requirement or, perhaps, reluctant to ask al-Tirjālī to write such a letter, ʿAbd al-Raḥmān presented the Fāsī muftī with his own version of the facts, for which reason, al-Tirjālī asserted, the latter refused to issue a fatwā directly addressing the issue of whether or not Sālim was ʿAlī's son. But the muftī did give ʿAbd al-Raḥmān a letter – designated by al-Tirjālī as a quittance (*barāʾa*) – pointing to a possible error in the latter's analysis of the hearsay testimony included in Sālim's document. In his letter, the muftī cited a case involving hearsay testimony mentioned in the chapter on testimony in the *Kitāb al-Tabṣira* of al-Lakhmī (d. 478/1075).[68] According to al-Lakhmī, if two professional witnesses testify regarding a rumor that is widespread in their town, the qāḍī must seek confirmation of that rumor from a third professional witness before passing judgment. Al-Lakhmī added that if two other professional witnesses deny the existence of the rumor, then the original testimony may not serve as the basis for a judicial decision.[69]

ʿAbd al-Raḥmān conveyed this letter to al-Tirjālī and suggested that the point of law raised by the muftī was relevant to the present case. In his view, the *istirʿāʾ* document submitted by Sālim (which contained testimony about a widespread rumor) was contradicted by the testimony of professional witnesses in ʿAbd al-Raḥmān's third document. For this reason, ʿAbd al-Raḥmān contended, Sālim's document properly could not serve as the basis for any judicial decision.[70]

To fend off the consequences of the Fāsī muftī's mention of the earlier case, al-Tirjālī argued that there was an important difference between the two cases (employing a rhetorical technique known as *dissociation*) and that his conclusion in the present case was not incompatible with that of the earlier one. Demonstrating his familiarity with the *Tabṣira*, the *mustaftī* explained that al-Lakhmī's stipulation was sound but had no bearing on the present case, because the two cases dealt with different factual circumstances: al-Lakhmī had cited a case in which two witnesses conveyed hearsay testimony regarding a person who was absent in another town, and, subsequently, two professional witnesses gave contradictory testimony. In the present case, all of the testimony relating to the dispute was given by witnesses who were residents of the same town. Al-Lakhmī's stipulation, al-Tirjālī continued, does not apply in the present case, in which, confronted with

[66] Ibid., vol. 10, 365, ll. 25–6.

[67] See David S. Powers, "On Judicial Review in Islamic Law," *Law and Society Review*, 26 (1992), 315–41.

[68] The *Tabṣira* is a commentary on the *Mudawwana*; see Makhlūf, *Shajara*, vol. 1, 117; C. Brockelmann, *Geschichte der arabischen Litteratur*, 2 vols plus 3 supplements (Leiden: E.J. Brill, 1937–49), vol. 1, 383, *Supplement*, vol. 1, 661. On hearsay testimony in connection with paternity, see note 38, above.

[69] *Miʿyār*, vol. 10, 365 (l. 25)–6 (l. 8).

[70] Ibid., vol. 10, 366, ll. 9–10.

two contradictory assertions, he was obliged to determine which had greater probative value, a determination that he made by examining the character of the respective witnesses and assessing the legal value of their respective testimonies. With regard to character, he determined that the witnesses who testified on behalf of Sālim were more closely connected to (*amass bi-*) ʿAlī, were older, and were more veteran residents of the town than were the witnesses who testified on behalf of ʿAbd al-Raḥmān (thereby demonstrating his understanding of *ʿadāla* or "integrity"). With regard to the legal value of the testimony, he determined that the testimony given on behalf of Sālim contained no contradiction. For these reasons, he concluded, the differences between the present case and the case mentioned by al-Lakhmī in his *Tabṣira* outweighed any similarities between them.[71]

The Search for Judicial Consensus and Doctrinal Support

Consultation with Judicial Advisors (shūra) *and Search for Doctrinal Support*

It is understandable that by this point in the litigation, the qāḍī was experiencing a certain measure of judicial anxiety. The testimony presented on behalf of Sālim was based on hearsay, and its validity had been challenged by a Fāsī jurist; Sālim himself had been accused of giving false testimony; and there was no dearth of documentary evidence that might be construed as supporting the maintenance of the existing state of affairs. At this time, al-Tirjālī consulted with several local jurists – presumably muftīs attached to his court – who corroborated the soundness of his legal reasoning, thereby establishing a local consensual base for his impending judgment.

Al-Tirjālī must have realized that his interpretation of al-Lakhmī was open to challenge, for which reason it was important that he adduce a judicial precedent that would provide positive doctrinal support for his judgment. To this end, he turned to earlier court practice, documented in a text containing a series of "Questions" (*Asʾila*) submitted by the Maghribī jurist, ʿIyāḍ (d. 544/1149),[72] to the Cordovan jurist, Ibn Rushd al-Jadd (d. 520/1126).[73] One case mentioned in this

[71] Ibid., vol. 10, 366, ll. 11–16.

[72] See al-Qāḍī Abū al-Faḍl ʿIyāḍ b. Mūsā b. ʿIyāḍ al-Yaḥsubī, known as Qāḍī ʿIyāḍ, *Madhāhib al-ḥukkām fī nawāzil al-aḥkām* (Beirut: Dār al-Garb al-Islāmī, 1990), 54–5. For biographical details, see Makhlūf, *Shajara*, vol. 1, 140, no. 411; Henry Toledano, *Judicial Practice and Family Law in Morocco* (Boulder, CO: Social Science Monographs), 104, note 44. We will encounter ʿĪyāḍ again in chapter five.

[73] Abū al-Walīd Muḥammad b. Aḥmad Ibn Rushd, the grandfather of Averroes and a highly esteemed and frequently quoted Mālikī jurist. His most important works include a commentary on the *Mudawwana* entitled *al-Muqaddimāt al-mumahhidāt li-bayān mā iqtaḍathu rusūm al-Mudawwana min al-aḥkām*. See Makhlūf, *Shajara*, vol. 1, 129, no. 376; Toledano, *Judicial Practice*, 52, note 3; Vincent Lagardère, "Abū l-Walīd b. Rušd qāḍī al-quḍāt de Cordoue," *Revue des Etudes Islamiques*, LIV (1986), 203–24.

text refers to a man who owned a female slave who gave birth to a son. Many years later, the slave-owner insisted that the child born to his female slave was his slave (*ghulām*), although the latter contended, "I am your son (*ibnuka*) by a free woman who is the daughter of two free persons." Two sets of testimony were presented on behalf of the claimant, one by a number of men who were not professional witnesses and the other by an unspecified number of men who were. The former group offered their testimony on the basis of the slave-owner's acknowledgement of the child as his son; the latter group testified on the basis of a widespread rumor to the effect that the child was his son. ʿIyāḍ asked Ibn Rushd whether the hearsay testimony conveyed by the professional witnesses was acceptable and, further, whether it made any difference if the person who was the object of the hearsay testimony was dead or alive. When al-Tirjālī presented this case to his legal advisors, he asked them whether it was not, in fact, more relevant to the case at hand than the case cited by al-Lakhmī. Curiously, however, he did not indicate their response.[74] (It also should be noted at this point that al-Tirjālī, in his *istiftā'*, reproduced only the question posed to Ibn Rushd but not his answer, perhaps because the answer was equivocal and might have been taken to indicate that hearsay testimony conveyed by professional witnesses was *not* sufficient to establish paternity; see below).[75]

Futyā

Al-Tirjālī was not satisfied merely with local consensus. Sensitive to the gravity of the case and to the possible social and political repercussions of his impending judgment, the qāḍī sought corroboration for his legal analysis from a prominent Fāsī muftī, Ibrāhīm b. ʿAbdallāh al-Yaznāsinī.[76] For this purpose, al-Tirjālī wrote his long and detailed narrative summary of the facts of the case, including summaries of all the relevant testimonial evidence, taking care to indicate those aspects of the case about which he was uncertain. At the end of the *istiftā'* – which has served as the basis of the present reconstruction – al-Tirjālī asked the muftī to respond to three questions: Was his refutation of the arguments advanced by ʿAbd al-Raḥmān legally sound? Did Sālim's denial that the slave named Maymūna was his mother negate his credibility as a witness – either absolutely or in part? And what bearing on the case – if any – did the quittance issued by the Fāsī mufti have?[77]

Al-Yaznāsinī, beginning his response with an unexplained allusion to "pressure from his [viz., al-Tirjālī's] master"[78] (perhaps someone, such as the sulṭān, who wanted al-Tirjālī to rule in favor of ʿAbd al-Raḥmān), immediately committed himself to a legal conclusion. In the course of his short response, he gratuitously

[74] *Miʿyār*, vol. 10, 366 (l. 16)–7 (l. 1).

[75] See Qāḍī ʿIyāḍ, *Madhāhib al-ḥukkām*, 54. This fatwā may also be found in *Miʿyār*, vol. 10, 156–57; and in Muḥammad b. Aḥmad Ibn Rushd, *Fatāwā Ibn Rushd*, 3 vols (Beirut: Dār al-Gharb al-Islāmī, 1987), vol. 2, 1081–82.

[76] On him, see note 15, above.

[77] *Miʿyār*, vol. 10, 367, ll. 1–10.

[78] Ibid., vol. 10, 367, l. 11. Text: "*ḍaghṭa min ṣāḥibihi*," alternatively, "pressure from his colleague."

offered his view on Sālim's legal status: Sālim's filiation to ʿAlī was established, in the first instance, by the testimony confirming the widespread rumor to the effect that they were father and son, and, further, by the corroborating testimonies contained in Sālim's *istirʿāʾ* document. Taken together, the muftī explained, these two testimonial declarations attained the legal level of epistemological certainty known as *al-tawātur al-maʿnāwī*,[79] that is, testimonies whose exact wording differs but that are mutually corroboratory with regard to their essential meaning and that are transmitted by a sufficient number of witnesses to preclude the possibility of error. On the other hand, the muftī regarded as legally inconsequential both Tāwatarā's acknowledgement that Sālim was "her brother" and Muḥammad's acknowledgement to the same effect.[80]

Turning to the three questions posed by the *mustaftī*, al-Yaznāsinī responded perfunctorily as follows: (1) There is no contradiction between the testimony contained in Sālim's *istirʿāʾ* document (specifically, the testimony asserting that Sālim is ʿAlī's son) and the testimony contained in ʿAbd al-Raḥmān's first document (specifying that ʿAlī had no heir other than Raḥḥū, Muḥammad, and Tāwatarā), for the reasons adduced by al-Tirjālī; and even if one were to concede, for the sake of argument, that the testimonies contained in the two documents were contradictory, Sālim's claim would prevail over that of ʿAbd al-Raḥmān, because Mālikī doctrine accords greater credence to a positive assertion than it does to a negative one. Turning to the critical legal issues, al-Yaznāsinī explained that Sālim's affiliation to ʿAlī was not undermined by the fact that his mother had been a slave belonging to Tāwatarā. Rather, (a) ʿAlī became liable for Maymūna from the moment that sexual contact occurred (*li-annahu bi-nafs al-masīs dakhalat fī ḍamānihi*) and owed his daughter a sum of money equal to the slave's market value (*lazimathu al-qīma*); (b) Maymūna became an *umm walad* (the first reference to this key term in either the *istiftāʾ* or the response); and (c) the female slave's market value was to be determined on the basis of her value on the day that intercourse occurred (because that is when the unlawful use occurred). There was no need, the muftī added, for a judicial decision (*ḥukm*) declaring Sālim's freedom.[81] (2) Sālim's denial of the fact that the slave named Maymūna was his mother does not impugn his credibility as a witness, because, at the time of his birth he was legally a minor and, by definition, did not qualify as a reliable witness.[82] (3) Finally, al-Yaznāsinī corroborated the soundness of al-Tirjālī's analysis of the quittance written by the unnamed Fāsī muftī and submitted as evidence by ʿAbd al-Raḥmān. Confirming al-Tirjālī's argument that the legal issue discussed by

[79] On this term, see Wael Hallaq, "On Inductive Corroboration, Probability, and Certainty in Sunnī Legal Thought," in *Islamic Law and Jurisprudence: Studies in Honor of Farhat J. Ziadeh*, ed. Nicholas Heer (Seattle: University of Washington Press, 1990), 3–32, esp. 19–21.

[80] *Miʿyār*, vol. 10, 367, ll. 11–16. The acknowledgements were legally inconsequential because they were indirect. A person who recognizes someone as being his brother cannot attribute to the beneficiary the status of being the son of his own father, without the latter's approval. In the absence of such approval, the beneficiary has no rights except as regards the author of the acknowledgement. See *EI*², s.v., Iḳrār.

[81] *Miʿyār*, vol. 10, 367, ll. 16–22.

[82] Ibid., vol. 10, 367, ll. 22–3.

al-Lakhmī had no bearing whatsoever on the case at hand, al-Yaznāsinī assured al-Tirjālī that his legal analysis of the case had been exemplary.[83]

Discussion

Shubha

As in other societies, levels of awareness among Muslims of the prevailing laws, norms, and values vary from one individual to the next and may be affected by differences in class, gender, education, and personal experience. Whereas some aspects of Mālikī legal doctrine were known to most Muslims in fourteenth-century Morocco, others – such as the notion of *shubha* as applied to sexual activity – were known only to a relatively small number of jurists and judges. In the case examined here, many of the litigants and witnesses involved in the dispute appear to have been operating under the erroneous assumption that sexual relations between a man and a female slave belonging to his daughter called for the *ḥadd* punishment for fornication; conversely, few of them appear to have been familiar with the legal concept of *shubha* as applied to this category of sexual relation. In other words, our case points to a gap between social practice and the law: members of the local Muslim community believed that sexual relations between a man and his daughter's slave entailed the *ḥadd* punishment for fornication, whereas Mālikī doctrine does not impose any punishment for such relations. It was through litigations such as the one that we have examined that Muslim jurists gradually filled such gaps. Together, the qāḍī and the muftī were sending an important signal to Muslim men and women: although technically illegal, sexual intercourse between a man and a virgin slave belonging to his daughter was not punishable. But that allowance was accompanied by responsibilities similar to those associated with a man's right to engage in sexual intercourse with a slave that he himself owned. Not only must he compensate his daughter for the decrease in the market value of her slave as a result of the loss of virginity, but also, if he acknowledged impregnating the slave, he was required to purchase her from his daughter, whereupon the slave acquired the status of an *umm walad* and the child was considered the freeborn son of its father – with all attendant legal rights and obligations. In this manner, the notion of *shubha*, as defined by Muslim jurists, extended the range of a man's sexual activity beyond the parameters of polygyny and concubinage, embodying a "policy" that not only reinforced patriarchal interests but also gradually transformed outsiders who had been brought into the Abode of Islam (*dār al-islām*) as slaves into freeborn members of the Muslim community, thereby promoting the biological and social reproduction of that

[83] Ibid., vol. 10, 367, ll. 24–6.

community.[84] By articulating, announcing and disseminating Mālikī legal norms and values, qāḍīs and muftīs contributed to the shaping and re-shaping of what it meant for a particular society to be "Islamic" at a given place and time in history.

The Work of the Qāḍī

Had ʿAlī b. Abī al-ʿUlā' been alive at the time of Sālim's release from prison, his oral acknowledgement or denial in the presence of reliable witnesses would have been sufficient to settle the paternity claim. But ʿAlī was dead, and he apparently never had formally acknowledged or denied Sālim in the presence of trustworthy witnesses. His failure to do so makes the case interesting to the modern observer, for it necessitated some other method of determining, first, whether or not ʿAlī and Maymūna had had sexual intercourse and, second, whether ʿAlī had fathered Sālim – an event that could have important financial and social consequences.

Certain aspects of the fourteenth-century Maghribī "legal sensibility"[85] are revealed in the efforts of the legal agents and litigants to "determine the indeterminable."[86] One striking feature is the qāḍī's reliance on the local community to determine who is or is not a member of a particular family and his willingness to accept the collective voice of the community over that of family members. Al-Tirjālī charged the litigants to produce testimonial evidence, placing the burden of fact-finding on them and pushing the fact-finding process down to the local level.[87] In response to the qāḍī's charge, the litigants identified members of the community who possessed local knowledge (in this case, indirect and mostly second-hand) that might support one or another version of the facts. Once witnesses had been identified, their knowledge was "translated" into the language and terminology of the law.[88] The process of translation was carried out, first by the notary who recorded their testimony and, at a later stage, by the qāḍī himself. After listening to the testimony (or reading the document in which it was inscribed), al-Tirjālī examined the status and character of the witnesses, paying careful attention to social and demographic factors (as, for example, personal reputation, age, relationship to the litigant, and length of residence in the town or village); any of these factors might constitute grounds for rejection of a witness' testimony.[89] He

84 On the significance of *shubha*, see further G.-H. Bousquet, *L'éthique sexuelle de l'Islam* (2nd edn, Paris: G.P. Maisonneuve et Larose, 1966), 62 ff.

85 The term is taken from Geertz, *Local Knowledge*, 175.

86 The phrase echoes the title of the second chapter of Rosen, *The Anthropology of Justice*.

87 Cf. Rosen, *The Anthropology of Justice*, 37, 65.

88 On law as a process of "translation," see James Boyd White, *Justice as Translation: An Essay in Cultural and Legal Criticism* (Chicago: University of Chicago Press, 1990).

89 We are dealing here with what anthropologists refer to as a "multiplex" community in which it is taken for granted that people living in a quarter have a deep and intimate knowledge of what goes on "behind closed doors." See Max Gluckman, *The Judicial Process Among the Barotse of Northern Rhodesia* (Manchester: Manchester University Press, 1955), 18–19; Richard Antoun, *Arab Village: A Social Structural Study of A Transjordanian Peasant Community* (Bloomington: Indiana University Press, 1972), 68–9, 78, 82, and 164.

then interrogated the witnesses, placing their testimonies into legally relevant categories, and, in several instances, asking specific witnesses to reformulate their statements. The important evidentiary point corroborated by this case is that hearsay testimony apparently was sufficient to establish paternity, provided that it met certain qualitative and quantitative conditions.[90]

In classifying the truth-claims of the witnesses' testimony, al-Tirjālī drew upon a wide range of hermeneutical tools – such as, the assumption that a positive assertion prevails over a negative one, the techniques of harmonization and dissociation, and common sense (for example, a child cannot know with certainty the legal status of its mother at the time of its birth). The qāḍī also sought to explain the actions and utterances of the litigants on the basis of his understanding of typical human behavior, for example, fear of punishment (invoked as an explanation for ʿAlī's failure to acknowledge Sālim and for Sālim's assertion that his mother had been a freeborn woman) and sexual desire (he took it for granted that a free Muslim man who had access to a female slave belonging to a member of his family would engage in sexual relations with her). Similarly, he drew upon his understanding of customary social practice, with regard to parents and children, to explain ʿAlī's "failure" to mention Sālim in the document in which he designated a testamentary guardian for his "minor children".

During the course of the litigation, al-Tirjālī engaged in complex forms of legal analysis (an activity that usually does not manifest itself in a judgment, or *ḥukm*), demonstrating his knowledge of, and ability to manipulate, legal discourse. Although the underlying legal concept that drove his analysis of the case – the notion of *shubha* – was straightforward (at least to the *mustaftī* and the muftī) and required little discussion, the qāḍī's knowledge of legal doctrine is reflected in his use of an earlier case to refute ʿAbd al-Raḥmān's argument regarding the fourth document. Similarly, in response to the *barāʾa* issued by the unnamed Fāsī muftī, he drew upon his knowledge of al-Lakhmī's *al-Tabṣira* to argue that the point raised by the muftī was not relevant to the case at hand, engaging in a form of legal reasoning known as *dissociation*. Subsequently, he invoked twelfth-century court practice, citing the "Questions" of ʿIyāḍ to Ibn Rushd in an effort to corroborate his analysis of the case.

The Art of Judicial Narrative

I have used al-Tirjālī's letter to al-Yaznāsinī as a lens through which to observe the work of the qāḍī and the operation of his court in fourteenth-century Morocco. But a lens is not always transparent, and, depending upon its construction, it may serve either to sharpen or distort one's perception of the image upon which

[90] On hearsay testimony in connection with claims of paternity, see note 38, above.

attention is focused. Most of what I know about the case of *Sālim v. the children of ʿAlī b. Abī al-ʿUlā*ʾ is mediated by al-Tirjālī's narrative composition, the *istiftā*ʾ, which was written with a clear illocutionary purpose. At some point early on in the litigation, al-Tirjālī committed himself to a ruling in favor of Sālim, and this commitment shaped his subsequent handling of the case and his formulation of the *istiftā*ʾ. The exact moment at which this commitment occurred is beyond my grasp. And I do not know for sure whether it was made on the basis of purely legal considerations and/or on the basis of extra-legal considerations such as ethics, politics, personal sentiment or utility. The decision no doubt was influenced by the fact that al-Tirjālī was situated within a complex network of ties that bound him to members of the local community, to political authorities, and to other jurists. It surely would have been difficult for him to disregard the testimony of the ninety members of the local community who testified on behalf of Sālim. And the political activities of the House of Abū al-ʿUlāʾ, especially the family's adversarial position vis-à-vis the Marīnid Sultan, may be related to the cryptic reference to "pressure" at the beginning of al-Yaznāsinī's response.

Be that as it may, once al-Tirjālī had committed himself to a specific judicial outcome, he did everything in his power as a jurist to secure the desired result, seeking to correlate general legal concepts with the "facts" of the case so as to produce a judgment that addressed local needs and also was grounded in Mālikī legal norms. One discerns a clear pattern in the qāḍī's interrogation of the two sets of witnesses who testified on behalf of Sālim and ʿAbd al-Raḥmān, respectively. Al-Tirjālī took extraordinary efforts to guarantee the validity of the testimony submitted by Sālim's witnesses – regardless of any defects. Thus, when nine of Sālim's witnesses reported having heard Tāwatarā refer to Sālim as "her brother" in a manner that was equivocal, al-Tirjālī intervened to have them specify that Tāwatarā had used the term "brother" to signify common descent and not common humanity. When a witness who testified on behalf of Sālim erroneously referred to Maymūna as "ʿAlī's" female slave, al-Tirjālī chose not to disqualify the witness. Similarly, the qāḍī drew upon his familiarity with Sālim's life (for example, his absence from home when the death-and-inheritance document was inscribed) to dismiss testimony that was potentially damaging to his case. And confronted with an apparent contradiction in Sālim's testimony that threatened to undermine his credibility, al-Tirjālī again drew upon his training as a jurist to harmonize and neutralize that contradiction by invoking Sālim's status as a slave to discount his statement.

At the same time, al-Tirjālī drew upon his knowledge of Mālikī procedural law to reverse the thrust of testimony submitted on behalf of ʿAbd al-Raḥmān. When thirteen of ʿAbd al-Raḥmān's witnesses testfied that ʿAlī "did not have a child by the name of Sālim," al-Tirjālī first rejected ten of these witnesses as unacceptable and then elicited supplementary testimony from the three acceptable witnesses in which they reformulated their testimony – "ʿAlī was not known to have any child except for Raḥḥū, Muḥammad, and Tāwatarā" – a formulation that the qāḍī more easily could harmonize with testimony *supporting* Sālim's filiation to ʿAlī. Further, al-Tirjālī succeeded in coaxing from the third acceptable witness – taking care to identify him as "the best of them with regard to status" – a supplementary statement in which the witness asserted that Maymūna sometimes served as a slave in ʿAlī's house, thereby establishing ʿAlī's opportunity to engage in sexual relations with her, the equivalent, in this context, of the western notion of "probable cause."

Also noteworthy is the striking disparity between the epistemological standard that the qāḍī applied to the testimony of witnesses, on the one hand, and his implicit and unquestioned claim to possess knowledge of the state of mind of both ʿAlī and Sālim, on the other. It was on the basis of his claim to possess knowledge of ʿAlī's state of mind on his deathbed that al-Tirjālī advanced an explanation of ʿAlī's deathbed declaration, and that he "determined" that ʿAlī's failure to mention Sālim in his last will and testament resulted from his fear of the consequences of what he erroneously believed to have been an unlawful act of intercourse with Maymūna: stoning! And it was on the basis of his claim to know Sālim's state of mind that he dismissed the legal relevance of Sālim's claim that his mother had been a freeborn woman. Al-Tirjālī, however, could not possibly have known either ʿAlī's state of mind or Sālim's.

The illocutionary purpose of al-Tirjālī's letter to al-Yaznāsinī is reflected in certain rhetorical strategies that he employed in the "staging" of the *istiftāʾ*. Inasmuch as Sālim's claim that his mother had been a free woman, offered in response to ʿAbd al-Raḥmān's initial deposition, threatened to undermine his credibility as a witness, it is noteworthy that al-Tirjālī formulated Sālim's statement in a manner that obscures his role as the person who solicited the statement. Further, al-Tirjālī summarized and arranged the information contained in the document submitted by Sālim (much of which was legally irrelevant) in a manner that had the effect of thrusting upon the reader successive waves of testimony that appear to support Sālim's claim. And in an effort to establish a motive for ʿAlī's refusal to acknowledge Sālim, he was careful to include in the *istiftāʾ* testimony regarding a deathbed statement attributed to ʿAlī by a witness rejected by the qāḍī as unacceptable.

Notwithstanding al-Tirjālī's handling of the witnesses, his claim to possess knowledge of the litigants' respective states-of-mind, and the rhetorical strategies that he employed, an outcome in favor of Sālim was not inevitable. In this regard, I would like to draw attention to two potentially significant "omissions" in the staging of the *istiftāʾ*. The first omission relates to the fatwā that ʿAbd al-Raḥmān solicited from the Fāsī muftī and submitted to al-Tirjālī. In his *istiftāʾ*, al-Tirjālī did not mention the name of the muftī, purported that the muftī's response to ʿAbd al-Raḥmān's solicitation was not a true fatwā but merely a "*barāʾa*," and focused his attention exclusively upon the muftī's citation of the *Tabṣira* of al-Lakhmī (see above). Fortuitously, a copy of the so-called *barāʾa* was available to al-Wansharīsī (the compiler of the *Miʿyār*), who, recognizing its relevance to the present case, included it in his compilation, placing it immediately before al-Tirjālī's *istiftāʾ*.[91]

[91] *Miʿyār*, vol. 10, 360 (l. 4)–1 (l. 24).

This text – partially translated in the Introduction to this book – sheds important new light on the case. The *istiftāʾ* specifies the name of the Fāsī muftī as Sīdī Miṣbāḥ b. Muḥammad b. ʿAbd Allāh al-Yāliṣūtī (d. 750/1349).[92] In addition, it contains a number of "facts" relating to the case that were not mentioned by al-Tirjālī. We learn that Sālim was a "ruddy youth"; that, at the time of the litigation, Tāwatarā (identified here as *fulāna*) was a major possessed of discernment (*al-kabīra al-rashīda*); that Maymūna belonged to "the lowest class of servants," in which capacity she performed multiple functions without ever being veiled; that she was the mother of several children, in addition to Sālim, and that, after giving birth to Sālim, her master arranged for her to marry a man; and, finally, that ʿAlī (identified here as *al-rajul al-mutawaffā*) was known for his virtue (*faḍl*) and reportedly was not the type of man who would take a concubine belonging to a third party for the purpose of sexual intercourse. Further, the *istiftāʾ* raises several questions about the nature of the hearsay testimony presented on behalf of Sālim: (a) the witnesses did not specify how long the rumor about which they testified had been in circulation; (b) their testimonies were of differential quality (for example, some testified merely to "hearsay" [*samāʿ*], others to "hearsay that was widespread" [*al-samāʿ al-mustafīḍ*]; and still others – although these were exceptional – to "hearsay that was widespread among upright witnesses and others"); (c) the witnesses were not present at the acknowledgement about which they testified.[93] As for al-Yāliṣūtī's response, to the best of my knowledge, there is nothing about either its form or content that would disqualify it as a fatwā. And it, too, contains information not mentioned by al-Tirjālī. Especially relevant is the muftī's closing statement, "The claimant's affiliation [to ʿAlī] is null and void unless he produces apodictic testamentary evidence to the effect that his father acknowledged him during his lifetime [as his child] by his daughter's female slave, in which case his affiliation is established, since there is uncertainty (*shubha*) with regard to him and her property."[94] This first omission suggests that the testimony presented on behalf of Sālim was contestable on the grounds that it did not constitute apodictic testimonial evidence (*bayyina qāṭiʿa*).

As for the second omission, it will be recalled that al-Tirjālī consulted with his local advisors about the resemblance between the present case and a similar case mentioned in a question posed by ʿIyāḍ to Ibn Rushd (see above). In the *istiftāʾ*, however, al-Tirjālī reproduced only the question, not the answer – and with good reason. In the earlier case, ʿIyāḍ had asked whether the testimony of trustworthy professional witnesses about a widespread rumor was sufficient to establish paternity. To this question, Ibn Rushd responded that the legal assessment depends on whether the reputed father is alive or dead. If he is alive, then hearsay testimony

[92] See Aḥmad Bābā al-Tunbuktī, *Kitāb nayl al-ibtihāj bi-taṭrīz al-dībāj* (Cairo: n.p., 1932), 344; Badr al-Dīn al-Qarāfī, *Tawshīḥ al-dībāj wa-ḥilyat al-ibtihāj* (Beirut: Dār al-Gharb al-Islāmī, 1983), 258, no. 283; Ibn Marzūq, *El Musnad: Hechos Memorables de Abū L-Ḥasan Sultan de los Benimerines*, tr. and ed. Marià J. Viguerra (Madrid: Instituto Hispano-Árabe de Cultura, 1977), 510.

[93] *Miʿyār*, vol. 10, 360 (l. 4)–1 (l. 10).

[94] Ibid., vol. 10, 361, ll. 21–2.

that does not attain the level of certain knowledge (*ʿilm*) is not sufficient to establish paternity, because the reputed father may deny the rumor at any time. As for the case in which the reputed father is dead, Ibn Rushd added:

> As you know, however, there are three different opinions on this matter [in the case in which the father] is dead: First, that he [viz., the child] is entitled to property but not to the establishment of filiation – this is the doctrine of Ibn al-Qāsim; second, that paternity is established and he is entitled to property; and third, that paternity is not established and he is not entitled to property, because property does not become obligatory until after the establishment of paternity ... [95]

One might conclude from Ibn Rushd's summary that the majority view of Mālikī jurists is that the hearsay testimony of professional witnesses is insufficient to establish paternity in a case in which the reputed father is dead. Had this been al-Tirjālī's point of departure, he would have had to disregard all of the testimony contained in Sālim's *istirʿā*-document, which would have made inevitable a decision for ʿAbd al-Raḥmān.

Kadijustiz *or Qāḍī-Justice?*

We do not know the final outcome of this case, although it is likely that al-Tirjālī followed al-Yaznāsinī's recommendation and declared Sālim to be the legitimate son of ʿAlī b. Abī al-ʿUlāʾ. But al-Tirjālī's handling of the case and the two omissions that we have identified suggest that the qāḍī was motivated by extra-legal considerations, perhaps "pressure" that was being exerted on him by an unnamed third party. Clearly, there were strong legal grounds for a decision *against* Sālim. His reputed father had never acknowledged him while alive, and the testimonial evidence submitted on his behalf was not apodictic. Why did the qāḍī ignore the position attributed to Ibn al-Qāsim, according to which Sālim was entitled to property but not to filiation?

We might have expected al-Yaznāsinī to address this and other important legal questions in his fatwā. But the muftī failed to give serious consideration to the views expressed by his Fāsī colleague, al-Yāliṣūṭī, in his so-called *barāʾa*. Al-Yaznāsinī's fatwā might have been an occasion for thought and argument. Instead, it was a perfunctory performance in which the muftī did nothing more than rubber-stamp the conclusions of the qāḍī. Even if we agree with the outcome, we must nevertheless question the process by which this outcome was reached.

Some would argue that al-Tirjālī arrived at the correct solution to this case, others that he did not. It is difficult to choose between these two views, in part because we do not have all of the relevant facts that would be necessary to make such a determination. Our source sheds little light on the litigants' economic

[95] Qāḍī ʿIyāḍ, *Madhāhib al-ḥukkām*, 54. See also Qurṭubī, *Kāfī*, 468, ll. 3–4.

situations, the particular circumstances of their lives, or the social connections between and among them. We can, however, speculate.

Some might assume that al-Tirjālī was a benevolent and fair-minded man who had compelling reasons to decide in favor of Sālim. They might well say that qāḍīs should craft legal decisions tailored to the specific needs and circumstances of the litigants. If established legal doctrine appears to be in conflict with claims of justice and equity, qāḍīs should use their judicial discretion to strike a balance between these two norms.

In the present case, supporters of al-Tirjālī would continue, the qāḍī used the law as a tool for reaching what he regarded as a just and equitable decision. Al-Tirjālī was not a slave of the law but its master. He gave legal effect to a relationship that had been recognized by all the parties involved in the dispute, as evidenced by their conduct and behavior: members of the family of ʿAlī b. Abī al-ʿUlāʾ clearly had treated Sālim as one of their own, and ʿAlī surely had regarded Sālim as his son. By assuming ʿAlī's ignorance of the law, the qāḍī sought to preserve his good name. When he declared Sālim to be ʿAlī's son, the qāḍī gave effect to ʿAlī's true intent and prevented ʿAbd al-Raḥmān and Tāwatarā from committing an injustice against their brother. Asserting his right to intervene in the intimate affairs of a Muslim family, the qāḍī ignored the letter of the law in order to legitimize a *de facto* familial relationship. The decision that he crafted may not have been doctrinally pure, but it was just and equitable. To achieve justice and equity, the qāḍī engaged in creative jurisprudence, choosing among several available legal precedents. A legal system that gives qāḍīs wide discretion to render a decision without formal legal constraints will in the long run achieve more "just" results.

Readers who disagree with this view would condemn al-Tirjālī's decision on the ground that it was achieved at the expense of judicial honesty. Granted, there may have been considerations of equity, but the qāḍī concealed any such considerations behind a façade of legal reasoning. He knew the result that he wanted to reach and tried to find legal authority and support for the desired outcome. He reached this result at the expense of the legal order that he was mandated to uphold. If all qāḍīs functioned thus, the law would become unreliable. If al-Tirjālī were not a fair-minded and benevolent man, his decision would be unfair. For every "good" qāḍī who engages in the creative manipulation of legal doctrine in an effort to reach the "correct" result, there is a "bad" qāḍī who will engage in the creative use of legal doctrine to reach a "bad" result. If qāḍīs are permitted to engage in creative jurisprudence, the result will be abuse and corruption. Further, if qāḍīs sometimes follow well-established legal doctrine and sometimes ignore it, the community will remain ignorant of what the law "is", and individuals will not know how to behave. Judicial creativity, proponents of this view conclude, undermines the stability and predictability of the legal system. For these reasons, qāḍīs should base their decisions on well-established legal doctrine, regardless of considerations of equity.

My view is that whether one applauds or condemns al-Tirjālī's handling of this case, the justice he dispensed was neither arbitrary nor unprincipled. His assessment of the testimonial evidence was informed by his training as a jurist. Like judges in other cultures, he sought to locate legal authority for his ruling in established sources and earlier authorities. He focused on substantive legal doctrines and on the factual similarities to and differences from prior cases; he emphasized antecedent concepts; and he employed a mode of judicial reasoning that might result in increasingly refined modes of legal analysis.[96] In this regard, I maintain, he was not exceptional, although further research is required on this point.

Whatever the principal aims of qāḍīs may have been, their work involved both the invocation of underlying socio-cultural assumptions and the manipulation of legal discourse. And whatever consequences their decisions may have had for litigants, qāḍīs sought to ground their judgments in reliable knowledge (*ʿilm*) and in the authority of Islamic legal doctrine.[97] Indeed, the very existence of the *istiftāʾ* points to the importance attached to the reasoned justification of judicial decisions in the Maghrib in the eighth/fourteenth century. Perhaps more than anything else, this emphasis on reasoned justification belies the Weberian notion of *kadijustiz* and the stereotype of the Muslim qāḍī as an unprincipled agent who dispenses justice according to considerations of individual expediency rather than doctrinal consistency.[98]

[96] Cp. Rosen, *The Anthropology of Justice*, 40, 45, 50, 55, 56–7, 74.
[97] Cp. ibid., 17–19, 26, 41, 44–5, 50, 55, 66, 73.
[98] See *Max Weber on Law in Economy and Society* (New York: Simon and Schuster, 1967), 213 ff.; David S. Powers, "*Fatwās* as Sources for Legal and Social History: A Dispute over Endowment Revenues from Fourteenth-Century Fez," *al-Qanṭara*, XI (1990), 295–341, esp. 326–30; my conclusions in this chapter corroborate those of Irene Schneider in her "Die Merkmale der idealtypischen *qāḍī*-Justiz-Kritische Anmerkungen zu Max Webers Kategorisierung der islamischen Rechtsprechung," *Der Islam*, 70 (1993), 145–59.

TWO

From Almohadism to Mālikism: The Case of al-Haskūrī, the Mocking Jurist, *ca.* 712–716/1312–1316

Do not make game of God's revelations. (Q. 2:231)

The person who will receive the most severe punishment on the Day of Resurrection is the scholar whose knowledge did not benefit him. (prophetic *ḥadīth*)

Avert the *ḥudūd* punishments in cases of uncertainty. (prophetic *ḥadīth*)

The case analyzed in chapter one dealt with an alleged sexual union between ʿAlī b. Abī al-ʿUlāʾ, a distinguished member of his community, and a female slave named Tāwatarā, who belonged to ʿAlī's daughter. ʿAlī had no legal training, and because of his unfamiliarity with the doctrine of *shubha*, he believed that he had committed *zinā*, or fornication. His ignorance – and that of others – played an important role in the case. Our attention was primarily focused on the qāḍī, who was called upon to weigh two conflicting versions of the facts. He demonstrated his skills as a jurist through his handling of Mālikī legal doctrine and the rules of judicial procedure, even if his treatment of the legal issues was driven by palpable but unidentified extra-legal issues.

The case to be examined in this chapter is in one respect similar to that in chapter one: the charge is fornication. But the defendant, al-Haskūrī, was accused of engaging in sexual relations with his former wife after having repudiated her on three occasions. More important, al-Haskūrī was not a layman but a distinguished jurist. Indeed, he was one of the few jurists at the beginning of the eighth/fourteenth century who claimed to be a *mujtahid*, a claim that was contested by many of his colleagues. When he was charged with committing fornication, al-Haskūrī used – most would say, abused – his knowledge of the law by invoking the doctrine of *shubha* in an effort to extricate himself from his predicament.

Whereas in chapter one our attention was focused on the work of the qāḍī, here our attention shifts initially to the work of two muftīs asked by a qāḍī to determine the fate of al-Haskūrī. Each muftī issued a detailed opinion in which he provided a reasoned justification for a specific punishment. The two recommendations were widely divergent, forcing the qāḍī to choose between the death penalty or a lesser punishment. Ultimately, the case made its way to the *majlis* of the Marīnid sulṭān, thereby affording us a measure of insight into the relationship between Muslim jurists and the state. Exceptionally, we know the outcome of the case, and it will become clear that the qāḍī's decision here, as in the previous case, was driven by extra-legal considerations. Once again these extra-legal considerations are not specifically mentioned in our source, although they lie close to the surface of our text.

Background: al-Haskūrī

Mūsā b. Yamwīn al-Haskūrī was born some time in the second half of the seventh/thirteenth century. His *nisba* indicates that he was a member of the Berber tribe of Haskūra, which was settled in the high valley of Tansift and the Wādī al-ʿAbīd, on the two slopes of the mountain range that links the Great Atlas, home of the Maṣmūda, with the Central Atlas, home of the Ṣanhāja of Tadla. The tribe of Haskūra occupied a strategic position on the trade route that linked Fez, Sijilmasa, and Sus. Although they were of Ṣanhāja origin, it became customary to associate them with the Maṣmūda as a result of their support for the Almohads.[1]

Although we do not know the exact date on which al-Haskūrī was born, his birth must have taken place a generation or so after the Marīnids replaced the Almohads as the rulers of the far Maghrib (see Introduction). There was a school for Qur'ānic exegesis in Haskūra, and Mūsā may have received his early intellectual formation in this former Almohad stronghold. Like other talented youth from the countryside, however, he was drawn to Marīnid Fez, where he no doubt studied in one of the *madrasa*s for which that city was becoming famous. By the beginning of the eighth/fourteenth century, he had developed a reputation as "one of the leading scholars of Fez."[2]

Al-Haskūrī was renowned for his powerful memory. The biographer Ibn al-Qāḍī reports that he committed to memory not only the *Kitāb* of the grammarian Sībawayhi (d. *ca.* 177/793) but also the *Ṣaḥīḥ* of the traditionist Muḥammad b. Ismāʿīl al-Bukhārī (d. 256/870), both substantial texts. As a result of the latter accomplishment, he acquired the nickname "al-Bukhārī."[3] The young jurist apparently had a charismatic personality and he not only attracted a following among the laymen of Fez but also had a notable influence on the judges and magistrates of the city. While climbing the ladder of scholarly success, however, al-Haskūrī appears to have antagonized some of his colleagues by challenging the

[1] *EI*², s.v. Maṣmūda.

[2] This observation is made by the modern editor of the *Miʿyār*, Muḥammad al-Ḥajjī, at vol. 4, 493, note 1.

[3] See Aḥmad Ibn al-Qāḍī al-Miknāsī (d. 1025/1616), *Durrat al-Ḥijāl fī Asmāʾ al-Rijāl*, ed. Muḥammad al-Aḥmadī Abū al-Nūr (Cairo: Dār al-Turāth, 1390/1970), vol. 3, 3–5; idem, *Jadhwat al-iqtibās fī dhikr man ḥalla min al-aʿlām madīnata Fās*, 2 vols (al-Ribāṭ: Dār al-Manṣūr li'l-Ṭibāʿa wa'l-Warāqa, 1973–74), vol. 1, 345–6, no. 365 (where his *kunya* is specified as al-Najjār, no doubt a typographical error).

conventions that were associated with Islamic piety and knowledge. His colleagues began to criticize the bold manner in which he treated scholarship (*ʿilm*), scholars (*ʿulamāʾ*), and prophetic *ḥadīth* and they challenged his claim to possess the qualifications to exercise *ijtihād.* As portrayed by his critics, al-Haskūrī was a bold, brash, and impetuous man who was willing to push matters to their limit – and beyond.

In the year 714/1314, al-Haskūrī was accused of engaging in *zinā*, or fornication. The allegation resulted in a court litigation, during the course of which a paper record was created that included two judicial opinions issued by colleagues of the accused and a letter that the second colleague wrote to the Marīnid Sulṭān, Abū Saʿīd ʿUthmān (r. 710–32/1310–31). Of special importance, the judicial opinions mention documents relating to the case, specify the names of the protagonists in the dispute, and refer to the dates on which key events took place. This paper record was preserved by unknown parties for over a century – during which time it may have been exposed to editing – and eventually found its way into the hands of al-Wansharīsī, who included copies of the two opinions and the letter in his *Kitāb al-Miʿyār*, compiled approximately 150 years after the events in question took place. These materials, preserved by al-Wansharīsī because of their jurisprudential value to judges and jurists, serve as the starting-point and major source for the present historical reconstruction.[4]

The available documentation allows us to follow the case from a micro-level event, the accused jurist's sexual relations with his wife, to a macro-level event, a request for the intervention of the sulṭān. Although the case itself is no doubt exceptional – indeed, extraordinary – it is nevertheless extremely useful for the purposes of historical investigation because in responding to it, the agents of the legal system were called upon to articulate the institutional structures and social, cultural, and legal values that defined their community as Islamic. By following this case from beginning to end, I shall attempt to identify these structures and values and to provide a "thick" empirical description of the legal culture that prevailed in eighth/fourteenth-century Fez. I shall also endeavor to pierce the surface level of the available documentation in an effort to determine if there may be a story buried and untold inside the story that we have, that is, to draw attention to the socially constructed nature of our documentation in an effort to expose motives, thinking, and behavior that may have been obscured or distorted by the person or persons who were responsible for its production.

The Facts of the Case

In the year 712/1312, al-Haskūrī married a certain ʿĀʾisha bt. ʿUmar b. ʿAbd al-Salām al-Yafrinī. The marriage was performed in the presence of Mālikī

[4] On the compilation of the *Miʿyār*, see Introduction. For a brief summary of the fatwā analyzed in the present essay, see V. Lagardère, *Histoire et Société en Occident Musulman au Moyen Age: Analyse du Miʿyār d'al-Wanšarīsī* (Madrid, 1995), 334–5, no. 179.

witnesses whose names were recorded at the end of the marriage contract (*rasm al-ṣadāq*), dated 3 Rabī I 712/9 July 1312.[5] Almost immediately the marriage failed, for reasons unspecified in the *Miʿyār*, and over the course of the next two years a complicated process of divorce unfolded, as shown in a series of statements inserted between the lines of the marriage contract and in an additional document.[6] As is well known, if a Muslim man wants to divorce his wife, he must repudiate her three times over the course of three separate menstrual periods, free of sexual intercourse; thereafter, he is forbidden to remarry his former wife and have sexual relations with her unless she marries another man, consummates that marriage, and is divorced by him, a process known as *taḥlīl*.[7]

That the dissatisfaction with the marriage was primarily ʿĀʾisha's is suggested by the nature of the first of the three required repudiations. According to Islamic law, the only circumstance in which a woman may initiate a divorce is one in which she is willing to compensate her husband for granting her a release by renouncing all financial claims that she may have against him, a procedure known as *khulʿ*.[8] Such a divorce is regarded as *bāʾin*, that is, definite and irrevocable: in a divorce of this type, the husband cannot take back his wife during her *ʿidda*, or waiting period; and once the waiting period has expired, a new marriage is necessary if the former husband and wife wish to return to each other. When ʿĀʾisha offered to make such a renunciation (on terms that are not specified in our source), al-Haskūrī accepted the offer, and on 11 Ramaḍān 712/10 January 1313, only six months after they had been married, al-Haskūrī granted ʿĀʾisha a *khulʿ* divorce, whereupon a statement to that effect was inserted in writing between the lines of the marriage contract.[9] Curiously, despite the definitiveness and irrevocability of a *khulʿ* divorce, al-Haskūrī treated this divorce as if it were revocable (*rajʿī*), taking ʿĀʾisha back (*murājaʿa*) by resuming sexual relations with her prior to the expiration of her waiting period of four months and ten days. In apparent disregard for this irregularity, someone inserted the following statement between the lines of the marriage contract, "He took back ʿĀʾisha after that type of divorce."[10]

On 10 Rabīʿ I 713/5 July 1313, nearly one year subsequent to the marriage and six months after the initial divorce, al-Haskūrī granted ʿĀʾisha a second divorce, this one of the type known as *tamlīk*, that is, a divorce in which a husband says to

[5] *Ṣadāq* literally means "dower". However, Mālikī jurists often use this term to signify the marriage contract. On this usage, see Henry Toledano, *Judicial Practice and Family Law in Morocco: The Chapter on Marriage from Sijilmāsī's* al-ʿAmal al-Muṭlaq (Boulder, CO: Social Science Monographs, 1981), 87, note 155, 137. The *rasm al-ṣadāq* or marriage contract is not transcribed in our source, although the *mustaftī* indicates that he examined the document.

[6] *Miʿyār*, vol. 4, 493, ll. 15 ff.

[7] On *taḥlīl*, see Ibn Rushd, *The Distinguished Jurist's Primer* [= *Bidāyat al-Mujtahid*], tr. Imran Ahsan Khan Nyazee and Muhammad Abdul Rauf, 2 vols (Reading, UK: Garnet Publishing, 1996), vol. 2, 103–5; cf. Joseph Schacht, *An Introduction to Islamic Law* (Oxford: Clarendon Press, 1964), 164; *Chapters on Marriage and Divorce: Responses of Ibn Ḥanbal and Ibn Rāhwayh*, tr. with introduction and notes by Susan A. Spectorsky (Austin: University of Texas Press, 1993), 28 ff.; *EI*², s.v., Muḥallil.

[8] On *khulʿ* divorce, see Ibn Rushd, *The Distinguished Jurist's Primer*, vol. 1, 79–83. Cf. Spectorsky (tr. and ed.), *Chapters on Marriage and Divorce*, 27–59, esp. 50–2.

[9] *Miʿyār*, vol. 4, 493, ll. 18–19.

[10] Ibid., vol. 4, 493, ll. 22–3.

his wife, "Your matter is in your hands" (*amruki bi-yadiki*), thereby transferring to her the power to initiate divorce. When such a clause is inserted in the marriage contract, it empowers the woman to pronounce an irrevocable repudiation of her marriage; if, subsequent to the expiration of her waiting period, her former husband wishes to take her back, he must remarry her (although *taḥlīl* is not required).[11] As was the case with the first divorce, however, al-Haskūrī appears to have ignored the definitive nature of the *tamlīk* divorce and to have resumed sexual relations with ʿĀʾisha. Once again the sentence, "He took back ʿĀʾisha after that type of divorce" was inserted between the lines of the marriage contract.[12]

A little over a year later, on 13 Ṣafar 714/29 June 1314, al-Haskūrī granted ʿĀʾisha a third divorce, this one, like the first, a *khulʿ* divorce. Once again, the divorce was irrevocable. In addition, however, this was the third repudiation that al-Haskūrī had pronounced, so that even if one condoned his treatment of irrevocable divorces as revocable ones, this divorce was final in a double sense: al-Haskūrī would have to remarry ʿĀʾisha in order to resume legitimate sexual relations with her, and he could not do so until ʿĀʾisha had first undergone the process of *taḥlīl*. If al-Haskūrī resumed sexual relations with ʿĀʾisha without her first having experienced *taḥlīl*, he would have committed fornication (*zinā*). To emphasize the finality of the divorce, the following sentence was inserted between the lines of the marriage contract, "She henceforth is not permissible to him until she marries a husband other than him."[13]

Al-Haskūrī, it will be recalled, was a distinguished jurist who would have been familiar with the specifications of Islamic divorce law. For this reason it is remarkable that he continued intimate relations with ʿĀʾisha as if the two were still married. To make matters worse, ʿĀʾisha may have become pregnant subsequent to the third divorce (see below).[14] Be that as it may, when it became known that al-Haskūrī was still having sexual relations with ʿĀʾisha after the third repudiation, someone brought the matter to the attention of the authorities and accused al-Haskūrī of committing *zinā*, or fornication. We do not know the identity of the person or persons who initiated the complaint. It may have been ʿĀʾisha's father, one of her brothers, or another male agnatic relative; or perhaps it was a jealous colleague or a political enemy. Our source also does not mention the name of the qāḍī to whom the complaint was brought, although he is identified in a biographical dictionary as al-Zamīnī.[15]

[11] Ibid., vol. 4, 493, l. 19. On *tamlīk* divorce, see Ibn Rushd, *The Distinguished Jurist's Primer*, vol. 2, 84–8. Cf. Spectorsky (tr. and ed.), *Chapters on Marriage and Divorce*, 48–9. Note: If a *tamlīk* is only a promise made by the husband after the conclusion of the marriage, then she may pronounce only one revocable repudiation (see Toledano, *Judicial Practice*, 40).

[12] *Miʿyār*, vol. 4, 493, ll. 22–3.

[13] Ibid., vol. 4, 493, ll. 20–1. Cp. Ibn al-Qāḍī, *Durrat al-Ḥijāl*, vol. 3, 4 (l. 5) where it is specified that this sentence (which is in fact a quotation from Qurʾān 2:230) was one of the clauses of the marriage contract (*min fuṣūlihi*).

[14] *Miʿyār*, vol. 4, 501, ll. 8–10.

[15] See Ibn al-Qāḍī, *Durrat al-Ḥijāl*, vol. 3, 4; idem, *Jadhwat al-iqtibās*, vol. 1, 346, no. 365 (where the name of the qāḍī appears as al-Zurayhinī).

On 12 Rabīʿ II 714/26 July 1314,[16] approximately one month after the third divorce, al-Haskūrī granted ʿĀʾisha yet another divorce, claiming that this one – the fourth that he had issued – was revocable; presumably, the witnesses who attested to this repudiation were not the same witnesses who had attested to the first three repudiations. An independent document verifying and authenticating this divorce was drawn up ten days later, on 22 Rabīʿ II 714/5 August 1314.[17]

It must have been shortly thereafter that the qāḍī al-Zamīnī summoned al-Haskūrī to his court and questioned him about his marital status. When the qāḍī asked how it was that al-Haskūrī found himself in his current predicament, al-Haskūrī initially responded by claiming that ʿĀʾisha had deceived him subsequent to the third divorce of 13 Ṣafar 714/29 June 1314. "My wife disappeared from me for a period of time," he asserted, "and [upon her return,] she claimed that she had married another man. I believed her."[18] If al-Haskūrī's statement were true, it would account for his otherwise inexplicable behavior and shift the burden of proof to ʿĀʾisha. But when the qāḍī summoned witnesses to verify al-Haskūrī's claim, he retracted his statement, presumably reluctant to lie in the presence of professional witnesses.[19]

Increasingly concerned about his situation, al-Haskūrī now made a dramatic shift in his defense strategy. Asked by al-Zamīnī to justify his having taken back ʿĀʾisha after three separate repudiations, he responded, "I have adopted the doctrine of those who say that *khulʿ* divorce constitutes [merely] an annulment (*faskh*), the doctrine of Ibn ʿAbbās – may God be pleased with him."[20] Now, in Islamic law, an annulment is not equivalent to a divorce and would *not* count as one of the three divorce utterances, although it does have other consequences (see below).[21] And Ibn ʿAbbās (d. 68/687–88) is indeed reported to have held the view attributed to him by al-Haskūrī – although the point had been disputed by early scholars.[22] If one adopts the doctrine of Ibn ʿAbbās on this point, it is possible to argue that only the second of the three divorces specified between the lines of the marriage contract, that is, the *tamlīk* divorce of 10 Rabīʿ I 713/5 July 1313, would count as a divorce utterance. According to this line of reasoning, al-Haskūrī would have repudiated ʿĀʾisha only once, by *tamlīk*, allegedly revocable; and because he took her back during her waiting period, he was still legally married to her when he issued the "second" single repudiation of 12 Rabīʿ II 714/26 July 1314 – in fact the fourth divorce utterance. Thus, there would be no grounds for applying the stoning penalty.

16 *Miʿyār*, vol. 4, 493, ll. 23–5. 17 Ibid., vol. 4, 493, ll. 23–4.

18 Ibid., vol. 4, 499, ll. 15–17 (as reported by al-Sarīfī, on the basis of someone "trustworthy").

19 Ibid., vol. 4, 499, ll. 17–18. 20 Ibid., vol. 4, 494, ll. 1–4.

21 "*Ṭalāḳ*, which is the exclusive right of the man, brings about the dissolution of the marriage by a simple unilateral declaration. It always presupposes a validly formed contract. Dissolution of marriage by way of *faskh* takes place at the instance of the wife or her relatives. It generally comes about by judicial process ... " (*EI²*, s.v., Fas<u>kh</u>) See further, Ibn Rushd, *The Distinguished Jurist's Primer*, vol. 2, 84; ʿAlī al-Khafīf, *Furaq al-zawāj fī l-madhāhib al-islāmiyya* (Cairo, 1958).

22 See Ibn Rushd, *The Distinguished Jurist's Primer*, vol. 2, 82; Spectorsky (tr. and ed.), *Chapters on Marriage and Divorce*, 48–9, 108. Ibn ʿAbbās' position on *khulʿ* was held by Ibn Taymiyya, a contemporary of al-Haskūrī; and Ibn Taymiyya says that it was the view of the Ẓahirī jurist Ibn Ḥazm. See *Majmūʿ Fatāwā Shaykh al-Islām Aḥmad Ibn Taymiyyah*, ed. ʿAbd al-Raḥmān b. Muḥammad b. Qāsim al-ʿĀṣimī al-Najdī, 35 vols (Riyadh: Maṭābiʿ al-Riyāḍ, 1381–86/1961–67), vol. 32, 289–335. I am grateful to Yossi Rapoport for bringing this reference to my attention.

The Response of al-Ṣughayyir

Because the case involved a prominent member of the community and might require the application of the death penalty, the qāḍī al-Zamīnī decided to consult with a jurist before issuing his judgment. He sent a summary of the facts of the case to Abū al-Ḥasan ʿAlī b. Muḥammad b. ʿAbd al-Ḥaqq al-Zarwīlī, known as al-Ṣughayyir (d. 719/1319, reportedly at the age of 100).[23] Al-Zamīnī seemingly had made an excellent choice, for al-Ṣughayyir had had a long and distinguished career. His biographers describe him as a short man, tan of complexion, lightly bearded, and with a preference for fine white clothes. As a youth he studied with Abū al-Faḍl Rāshid b. Abī Rāshid al-Walīdī,[24] Abū al-Ḥasan b. Sulaymān, and Abū ʿImrān al-Ḥawrānī; and his students included al-Yafrānī, al-Saṭṭī, and al-Tasūlī. Like al-Haskūrī, he was a Berber and was renowned for his powerful memory, a quality that no doubt enhanced his scholarly prestige. Indeed, he reportedly astonished his colleagues by reciting from memory eight texts that would be placed in front of him at his study circle, some short (for example, the *Kitāb Ṣadr al-Dawla* and texts by Ibn Yūnis, al-Lakhmī, al-Bājī, Ibn Abī Zamanayn, and others) and others long (for example, the *Kitāb al-Tafāṣīl* of Ibn Rushd). He also had committed to memory the *Tahdhīb* of al-Barādhiʿī and the *Tanqīḥāt* of al-Qarāfī. His prestige was so great that 100 students regularly attended his study session at the Jāmiʿ al-Ajdaʿ in Fez, necessitating that al-Ṣughayyir, whose voice was weak, sit on a high chair so that all could hear him.

Several details mentioned in the biographical dictionaries suggest that al-Ṣughayyir combined the study of law with the practice of mysticism. In the Maghrib and elsewhere, the legal genre known as *uṣūl al-fiqh*, originally a form of legal reasoning, came to be used as a tool for reconciling mysticism and normative Islam. Many opposed this practice, however, and al-Ṣughayyir reportedly offended some of his colleagues by "embroidering" his study sessions with references to

[23] On al-Ṣughayyir, see Ibn Farḥūn, *Kitāb al-Dībāj al-mudhahhab fī maʿrifat aʿyān ʿulamāʾ al-madhhab* (Cairo: Dār al-Turāth, 1932), 212–13; al-Wansharīsī, *Wafayāt*. In *Alf sana min al-wafayāt fī thalātha kutub*, ed. M. Ḥijjī (Rabat: Dār al-Maghrib li'l-ta'līf, 1396/1976), 102–03; Ibn al-Qāḍī, *Durrat al-Ḥijāl*, vol. 3, 243, no. 1260; idem, *Jadhwat al-iqtibās*, vol. 2, 472, no. 521; Ibn al-Khaṭīb, *al-Iḥāta fī akhbār Gharnāṭa*, ed. Muḥammad ʿAbd Allāh ʿInān, 2 vols (2nd edn, Cairo: Maktabat al-Khānjī, 1393/1973), vol. 1, 372–73; Muḥammad b. Muḥammad Makhlūf, *Shajarat al-nūr al-zakiyya fī ṭabaqāt al-mālikiyya*, 2 vols (2nd edn, Beirut: Dār al-Kitāb al-ʿArabī, *ca.* 1975), vol. 1, 215, no. 757; Mohamed b.A. Benchekroun, *La vie intellectuelle marocaine sous les Mérinides et les Waṭṭāsides (XIIIe XIVe XVe XXVIe siècles)* (Rabat, 1974), 172–7. Muḥammad al-Manūnī, *Waraqāt ʿan ḥaḍārat al-Marīniyyīn* (Rabat: Kulliyyat al-Ādāb wa'l-ʿUlūm, 1996), 294–6; al-Ziriklī, *Aʿlām*, 8 vols (5th edn, Beirut: Dār al-ʿIlm li'l-Malāyin, 1980), vol. 4, 334. For other fatwās issued by this jurist, see *Miʿyār*, vol. 3, 41, 373; 4, 363.

[24] Al-Walīdī (d. *ca.* 695/1295–96, reportedly at the age of 120) was the author of a commentary on the *Mudawwana* and of *al-Ḥalāl wa'l-Ḥarām*, ed. ʿAbd al-Raḥmān al-ʿUmrānī al-Idrīsī (Rabat: Maṭbaʿat Faḍāla al-Muḥammadiyya, 1410/1990). For biographical details, see ibid., 30 ff.; Ibn al-Qāḍī, *Jadhwat al-iqtibās*, vol. 1, 196–7, no. 156; al-Tunbuktī, *Nayl al-ibtihāj*, 117; Makhlūf, *Shajarat al-nūr al-zakiyya*, vol. 1, 201, no. 685; Manūnī, *Waraqāt*, 294, 302. We will analyze a fatwā issued by al-Walīdī (see *Miʿyār*, vol. 8, 11 ff.) in chapter three.

uṣūl al-fiqh.[25] In addition, the term *quṭb* ("axis" or "pole"), generally applied to the sufi saint identified as the "Axis of the Age," was applied to al-Ṣughayyir, who is remembered as "one of the axes (*aqṭāb*) around whom fatwā revolved during his lifetime."[26] Finally, a favorite sufi pun juxtaposes the notions of *ʿilm* and *ʿamal*, theoretical knowledge and exemplary action. Ibn al-Khaṭīb (d. 776/1375) reports that al-Ṣughayyir combined *ʿilm* and *ʿamal* in a manner that was unique, adding that this legendary jurist "had no peer (*mā ʿāṣarahu mithluhu*) during his lifetime or thereafter."[27]

Al-Ṣughayyir was appointed qāḍī of Tāzā by the fifth Marīnid, Abū Yaʿqūb Yūsuf (r. 685–706/1286–1307) despite the availability of more senior candidates for the position, and he subsequently was appointed chief qāḍī of Fez by the Sulṭān Abū al-Rabīʿ Sulaymān (r. 708–10/1308–10).[28] He was no doubt loyal to his Marīnid patrons. In his capacity as muftī, he received questions from all regions of the Maghrib, and his responses were noted for their concision and "omission of needless speech."[29] As mentioned, by the end of his lifetime, al-Ṣughayyir had developed a reputation as one of the greatest jurists of his age. In short he possessed all of the qualifications of, and personified, the notion of the "legal man."[30] Of his judicial character, it is noteworthy in the present context that he had a reputation for "severity and harshness in justice."[31]

[25] On Mālikī resistance to the introduction of *uṣūl al-fiqh* in al-Andalus and the Maghrib, see Benchekroun, *La vie intellectuelle marocaine*, 453; Vincent Cornell, *Realm of the Saint: Power and Authority in Moroccan Sufism* (Austin: University of Texas Press, 1998), 15; see also Maribel Fierro, "The Legal Policies of the Almohad Caliphs and Ibn Rushd's *Bidāyat al-Mujtahid*," *Journal of Islamic Studies*, 10:3 (1999), 226–48.

[26] Ibn Farḥūn, *Dībāj*, 212; Ibn al-Qāḍī, *Jadhwat al-iqtibās*, vol. 2, 472, no. 521; Manūnī, *Waraqāt*, 296 (citing Ibn al-Khaṭīb).

[27] Makhlūf, *Shajara*, vol. 1, 215, no. 757; Manūnī, *Waraqāt*, 296.

[28] See *EI*², s.v., Marīnids.

[29] Al-Ṣughayyir's fatwās were compiled into a book by his student, al-Tasūlī (d. 749/1348–49) and subsequently rearranged according to legal categories by Ibrāhīm b. Hilāl b. ʿAlī al-Ṣanhājī (d. 903/1497–98), who gave it the title, *al-Durr al-nuthayyir ʿalā ajwibat Abī al-Ḥasan al-Ṣughayyir* (published in Fez as a lithograph in 1318/1900–01). See Benchekroun, *La vie intellectuelle marocaine*, 177.

[30] Muslim jurists were expected to manifest the values of the Islamic educational system in their personal conduct and public behavior. The ethical and personal qualities expected of a jurist included self-reliance, generosity, humility, a smiling and untiring nature, a strong will, freedom from greediness and ambition, and avoidance of forbidden actions. It was the combination of these two elements – the reception of *ʿilm* from distinguished scholars who were themselves embodiments of the "legal man" and the cultivation of exemplary ethical and moral qualities – that conferred prestige and authority upon the jurist. The closer one came to the ideal of perfection, the greater one's authority. On the notion of the legal man, see M. Khalid Masud, "*Ādāb al-Muftī*: The Muslim Understanding of Values, Characteristics, and Role of a *Muftī*," in *Moral Conduct and Authority: The Place of Adab in South Asian Islam*, ed. Barbara Daly Metcalf (Berkeley: University of California Press, 1984), 124–50; cf. William A. Graham, "Traditionalism in Islam: An Essay in Interpretation," *Journal of Interdisciplinary History*, 23 (1993), 495–522.

[31] Al-Wansharīsī, *Wafayāt*, 102–3. Al-Ṣughayyir's harsh judicial temperament manifested itself in an incident that occurred in Fez in 709/1309, shortly after he had been appointed chief qāḍī. When he was informed that the Naṣrid ambassador to the Marīnid court had been discovered with wine on his breath, al-Ṣughayyir ordered that the diplomat be flogged in public. See Ibn Khaldūn, *Kitāb al-ʿIbar*, 7 vols (Beirut: Dār al-Kitāb al-Lubnānī, 1959), vol. 7, 500–1. Translated by de Slane as *Histoire des Berbères et des dynasties musulmanes de l'Afrique Septentrionale*. 4 vols (Paris: P. Geuthner, 1925–56), vol. 4, 185–6.

After studying the case, al-Ṣughayyir wrote a judicial opinion that was characteristically concise and to the point. The first and primary issue that he addressed was the status of the single, revocable repudiation that al-Haskūrī had issued on 12 Rabīʿ II 714/26 July 1314. To evaluate the status of this legal act, al-Ṣughayyir speculated about al-Haskūrī's state of mind when he made the repudiation. There were two possibilities: (1) al-Haskūrī regarded this as a fourth repudiation, or (2) al-Haskūrī regarded this as only a second repudiation, because the first and third "divorces" were not divorces but annulments.[32]

As for the first possibility, the jurist explained that al-Haskūrī had already issued three irrevocable divorces, so that he no longer had the power to take back ʿĀʾisha and to resume sexual relations with her except after an intermediate marriage and divorce, and then only with the consent of her *walī*, or marriage guardian.[33] The repudiation of 12 Rabīʿ II 714/26 July 1314 was therefore of no legal import whatsoever. As for the second, and more likely, possibility, the jurist argued that if this were what al-Haskūrī had had in mind, then he must be labeled a liar, for two reasons: first, because the middle repudiation that he characterized as being revocable was in fact irrevocable and, second, because whereas he asserted that only ten days had passed between the date of the second and fourth repudiations, in fact, thirteen months had passed between these two dates.[34] In sum, the law was clear and unequivocal: despite having repudiated ʿĀʾisha three times, al-Haskūrī had continued to live with her and to have sexual relations with her – the latter point was undisputed – thereby engaging in fornication on either construction of his mind.[35]

All that remained for al-Ṣughayyir was to determine the appropriate punishment. The penalty for fornication is 100 stripes for a free man who had been a virgin at the time of the illegal act (plus exile, according to Mālik), but stoning for someone like al-Haskūrī, who was *muḥṣan*, that is, someone who had already experienced intercourse in a valid marriage.[36] Despite his aforementioned reputation for judicial severity, however, al-Ṣughayyir recommended that al-Haskūrī be given painful stripes and sentenced to life in prison, but that he should not be stoned.[37] No doubt sensitive to the accusation that he was being unduly lenient, al-Ṣughayyir offered a point-by-point justification of the recommended punishment, holding the matter of life-imprisonment for the last.

[32] *Miʿyār*, vol. 4, 494, ll. 5–11.

[33] According to the Mālikīs, the presence of a *walī* is one of the preconditions of a valid marriage, although the point was disputed by Abū Ḥanīfa and other jurists. See Ibn Rushd, *The Distinguished Jurist's Primer*, vol. 2, 9–13; Toledano, *Judicial Practice*, 54 ff.; Spectorsky (tr. and ed.), *Chapters on Marriage and Divorce*, 9–14; *EI²*, s.v. Nikāḥ.

[34] Recall that the second divorce occurred on 10 Rabīʿ I 713/5 July 1313, as specified between the lines of the marriage contract; and that the fourth divorce occurred on 12 Rabīʿ II 714/26 July 1314, as specified in the second, independent document drawn up ten days later on 22 Rabīʿ II 714/5 August 1314.

[35] *Miʿyār*, vol. 4, 494, ll. 12–15.

[36] On *zinā*, see chapter one, note 17; Ibn Rushd, *The Distinguished Jurist's Primer*, vol. 2, 523–7. On the stoning penalty and its connections to Jewish law, see John Burton, *An Introduction to Hadith* (Edinburgh: Edinburgh University Press, 1994), 81–91.

[37] *Miʿyār*, vol. 4, 494, ll. 15–16.

Painful Stripes

The divorce of 12 Rabīʿ II 714/26 July 1314, which is contained in a second, independent document, constitutes an acknowledgement (*iqrār*) by al-Haskūrī of his having had intercourse with ʿĀʾisha after having irrevocably divorced her. Thus, al-Ṣughayyir reasoned, al-Haskūrī should receive painful stripes.[38]

No Stoning

Al-Ṣughayyir avoided the necessity of imposing the stoning penalty by invoking the important and critical legal notion of *shubha*, already encountered in chapter one. It will be recalled that the word *shubha* signifies a "likeness" or "resemblance"; as a technical legal term, it refers to uncertainty or doubt resulting from a resemblance between an unlawful action and a lawful one. Because of the resemblance between the two actions, Islamic law exempts the wrongdoer from the normal punishment while continuing to regard the action in question as unlawful. With regard to *zinā*, or fornication, Muslim jurists had identified a dozen or so circumstances of sexual intercourse to which the notion of *shubha* applied, including that of a man who has intercourse with a woman whom he mistakenly believed to be his wife.[39]

The jurists' understanding of the notion of *shubha* was based upon their interpretation of a statement attributed to the Prophet Muḥammad, "Avert the *ḥudūd* punishments in cases of uncertainty (*idraʾū al-ḥudūd biʾl-shubuhāt*)."[40]

[38] Ibid., vol. 4, 494, ll. 17–19.

[39] On *shubha*, see Ibn Rushd, *The Distinguished Jurist's Primer*, vol. 2, 521–3; David Santillana, *Istituzioni di Diritto Musulmano Malichita*, 2 vols (Roma: Istituto per L'Oriente, 1938), vol. 1, 343; Schacht, *Introduction*, 176 ff.; *EI*², s.v., Shubha; J.N.D. Anderson, "Invalid and Void Marriages in Hanafi Law," *Bulletin of the School of Oriental and African Studies*, 13:2 (1950), 357–66, esp., 360, note 2; see also chapter one, pp. 29–30.

[40] *Miʿyār*, vol. 4, 494, l. 20 (the *ḥadīth* is cited at ibid., 4, 495, l. 2). This *ḥadīth* does not appear in this form in any of the canonical collections. Rather, one finds *bāb al-sitr ʿalā al-muʾmin wa-dafʿ al-ḥudūd biʾl-shubuhāt* (Ibn Māja, *Ḥudūd*, 5); *wa-kuntu udāriʾu minhu baʿḍ al-ḥadd* (Bukhārī, *Ḥudūd*, 31; Tirmidhī, *Ḥudūd*, 51); "*Idraʾūʾl-ḥudūd ʿaniʾl-muslimīn mā istaṭaʿtum*" (Dārimī, *Ṣalāt*, 114; Tirmidhī, *Ḥudūd*, 2); *fa-daraʾa ʿanhā rasūl allāh al-ḥadd* (Tirmidhī, *Ḥudūd*, 22; Ibn Māja, *Ḥudūd*, 3; Ibn Ḥanbal, *Musnad*, 6 vols (Cairo, 1895; reprinted Beirut: al-Maktab al-Islāmī li'l-Ṭibāʿa wa'l-Nashr, 1969), IV, 218 (or 318)); *idfaʿū ʾl-ḥudūd mā wajadtum lahu madfaʿan* (Ibn Māja, *Ḥudūd*, 5). For a convenient summary of the different versions, with attention to transmission history, see al-Zaylaʿī (d. 762/1360–61), *Naṣb al-rāya li-aḥādīth al-hidāya*, 4 vols (1st edn [S.l.]: al-Majlis al-ʿIlmī, 1357/1938), vol. 3, 309–10. As for the formulation "*idraʾū al-ḥudūd fīʾl-shubuhāt*", it appears in later texts, for example, al-Khaṭīb al-Baghdādī (d. 463/1070–71), *Taʾrīkh Baghdād* (Cairo: Maṭbaʿat al-Khānjī; and Baghdad, al-Maktaba al-ʿArabiyya, 1349/1931), vol. 9, 303, no. 4844 (the poet, Ṣāliḥ b. ʿAbd al-Quddūs al-Baṣrī, upon being summoned by al-Mahdī and accused of *zandaqa* in his poetry, denies authorship of the relevant verse and protests – in vain, "Do not shed my blood for something doubtful, for the Prophet – may God bless him and grant him peace, said, '*idraʾū al-ḥudūd biʾl-shubuhāt*'"); Ibn Rushd, *The Distinguished Jurist's Primer*, vol. 2, 522; al-ʿAjlūnī al-Jarrāḥī (d. 1162/1748–49), *Kashf al-khafāʾ wa-muzīl al-ilbās*, 2 vols in 1 (Beirut: Dār Iḥyāʾ al-Turāth

Al-Ṣughayyir chose to interpret this prophetic *ḥadīth* as broadly as possible, glossing its meaning as follows: "The sacred law is magnanimous with regard to the *ḥudūd* punishments in cases of fornication."[41] In his view, *any* uncertainty constituted grounds to avert the application of the *ḥudūd* punishments. Thus, he explained, one finds in the *Mudawwana* and other Mālikī legal texts that the *ḥadd* punishment for fornication is averted in the case of someone who acknowledges having fornicated but subsequently denies the acknowledgement, thereby creating uncertainty. Similarly, the stoning penalty is averted in the case of a man who repudiates his wife three times while on a journey, as established by testimonial evidence (*bayyina*), but reaches his destination before the witnesses do, whereupon he acknowledges having had intercourse with his wife and denies having repudiated her; only then do the witnesses arrive. In this case, the divorce is considered to be effective, but the man should not be stoned because of the uncertainty or *shubha*.[42]

The prophetic dictum and the case material found in the *Mudawwana* provided al-Ṣughayyir with textual authority that was, in his mind, sufficient to avert the application of the stoning penalty. In the present case, the jurist asserted, uncertainty was created by al-Haskūrī's claim to have adopted the doctrine of Ibn ʿAbbās, according to which *khulʿ* constitutes an annulment and not a divorce. By invoking this doctrine, al-Haskūrī acquired a status similar to that of a person who acknowledges having fornicated but subsequently retracts or denies his acknowledgement. For this reason he should not be stoned, because, as al-Ṣughayyir explained, "blood should not be shed in cases of doubt."[43] But the averting of the stoning penalty did not mean that al-Haskūrī should go unpunished. As mentioned, al-Ṣughayyir recommended that he should be severely beaten.

To persuade his audience, al-Ṣughayyir had to consider potential objections to his reasoning. At a critical juncture in his argument he invoked the authority of the distinguished twelfth-century Cordovan jurist, Ibn Rushd al-Jadd (d. 520/1126) who had once issued a fatwā in which he called for the imposition of the *ḥadd* punishment in a case involving *mutʿa*, or temporary marriage.[44] To ensure that Ibn Rushd's fatwā would not be invoked by another jurist as a precedent for *applying* the *ḥadd* punishment in the present case, al-Ṣughayyir had to demonstrate that the two cases were not analogous. No doubt taking for granted his audience's familiarity with Ibn Rushd's fatwā, al-Ṣughayyir represented it briefly as follows:

al-ʿArabī, 1351–52/1932–33; reprinted Beirut, Dār al-Kutub al-ʿIlmiyya, 1408/1988), vol. 1, 71–2; Ibn Ḥajar al-ʿAsqalānī, *Talkhṣīṣ al-ḥabīr* (Cairo: Muʾassasat Qurṭubah: Dār al-Mishkāh, 1416/1995), vol. 4, 104–5; al-Muttaqī al-Hindī (d. 975/1567–68), *Kanz al-ʿummāl fī sunan al-aqwāl wa'l-afʿāl* (Beirut: Muʾassasat al-Risāla, 1399/1979), vol. 5, 305, no. 12957 (Abū Muslim al-Kajjī [d. 292/904], on the authority of ʿUmar b. ʿAbd al-ʿAzīz: *mursal*), 309, no. 12972, where the context has the effect of reversing the meaning of the prophetic dictum ("*idraʾū al-ḥudūd bi'l-shubuhāt wa-aqīlū al-kirāma ʿatharātihim illā fī ḥadd min ḥudūd allāh*").

41 *Miʿyār*, vol. 4, 494, l. 22.

42 Ibid., vol. 4, 494–5.

43 Ibid., vol. 4, 495, l. 6. We will encounter the phrase "blood should not be shed in cases of doubt" again in chapter five.

44 *Miʿyār*, vol. 4, 495, ll. 10–12.

[As for the fatwā] that Ibn Rushd issued in his responsa (*ajwiba*) with regard to the application of the *ḥudūd* punishments to someone who concluded a marriage of the type [known as] *mutʿa*, that case is not similar to this one, because the man in that case, according to what [the *mustaftī*] said, married without a legal guardian (*walī*) and for one-half of a dirham, and the two of them contracted [the marriage] on the basis of the testimony of persons who did not meet the qualification of *ʿadāla* (*ghayr al-ʿudūl*).[45] And for this reason, [Ibn Rushd] issued a fatwā calling for the *ḥadd* punishment. The *mutʿa* marriage that the remainder of those who, exceptionally, declare permissible, is a marriage for a [specified] period of time that is accompanied by all of the stipulations of a [regular] marriage. [A person who concludes a marriage of the latter type,] according to the *Mudawwana*, deserves only the discretionary punishment (*ʿuqūba*) for *mutʿa*, according to this interpretation.[46]

This brief representation obscures several details mentioned in the full version of the fatwā: the defendant was a scholar (*min ahl al-maʿrifa*) who had fallen in love with a woman who was socially inappropriate and therefore inaccessible to him. Although he claimed to have contracted a *mutʿa* marriage,[47] he had not fulfilled any of the three conditions required for a valid marriage (having a legal guardian, a dower, and two upright witnesses); in other words, the "marriage" that he claimed to have contracted was nothing more than an agreement to have sexual relations with a woman in return for monetary compensation, behavior which constitutes not *mutʿa* but *zinā*.[48] And since no *shubha* existed regarding this act of fornication, Ibn Rushd called for the application of the *ḥadd* punishment. Without explicitly saying so, al-Ṣughayyir implied that the difference between the two cases lay in the fact that in the earlier case no *shubha* existed regarding the act of fornication, whereas in the present case there was *shubha*, so that the averting of the *ḥadd* punishment was justified.[49]

[45] According to Ibn ʿAbbās, "There is no marriage without two *ʿadl* witnesses and a supervising guardian." The report is cited in Ibn Rushd, *The Distinguished Jurist's Primer*, vol. 2, 20. For testimony to be acceptable, the witness must meet five qualifications: puberty, Islam, freedom, absence of an accusation, and *ʿadāla*. Although the definition of *ʿadāla* was disputed, the majority held that it required that the witness abide by the prescribed obligations and recommendations and avoid prohibited and disapproved acts (ibid., vol. 2, 556). Cf. *EI²*, s.v., Nikāḥ.

[46] *Miʿyār*, vol. 4, 495, ll. 10–15.

[47] Note: *mutʿah* marriage was a Shīʿī institution that was recognized only exceptionally by Sunnī jurists. Those Sunnī jurists who did accept the institution required the fulfillment of all the conditions of a normal marriage, that is, having a legal guardian, paying a dower, and summoning witnesses. Among the Shīʿīs, on the other hand, *mutʿah* required only a token dower, such as half a dirham, and nothing else. In the case discussed by Ibn Rushd, the parties to the union appear to have invoked Shīʿī law. Al-Ṣughayyir, however, treated the case according to Sunnī law, which meant that the "marriage" that the young man claimed to have contracted was nothing more than an agreement to have sexual relations with a woman in return for monetary compensation, that is, *zinā*, or fornication. On *mutʿa*-marriage, see Arthur Gribetz, *Strange bedfellows:* mutʿat al-nisāʾ *and* mutʿat al-ḥajj*: a study based on Sunnī and Shīʿī sources of* tafsīr, aḥādīth, *and* fiqh (Berlin: K. Schwarz, 1994).

[48] For the full Arabic text of this fatwā, see *Fatāwā Ibn Rushd*, vol. 1, 461–9. In the case discussed by Ibn Rushd, the parties to the union appear to have invoked Shīʿī law.

[49] *Miʿyār*, vol. 4, 495, ll. 12–13.

Further, al-Ṣughayyir claimed to have found positive support for the imposition of a lesser punishment in this very same fatwā, in which Ibn Rushd mentions the existence of a disagreement among jurists regarding the status of *mutʿa* marriage. Although there existed a consensus that this type of marriage had been prohibited by the Prophet, some scholars exceptionally regarded it as permissible on the condition that it is concluded for a specified period of time and "is accompanied by all of the stipulations of a [regular] marriage."[50] Moving beyond the fatwā of Ibn Rushd, al-Ṣughayyir noted that according to the *Mudawwana*, a man who concludes a *mutʿa* marriage receives only the lesser, discretionary punishment for *mutʿa*, not the *ḥadd* punishment for fornication.[51] Similarly, he implied, al-Haskūrī should be flogged but not stoned.

Life-Imprisonment[52]

Al-Ṣughayyir's recommendation that al-Haskūrī be sentenced to life-imprisonment was not directly related to the issue of fornication, but rather to the fact that al-Haskūrī was a leading jurist of Fez who regularly issued fatwās. His personal behavior and conduct were totally inappropriate for a jurist and muftī responsible for instructing other Muslims on how to conduct their affairs, for he had not only fornicated but also offered conflicting testimony, lied about his circumstances, and used his professional knowledge in an effort to subvert the *sharīʿa*, or sacred law of Islam. Al-Ṣughayyir wrote, "He is known to have corrupted the religion of the masses with his fatwās."[53] To mitigate the damage done to Muslim society by al-Haskūrī's behavior, al-Ṣughayyir argued, it was incumbent upon the authorities to incarcerate him for the rest of his life. Further, upon his arrival at the prison, the authorities should inform him that he would be beaten severely if he were discovered issuing fatwās or speaking about *iftāʾ* during his incarceration. Interestingly, al-Ṣughayyir left open the possibility of rehabilitation, specifying that al-Haskūrī might be released from prison if he reformed himself and agreed to abstain from issuing fatwās in the future.[54]

At this point, al-Ṣughayyir's statement ends abruptly with the affirmation of Divine unity, "God guides to [the truth] – He has no partner."

[50] Ibid., vol. 4, 495, ll. 13–15. On *mutʿah*, see Ibn Rushd, *The Distinguished Jurist's Primer*, vol. 2, 67–8; cf. Gribetz, *Strange bedfellows*; *EI*[2], s.v. Mutʿah.

[51] See Saḥnūn, *Mudawwana* (1st edn, al-Maṭbaʿa al-Khayriyya, 1324), vol. 4, 380: "*Wa-kadhālika nikāḥ al-mutʿa ʿāmidan lā yuḥaddūna fī dhālika wa-yuʿāqabūna*."

[52] The notion of imprisonment for life as a punishment for crime was a relatively late development in Islamic law; see Irene Schneider, "Imprisonment in pre-classical and classical Islamic Law," *Islamic Law and Society*, 2 (1995), 157–73.

[53] *Miʿyār*, vol. 4, 495, ll. 16–17.

[54] Ibid., vol. 4, 495, l. 18.

Ibrāhīm al-Sarīfī's Refutation of al-Ṣughayyir

After receiving the response (*jawāb*) of al-Ṣughayyir but before taking any judicial action, the qāḍī al-Zamīnī consulted with another jurist and asked him to examine the contents of al-Ṣughayyir's response from beginning to end. This second jurist was the scholar, professor, and muftī, Abū Isḥāq Ibrāhīm b. ʿAlī al-Maʿāfirī al-Sarīfī al-Ghāzī (d. Rajab 716/September–October 1316). Biographical details relating to this jurist are scarce.[55] His *nisba*, al-Maʿāfirī, suggests that he was of Arab origin, and he may have been an immigrant from al-Andalus.[56]

From the nature of his response, it is clear that al-Sarīfī had in front of him either the original opinion issued by al-Ṣughayyir or a copy thereof. The judicial "leniency" (flogging and life imprisonment!) manifested by al-Ṣughayyir so infuriated al-Sarīfī that he wrote a long and detailed treatise in which he not only refuted the specific arguments advanced by al-Ṣughayyir but also raised and expounded upon four general jurisprudential issues, thus making his treatise an interesting example of how actual cases shaped the development of Mālikī legal doctrine. These issues were: (1) whether one can or should construct a legal argument on the basis of an opinion that is disputed within a particular law school; (2) whether *khulʿ* constitutes a divorce or an annulment; (3) how to interpret and apply the prophetic dictum, "Avert the *ḥudūd* punishments in cases of uncertainty"; and (4) how to weigh the strength of a defendant's initial claim (*aṣl*) against that of a preponderant judicial presumption (*ghālib*).

Because al-Sarīfī and al-Ṣughayyir were contemporaries (who died within three years of each other), it is likely that they were familiar with one another, although our sources are silent about the nature of their relationship. At the outset of his treatise al-Sarīfī established that al-Ṣughayyir had deviated from the straight path for reasons that were inexplicable. "I do not know," he wrote, "what induced this muftī – may God guide him to the truth – to do what he did."[57] At issue was the judicial methodology by means of which al-Ṣughayyir had reasoned his way to a legal conclusion. According to al-Sarīfī, al-Ṣughayyir had analogized legal issues that were in fact distinct and had differentiated legal issues that were in fact similar; abandoned the true subject of the case, that is, divorce, invoking irrelevant issues such as *mutʿa*; and failed to cite the views of the eponym of the Mālikī school, Mālik b. Anas, and his followers. Such errors apparently were uncharacteristic of al-Ṣughayyir, and the only explanation that al-Sarīfī offered was that his contemporary either had sought to expedite the resolution of the case or had been afflicted by an unspecified anxiety. In either case, al-Sarīfī asserted, "[his honor] ha[d] been defiled."[58]

[55] On al-Sarīfī, see Ibn al-Qāḍī, *Laqṭ al-farāʾid min lufāẓat ḥuqaq al-fawāʾid* (Rabat: Dār al-Maghrib li'l-Taʾlīf, 1396/1976), 174; idem, *Durrat al-Ḥijāl*, vol. 1, 177, no. 229 (where his name is given as al-Sharīfī).

[56] See *EI*², s.v. Maʿāfir. A certain Abū al-Ḥasan ʿAlī al-Maʿāfirī was an Andalusian Mālikī scholar who was born in Malaga but later moved to Jerusalem, where he died in 605/1208. See *EI*², s.v. al-Maʿāfirī. I wish to thank Maribel Fierro for this observation.

[57] *Miʿyār*, vol. 4, 496, l. 1.

[58] Ibid., vol. 4, 496, ll. 1–6.

The primary object of al-Sarīfī's animus, however, was the accused, Mūsā b. Yamwīn al-Haskūrī, a jurist who claimed to be capable of exercising independent reasoning (*ijtihād*) but who, according to al-Sarīfī, used his knowledge of the law for unlawful purposes, thereby expressing disdain for, even mocking, Islam. Al-Haskūrī's violation of Islamic ethical norms was as serious as, if not more than, his sexual transgression, for it threatened to undermine the legitimacy of the Marīnid judicial system, which depended on the integrity of those who participated in it. It was a basic tenet of the system of ethical and legal training that produced muftīs that a Muslim scholar would use his knowledge (*ʿilm*) to sustain and reproduce a society in which individual behavior manifests submission to God (*islām*) and in which individuals act in accordance with the prescriptions recorded in the Qurʾān and the *sunna* of the Prophet.[59] As mediators between the Sacred Law and the masses of Muslim laymen (*ʿawāmm*), it is the special responsibility of experts in legal knowledge (*ʿulamāʾ*) to adhere to the highest standards of Islamic conduct and to use their knowledge for positive purposes.[60] The reverse side of this judicial ethos is reflected in a cautionary prophetic *ḥadīth* related on the authority of Abū Hurayra: "The Messenger of God said, 'The person who will receive the most painful punishment on the Day of Resurrection will be the scholar whose knowledge did not benefit him.' "[61] Al-Haskūrī was, in the eyes of al-Sarīfī, a misguided scholar, and, acting upon his religious obligation to "command good and forbid evil," al-Sarīfī sought to expose his colleague in as public a manner as possible. He made no attempt to hide his contempt for al-Haskūrī, to whom he refers almost exclusively throughout his treatise with pejorative epithets such as liar, deceiver, sower of confusion and deception, forsaken one, wretch, and enemy of God.

Serial Refutation of al-Ṣughayyir's Response

Punishment

In a point-by-point analysis of al-Ṣughayyir's opinion, al-Sarīfī cited the jurist's words verbatim and refuted his arguments. He began by quoting al-Ṣughayyir's

[59] On *adab al-muftī*, see M. Khalid Masud, "*Ādāb al-Muftī*: The Muslim Understanding of Values, Characteristics, and Role of a *Muftī*," 124–50.

[60] On knowledge, see the fundamental work of Franz Rosenthal, *Knowledge Triumphant* (Leiden: E.J. Brill, 1970), esp. 240 ff.

[61] Text: *Ashaddu ʾl-nās ʿadhāban yawma al-qiyāma ʿālim lam yanfaʿhu ʿilmuhu*; see Ibn Māja, *Sunan*, ed. Muḥammad Fuʾād ʿAbd al-Bāqī, 2 vols (Cairo: ʿĪsā al-Bābī al-Ḥalabī, 1972), vol. 1, 92 (no. 250), 93 (no. 253), 95 (no. 258), 96 (nos. 259–60), vol. 2, 1261 (no. 3837), 1263 (no. 3843); al-ʿAjlūnī al-Jarrāḥī, *Kashf al-khafāʾ*, vol. 1, 131, no. 376. One also finds the Prophet saying, *allāhummā innī aʿūdhu bika min ʿilm lā yanfaʿu*; see Nasāʾī, *Sunan bi-sharḥ al-Suyūṭī*, ed. Ḥasan Muḥammad al-Masʿūdī, 8 vols (Cairo: al-Maktaba al-Tijāriyya al-Kubrā, n.d.), vol. 8, 254–5, 263, 284–5; Ibn Ḥanbal, *Musnad*, vol. 3, 192, 255, 283, vol. 4, 371, 381.

recommendation, "As for the bodily punishment that he deserves, painful stripes and life-imprisonment." Al-Sarīfī noted, first, that these words are in fact the words of Ibn Rushd, cited by al-Ṣughayyir without proper attribution, in the aforementioned fatwā issued by the Andalusian jurist regarding a man who claimed to have contracted a *mutʿa* marriage. Al-Ṣughayyir not only failed to acknowledge his source but also misrepresented him, for, al-Sarīfī explained, if one refers to the full text of Ibn Rushd's fatwā, one finds that he made the following recommendation with regard to the defendant in that case: "If he is a virgin, he should be beaten severely *after* the *ḥadd* punishment has been applied, and he should be put in prison for a long time, because of his disdain for religion and his deception of the Muslims" (emphasis added). Thus, one finds that in the case treated by Ibn Rushd, the defendant (who was a jurist) had not only fornicated but also made light of religion and deliberately confused (*talbīs*) others, an action that Muslim scholars associate with the work of Satan.[62] For the first offense, Ibn Rushd argued, he should receive the *ḥadd* punishment for fornication, which, for a virgin, is flogging; for the second offense he should receive a discretionary punishment, namely, painful stripes and a lengthy imprisonment.[63]

The legal cause for the recommended punishment

Al-Sarīfī next cited the legal ground (*ʿilla*) upon which al-Ṣughayyir recommended a severe beating. According to al-Ṣughayyir, al-Haskūrī had either implicitly acknowledged having had intercourse with ʿĀʾisha after three repudiations or openly acknowledged having had intercourse with her, as evidenced by the second, independent divorce document, dated 22 Rabīʿ II 714/6 July 1314, which was subsequent to the three separate repudiations. Yet, notwithstanding the implicit and explicit evidence, which constitutes grounds for the stoning penalty in the case of someone who is *muḥṣan*, al-Ṣughayyir recommended only a severe beating. In doing so, he treated al-Haskūrī as if he had revoked his acknowledgement despite the fact that al-Haskūrī had invoked as an excuse something to which no *shubha* applied. This recommendation, according to al-Sarīfī, constituted "plain negligence and a repugnant error."[64]

No stoning

Finally, al-Sarīfī argued that al-Ṣughayyir's assertion that al-Haskūrī "should not be stoned" directly contradicts the legal doctrine of the Mālikī school. As support

[62] See Ibn al-Jawzī (d. 597/1200–01), *Al-Nafīs fī takhrīj aḥādīth Talbīs Iblīs*, ed. Yaḥyā b. Khālid b. Tawfīq (Jīzah: Maktabat al-Tarbiyya al-Islāmiyyah, 1994).
[63] *Miʿyār*, vol. 4, 496, ll. 6–10.
[64] Ibid., vol. 4, 496, ll. 11–15.

for this assertion, he cited a case from the *Mudawwana* in which Mālik called for the application of the *ḥadd* punishment for fornication in the case of a man who had intercourse with a woman whom he previously had divorced by means of three irrevocable repudiations, without there having been an intervening marriage; it is further stipulated that the man knew that his conduct was forbidden.[65] Al-Sarīfī added that this case was discussed by leading authorities of the Mālikī school and that he was not aware of a single authority who had adopted the view espoused by al-Ṣughayyir.[66]

Applied Jurisprudence

Having completed his refutation of al-Ṣughayyir, al-Sarīfī now turned to four general jurisprudential issues raised by the case.

"Respect for disagreement is the weakest principle of the school"

Al-Haskurī defended himself by invoking a minority opinion attributed to Ibn ʿAbbās according to which *khulʿ* constitutes an annulment and does not count as one of the three repudiations that a man is allowed before being irrevocably divorced from his wife. Al-Sarīfī chastised al-Haskūrī for his failure to take into account the jurisprudential consideration that "disagreement is the weakest of all the principles in the school doctrine"; that is, an argument based upon a minority or isolated opinion has less validity than an argument based upon the consensual agreement of scholars belonging to the school.[67]

To illustrate his point, al-Sarīfī cited the following case: a man divorced his wife saying, "I divorce you definitively [*al-batta*]," instead of saying, "I divorce you three times [*al-thalāth*]." There had been an early disagreement within the Mālikī school over whether or not the word *al-batta* is divisible into parts, that is, whether or not it counts as one divorce or as three.[68] In the *Mudawwana*, Saḥnūn

[65] See Saḥnūn, *Mudawwana* (al-Maṭbaʿa al-Khayriyya, 1324), vol. 4, 380: "He should be given the *ḥadd* punishment and the child should not be affiliated to him."

[66] *Miʿyār*, vol. 4, 496, ll. 17–21.

[67] Ibid., vol. 4, 496–7. Cf. Lutz Wiederhold, "Legal Doctrines in Conflict: The Relevance of *Madhhab* Boundaries to Legal Reasoning in the Light of an Unpublished Treatise on *Taqlīd* and *Ijtihād*," *Islamic Law and Society*, 3:2 (1966), 234–304.

[68] Mālik held that divorce with *batta* is triple and definite. See Mālik, *Muwaṭṭaʾ Yaḥyā b. Yaḥyā*, 4 vols (Cairo, 1379/1959), vol. 3, 166; *Muwaṭṭaʾ Imām Mālik*, tr. Muhammad Rahimuddin (Pakistan: Sh. Muhammad Ashraf, 1980), 245: No. 1121, "Abū Bakr b. Abī Ḥazm reported that ʿUmar b. ʿAbd al-ʿAzīz asked what people said about triple divorce at one time. Abū Bakr said: Abān b. ʿUthmān deemed it one divorce. ʿUmar b. ʿAbd al-ʿAzīz said: Had a thousand divorces been valid, *battah* would not have retained any of them. He who pronounced *battah* reached the extreme"; no. 1122, Ibn Shihāb reported that Marwān b. Ḥakam ordered that *battah* carried three divorces." See also Ibn Rushd, *Fatāwā*, vol. 1, 461–9; Spectorsky (tr. and ed.), *Chapters on Marriage and Divorce*, 30–1; Manuela Marín, *Mujeres en al-Ándalus* (Madrid: Consejo Superior de Investigaciones Científicas, 2000), 468–71.

is reported to have held that a man who wants to divorce his wife only once but who uses the word *al-batta* in fact divorces her three times, irrevocably.[69] The majority position within the school requires an intervening marriage before such a man may remarry his former wife and resume sexual relations with her; if he resumes sexual relations without there having been an intervening marriage, the couple has committed fornication, and the stoning penalty should be applied. But this was not the unanimous position of the school, for Aṣbagh (d. 225/839) reportedly withheld the stoning penalty in such a case, irrespective of whether the man was knowledgeable or ignorant of the law, presumably because the disagreement over the legal significance of the word *al-batta* created uncertainty. Aṣbagh also demonstrated leniency in the case of a fornicator who is ignorant of the law, treating him like a foreigner who has no knowledge of the law and therefore is not legally responsible for his actions.[70]

Lest one opt for leniency on the strength of the minority position attributed to Aṣbagh, al-Sarīfī distinguished the earlier Mālikī case law from the case at hand. Unlike the fornicator with respect to whom Aṣbagh withheld the stoning penalty, the perpetrator in the present case, al-Haskūrī, was a jurist who claimed the ability to exercise independent reasoning (*ijtihād*). For this reason, the minority opinion attributed to Aṣbagh does *not* provide any support whatsoever for the present case, al-Sarīfī reasoned.

Khulʿ: divorce or annulment?

Al-Sarīfī now turned to al-Haskūrī's argument that he should not be stoned because of the uncertainty (*shubha*) regarding the status of *khulʿ*, that is, the disagreement as to whether *khulʿ* constitutes a divorce utterance (the majority position) or an annulment (as held by Ibn ʿAbbās). The latter position, he retorted, is a "delusion." While he did not contest the fact that Ibn ʿAbbās regarded *khulʿ* as constituting an annulment, he wrote that the legal consequences of this view rendered al-Haskūrī's position *less* tenable rather than more. Let us assume, al-Sarīfī suggested, that *khulʿ* does indeed constitute an annulment. As with any contract, if a marriage contract is annulled, it is as if the marriage never existed, and the woman assumes the status of a stranger with respect to the man.[71] If, subsequently, the man wants to marry the same woman, he must do everything that is required to produce a valid marriage, that is (1) negotiate the marriage with the woman's marriage guardian, or *walī*; (2) pay a dower (*ṣadāq*); and (3) summon two qualified witnesses to attest to the marriage. Al-Haskūrī had not fulfilled any of these requirements.

[69] Saḥnūn, *al-Mudawwana al-kubrā*, 16 vols in 7 (Cairo, 1303/1905–06), vol. 5, 77 ff.
[70] *Miʿyār*, vol. 4, 497, ll. 3–10.
[71] On *faskh*, see Ibn Rushd, *The Distinguished Jurist's Primer*, vol. 2, 84; Schacht, *Introduction*, 121, 148, 152, 154; *EI*², s.v. Faskh.

But that was not all. The witnesses who had attested to the marriage between al-Haskūrī and 'Ā'isha on 3 Rabī' I 712/9 July 1312 had done so on the basis of Mālikī doctrine (according to which *khul'* constitutes a divorce). A full two years would pass before al-Haskūrī, coming before the judge who heard the case, claimed to "have adopted the doctrine of Ibn 'Abbās." Al-Sarīfī viewed this statement as an attempt to convince the court that he had sincerely believed it possible to marry under one doctrine yet live by another – a situation that would be patently ridiculous. Al-Sarīfī remarked with disdain that the "troublemaker sowed the utmost amount of confusion and deception," and that there was no upright witness who would give testimony regarding a marriage contract according to the doctrine of Ibn 'Abbās.[72]

Returning to the Ibn Rushd fatwā and its potential relevance to the present case, al-Sarīfī conceded that there was a superficial similarity between the two cases, in that both of the accused men sought legal support for their actions by invoking the doctrine of a *madhhab* other than the one to which they were formally affiliated.[73] It may be possible to excuse the person who contracted the *mut'a* marriage if his motives were sincere, but one could not do the same for al-Haskūrī, whose sole motive, according to al-Sarīfī, was to mock Islam and manipulate religion, as reportedly was his custom, both in private and in public.[74] Al-Sarīfī concluded this section of his argument as follows:

> Anyone who is familiar with what [al-Haskūrī] does in private [should] declare with certainty the evil [that he does] in public, even if he manifests goodness [in public]. Further, this question is the clearest testimony against him for he married this woman four times and he said on the fourth occasion that he married her according to the doctrine of Ibn 'Abbās. In truth, however, he did not marry her nor did he render her licit (*istabāḥā*) according to the doctrine of either one of the two scholars [viz., Mālik or Ibn 'Abbās]. He is a fornicator, according to consensus, ... if he acknowledged intercourse, or [if] testimonial evidence – or its equivalent – was brought against him, as will follow, if God wills. For, verily, he entered the state of marriage and in that fashion he rendered licit that which he rendered licit from among the sacred things of the Exalted God, and this is a more serious matter for him ... No one would judge [this person] favorably in this case and lend credence to him, on account of the mockery that he manifested in it – except a simpleton who is devoid of the capacity to accept the religion of truth [*al-fiṭra*][75] or a dissimulator who is indifferent to religion – may God save us from that![76]

[72] *Mi'yār*, vol. 4, 497, ll. 15–25. Note: On the part of the husband, the *khul'* is regarded as an undertaking under oath, so that he cannot withdraw an offer of *khul'* which has been made. See Schacht, *Introduction*, 164.

[73] *Mi'yār*, vol. 4, 498, ll. 12–13. See again Wiederhold, "Legal Doctrines in Conflict," esp. 242 ff.

[74] *Mi'yār*, vol. 4, 498, ll. 13–15.

[75] On this term, see Lane, *Arabic-English Lexicon* (London: Williams and Norgate, 1863), s.v. f-ṭ-r; Wael Hallaq, "Ibn Taymiyya on the Existence of God," *Acta Orientalia* (1991): 49–69, esp. 55 ff.

[76] *Mi'yār*, vol. 4, 498, ll. 15–23.

Interpretation of the prophetic dictum

In his fatwā, al-Ṣughayyir had justified his averting the *ḥadd* punishment for fornication on the ground that "the sacred law is magnanimous in the matter of *ḥudūd* punishments, for it averts them in cases of uncertainty," alluding to the well known and widely cited prophetic *ḥadīth* that establishes a key jurisprudential principle (see above). Al-Sarīfī took exception to al-Ṣughayyir's generous interpretation of this dictum. "How ugly this statement is!"[77] he exclaimed, for al-Ṣughayyir had interpreted and understood the prophetic *ḥadīth* as if it applies to *every* uncertainty, when, in fact, it is necessary to distinguish different degrees of uncertainty, some of which make it necessary to avert the *ḥudūd* punishments while others do not. To clarify the matter, al-Sarīfī quoted the exact words attributed to the Prophet, "*idraʾū al-ḥudūd fī'l-shubuhāt*," drawing attention to the fact that the Prophet used the terms "*ḥudūd*" and "*shubuhāt*" in a general manner without specifying exactly which *ḥudūd* punishments are to be averted (there are five: unlawful intercourse, false accusation of unlawful intercourse, drinking wine, theft, and highway robbery), also without specifying the threshhold of uncertainty required to avert a particular *ḥadd* punishment.[78] In an apparent criticism of al-Ṣughayyir's intellectual powers, al-Sarīfī commented that the task of making these determinations and filling in this gap in the law is solely that of a *mujtahid*, who uses his expert knowledge to inform the judicial authorities of the specific course of action to be taken.[79]

Preferring a narrower interpretation of the prophetic dictum, al-Sarīfī invoked the authority of Mālik b. Anas. In a case mentioned above, Mālik was asked about a man who had divorced his wife using the word *al-batta* instead of *al-thalāth*, and neither Mālik nor any of his companions had invoked uncertainty (*shubha*) as a ground for averting the stoning penalty for fornication. Indeed, al-Sarīfī observed, Mālik unequivocally stated, "He should be stoned," even though the school's disagreement about the legal significance of *al-batta* constituted uncertainty. How much the more so in the present case, in which al-Haskūrī made *three* separate repudiations, with the result that, according to the unanimous opinion of Mālikī jurists, it is forbidden for him to remarry his former wife without an intervening marriage (*taḥlīl*), as specified explicitly and unequivocally in Q. 2:229–30.[80]

Al-Sarīfī's narrow interpretation of the prophetic dictum was unaffected by al-Haskūrī's claim to be an adherent of the doctrine of Ibn ʿAbbās. Let us suppose for the sake of argument, al-Sarīfī suggested, that that "sower of confusion" was in fact a *bona fide* follower of the doctrine of Ibn ʿAbbās. Mālik still would apply the stoning penalty to him because of his duplicity and insincerity: it will be

[77] Ibid., vol. 4, 499, ll. 1–2. We will have occasion to discuss in greater detail "the sacred things of the Exalted God" (*ḥurumāt allāh*) in chapter five.

[78] See *EI*², s.v. Ḥadd.

[79] *Miʿyār*, vol. 4, 499, ll. 3–7. On the problem of *ijtihād*, see Wael B. Hallaq, "Was the Gate of *Ijtihād* Closed?" *International Journal of Middle East Studies*, 16 (1984), 3–41.

[80] *Miʿyār*, vol. 4, 499, ll. 7–11.

recalled that at the time of his marriage al-Haskūrī had identified himself as a follower of the doctrine of Mālik, the doctrine of the witnesses whom he had summoned to attest to the marriage – and not as a follower of the doctrine of Ibn ʿAbbās. Further, it will be remembered that upon questioning by the qāḍī al-Zamīnī, al-Haskūrī initially claimed to have been deceived by his wife but later retracted his statement when authorized witnesses were summoned to verify it. It was only then, that is, more than two years after the marriage, that al-Haskūrī shifted his defense strategy, claiming to be an adherent of the doctrine of Ibn ʿAbbās. This was an important point for al-Sarīfī, for it exposed al-Haskūrī, dubbed here "the enemy of God," as a liar, with the result that nothing that he said about the case could be trusted.[81]

The exposure of al-Haskūrī as a liar raised the issue of his potential repentance. Although the widespread opinion among Mālikī jurists holds that a person who gives false testimony should be punished even if he has subsequently repented, a minority view holds that he should not be. Should al-Haskūrī be offered the option of repenting and, if he chose to repent, should he be spared punishment? Absolutely not, al-Sarīfī asserted, because the transgression committed by a person who gives false testimony and then repents is not the same as that committed by al-Haskūrī, who, when the discrepancy in his assertions was exposed, lied rather than repented, thereby committing an abomination (*aẓīman*). Leniency cannot be granted in the case of al-Haskūrī, and anyone who made such an argument in this case, al-Sarīfī pronounced, has "strayed entirely from the mark."[82]

As further support for his narrow interpretation of the prophetic dictum and for his insistence that the *ḥudūd* punishments are not to be avoided in *all* cases in which there is uncertainty, al-Sarīfī cited five examples of earlier cases decided by Mālik b. Anas. In all five cases (and, al-Sarīfī averred, many more could be cited), there was some *shubha* or uncertainty regarding the charge; in all five cases, however, Mālik called for the application of the *ḥadd* punishment.[83] Clearly, the

81 Ibid., vol. 4, 499, ll. 11–19.

82 Ibid., vol. 4, 499–500.

83 The cases are as follows: (1) A man who fornicated with a Muslim concubine (*amat al-islām*) [belonging to a third party] claimed ignorance of the law in defense of his behavior. Mālik rejected this argument and did not liken the perpetrator to a foreigner, for whom ignorance legitimately may be invoked as an excuse. *Ad minorum ad majorum*: if Mālik saw no grounds for taking uncertainty into consideration here, there surely would be no grounds for doing so in the case of al-Haskūrī (ibid., vol. 4, 500, ll. 2–5). (2) Theft is held to occur if a responsible person takes by stealth, out of a secured place (*ḥirz*), an object which has a value exceeding a certain minimum amount and to which he has neither the right of ownership nor quasi-ownership (see Ibn Rushd, *The Distinguished Jurist's Primer*, vol. 2, 536 ff., esp. 540–2; Schacht, *Introduction*, 179–80). In one case, several witnesses disagreed about the value of an object that had been stolen. Mālik held that if two witnesses endowed with eyesight agreed on its value, the offender's hand should be amputated, notwithstanding the disagreement of the other witnesses regarding the value of the object. Commenting on this case, al-Sarīfī observed that Mālik did not take into consideration the uncertainty created by the disagreement among the witnesses (although he conceded that other Mālikī jurists did so) [*Miʿyār*, vol. 4, 500, ll. 5–8]. (3) A man climbed over the wall of a house and seized certain household items. When he was apprehended, the man claimed that the items were his property. Initially, the owner of the house accepted the intruder's word, but later he brought charges

documented practice of the founding Imām of the Mālikī school points unequivocally to a narrow interpretation of the prophetic dictum. It is against this background, al-Sarīfī said, that one must assess the validity of al-Ṣughayyir's assertion, "The sacred law is magnanimous with regard to the *ḥudūd* punishments in cases of fornication, for it averts them in cases of uncertainty." This statement, al-Sarīfī suggested, must be understood in its proper jurisprudential context. On the basis of his reading of Mālikī sources al-Sarīfī determined that some uncertainties are strong and require averting the *ḥudūd* punishments while others are weak and do not. As noted, it is the task of the qualified *mujtahid* to distinguish strong uncertainties from weak ones.[84]

What about the cases cited by al-Ṣughayyir in which earlier jurists did invoke uncertainty as grounds for averting the *ḥudūd* punishments, as, for example, the case in which a person who was traveling divorced his wife by means of testimonial evidence but subsequently denied the divorce and acknowledged having had intercourse with her? Here, al-Sarīfī asserted that al-Ṣughayyir had committed a jurisprudential error. The proper ruling, following al-Māzarī (d. 536/1141),[85] was that a person who acknowledges an act of fornication is judged on the strength of the testimonial evidence (*al-bayyina*).[86]

Similarly, what must one do with al-Ṣughayyir's assertion that al-Haskūrī's legal status was similar to that of a person who acknowledged fornication but subsequently retracted his acknowledgement or denied the offence, with the result that the stoning penalty should be averted from him? Al-Sarīfī retorted that al-Ṣughayyir had committed a jurisprudential error – "an outright delusion and a mistake:"[87] the offender should be stoned.[88]

At this point al-Sarīfī introduced critical information relating to the case that had not been mentioned by al-Ṣughayyir in his response. "I have learned," al-Sarīfī wrote, that ʿĀ'isha is pregnant, presumably as a result of intercourse with al-Haskūrī.

against him. According to Mālik, the houseowner's acceptance of the defendant's assertion is outweighed by the *ghālib*, that is, the preponderant judicial assumption regarding the defendant's manifest behavior, which identifies him as a thief and makes the *ḥadd* punishment obligatory (ibid., vol. 4, 500, ll. 8–12. See Saḥnūn, *Mudawwana* (al-Maṭbaʿa al-Khayriyya, 1324), vol. 4, 413–15). (4) A man claimed to have purchased a concubine from her master prior to having intercourse with her. The master denied having sold the concubine to the man. Disregarding the uncertainty, Mālik held that the *ḥadd* punishment should be applied (*Miʿyār*, vol. 4, 500, ll. 12–13; see Saḥnūn, *Mudawwana* (al-Maṭbaʿa al-Khayriyya, 1324), vol. 4, 380). (5) A woman married and then divorced. Four years and eight months subsequent to the divorce, she married another man and five months later gave birth. Thus, the child was born more than five years (the maximum period of gestation allowed by the Mālikīs) after her divorce from her first husband, but less than six months (the minimum period of gestation) after her marriage to her second husband. Mālik called for the application of the *ḥadd* punishment for fornication and held that the child should not be affiliated to either of the two husbands (although al-Qābisī reportedly held a dissenting view) [*Miʿyār*, vol. 4, 500, ll. 13–15]. [84] Ibid., vol. 4, 500, ll. 16–18.

[85] Abū ʿAbdallāh Muḥammad b. ʿAlī al-Māzarī, a distinguished Mālikī jurist who was the student of al-Lakhmī (d. 418/1085) and the teacher of Qāḍī ʿIyāḍ (d. 544/1149). He reportedly attained the rank of *mujtahid fī'l-fatwā* and was the author of *Kitāb al-Taʿliqah ʿalā al-Mudawwana*. See Ibn Farḥūn, *Dībāj*, 279; Makhlūf, *Shajara*, vol. 1, 127, no. 371; Toledano, *Judicial Practice*, 101 n. 29.

[86] *Miʿyār*, vol. 4, 500, ll. 18–22. [87] Ibid., vol. 4, 501, l. 1.

[88] Ibid., vol. 4, 500 (bottom)–1 (top).

(Al-Sarīfī expressed surprise at al-Ṣughayyir's failure to mention this fact and was loath to speculate about the reasons for this lapse.)[89] Was 'Ā'isha's pregnancy of greater probative value than al-Haskūrī's denial that he had intercourse with her subsequent to the third repudiation? Yes, according to al-Sarīfī. And in support of this conclusion, he cited three additional cases which share as their common denominator the rejection of a claim that intercourse had *not* occurred between a man and his wife or between a man and a woman whom he was accused of having raped.[90] These examples show that the cases were decided by adherence to commonly accepted legal presumptions (for example, a man who has been married for twenty years is legally presumed to have had intercourse with his wife). In the present instance, the accepted legal presumption is that al-Haskūrī had intercourse with 'Ā'isha after taking her back following the third repudiation, as evidenced by her pregnancy and notwithstanding his denial. It follows, al-Sarīfī concluded, that al-Haskūrī should receive the *ḥadd* punishment and the child should not be affiliated to him.

Initial claim (*aṣl*) versus preponderant judicial presumption (*ghālib*)

Most of the cases cited by al-Sarīfī share with the case under consideration one important factor: the problem of making a legal determination as to whether or not

89 Ibid., vol. 4, 501, ll. 8–10.

90 The cases are as follows: (1) Citing a statement attributed to a certain 'Abd al-Malik in the *Kitāb Muḥammad* – probably the *Mawwāziyya* of Muḥammad b. Mawwāz (Muḥammad b. Ibrāhīm, known as Ibn al-Mawwāz, d. 281/894 or 269/882, was an Alexandrian jurist who reportedly studied with Ibn al-Mājashūn and Ibn 'Abd al-Ḥakam. See Toledano, *Judicial Practice*, 64, note 51; Ibn Farḥūn, *Dībāj*, 232; Makhlūf, *Shajara*, vol. 1, 68, no. 72), al-Sarīfī adduced the case of a man who was caught fornicating, as established by testimonial evidence, after his having spent a long time with his wife. In an effort to reduce the punishment from stoning to flogging, the accused man asserted that he had not had intercourse with his wife since marrying her (and was therefore a virgin at the time of his fornication). Holding that the presumption of intercourse prevails over the fornicator's denial, 'Abd al-Malik called for imposition of the stoning penalty: even if the man had spent only a single night with his wife, he was guilty of fornication, a view reportedly held by several earlier scholars (*Mi'yār*, vol. 4, 501, ll. 17–20; cf. Saḥnūn, *Mudawwana* (al-Maṭba'a al-Khayriyya, 1324), vol. 4, 397. (2) From the *Mudawwana*: A woman was caught fornicating after having been married for twenty years, during which time she had made no claim regarding her husband's failure to consummate their marriage. Only now, facing the possibility of stoning, did she make such a claim. Although she might have made this claim after the first night of marriage, she cannot do so after twenty years, and the *ḥadd* punishment is applied, even if the husband corroborates her claim (*Mi'yār*, vol. 4, 501, ll. 20–3; cf. Saḥnūn, *Mudawwana* (al-Maṭba'a al-Khayriyya, 1324), vol. 4, 208; Abū al-Walīd Sulaymān b. Khalaf al-Bājī, *al-Muntaq'a sharḥ Muwaṭṭa' Imām Dār al-Hijra Sayyidunā Mālik b. Anas* (Cairo: Maṭba'at al-Sa'āda, 1332/1914; reprinted Dār al-Kitāb al-Islāmī, 1990), vol. 3, 333). (3) From the *Kitāb* of al-Lakhmī (perhaps the *Tabṣirah*, a commentary on the *Mudawwana*; on al-Lakhmī [d. 478/1075], see Ibn Farḥūn, *Dībāj*, 203; Makhlūf, *Shajara*, vol. 1, 117, no. 326; Toledano, *Judicial Practice*, 63, note 44): a man kidnapped a woman in the presence of eyewitnesses, spent the night with her, and subsequently denied having intercourse with her. Al-Lakhmī called for imposition of the *ḥadd* punishment on the strength of the eyewitness testimony regarding the abduction. According to al-Lakhmī this particular problem, in which the preponderant judicial presumption (intercourse) is contradicted by the man's initial claim, is treated in the lawbooks in a chapter devoted to "adjudication on the basis of an indicator" (*Mi'yār*, vol. 4, 501, ll. 23–6).

a man has had intercourse with a woman – a private and delicate matter. Mālikī legal doctrine deals with this problem by making legal presumptions based upon certain inferences regarding the behavior of individuals: on the one hand, if a woman is not married, a presumption of continuity exists regarding her virginity (*istiṣḥāb al-bakāra*) until such time as evidence establishes a change in her condition.[91] On the other hand, once a woman enters her husband's house and is alone with him overnight, the *ghālib*, or preponderant judicial presumption, holds that intercourse has taken place, despite the fact that it is possible – albeit highly unlikely – for a man to abstain from deflowering his wife for a long time and despite the fact that virginity is a matter that can be determined through a physical examination (*amrun ḥissī*).[92]

This segment of al-Sarīfī's analysis reveals another stratagem used by al-Haskūrī in an attempt to escape stoning, for al-Sarīfī undertakes to determine whether or not al-Haskūrī had intercourse with ʿĀʾisha after taking her back subsequent to the third divorce. Should one adopt the defendant's initial claim (*aṣl*), that is, al-Haskūrī's denial of intercourse, or should one follow the preponderant judicial presumption (*ghālib*), according to which intercourse is assumed to have taken place if she entered his house and was alone with him for one night? In the present case, al-Sarīfī declared, there is no question as to whether it is the *aṣl* or *ghālib* that applies, for it is agreed upon that "the poor fellow" (*miskīn*) sexually penetrated ʿĀʾisha several times, legally before and illegally after the third repudiation, as established in a certified judicial document (*al-ḥukm al-maqṭūʿ bihi*) – which I understand as a reference to his having acknowledged taking back ʿĀʾisha a fourth time. The legal determination regarding events after the third repudiation must be based upon the preponderant judicial presumption of intercourse, so long as no change occurred in al-Haskūrī's physical condition that would have made intercourse impossible for him. Alluding to al-Ṣughayyir without mentioning his name, al-Sarīfī scoffed that only a person "whose mind contains weakness and disorder and who is ignorant of human sexual desire" (literally: that which is required by unblemished natures and sound temperaments) would assert that al-Haskūrī did not have intercourse with ʿĀʾisha. Further, the presumption of intercourse is reinforced by several indicators, including the discrepancies in the statements uttered by al-Haskūrī in the presence of the qāḍī al-Zamīnī (who nevertheless treated him as one who acknowledged having unlawful intercourse), the confusion that he attempted to sow by invoking the doctrine of Ibn ʿAbbās, and

[91] *Istiṣḥāb* literally signifies "escorting" or "companionship." Muslim jurists use the term in a technical sense to refer to a rational proof that "may be employed in the absence of other indications; specifically, those facts, or rules of law and reason, whose existence or non-existence had been proven in the past, and which are presumed to remain so for lack of evidence to establish any change" (Kamali, *Principles*, 297). See further Ignaz Goldziher, "Das Prinzip des *Istiṣḥāb* in der Muhammedanischen Gesetzwissenschaft," *Vienna Oriental Journal*, 1 (1887), 228–36; Wael B. Hallaq, *A History of Islamic Legal Theories: An Introduction to* Uṣūl al-Fiqh (Cambridge: Cambridge University Press, 1997), 113–15.

[92] *Miʿyār*, vol. 4, 502, ll. 4–7.

a detail mentioned now for the first time, to wit, that al-Haskūrī was known to be heterosexual (lit.: "he loved women and experienced sexual desire for them").[93]

Focusing his attention on the relationship between the defendant's initial claim (*aṣl*) and the preponderant judicial presumption (*ghālib*), al-Sarīfī cited analogous cases and invoked earlier authorities to support his assertion that the *ghālib* takes precedence over the *aṣl*. In one case, a woman who claimed to be a virgin was accused of committing fornication by four witnesses. Although her claim to virginity was corroborated by the female experts who were summoned to examine her, Mālik nevertheless rejected the experts' assertion and called for the application of the *ḥadd* punishment on the strength of the witness testimony.[94] Once again, the defendant's initial claim was superseded by the testimonial evidence; again, the "correct" answer was linked to adherence to the authorized professional norms of Muslim jurists.

Al-Sarīfī now suggested that it was possible to change the terms of the argument in the present case and to hold that the *aṣl* was in fact intercourse so that the *aṣl* and the *ghālib* coincide. "And this is the truth," he declared, "in which there is no doubt,"

> because this woman was sexually penetrated by that poor fellow previously, many times, and it is absolutely impossible for him to deny having had intercourse with her. If this is the case, then there is a presumption of continuity regarding the existence of intercourse (*fa-wujūd al-waṭ' mustaṣḥab*) until one hears about some obstacle [to intercourse], and nothing has been heard that would necessitate denying (?) credence to him in the matter.[95]

Al-Sarīfī cited an additional case which sheds light on the relationship between the *aṣl* and the *ghālib* but concluded that the case was superfluous as far as al-Haskūrī was concerned because the latter sowed confusion, treated as permissible that which was not permissible with respect to himself and others, and was a demonstrated liar, so that none of his claims in the matter should be accepted.[96]

Taking solace in the sufferings of past jurists

Al-Haskūrī, it will be remembered, was a prominent jurist, and his behavior, once it became known, no doubt raised serious questions about his character, integrity, and judicial competence. When his followers began to doubt him, al-Sarīfī reported, al-Haskūrī explained his situation by comparing himself to two great Imāms of the past who had been flogged for political transgressions. The first was Saʿīd b. al-Musayyab al-Makhzūmī (d. *ca*. 94/712–13), one of the "seven jurists of Medina," renowned for his piety and for his knowledge of *ḥadīth*, *fiqh*, and *tafsīr*.

[93] Ibid., vol. 4, 502, ll. 7–16. Text: *ḥubbuhu li'l-nisā' wa-shahawātuhu lahunna*. I wish to thank Maribel Fierro for helping to clarify the meaning of the Arabic text.
[94] Ibid., vol. 4, 502 (l. 17)–3 (l. 4). [95] Ibid., vol. 4, 503, ll. 4–8. [96] Ibid., vol. 4, 503, ll. 8–16.

Ibn al-Musayyab's desire for independence from the political authorities resulted in two floggings: sixty strokes following his refusal to recognize Ibn al-Zubayr, and additional strokes as a result of his refusal to pay allegiance to the sons of ʿAbd al-Malik, al-Walīd and Sulaymān.[97] The second Imām spoken of by al-Haskūrī was none other than Mālik b. Anas. In 145/762, an ʿAlid pretender to supreme power, Muḥammad b. ʿAbdallāh, staged a coup and made himself master of Medina. Although Mālik did not play an active role in the rebellion, he issued a fatwā in which he declared that homage paid to the ʿAbbāsid caliph al-Manṣūr had been given under compulsion and therefore was not binding. When the rebellion failed in 147/763, Mālik was flogged by the governor of Medina, Jaʿfar b. Sulaymān, and suffered a dislocated shoulder. Mālik's punishment is reported to have increased his prestige.[98] By comparing himself to Mālik and Ibn al-Musayyib, al-Haskūrī magnified his stature in the eyes of his lay followers, who strove even more diligently to follow his words and actions. This development, wrote al-Sarīfī, was "the greatest calamity that ha[d] occurred in religion."[99]

Ḥadd punishments are not applied in cases of doubt

At the end of his treatise, al-Sarīfī returned to the subject of *shubha* and to the fatwā issued by Ibn Rushd with regard to the case of *mutʿa*. He sharply criticized al-Ṣughayyir, asserting that his knowledge of the legal doctrine of *shubha* was weak and that he apparently had not studied the relevant chapters of the law. *Ipso facto*, there was nothing objectionable about al-Ṣughayyir's statement, "The *ḥadd* punishments are not applied when there exists doubt" (*bi'l-shakk*), a prophetic dictum that may be invoked when there is a sound reason to do so. "But what doubt," al-Sarīfī asked, "exists in our case in the eyes of the jurists?" In a similar case, Mālik had called for the stoning penalty.[100]

Al-Sarīfī concluded by returning to al-Ṣughayyir's reference to the fatwā issued by Ibn Rushd. It will be remembered that al-Ṣughayyir had invoked this fatwā in order to distinguish it from the present case. And the distinction identified by al-Ṣughayyir served as the ground on which he had reached the conclusion that one should *not* apply the *ḥadd* punishment to al-Haskūrī. To demonstrate that al-Ṣughayyir had identified a false or irrelevant distinction and thus had reached a baseless conclusion, al-Sarīfī quoted the exact words of the relevant section of al-Ṣughayyir's fatwā, as follows:[101]

> And consider the fatwā issued by Ibn Rushd – may God have mercy on him – in his responsa (*ajwiba*), namely, the application of the *ḥadd* punishment to someone who

[97] See *EI²*, supplement, s.v. Fuḳahāʾ al-Madīna al-Sabʿa, and the sources cited there.

[98] Text: *mā zāla Mālik baʿda dhālika al-ḍarb fī rifʿatin min al-nās wa-ʿuluwwin min amrihi wa-iʿẓāmi al-nās lahu wa-ka-innamā kānat tilka al-siyāṭ allatī ḍuriba bihā ḥilyan ḥuliya bihi*. See Ibn ʿAbd al-Barr al-Qurṭubī (d. 463/1070–71), *al-Intiqāʾ fī faḍāʾil al-thalātha al-aʾimma al-fuqahāʾ* (Cairo, Maktabat al-Qudsī, 1350), 43–4; *EI²*, s.v. Mālik b. Anas, and the sources cited in the bibliography.

[99] *Miʿyār*, vol. 4, 503, ll. 16–23. [100] Ibid., vol. 4, 504, ll. 9–14. [101] Ibid., vol. 4, 504, ll. 15 ff.

engages in a *mutʿa*-marriage.[102] But our case is not like that one. Because that one [viz., the perpetrator in the *mutʿa*-case], according to what he [viz., the *mustaftī*] said, married without a *walī*, and for one-half of a dirham, and the contract [was witnessed by men] who did not meet the qualification of *ʿadāla*.

And for this reason, [Ibn Rushd] issued a fatwā calling for the *ḥadd* punishment. And the *mutʿa* marriage which is permitted, exceptionally, by those who permit it, is specifically a marriage for a specified time, in which all of the stipulations of marriage are fully present.[103]

Al-Sarīfī called the manner in which al-Ṣughayyir distinguished the two cases juristic "negligence." In fact the resemblance (*tashbīh*) between the two cases was stronger than the alleged difference, he wrote. One aspect of al-Ṣughayyir's negligence was his failure to cite the full text of Ibn Rushd's fatwā, which specifies that the defendant in the *mutʿa* case responded to the charges brought against him by making the following points: (1) A *mutʿa* marriage does *not* require a *walī*: Indeed, all that is required is the consent of the woman, who may lease her body in the same manner that she may lease property belonging to her; a *walī* is required only when a man acquires permanent ownership of his wife's vulva in a sound and valid marriage. (2) The half dirham paid as dower is, in fact, regarded as a proper dower by some jurists; and those jurists who, exceptionally, regard *mutʿa* as permissible do not apply the *ḥadd* punishment for even the smallest bridewealth. (3) The witnesses that the defendant summoned were the only witnesses available. He, himself, said of this fact that he hoped that their presence alone was sufficient to make his actions legal regardless of their qualifications. "Perhaps God will accept this excuse from me," he said. Further in the fatwā of Ibn Rushd, one finds that the defendant also put forward as an excuse for his behavior the difference in status between the woman and him, which, he claimed, made it impossible for them to marry in a sound and valid manner. He said that he thought that basing his behavior on a disputed point "was preferable to fornication."[104]

Ibn Rushd, however, *rejected* these arguments and called for the imposition of the *ḥadd* punishment. One important reason why he did so was the *mustaftī*'s characterization of the defendant in the *mutʿa* case as "one of the people of knowledge and education." More than anything else, what troubled Ibn Rushd (and, subsequently, al-Sarīfī) was the fact that a person possessing *ʿilm* would use his knowledge for un-Islamic purposes. The transgressions of the defendant in the *mutʿa* case and of al-Haskūrī were intolerable, for if educated Muslims behave in this manner, what can be expected of laymen? Suggesting that the Prophet himself had anticipated this problem, Ibn Rushd cited toward the end of his response the aforementioned prophetic *ḥadīth*, "The person who will receive the most severe punishment on the Day of Resurrection is the scholar whose knowledge did not benefit him."[105]

[102] See note 48, above.
[103] Ibid., vol. 4, 504, ll. 15–18. Cp. Ibn Rushd, *Fatāwā*, vol. 3, 1535 ff.
[104] *Miʿyār*, vol. 4, 504 (l. 16)–5 (l. 5); Ibn Rushd, *Fatāwā*, vol. 3, 1536.
[105] *Miʿyār*, vol. 4, 505, ll. 6–7. Cp. Ibn Rushd, *Fatāwā*, vol. 3, 1537. For references, see note 61, above.

Al-Sarīfī quoted Ibn Rushd's description of the defendant in the *mutʿa* case:

> His knowledge and education (*ṭalabuhu*) are a proof against him which necessitate his shame in this world and the next and which cause him to descend to the worst of all levels [of Hell]. This is because he knew what is right but opposed it; and what is correct but contradicted it; and what is forbidden but rushed into it, in order to slander the Exalted God, disdain his limits (*ḥudūd*), and mock his religion.[106]

If Ibn Rushd treated the defendant in this case as a fornicator, compared his behavior to that of prostitutes in pre-Islamic Arabia, gave no consideration to the excuses that he put forward, paid no attention to the claim of *shubha*, and called for the application of the *ḥadd* punishment, then it was even more appropriate, al-Sarīfī concluded, that the *ḥadd* punishment be applied in the case of al-Haskūrī, that "criminal" who did not pay even a nominal bridewealth, did not summon witnesses, and did not negotiate the marriage with a *walī*. Further, al-Haskūrī crossed *madhhab* boundaries to justify his actions but failed to live up to the requirements of the doctrine to which he claimed to adhere, the doctrine of Mālik b. Anas! Finally, the discrepancies in his statements made in the presence of the qāḍī al-Zamīnī established beyond any question that he was a liar.[107]

Al-Haskūrī's case and that of the offender in Ibn Rushd's fatwā admittedly were analogous in that each man invoked the doctrine of a law school to which he did not belong. Unlike his counterpart, however, al-Haskūrī had no objective other than to mock religion and to attribute mendacity to Ibn ʿAbbās, "the righteous man of the *umma*."[108] On balance, therefore, the *mutʿa* perpetrator was in a *better* position than al-Haskūrī and manifested more *taqwā*, or fear of God. If the acknowledgement of intercourse by the accused in the *mutʿa* case constituted grounds for the *ḥadd* punishment, then al-Haskūrī certainly deserved the same punishment, al-Sarīfī emphasized. All of this could be traced back to Mālik and his companions, and anyone who sought support for a contrary position elsewhere was being stubborn and wasting his time.[109] Al-Sarīfī concluded: "And God is the Master of success and guidance, and the Champion of his Messengers and of those who believe in the life of this world and in the day on which the testimony will be given. May God pray for our master Muḥammad, his family, and his Companions, and grant them peace."[110]

Judicial Action

The qāḍī al-Zamīnī now had in front of him two judicial opinions on the basis of which he might decide the fate of al-Haskūrī. Both jurists agreed that al-Haskūrī had committed *zinā* or fornication. But they disagreed regarding the appropriate

[106] *Miʿyār*, vol. 4, 505, ll. 7–10; cp. Ibn Rushd, *Fatāwā*, vol. 3, 1537.
[107] *Miʿyār*, vol. 4, 505, ll. 10–19.
[108] Ibid., vol. 4, 505, ll. 19–24.
[109] Ibid., vol. 4, 505 (l. 24)–6 (l. 4).
[110] Ibid., vol. 4, 506, ll. 4–6.

punishment. Notwithstanding his reputation for severity and harshness in judgment, al-Ṣughayyir recommended a severe beating and life-imprisonment, whereas al-Sarīfī recommended that the stoning penalty be implemented. Which was the better and more persuasive opinion? Which better served the goal of reinforcing the moral and legal norms of Marīnid society? Upon which opinion should the qāḍī base his *ḥukm*, or judgment?

From the standpoint of strict judicial logic, the first muftī's opinion appears to have been severely flawed, whereas that of the second was rigorously argued, meticulously documented, and firmly grounded in authoritative sources. As is true of most if not all of the fatwās preserved in the *Miʿyār*, our text does not specify what judicial action was taken by the qāḍī who requested the fatwā. In the present instance, however, we are fortunate in that al-Haskūrī was a well-known scholar who merited an entry in the biographical dictionary of Ibn al-Qāḍī (d. 1020/1616), where we read that he was flogged (*ḍuriba*), in partial conformity with the recommendation of al-Ṣughayyir.[111] Al-Zamīnī's decision to follow the opinion that was technically flawed at the expense of the opinion that was technically and juridically more rigorous may be explained – tentatively – by the following factors.

First, there is the nature of the evidence. The evidentiary requirements to establish fornication are extremely high: four eyewitnesses to the act or an acknowledgement by the accused. In the present case, there were no eyewitnesses to the act, nor did al-Haskūrī explicitly acknowledge having had intercourse with ʿĀʾisha subsequent to the third repudiation. Rather, he merely acknowledged having "taken her back" subsequent to the third repudiation. The leap from "taking her back" to his having had intercourse with her is based on a legal presumption that *if* he "took her back," he must have had sexual intercourse with her. But a legal presumption constitutes only probable knowledge (*ẓann*) and not the apodictic certainty (*qaṭʿ*) required to establish fornication. The judge reasonably may have concluded that the requisite evidentiary grounds for application of the *ḥadd* punishment had not been established. To this must be added al-Haskūrī's denial that he had had intercourse with ʿĀʾisha subsequent to the third repudiation, a denial which created a level of *shubha* which arguably was sufficient to avert implementation of the *ḥadd* punishment.[112] In addition, the very fact that two muftīs disagreed over whether or not *shubha* was present in this case constituted a second level of *shubha*.

Second, the qāḍī may have weighed the logical precision and technical rigor of al-Sarīfī's opinion against its emotional tenor. In sharp contrast to Ibn Rushd and al-Ṣughayyir, al-Sarīfī adopted a haughty and condescending tone that at times sounded vindictive. He referred to al-Haskūrī not in the objective and neutral

[111] Ibn al-Qāḍī, *Durrat al-Ḥijāl*, vol. 3, 4.

[112] The case for *shubha* was perhaps stronger than al-Sarīfī suggested. Islamic legal doctrine generally holds that *shubha* does in fact exist if a man divorces his wife three times but continues to live with her, believing, for whatever reason, that she is still his wife. See, for example, ʿAbd al-Raḥmān al-Jarīrī, *Kitāb al-Fiqh ʿalā al-madhāhib al-arbaʿ*, 5 vols (Cairo: Dār al-Irshād li'l-Ṭibāʿa wa'l-Nashr, 1980), vol. 5, 76–7.

terms that are the standard coinage of judicial opinions ("the man," "the defendant"), but in negative, emotional and value-laden terms ("liar," "deceiver," "sower of confusion and deception," "forsaken one," and "criminal"). The cumulative effect of demonizing al-Haskūrī was that al-Sarīfī unwittingly exposed himself as an extremist whose anger and hatred might well have jeopardized his judicial objectivity, or at least the appearance of it. Al-Ṣughayyir, on the other hand, manifested a greater measure of judicial objectivity and cool-headedness, notwithstanding his reputation for judicial harshness and severity.

Third, before enacting his judgment, the qāḍī may have taken into consideration the attitudes and feelings of his constituency, the Muslim community of Fez in general and the jurists in particular. Under any circumstances, the stoning of a member of the Muslim community would have been exceptional. When the accused was a leading jurist of Fez, the execution would have been extraordinary. Al-Zamīnī's primary goal was not necessarily absolute truth or legal logic; more likely, he sought to put an end to communal unrest and to re-establish communal harmony. Only an outcome that was acceptable to a broad cross-section of the community would have served to support and reinforce the authority of the qāḍī. Al-Zamīnī also may have been concerned about establishing a dangerous precedent. If he stoned al-Haskūrī in the present instance, he would have to stone other fornicators in the future.

Finally, al-Zamīnī had to keep in mind the position of the Marīnid sulṭān, who would be responsible for implementation of the stoning penalty. It will be recalled that there were strong ties of loyalty between the Marīnid sulṭāns and al-Ṣughayyir. Abū Yaʿqūb Yūsuf had appointed al-Ṣughayyir qāḍī of Tāza, despite the availability of more senior candidates; and Abū al-Rabīʿ Sulaymān had appointed him as chief qāḍī of Fez. Also, al-Ṣughayyir was perhaps the most distinguished jurist of his day, whereas al-Sarīfī may have been an outsider and newcomer to Fez. Al-Zamīnī would have weighed these factors carefully before issuing his judgment.

Al-Sarīfī's Letter to the Marīnid Sulṭān with regard to al-Haskūrī

The early Marīnid sulṭāns sought to draw attention to their religious authority by adopting the title *amīr al-muslimīn* or Commander of the Muslims; and beginning with Abū ʿInān (r. 749–59/1348–59) they would add the epithet *amīr al-muʾminīn* or Commander of the Believers, which implied leadership of the Muslim community at large.[113] As agents of caliphal authority, it was the task of the sulṭān *inter*

[113] See *EI*[2], s.v. Marīnids; Manūnī, *Waraqāt*, 81. Beginning with the Seljuks, Muslim rulers adopted the title of Sulṭān, accompanied by epithets such as al-Muʿaẓẓam. Although the various sulṭāns of the Muslim world were first and foremost temporal rulers, they sometimes exercised religious authority as well, for which they found support in the tradition, "The sultan is the shadow of God upon His earth, with whom all the oppressed find refuge" (cited in H.A.R. Gibb, "Constitutional Organization," in *Law in the Middle East*, ed. Majid Khadduri and Herbert Liebesney [Washington, DC: Middle East Institute, 1955], 3–27, at 21; cf. *EI*[2], s.v. Sulṭān).

alia to supervise the office of muftī.[114] For this reason, it is not surprising that al-Sarīfī, who regarded al-Zamīnī's decision in this case as a gross miscarriage of justice, would write a letter to Abū Saʿīd ʿUthmān b. Yaʿqūb b. ʿAbd al-Ḥaqq (r. 710–32/1310–31), the Marīnid Sulṭān.

Whereas al-Sarīfī's earlier treatise had focused almost exclusively on al-Haskūrī's sexual transgression and its judicial consequences, his letter to the Marīnid Sulṭān, which properly belongs to the literary genre known as "advice for rulers" (*naṣīḥat al-mulūk*),[115] focused largely on al-Haskūrī's *ethical* failure as a jurist and scholar and on the danger that he posed to a God-fearing Muslim society. Not only the subject but also the tone and rhetorical register of the letter to Abū Saʿīd ʿUthmān differed from that of al-Sarīfī's earlier writing. In an apparent effort to stroke the ego of the Marīnid Sulṭān, al-Sarīfī elevated his title from Commander of the Muslims to Commander of the Believers (*amīr al-muʾminīn*), "May God grant success to the Commander of the Believers, guide him, and render him victorious."[116] Al-Sarīfī referred to al-Haskūrī by name only once, and, at that, only by nickname: at the very outset of the letter, he called him "al-Bukhārī the deceiver (*al-muḍillu*)."[117] And unlike his earlier treatise, al-Sarīfī's letter to the Sulṭān contains several artfully chosen citations from the Qurʾān, metaphors, and references to the pious models of great figures of the Muslim past.

At the very outset of his letter, al-Sarīfī explained to the Sulṭān that al-Haskūrī's fornication was only the latest in a series of objectionable acts that had concerned the muftī and his colleagues for some time. Without providing any details, he referred to al-Haskūrī's "audacity with regard to knowledge, scholars, and the

[114] In the *Muqaddima*, the historian Ibn Khaldūn (1332–1406) offers the following brief statement regarding the office of the muftī: "As to the office of the muftī, the caliph must examine the religious scholars and teachers and entrust it only to those who are qualified for it. He must help them in their task, and he must prevent those who are not qualified for the office from [becoming muftīs]. [The office of muftī] is one of the [public] interests of the Muslim religious community. [The caliph] has to take care, lest unqualified persons undertake to act as [muftī] and so lead the people astray ... [T]eachers and muftīs must have some restraining influence in them that tells them not to undertake something for which they are not qualified, so that they may not lead astray those who ask for the right way or cause to stumble those who want to be guided. A tradition says: 'Those of you who most boldly approach the task of giving fatwās are most directly heading toward hell.' The ruler, therefore, has supervision over [muftīs and teachers] and can give, or deny, them permission to exercise their functions, as may be required by the public interest." Ibn Khaldūn, *The Muqaddimah: An Introduction to History*, trans. Franz Rosenthal, 3 vols (Princeton: Princeton University Press, 1958), vol. 1, 451–2.

[115] On this genre in the Maghrib, see Jacques Berque, *Ulémas, fondateurs, insurgés du Maghrib, xviie siècle* (Paris: Sindbad, 1982), 121–2, 148, 242, 245–6; Henry Munson, Jr, *Religion and Power in Morocco* (New Haven: Yale University Press, 1993), 50–2; Abdelfattah Kilito, "Speaking to Princes: Al-Yusi and Mawlay Ismaʿil," in *In the Shadow of the Sultan: Culture, Power, and Politics in Morocco*, ed. Rahma Bourqia and Susan Gilson Miller (Cambridge, MA: Harvard University Press, 1999), 30–46; see generally *EI*², s.v., Naṣīḥat al-Mulūk; A.K.S. Lambton, "Islamic Mirrors for Princes," *Quaderno dell'Accademia Nazionale dei Lincei*, 160 (1971), 419–42; *Ghazālī's Book of Counsel for Kings* (*Naṣīḥat al-Mulūk*), trans. F.R.C. Bagley (London: Oxford University Press, 1964); *The Sea of Precious Virtues (Baḥr al-Favāʾid): A Medieval Islamic Mirror for Princes*, trans. Julie Scott Meisami (Salt Lake City: University of Utah Press, 1991).

[116] *Miʿyār*, vol. 4, 506, ll. 13–14.

[117] Ibid., vol. 4, 506, l. 15; cf. above, vol. 4, 506, l. 10, where the editor's rubric has "*al-muftī al-ʿābith*" (the mocking muftī).

ḥadīth of the Messenger of God."[118] He reported that al-Haskūrī had claimed that he was capable of exercising *ijtihād* although his colleagues apparently disagreed. He had called earlier imāms negligent whose model behavior was in fact to be emulated. He had attracted a following among the masses, described as "the gullible and the scoundrels," who trusted his judicial opinions and recommendations and regarded him as an honorable figure. Intoxicated by his growing power, al-Haskūrī had begun "to manipulate God's religion"[119] with no regard for the transgressions that he was perpetrating, and he had succeeded in deceiving not only laymen but also honorable and authoritative judges and magistrates. When al-Haskūrī had acted aggressively toward some laymen, they came to fear him, and, sensing their fear, he had caused them damage in their legal transactions. This, al-Sarīfī despaired, was "a catastrophe in matters of religion and this world, and it was a great cause of corruption."[120] And yet, al-Sarīfī asserted, no one, other than himself, was prepared to fulfill the obligation of commanding good and forbidding evil by denouncing al-Haskūrī. Hence, the present letter.

Al-Sarīfī compared al-Haskūrī to someone who has been infected with a "disease": although it was common knowledge that an insane asylum was preferable to a prison for the treatment of disease, al-Haskūrī's malady – stupidity and disobedience – could not be treated with the customary medications and his illness had defied all remedies. Al-Haskūrī's transgressions, compounded by his having engaged in fornication, necessitated the application of the *ḥadd* punishment. Once these corruptions had been exposed and had become common knowledge, it was necessary to ask the sulṭān to deal with the matter.[121]

The issue of punishment brought al-Sarīfī back to the details of the case and to the rules of evidence. As noted above, it appears that al-Haskūrī, in an effort to save himself, had claimed ignorance and denied having intercourse with ʿĀʾisha after the third repudiation, in effect denying or revoking his earlier acknowledgement. According to Mālikī doctrine, the *ḥadd* punishment for fornication must be applied if the alleged perpetrator acknowledges having had intercourse with a woman forbidden to him, or if four upright witnesses give eyewitness testimony regarding the act. However, opinions differ in the case in which the alleged perpetrator denies having had intercourse with the woman. In this circumstance, al-Sarīfī explained, "the most widespread and soundest [opinion], according to the authoritative jurists, is that he should receive the *ḥadd* punishment."[122] No consideration should be given to his claim of ignorance, not only because he was in fact a person whom one would expect to be knowledgeable about the rules regulating sexual relations but also because he had claimed to be a *mujtahid*. Further, his denial of intercourse should not be accepted after his two acknowledgements thereto. Alluding to al-Ṣughayyir, al-Sarīfī wrote that whoever accepted such a revocation was "remote from mindfulness of the law."[123]

118 Ibid., vol. 4, 506, ll. 17–18.
119 Ibid., vol. 4, 506, l. 20.
120 Ibid., vol. 4, 506, ll. 23–4.
121 Ibid., vol. 4, 506–7.
122 Ibid., vol. 4, 507, l. 6.
123 Ibid., vol. 4, 507, ll. 6–8.

Drawing on some of the statements included in his earlier opinion, al-Sarīfī informed the Sulṭān that subsequent to his flogging, al-Haskūrī had sought to keep his followers' trust by portraying himself as a righteous man of God who was being persecuted by hypocritical jurists, a common topos. Comparing himself to two model jurists of the past who had suffered for their beliefs, Mālik b. Anas and Saʿīd b. al-Musayyab, al-Haskūrī characterized himself as a persecuted wretch and the officials who had incarcerated him as "jailers" (in al-Sarīfī's eyes the latter were "angels"). And, apparently, in complaining about the flogging that he had received, he ignored its cause, to wit, his disdain and mockery of religion. Unfortunately, his followers and other "fools" continued to treat him as if he were acting in accordance with the law. Al-Sarīfī asserted that whoever would intercede on behalf of al-Haskūrī by recommending flogging and life-imprisonment instead of stoning would heap scorn and abuse on God because, according to the Prophet Muḥammad, God is cursed when a person intercedes to prevent the execution of one of His punishments.[124]

The community of Fez was divided into two factions: al-Haskūrī's supporters were lobbying for his release from prison while his opponents, headed by al-Sarīfī, demanded that he be put to death. By this point in time, al-Sarīfī no doubt realized that he had lost the battle with regard to the stoning of al-Haskūrī. His letter appears to have been written while the latter was still in jail but also on the verge of being released. Al-Sarīfī wanted to ensure that al-Haskūrī *complete* the lesser sentence that had been imposed upon him – life-imprisonment with harsh treatment – because, were he to be released, "gullible" people would seek guidance from him with the result that tyranny would prevail over knowledge and scholars (*wa-aẓharū ṣūlatan ʿalā al-ʿilm wa'l-ʿulamāʾ*).[125]

Given the division within the community, al-Sarīfī may well have viewed as even more important than usual the need to define the boundaries between proper and improper Islamic conduct, between God-fearers and God-rejectors, between good and evil, between those who support God and those who try to defeat him. Cleverly drawing upon the powerful rhetorical resources of the Qurʾān and *sunna*, he asserted, "[T]he party of God (*ḥizb allāh*)[126] will be victorious and will prosper" over the deceivers, and he invoked as support for this assertion God's statements in the Qurʾān, "I shall assuredly be the victor, I and My Messengers" (Q. 58:21).[127]

Lest the evildoers develop a false sense of security, al-Sarīfī cited Q. 7:96–7, "Do the people of the cities feel secure – Our might shall not come upon them at night while they are sleeping? Do the people of the cities feel secure – Our might shall not come upon them in daylight while they are playing?"[128] Indeed, this very verse reportedly had caused the Prophet Muḥammad himself to experience anxiety, with the result that he sought God's assurance lest His blessings pass, His vengeance appear suddenly, or His forgiveness be transformed – all this despite

[124] Ibid., vol. 4, 507, ll. 13–22. [125] Ibid., vol. 4, 507, ll. 23–5.
[126] The expression *ḥizb allāh* or "party of God" was used by Ibn Tūmart and Abū Madyan to characterize their followers. See V. Cornell, *Realm of the Saint*, 137.
[127] *Miʿyār*, vol. 4, 507, ll. 25–6. [128] Ibid. vol. 4, 508, ll. 6–7.

Muḥammad's inviolability, his being the Lord of Adam's children, and his being the best of creation. Similarly, ʿAlī, the Lord or *mawlā* of the Muslims and Muḥammad's *khalīfa* (sic), or successor, reportedly sought refuge with God from sins that would necessitate retribution, eliminate blessing, and give his enemies dominion over him.[129]

The reference to ʿAlī as *khalīfa* marked a critical transition from sacred history to mundane reality. Making another direct appeal to the Marīnid Sulṭān's ego and pretension to religious authority, al-Sarīfī reminded Abū Saʿīd ʿUthmān of his status as *khalīfa*, or representative of God on earth.[130] It was the Sulṭān who bore the ultimate responsibility for removing the "defect" that had been exposed within the Muslim community. In order to carry out this responsibility, the Sulṭān must situate himself within the chain of authority that leads back to the Prophet Muḥammad by putting the imāms of the ancients and their distinguished authorities between himself and God. The imāms of the past served as witnesses for and against the Sulṭān and as a *ḥujja*, or proof, in the eyes of God. If the Sulṭān followed their example, he assured himself of deliverance and redemption; if he ignored them, he would face divine punishment on the Day of Resurrection. Faced with this choice, al-Sarīfī indicated, the Sulṭān should consider God's description of the evildoer in Q. 25:58, "Upon the day the evildoer shall bite his hands, saying, 'Would that I had taken a way along with the Messenger! Alas, would that I had not taken So-and-So for a friend!' ..." The Sulṭān's response to the present case, al-Sarīfī warned, would determine *his* fate on the Day of Judgment.[131]

Al-Sarīfī advised the Sulṭān that as he contemplated his course of action he should keep in mind the model provided by the second caliph, ʿUmar b. al-Khaṭṭāb, who, despite the fact that his integrity (*ʿadl*) and truthfulness were of the highest standard, reportedly suffered from great anxiety regarding his fate in the Hereafter. As reported in a *ḥadīth*, shortly before he died, ʿUmar posed a question to those who were attending him: "'When the Day of Resurrection arrives and God causes me to stand in His presence, and He asks you about me, will you be witnesses to what that one [viz., Ibn ʿAbbās] said [about me]?'... To which [his attendants] replied, 'Yes.' Only then was ʿUmar's soul put at ease. He said, 'God is great' and died."[132]

Al-Sarīfī concluded by brazenly warning the Sulṭān that his ultimate salvation or damnation rested on the decision that he made regarding al-Haskūrī:

> All of this – even if [the matter] is difficult (*taʿadhdhara*) and its causes have been difficult for a long time, we implore the Exalted God that it will be a small thing on His part, sufficient in the presence of the Exalted God, for [even] a small measure of goodness, if one acts in accordance with it in order to magnify God, causes one to enter the Garden; just as a small measure of evil, if one acts in accordance with it in order to

[129] Ibid., vol. 4, 508, ll. 7–14.

[130] On the term *khalīfa* and its significance in early Islam, see Patricia Crone and Martin Hinds, *God's Caliph: Religious authority in the first centuries of Islam* (New York and Cambridge: Cambridge University Press, 1986).

[131] *Miʿyār*, vol. 4, 508, ll. 15–22.

[132] Ibid., vol. 4, 508–9.

> mock God's justice (*ḥaqq*), causes one to enter the Fire. No one, however, will be destroyed by God except for one who destroys [others].[133]

"This," al-Sarīfī concluded, "is the advice that I offer you."[134] In essence, he had told the Sulṭān that his failure to punish al-Haskūrī would constitute proof of his illegitimacy and would result in his punishment by God on the Day of Judgment. By delivering this information to the Sulṭān, al-Sarīfī sought to relieve his contractual obligation after it had become apparent to him that "none had denounced [al-Haskūrī] in [the Sulṭān's] presence or deemed great that which God magnified."[135] Significantly, in his signature, he identified himself as "the one who desires your welfare (*murīd al-khayr lakum*)."[136]

What action did the Sulṭān take? Yet another detail preserved in the biographical dictionary of Ibn al-Qāḍī indicates that the Sulṭān issued an order instructing his agents to release al-Haskūrī from prison and to send him into exile, perhaps because he regarded the popular jurist as a political threat. According to Ibn al-Qāḍī, al-Haskūrī traveled first to al-Andalus and then to Tūnis, capital of the Ḥafṣids (who, it should be noted, were the last torchbearers of Almohad doctrine).[137]

A story that is odd and possibly apocryphal is told by Ibn al-Qāḍī. During al-Haskūrī's travels, he reportedly entered a village and urinated in the local mosque. In response to the ensuing uproar, al-Haskūrī offered as a proof-text for the licitness of his behavior a *ḥadīth* of the Prophet. According to this *ḥadīth*, when the Prophet saw a bedouin urinating in a mosque, he said, "Leave him [alone]." When the man had finished his business, the Prophet called for water and poured it over the floor.[138] Now this *ḥadīth*, which may be found *inter alia* in the *Ṣaḥīḥ* of

[133] *Miʿyār*, vol. 4, 508, ll. 5–8. Al-Sarīfī's letter to Abū Saʿīd ʿUthmān bears a strong resemblance to a letter written by the Sufi Ibn ʿĀshir (d. 764/1362) to Abū ʿInān. In his letter, Ibn ʿĀshir gave the Sulṭān the following advice: "Know that God watches over you at every moment in time, at every hour, at every breath, and at every blink of the eye. [Know that] you must encounter Him, that He will ask you what you have done, and that His justice will envelop you. He will also ask you about the affairs of your subjects and what you have done for them." Cited and trans. by V. Cornell, *Realm of the Saint*, 144.

[134] *Miʿyār*, vol. 4, 509, l. 9.

[135] Ibid., vol. 4, 509, ll. 9–10.

[136] Ibid., vol. 4, 509, l. 11.

[137] Ibn al-Qāḍī, *Durrat al-Ḥijāl*, vol. 3, 4. Al-Haskūrī may have had family connections in Tūnis. Approximately a century earlier, a Moroccan scholar by the name of Muḥammad b. Shuʿayb al-Haskūrī (d. 664/1265) traveled to Egypt and then settled in Tunis and Qayrawan, where he taught law, held the office of qāḍī, and contributed to the revival of Mālikism.

[138] Ibid. vol. 3, 4. The *ḥadīth* may be found in Bukhārī, *Ṣaḥīḥ*, ed. Krehl, 4 vols (Leiden: E.J. Brill, 1862), vol. 1, 67, nos. 57–8, vol. 4, 119, no. 35, 141–2, no. 80; Muslim, *Ṣaḥīḥ*, ed. Muḥammad Fu'ād ʿAbd al-Bāqī, 5 vols (Cairo: Dār Iḥyā' al-Kutub al-ʿArabiyya, 1371/1955), vol. 1, 256, no. 98; Abū Dā'ūd, *Sunan*, ed. Muḥammad Muḥyī al-Dīn ʿAbd al-Ḥamīd, 4 vols (Cairo: al-Maktaba al-Tijāriyya al-Kubrā, 1369/1950), vol. 1, 103, no. 380; Tirmidhī, *Sunan bi sharḥ Ibn al-ʿArabī al-Mālikī*, ed. ʿAbd al-Wāḥid Muḥammad al-Tāzī, 13 vols (Cairo: al-Maṭbaʿa al-Miṣriyya, 1350/1931), vol. 1, 243–4; Nasā'ī, *Sunan*, vol. 1, 47–9, 175. The idea of pissing in a mosque may be a topos. For example, Wakīʿ b. al-Jarrāḥ quotes Abū Ḥanīfa as saying, with regard to legal reasoning, "Some analogies are uglier than pissing in a mosque." See al-Fasawī, *K. al-Maʿrifa wa'l-tārīkh*, ed. Akram Ḍiyā' al-ʿUmarī, 4 vols (3rd edn, Medina: Maktabat al-Dār, 1410/1989), vol. 1, 673; cited in Christopher Melchert, "How Ḥanafism Came to Originate in Kufa and Traditionalism in Medina," *Islamic Law and Society*, 6:3 (1999), 318–47, at 332.

al-Bukhārī, the famous traditionist from whom al-Haskūrī received his nickname, is customarily invoked in order to clarify the measures to be taken in order to remove an impurity from a mosque. Al-Haskūrī's invocation of this *ḥadīth* as proof that it is permissible to urinate on the floor of a mosque is a good example of what his critics called his depravity, to wit, his use of *ʿilm* for un-Islamic purposes.

Discussion

The case of al-Haskūrī sheds important light on the workings of the qāḍī court in eighth/fourteenth-century Fez. One important function of the qāḍī was to distinguish between competing versions of the "truth" in an effort to reach a judgment. To this end, he summoned both the plaintiff and the defendant to his court and gave each an opportunity to relate his (or her) respective versions of the facts. In the present case, the evidence against al-Haskūrī included two written documents attesting to legal actions carried out in the presence of, or verified by, upright witnesses: his marriage contract (*rasm al-ṣadāq*), in which the three repudiations were recorded interlinearly, and a second document recording the fourth repudiation.

Al-Zamīnī was called upon to reconcile conflicting legal norms. In the present instance, the central legal norm takes the form of the *maḥārim*, or sacred things of God, which include people – here, al-Haskūrī's wife, ʿĀʾisha (whose voice is notably absent from the historical record). When a Muslim man marries, he renders *ḥalāl*, or licit, to himself the body of his wife which is otherwise *ḥarām*, or forbidden. Any violation of the *ḥurma*, or sanctity, of a woman's body is a violation of the *ḥudūd*, or limits of God, for which the Qurʾān specifies severe punishments. Within the first century of Islam, however, the Muslim community in general and the jurists in particular manifested a repugnance for the application of these severe Qurʾānic sanctions. As a counter-norm, jurists established the principle that "blood should not be spilled in cases of doubt," a norm that derives its sanction and legitimacy from the prophetic dictum, *idraʾū ʾl-ḥudūd fī ʾl-shubuhāt*, "avert the *ḥadd* punishments in cases of doubt." The dictum was well known to judges and jurists, who treated it seriously. In the present instance, it appears to have prevailed.

In a sensitive and highly charged case such as this one, the qāḍī would not issue a judgment without first soliciting the opinion of one or more distinguished jurists. Thus, al-Zamīnī solicited the opinions of two well known and highly respected muftīs, al-Ṣughayyir and al-Sarīfī. Although the opinions issued by these two men are available to the modern historian in their written form, it is possible that they discussed or debated the case in public, either in the qāḍī's court, one of the *madrasas* of Fez, or the Friday mosque.[139] If so, the audience might have included,

[139] Under the Ḥafsids, muftīs reportedly issued their fatwās immediately after the Friday prayer, in the congregational mosque itself or at the entrance to the market; in either case, the audience would have been substantial (Brunschvig, *La Berbérie orientale*, vol. 2, 139). Note also that Ibn al-Qāḍī mentions a "dispute" (*munāzaʿa*) between the qāḍī and al-Haskūrī (*Jadhwat al-iqtibās*, vol. I, 346).

in addition to the judges and litigants, leading jurists, dignitaries, students, and perhaps interested members of the general public. Jurists debated critical legal issues using formal, rational arguments and complex modes of reasoning that were the standard tools of their art, for example, the citation of Qur'ān, *ḥadīth*, and earlier judicial authorities, comparing and distinguishing earlier cases, *a fortiori* argumentation, and the contextualization of authority statements. The institution of oral, in addition to written, debate was part of a public sphere that served as a buffer between the potentially coercive power of the ruler, on the one hand, and the Muslim inhabitants of Fez, on the other; although limited to the élite, this public sphere served the important function of articulating and reinforcing legal norms that may have been disseminated to the public at large.[140] This forum also constituted the arena within which regulatory control was exercised over the behavior of muftīs. The jurists themselves defined the standards of their craft and ensured that their colleagues possessed the requisite intellectual and moral qualifications, even though the sulṭān, in his capacity as Commander of the Muslims, exercised ultimate control over the activities of judges and muftīs.

The muftī, the qāḍī, and the sulṭān were situated within complex and overlapping hierarchies of power and religious authority. Muftīs acted independently, without appointment, on the strength of their reputations, and were embedded within a hierarchy of specialized religious knowledge, which, as early as the middle of the twelfth century, had taken firm shape.[141] The relationship between qāḍīs and muftīs was one of mutual dependence: the considered opinion of the muftī conferred religious legitimacy on the judgment of the qāḍī, but the muftī's opinion was not binding and required the power of the qāḍī and the ruler for execution. Thus, qāḍīs were in need of legitimacy that could be provided only by muftīs, and muftīs were in need of executive power that could be provided only by qāḍīs. Standing apart from and above both figures was the sulṭān, in whose person was embodied supreme executive power and a claim to supreme religious authority. In his capacity as the *khalīfa* of the Prophet Muḥammad, the sulṭān was the supreme religious and political authority in the society, responsible for the exercise of justice and for the behavior and actions of judges and jurists.[142]

The case that we have examined also opens a window on the prevailing social and cultural values of Muslim society in eighth/fourteenth-century Fez. Our knowledge of the bizarre behavior of al-Haskūrī (as portrayed by his detractors)

[140] Referring to modern, capitalist, industrial societies, Habermas defines the public sphere as an arena of deliberative exchange in which rational-critical arguments rather than inherited ideas or personal statuses serve as the basis of agreements and actions. See Jürgen Habermas, *The Structural Transformation of the Public Sphere* (Cambridge, MA: MIT Press, 1989); cf. Craig Calhoun, "Civil Society and the Public Sphere," *Public Culture*, vol. 5 (1993), 267–80.

[141] At the top of this hierarchy were those muftīs whose mastery of jurisprudence qualified them to derive solutions to new cases from the recognized sources of law; a middle category included those jurists who were capable of distinguishing between opinions that are in conformity with Mālikī doctrine and those that are not; and the bottom level included those jurists who were mere memorizers of legal doctrine. See Ibn Rushd, *Fatāwā*, vol. 3, 1494–1505, no. 549.

[142] Ibn Khaldūn, *The Muqaddima*, vol. 1, 461–2.

comes exclusively from two judicial opinions preserved in the *Mi'yār* of al-Wansharīsī and from a short biographical notice contained in the *Durrat al-Ḥijāl* of Ibn al-Qāḍī. Clearly al-Wansharīsī and Ibn al-Qāḍī made a conscious decision to memorialize al-Haskūrī. But to what end? The goal of the *madrasa* educational system was to produce individuals who would internalize the underlying norms and values of the *sharī'a* and develop the ability to reason and interpret the law. These skills were developed by means of an apprenticeship with teachers who were positive role models, abundant examples of which may be found in the ubiquitous biographical dictionaries. By contrast, al-Haskūrī was a negative role model, an antithesis or counter-model to the behavior expected of great scholars and teachers, an example of the *'ālim al-fāsiq* or "wicked scholar" repeatedly mentioned in Islamic sources.[143] His wickedness consisted of his use of *'ilm* to justify patently un-Islamic behavior, in the present instance, his violation of the *ḥurma*, or sanctity, of his wife, by continuing to have sexual relations with her after having repudiated her three times. Al-Haskūrī was an extreme example of how one should *not* behave, wherein lies his sole – and unwitting – social utility.[144]

The response of the jurists to al-Haskūrī's behavior highlights the status of religious knowledge as an important social, cultural, and religious value in eighth/fourteenth-century Fez. *'Ilm* was acquired through a process of apprenticeship with model scholars who themselves acquired their specialized knowledge in a similar manner, thereby situating the *'ālim*, or possessor of such knowledge, in a chain of religious authority that leads back to the Prophet and his Companions.[145] As we learn from the examples cited by al-Sarīfī in his letter to the Marīnid Sulṭān, the content of this *'ilm* was not only facts or information but also a world view at the center of which stands the concept of *taqwā*, that is, piety or consciousness of God. On the Day of Judgment, all Muslims will be called upon to answer to their Creator. If this inevitability applies to 'Alī, 'Umar b. al-Khaṭṭāb, and even Muḥammad himself, then it certainly applies to the Marīnid Sulṭān, al-Ṣughayyir, al-Sarīfī and al-Haskūrī. It follows that anyone who wishes to qualify as a scholar must manifest *taqwā* in his daily actions and conduct and in his treatment of others. Someone who claims to possess *'ilm* in fact does not unless he uses his knowledge to promote the goals and aims of Islam, that is to say, unless his knowledge manifests social utility and usefulness within the framework of the established ethics and values of Muslim society. Pseudo-knowledge, on the other hand, leads to tyranny and *fasād al-zamān*, or the corruption of the times.

It is against this background that we must seek to understand the severity of Ibn Rushd's response to the behavior of the defendant in the *mut'a* case and that of al-Sarīfī to the behavior of al-Haskūrī (while distinguishing between the quite different tone of the two responses), for both defendants claimed to be scholars

[143] For references, see Rosenthal, *Knowledge Triumphant*, 315 ff.

[144] Cf. Rosenthal's comment, "The socially unacceptable actions of a scholar nullify his usefulness for society" (ibid., 317).

[145] See note 30, above.

(*min ahl al-ʿilm wa'l-maʿrifa*) and al-Haskūrī, in addition, claimed the capability to exercise *ijtihād.* And yet both abused their status to advance their own interests, thereby threatening the moral fabric of Muslim society. As the aforementioned *ḥadīth* teaches, "The person who will receive the most painful punishment on the Day of Resurrection will be the scholar whose knowledge did not benefit him."

Postscript: A Hidden Agenda?

The reader who has followed the argument to this point hopefully will agree that we are dealing here with a real case, and not with the product of the fertile imagination of some jurist, invented from whole cloth for didactic purposes or otherwise. At the same time, it must be conceded that the materials preserved in our source were produced with an illocutionary purpose in mind – first and foremost, to make an example of al-Haskūrī. In addition, we cannot exclude the possibility that these materials were shaped by processes of selection, assemblage, and editing during the 150 year period between the event itself and the copying of the materials by al-Wansharīsī toward the end of the ninth/fifteenth century. For these reasons, we will never know what really happened. In what follows, I shall attempt to exercise my historical imagination in an effort to pierce the surface level of our documentation in order to expose a story that lies buried and untold inside the story that we have just related.

Our source portrays al-Haskūrī as an arrogant, supercilious, and manipulative man who was intoxicated with power and who thought that he could get away with anything. Having cultivated influence with the authorities, on the one hand, and the masses, on the other, he regarded himself as above the law and untouchable. Whatever reasons he may have had for behaving as he did, he regarded his colleagues as gullible jurists who could be manipulated by clever legal reasoning. At every stage of the case, he sought to deflect blame and responsibility on to others: ʿĀʾisha allegedly lied to him about having undergone the process of *taḥlīl*; his colleagues failed to appreciate his invocation of the doctrine of Ibn ʿAbbās; and the response of his village hosts to his urinating in the mosque was a result of their boorishness and unfamiliarity with the *sunna* of the Prophet. Alternatively, when he found himself with his back against the wall, he cast himself in the role of a persecuted martyr.[146]

How are we to explain the bizarre aspects of al-Haskūrī's behavior? He may have been a non-conformist who sought to challenge the tradition-bound and conservative society in which he lived, pushing the envelope, as it were, to the outer limits. Alternatively, it is possible that the experience of public humiliation and flogging triggered a spiritual transformation in al-Haskūrī, causing him to

[146] I wish to thank Patricia Crone for these observations.

become an eccentric ecstatic or holy fool (*majdhūb*).[147] Up until the time of his arrest, public flogging, and dispatch into exile, he identified himself first and foremost as a member of the *ʿulamāʾ* class. Thus, when he was accused of engaging in fornication, he defended himself by drawing upon his extensive knowledge of the law. But the public humiliation that he experienced may have engendered a spiritual crisis that transformed al-Haskūrī into a Malāmatī Sufi antinomian who sought to provoke people into a response by his outrageous acts – such as pissing in a mosque.[148]

What would al-Haskūrī have said in his own defense? It is difficult to answer this question because only rarely do we hear his voice and even then it is carefully mediated by an unseen narrator, either the *mustaftī* or the muftī. And we never hear the voice of ʿĀʾisha – who may be the key to whatever agenda lies buried within our source. For if al-Haskūrī was guilty of fornication, was not ʿĀʾisha as well? Not necessarily, since the charge of *zinā* here was based upon al-Haskūrī's acknowledgement following the third repudiation, which bound him but not her. But then there is the matter of ʿĀʾisha's pregnancy – passed over in silence by al-Zamīnī and al-Ṣughayyir, but mentioned, albeit in passing, by al-Sarīfī – an indisputable sign of her having had illicit sexual relations, presumably with al-Haskūrī. One wonders if al-Haskūrī may have been the victim of a plot hatched by jealous colleagues or political enemies.

There is reason to believe that al-Haskūrī may indeed have been the victim of such a plot.[149] It will be recalled that he was born some time in the second half of the seventh/thirteenth century, shortly after the Marīnids (who were Zanāta Berbers) replaced the Almohads (who were Maṣmūda) as rulers of the far Maghrib. Under the Marīnids Mālikism replaced Ẓāhirism (see Introduction).[150] The Almohads offered stiff resistance to the Marīnids, who eventually prevailed, but only after suppressing the powerful religious and intellectual élites that had been trained by the Almohads. Al-Haskūrī's *nisba* identifies him as a member of the tribe of Haskūra, Ṣanhāja Berbers with close ties to the Almohads.[151] He may have

147 *EI²*, s.v., Madjdhūb; Michael Dols, *Majnūn: The Madman in the Medieval Islamic World* (Oxford: Oxford University Press, 1992), chap. 13, "The Holy Fool."

148 V. Cornell notes that Malāmatī sufis had been operating in the Maghrib since the time of Abū Yiʿzza (d. 572/1177) (*Realm of the Saint*, 68–9) and that a high percentage of "upper-class Moroccan saints became interested in Sufism after experiencing a crisis of self-blame (*lawma*) or repentance (*tawba*)" (ibid., 108). On Malāmatīs in seventeenth-century Morocco, see Berque, *Ulémas, fondateurs, insurgés du Maghreb*, 129–31, 136, 140, 145–6. See generally *EI²*, s.v. Malāmatīya; J. Spencer Trimingham, *The Sufi Orders in Islam* (London: Oxford University Press, 1971), 264–9; Ahmet Karamustafa, *God's Unruly Friends: dervish groups in the Islamic later middle period, 1200–1550* (Salt Lake City: University of Utah Press, 1994), 13 ff.

149 If so, he was neither the first nor the last to be the subject of a cabal. See Berque, *Ulémas, fondateurs, insurgés du Maghreb*, 243.

150 See Manūnī, *Waraqāt*, 94, 236, 293, 405–8.

151 On the connections between the tribe of Haskūra and the Almohads, see Ambrosio Huici Miranda, *Historia politica del imperio almohade* (Tetuan, 1956–57); Brunschvig, *La Berbérie Orientale*, vol. 1, 15; vol. 2, 48, 289. However, Haskūrid support for the Almohads was not absolute; for references to their opposition to certain Almohad rulers or factions, see Mohammed Kably, *Société, pouvoir et religion au Maroc à la fin du Moyen-Age* (Paris: Maisonneuve et Larose, 1986), 307–9, 311.

received his early intellectual formation in this former Almohad stronghold. If so, upon his arrival in Fez, he may have been suspected of harboring Almohad sympathies. This suspicion would have been confirmed by his actual behavior, which suggests that he was following Almohad ideals of how a Muslim jurist should act: Al-Haskūrī had a special interest in prophetic *ḥadīth*, as evidenced in his having committed to memory the *Ṣaḥīḥ* of al-Bukhārī (hence, his nickname). He was one of only a handful of scholars active during the Marīnid period who claimed the right to exercise *ijtihād*. And he appears to have used his own marriage to make a public example of his unconventional views. Challenged to explain his behavior, he responded in typical Almohadian fashion by circumventing the Mālikī tradition in favor of an early opinion of Ibn ʿAbbās, thereby demonstrating his own distinctive understanding of Islamic divorce law.[152] Finally, the story of his pissing in a mosque constitutes yet another example of his deliberately making a spectacle of himself in an effort to demonstrate his unique abilities, as a *mujtahid*, to engage in a fresh examination of the original sources of Islamic law.[153]

152 The proposed link between al-Haskūrī and Almohadism may also help to explain the uncharacteristic judicial leniency manifested by al-Ṣughayyir, who, it will be recalled, had a reputation for harshness and severity in judgment. Like al-Haskūrī, al-Ṣughayyir also may have had pro-Almohad sympathies. It is reported that he was once asked by al-Ābilī, "What is your opinion of the Mahdī [viz., Ibn Tūmart]?" To which he responded, "A learned man and a supreme authority (*ʿālim sulṭān*)." The anecdote is cited in Kably, *Société, pouvoir et religion au Maroc*, 285. It may also be relevant in this regard that al-Ṣughayyir is said to have responded to the lack of sophistication manifested by Berber students who had only recently arrived from the countryside by manifesting "calmness, patience, and dignity." See Ibn Farḥūn, *Dībāj*, 212.

153 The interpretation advanced in this paragraph was suggested to me by Maribel Fierro. Possible support for the hypothesis that al-Haskūrī was a proponent of legal reform comes from an unexpected direction. At the same time that al-Haskūrī was advancing his radical ideas about *khulʿ* divorce, his more famous contemporary, Ibn Taymiyya (661–728/1263–1328) was advancing similarly radical ideas about other aspects of Islamic divorce law. In the Mamlūk empire, it had become common for a man to swear an oath to the effect that if he performed (or did not perform) a certain action, his wife would be triply divorced; if he subsequently performed (or did not perform) the action, he was considered to be irrevocably divorced from his wife. If he wanted to remarry her, she first would have to endure the process of *taḥlīl*, which Ibn Taymiyya regarded as an "abominable and corrupting" *ḥila*, or legal fiction. He sought to mitigate the effects of this socially repugnant procedure by arguing that a man who uttered such an oath might nevertheless violate it and perform an act of expiation in its place. This argument contradicted the established Sunnī consensus. In 718/1318, Ibn Taymiyya wrote a short treatise, *al-Ijtimāʾ waʾl-iftirāq*, in which he advanced a novel legal doctrine regarding divorce oaths (see Ibn Taymiyya, *al-Ijtimāʾ waʾl-iftirāq fīʾl-ḥilf biʾl-ṭalāq*, ed. Muḥammad ʿAbd al-Razzāq [Cairo: al-Manār Press, 1346/1926–27]; for a French translation, see H. Laoust, "Une *risāla* d'Ibn Taimiya sur le serment de répudiation," *Bulletin d'études orientales*, vols 7–8 [1937–38], 215–36). In this treatise Ibn Taymiyya sought to undermine the force of the reputed Sunnī consensus by identifying other Sunnī jurists who held a view similar to his own. In this connection, he mentions the names of several Mālikī jurists of the Maghrib who, he asserted, concurred with his opinion that a divorce oath might be expiated. The first name on his list is Abū Yaḥyā al-Haskūrī from Miltāna, no doubt a distortion of Milyāna, a town in western Tunisia (Ibn Taymiyya, *al-Ijtimāʾ waʾl-iftirāq*, 24). It is tempting to identify Abū Yaḥyā al-Haskūrī with the Mūsā al-Haskūrī of the present investigation. Admittedly, in Ibn al-Qāḍī, *Durrat al-Ḥijāl*, vol. III, 3, the *kunyā* of al-Haskūrī is given as Abū ʿImrān, but such discrepancies are not uncommon. And we know, also from Ibn al-Qāḍī, that Mūsā al-Haskūrī left Fez shortly after 714/1314, traveled to Tunisia, and was still alive in the year 723/1323. I wish to thank Yossi Rapoport for bringing this information to my attention and for sharing with me his unpublished essay, "Ibn Taymiyya on Divorce Oaths." For a discussion of scholarly disagreements over divorce in al-Andalus, see Marin, *Mujeres*, 468 ff.

All of this suggests that al-Haskūrī's colleagues may have been waiting patiently on the sidelines for an opportunity to rid themselves of a man who was regarded as a danger to the body politic. And al-Haskūrī was only too happy to oblige them. When it became known that he had repudiated ʿĀ'isha a fourth time, his enemies, realizing that they had caught al-Haskūrī in a net of his own weaving, immediately seized upon the opportunity to rid themselves of the mocking jurist. Their silence about ʿĀ'isha may have been an effort to protect her. And so her voice and her involvement in the alleged crime may have been excised from the historical record.

On the surface this case was about divorce and fornication. At a deeper level it was about defining the boundaries of legitimate *ijtihād*. Al-Haskūrī understood the role of the *mujtahid* as including the right to engage in a direct re-examination of the primary sources of Islamic law, such as the *sunna* and, presumably, also the Qur'ān; the right to base a new legal argument on a minority or isolated opinion within the Mālikī *madhhab*, or law school; and the right to transcend the boundaries of the *madhhab* in the search for a novel solution to a legal problem. His adversaries and critics had a much more limited (and, one might say, reasonable) understanding of *ijtihād*; and they viewed his actions as a sign or indicator of a serious decline in the level of legal skills possessed by Muslim jurists. If the door of *ijtihād* was open in the eighth/fourteenth century, it was merely ajar. The prevailing approach to legal interpretation was that of *taqlīd*, that is, faithful adherence to the doctrines of previous generations of scholars, or, what we might call, adherence to the rule of law.

THREE

A Riparian Dispute in the Middle Atlas Mountains, *ca.* 683–824/1285–1421

Muslims are partners in three things: water, fire, and pasture. (prophetic *ḥadīth*)

O Prophet of God, what thing is there that is not lawful to withhold?
He said, "Water". (prophetic *ḥadīth*)

Whoever is first to that in which no Muslim has preceded him,
he has prior claim to it. (prophetic *ḥadīth*)

Those living upstream retain [the water] until it reaches the ankles;
then they send [it down]. (prophetic *ḥadīth*)

In the cases analyzed in chapters one and two, the plaintiff and defendant were specific individuals who lived in or near Fez and were members of the urban bourgeoisie. In each instance, the case was settled in a timely manner and resulted in the issuance of a *ḥukm* or judgment. But the apparatus of Marīnid justice extended to rural communities living in the countryside outside of Fez and it included alternative means of dispute resolution.

In the present chapter, we will examine a dispute between two rural communities on the banks of a wadi in the Middle Atlas mountains, approximately 40 km south of Fez. We will follow these two communities in and out of the Marīnid courts as they attempted to resolve competing claims to vital water resources over nearly 150 years. During this period a series of qāḍīs and muftīs were called upon to deal with the interplay of Islamic law, on the one hand, and the changes in economic, climatic, and environmental conditions, on the other. Because the plaintiffs and defendants were communities rather than individuals and because the relevant facts could not be established with legal certainty, the case did not lend itself to a final judgment. But the jurists nevertheless attempted to resolve the dispute through a series of mediations that kept the process open and flexible. They drew upon established water law and constructed an increasingly intricate and sophisticated definition of water entitlement in the wadi.[1]

[1] For an initial, intelligent, treatment of this dispute, see Omar Benmira, "Qaḍāyā al-miyāh bi'l-maghrib al-wasiṭ min khilāl adab al-nawāzil," in *al-Ta'rīkh wa-adab al-nawāzil*, ed. Muḥammad al-Manṣūr and Muḥammad al-Maghrāwī (Rabat: al-Jam'iyya al-Maghribiyya li'l-Baḥth al-Ta'rīkhī, 1995), 77–85. I am grateful to Yehoshua Frenkel for drawing my attention to this essay.

The Geographical Setting

The walled town of Sefrou lies nestled in the foothills of the Middle Atlas mountains at an altitude of 850 m. As one leaves the town, heading eastwards, climbing higher into the mountains, irrigated gardens and orchards give way to terrain that becomes increasingly rocky, rugged and barren, dotted here and there with occasional scrub cedars.[2] Approximately 10 km east of Sefrou, at an altitude of 1150 m, one reaches the village of Zgane (Arabic: Azkān), just above a wadi of the same name. From this point, Wadi Zgane winds its way down the mountain in a northerly direction, past fields and orchards. Some 8 km below the village of Zgane, the wadi passes the town of Mazdgha (Arabic: Mazdagha) before it eventually disappears into Wadi Sebou and the Sāʾis plain that stretches for some 30 km until it reaches the outskirts of Fez.[3]

The ancient inhabitants of Zgane and Mazdgha may be described as "people without history," that is, people who have left little or no trace in the historical record.[4] Apart from a fourteenth-century eyewitness description of Wadi Zgane transcribed by al-Wansharīsī in the *Miʿyār*, a few lines in the *Description of Africa* by the sixteenth-century traveler Leo Africanus, and a brief notice in Ibn al-Aḥmar's *Buyūtāt Fās al-kubrā*, the very existence of these two settlements is largely unknown to the outside world and, probably, to a great many Moroccans as well. For at least 700 years, however, the Arabicized Berbers and peasants who inhabited the wadi that links the settlements eked out a living there. The ancestors of the present inhabitants of the wadi constructed an irrigation system composed of diversion dams, water-lifting devices, and canals that brought the normally abundant water to barley, flax, and hemp fields, to orchards in which olive, fig and mulberry trees were cultivated, and to mills where wheat was ground into grain. Although some of these products were used for local consumption, many were produced for outside markets. As suppliers of these agricultural products, the residents of Wadi Zgane were critical to the prosperity of Sefrou and Fez and no doubt were linked to their urban neighbors by networks of kinship and clientage that brought town and countryside into a single, integrated socio-economic system.[5]

Leo Africanus (d. *ca*. 957/1550) identified the location of these two settlements and the type of agriculture that was practiced in the area. Zgane, Leo observed, was a mountainous region located west of Jabal Slīliyū, east of Mount Sefrou, north of the mountains near the Malwīya river, and south of Fez. The region of the

[2] See *EI*², s.v. Ṣufrūy.

[3] In Arabic sources, the Berber topnonym Zgane is rendered as either "Azkān" or "Arjān"; and the Berber toponym Mazdgha is rendered "Mazdagha". In what follows, I render these toponyms in their Berber forms.

[4] The phrase is that of Eric Wolf, in his *Europe and the people without history* (Berkeley: University of California Press, 1982).

[5] On the relationship between Fez and the surrounding countryside during the Saʿdid period (1549–1637), see Muḥammad Mazīn, *Fās wa-bādiyatuhā: musāhama fī taʾrīkh al-maghrib al-saʿdī*, 2 vols (Rabat: Manshūrāt Kulliyāt al-ʿUlūm al-Insāniyya, 1406/1986), esp. vol. 2, 507–17.

Zgane mountains extended over an area that was 40 *mīl*s long and 15 *mīl*s wide.[6] Because of the intense cold, only the slopes facing Fez were inhabited. The area contained numerous olive groves and other fruit trees and was blessed with abundant natural springs that spilled into the wadi, allowing farmers to grow barley, flax, hemp, and, in Leo's time, mulberry trees. Eight *mīl*s northeast of Sefrou was Mazdgha, a walled town situated at the foothills of the Middle Atlas mountains. Although the houses in Mazdgha were of poor quality, each had a fountain of clear water. The town's inhabitants specialized in the production of porcelain pottery, which they marketed in Fez, located 12 *mīl*s to the north. The farmers of Mazdgha cultivated barley, flax, and hemp, and figs and other fruits.[7] A later source, Ibn al-Aḥmar, indicates that the inhabitants of Mazdgha were members of a Berber tribe (*qabīla*) that was responsible for the fortress (*qalʿa*) of Sefrou in the mountains of Bilād Būblān; the tribe was known for its learning and righteousness.[8]

The inhabitants of Zgane and Mazdgha no doubt traded with one another, intermarried, and came together for the purpose of common defense. They interacted on multiple fronts and expected those interactions to continue into the future. As neighbors, they were inclined to cooperate and they achieved cooperation by developing norms of neighborliness that promoted the aggregate welfare of both communities. Chronic but relatively minor disputes were resolved on the basis of informal norms, for example, the costs for repair of a fence are proportional to the number of livestock on the respective sides of the boundary line. When a neighbor violated one of these informal norms, the injured party might respond, first, by issuing a warning; second, by disseminating truthful negative gossip; and third, by using force. Under normal circumstances, these self-help measures made it possible for the residents of Zgane and Mazdgha to resolve their disputes on their own, without seeking the help of agents of the legal system.[9]

But circumstances are not always normal, and certain types of disputes are not amenable to resolution at the local level. The allocation of water resources during a shortage is a case in point. In a dispute over scarce water resources, the stakes tend to be high and the relevant technical issues complex. For these reasons, the

[6] One *mīl* = 4000 els = 1/3 farsakh = approx. 2 km. See Walther Hinz, *Islamische masse und Gewichte: Umgerechnet ins metrische system* (Leiden: E.J. Brill, 1955), 63.

[7] Al-Wazzān, *Waṣf Ifrīqīya*, 2 vols (Rabat, 1980), vol. 1, 362; Leo Africanus, *The History and Description of Africa and of the notable things therein contained*, tr. John Pory, ed. Robert Brown, 3 vols (London: The Hakluyt Society, 1896), vol. 2, 551–2; Leon Africano, *Descripcion de Africa y de las cosas notables que en ella se encuentran* (Imp. Imperio, 1952), vol. 1, 192–3.

[8] Ismāʿīl Ibn al-Aḥmar, *Buyūtāt Fās al-kubrā* (Rabāṭ: Dār al-Manṣūr li'l-Ṭibāʿa wa'l-Wirāqa, 1972), 8, 13. One prominent Mazdaghī in the eighth/fourteenth century was Abū al-Faḍl al-Mazdaghī. On his fall from grace, see Maya Shatzmiller, "Un texte relatif aux structures politiques mérinides: les cas du khaṭīb Abū 'l-Faḍl al-Mazdaghī (746/1345)," *Revue des Etudes Islamiques* (1977), 310–19; idem, *The Berbers and the Islamic State: The Marīnid Experience in Pre-Protectorate Morocco* (Princeton: Markus Wiener, 2000), 69–81. Closer to the present time, the tribe of Mazdgha split up into several segments, one of which currently occupies Mazdgha Jurf, the other Mazdgha al-Sūq.

[9] See Robert C. Ellickson, *Order Without Law: How Neighbors Settle Disputes* (Cambridge: Harvard University Press, 1991), 4, 55, 58–62, 218.

legal system has a comparative advantage over local communities as an agent of social control. In a dispute of this nature, neighboring communities may assert their formal legal rights and entitlements and seek the assistance of agents of the legal system, who attempt to resolve the dispute according to the norms of formal law.[10]

Some two and a half centuries prior to Leo Africanus, *ca.* 683/1284–85, the residents of Zgane and Mazdgha became embroiled in a dispute over the use of the waters of the wadi, and they challenged one another intermittently over the issue of water rights for the next 150 years, until at least 824/1421. Although Zgane and Mazdgha were off the beaten path, they were included within the jurisdiction of the Māliki courts. Conversely, local landowners had links to the Marīnid dynasty and they sought the assistance of the chief qāḍī of Fez when disputes over water broke out. The qāḍī, in turn, sent water experts to the wadi to survey the area between the two settlements. It was in the office of the chief qāḍī of Fez that scribes created the documentary record that has served as the basis of our analysis in the present chapter.

Our primary source for this dispute is the *Miʿyār* of al-Wansharīsī, which contains seven fatwās relating to the ongoing conflict, issued by distinguished jurists of Fez between *ca.* 683/1284–85 and 824/1421; attached to, or embedded in, these fatwās are an eyewitness description of the wadi, judicial certifications of several fatwās, records of witness testimony, and a document identified as an *iʿmāl*, perhaps a judicial implementation. Due to the vagaries of transmission, which involved frequent copying and re-copying, the documents do not appear in our source in the order in which they were issued. To facilitate their analysis, I have arranged them chronologically, as indicated in table 3.1.

By analyzing the dispute between the inhabitants of Zgane and Mazdgha, I hope to shed light on the relationship between law and economy in the Magrib in the period between *ca.* 1300 and 1500 CE. It is a truism that economic phenomena generally take place within a legal environment, and that legal norms and principles have economic consequences. But the manner in which law and economy interact is often difficult to specify and will vary over time and from one society to the next. Legal historians have posited several models to explain this relationship. According to one model, jurists invoke fixed and unchanging legal principles in apparent disregard for their economic consequences (at first glance, this model would appear to best fit the case of Muslim societies). According to another model, judges and jurists respond to changes in the economy by manipulating or reforming the law in an effort to provide support for entrepreneurs, that is, law serves as an instrument of class power (this model nicely describes the Tanzimat reforms of the late nineteenth century). According to a third model, judges and jurists create legal methods, institutions, and precedents to serve the needs of entrepreneurs and, over time, entrepreneurs "select" those methods, institutions and precedents that best serve their needs. If, for some reason, the law should come to serve as an obstacle to economic growth and efficiency, entrepreneurs

[10] Ibid., 257.

Table 3.1 Documents in Chronological Order (*Miʿyār*, vol. 8, 5–20)

Date	*Subject*	*Location*
undated (< 683/1284–85)	Response of al-Waryāghlī (d. 683/1284–85)	vol. 8, 10, ll. 11–23
undated < 695/1295–96	Response of al-Wālidī (d. *ca*. 695/1295–96)	vol. 8, 11, ll. 1–14
undated (< 719/1319–20)	Response of al-Ṣughayyir (d. 719/1319–20)	vol. 8, 11 (l. 15) – 12 (l. 9)
mid Rabīʿ I 721/9–19 April 1321	Description of wādī by eyewitnesses	vol. 8, 5 (l. 8) – 8 (l. 11)
mid Dhū al-Qaʿda 738/31 May – 9 June 1338	Certification of topographical description by al-Azdī (d. ??)	vol. 8, 8, ll. 13–17
25 Ramaḍān 739/6 April 1339	Witnesses certify al-Wālidī's handwriting and give testimony regarding his death	vol. 8, 11, ll. 3–8
late Ramaḍān 739/11 April 1339	Certification of al-Ṣughayyir's fatwā and authentication (*istiqlāl*) by al-Azdī	vol. 8, 12, ll. 10–16
mid Muḥarram 746/14–24 March 1345	Testimony regarding water usage	vol. 8, 8 (l. 24) – 9 (l. 8)
last decade Jumādā I 748/ 29 August – 7 September 1347	Testimony certified in presence of al-Jazūlī (d. 758/1357)	vol. 8, 9, ll. 10–18
24 Jumādā II 748/1 October 1347	*Taṣḥīḥ* and *iktifāʾ* by al-Jazūlī	vol. 8, 9, ll. 20–4
undated (< 750/1349–50)	Response of Muḥammad al-Yāliṣūtī (d. 750/1349–50)	vol. 8, 12 (l. 17) – 14 (l. 18)
undated (< 773/1371–72)	Response of al-Sarīfī (d. < 773/1371–72 = son's death date?)	vol. 8, 14 (l. 19) – 15 (l. 7)
ca. 792/1390 (possible mistake?)	*Istiqlāl* and *iʿmāl* of ʿAbdallāh al-Ṣanhājī (see *Shajara*, no. 855)	vol. 8, 9 (l. 24) – 10 (l. 5)
before 24 Rabīʿ I 824/29 March 1421	Response of ʿAbdallāh al-ʿAbdūsī (d. 847/1443–44)	vol. 8, 18 (l. 18) – 19 (l. 23)
24 Rabīʿ I 824/29 March 1421	Authentication of al-ʿAbdūsī's response + *istiqlāl* of al-Awrabī	vol. 8, 19 (l. 24) – 20 (l. 9)
before 19 Jumādā I 824/22 May 1421	Response of al-Tāzaghdrī (d. 831/1427–28)	vol. 8, 15 (l. 8) – 18 (l. 5)
19 Jumādā I 824/22 May 1421	Certification of al-Tāzaghdrī's response	vol. 8, 18, ll. 8–23
late Jumādā I 824/late May or early June 1421	*Iʿmāl* of Muḥammad al-Ṣanhājī [possibly AH 724?]	vol. 8, 8, ll. 17–21

will find a way to achieve their objectives, for example, through litigation, by circumventing the law, or by agitating to change the law. According to this third model, social and economic imperatives determine the content of the law. The reader may want to keep these three models in mind as we proceed with our analysis of the dispute.[11]

In an effort to better understand the dispute between the inhabitants of Zgane and Mazdgha, let us consider several long-term historical developments that unfolded during the Marīnid period.

Historical Background

We begin with the legal system. As explained in the Introduction, Mālikism experienced severe setbacks under the Almohads (524–667/1130–1269). The Mahdī Ibn Tūmart had established as the basis of his doctrine elements of the purest orthodoxy, that is, Qur'ān, *sunna*, and *ijmāʿ*. Ibn Tūmart was succeeded by ʿAbd al-Mu'min, who was proclaimed caliph in 524/1130. The third successor to ʿAbd al-Mu'min, Abū Yūsuf Yaʿqūb al-Manṣūr, issued an order banning the works of Mālikī substantive law (*furūʿ*) and calling for the burning of Mālikī legal texts, including the *Mudawwana* of Saḥnūn. This same caliph appointed a certain number of Ẓāhirī judges in the Maghrib and al-Andalus. At the same time, however, many Mālikīs continued to serve as qāḍīs and to issue judgments on the basis of the Mālikī *madhhab*.[12] As Abun-Nasr has put it, "although reliance on the manuals of the Muslim jurists was formally banned, the practical needs of justice led to the tacit toleration of the Malikite system."[13] With the rise of the Marīnid dynasty, Ẓāhirism fell from official favor and Mālikism experienced a revival as Mālikī doctrine spread throughout the Maghrib with the active support of the new dynasty. In an effort to solidify their control of the Maghrib and reinforce the legitimacy of their rule, the Marīnids gave substantial support to higher education in Fez, endowing numerous *madrasas* in which Mālikī scholars taught their students the fundamentals of law (*fiqh*) and jurisprudence (*uṣūl*).[14] And in an effort

[11] This paragraph draws on Joshua Getzler, "Rules Writ in Water: A Study in Industrialization of the Law," paper presented to the Law and History forum of the Faculty of Law, Tel Aviv University, 23 December 1998. I am grateful to my colleague, Ron Shaham, for bringing this essay to my attention and providing me with a copy.

[12] See *EI*², s.v.v. Mālikiyya, al-Muwaḥḥidūn; Maribel Fierro, "The Legal Policies of the Almohad Caliphs and Ibn Rushd's *Bidāyat al-Mujtahid*," *Journal of Islamic Studies*, 10.3 (1999), 226–48; Jamil M. Abun-Nasr, *A History of the Maghrib in the Islamic Period* (Cambridge: Cambridge University Press, 1987), 95, 97–8; Muḥammad al-Maghrāwī, "Khiṭṭat qaḍā' al-jamāʿa bi-Marākish al-muwaḥḥidiya," paper presented at the conference, "Marrakesh from its foundation to the end of the Almohad period," April 1988.

[13] Abun-Nasr, *A History of the Maghrib*, 95.

[14] See *EI*², s.v. Mālikiyya; Abun-Nasr, *A History of the Maghrib*, 116–17; according to Muḥammad al-Manūnī, *Waraqāt ʿan ḥaḍārat al-Marīniyyīn* (Rabat: Kulliyyat al-Ādāb wa'l-ʿUlūm, 1996), 271–82, Mālikism "replaced" Ẓāhirism, which is perhaps an overstatement.

to combat the influence of sufi saints in the countryside, the Marīnids recruited young men from rural districts for training in the *madrasas* of Fez, a policy which may have contributed to the incorporation of the countryside into the apparatus of justice.[15] This point is of special relevance to the present investigation, for this policy contributed to the Islamization of the Wadi Zgane irrigation system.

The dispute between the residents of Zgane and Mazdgha – as documented in our source – stretched over a period that was nearly coterminous with the reign of the Marīnids, who exercised control over Morocco from 656/1258 until 869/1465: the dispute began a generation after the Marīnids had seized power and continued until the generation immediately preceding their replacement by the Waṭṭāsids. The two centuries of Marīnid rule was a period of relative political stability, commercial prosperity, and intellectual achievement, during which Fez became one of the great cities of the Muslim world.[16]

Originally nomadic shepherds and breeders of sheep, the Marīnids, Berbers of the Zanāta tribe, frequented the area between Figuig and Sijilmāsa until the fifth/eleventh and sixth/twelfth centuries, when the arrrival of Arab tribes in the region triggered demographic disturbances that compelled them to migrate to the northern part of the Maghrib. Following the defeat of the Almohads at Las Navas de Tolosa in 609/1212, the Marīnids took advantage of the weakness of the ruling dynasty by claiming dues from major towns and charging protection fees. By the middle of the seventh/thirteenth century, the Marīnids had succeeded in physically occupying the large towns and settling therein: Meknès (642/1244); Fez (646/1248); Sijilmāsa (653/1255); and, finally, Marrakesh (668/1269), which had served as the Almohad capital. The Marīnid sulṭāns, who made Fez the seat of their administrative apparatus, used their political and military power to exploit the resources of the Moroccan countryside by distributing plots of land, in the form of *iqṭāʿ*s, to Berber soldiers and *amīr*s. The recipients of these *iqṭāʿ*s forced local farmers either to work for them (*iqṭāʿ tamlīk*) or to pay taxes (*iqṭāʿ jibāya*).[17]

The Wadi Zgane irrigation system no doubt had been in existence for one or more centuries prior to the arrival of the Marīnids in this area. Whatever the nature of the pre-Marīnid irrigation system and its manner of operation, it is clear that with the arrival of the Marīnids, significant changes took place in patterns of land ownership, investment in hydrology, and land usage. The *Miʿyār* specifies that a number of fields and diversion dams in the vicinity of Zgane were owned by

[15] On the connection between the countryside and Fez, see Vincent Cornell, *Realm of the Saint: Power and Authority in Moroccan Sufism* (Austin: University of Texas Press, 1998), 32 ff.

[16] On the Marīnids, see al-Manūnī, *Waraqāt*; Mohammad Kably, *Société, pouvoir et réligion au Maroc à la fin du Moyen-Age* (Maisonneuve et Larose, 1986); *EI*², s.v. Marīnids; Roger Le Tourneau, *Fez in the Age of the Marinides*, tr. Besse Alberta Clement (Norman: University of Oklahoma Press, 1961); Abun-Nasr, *A History of the Maghrib*, 103–18.

[17] Abun-Nasr, *A History of the Maghrib*, 103–18; *EI*², s.v. Marīnids; Omar Benmira, "al-Nawāzil wa'l-mujtamaʿ," PhD dissertation, Kulliyat al-ādāb bi'l-Rabāṭ, 1989, 321 ff.

individuals named Ibn Warāsin, Ibrāhīm al-Barīdī, and ʿUmar b. Raḥḥū,[18] all of whom may have received plots of land in the Wadi in the form of *iqṭāʿ*s. These men, whose names suggest that they were Berbers, invested significant financial resources in the agricultural infrastructure, building a series of diversion dams (*sudūd*, sg. *sadd*) and canals (*sawāqin*, sg. *sāqiya*)[19] that made it possible to increase the area of cultivated land and, perhaps, to introduce new crops that required greater amounts of water.[20] (In this connection Leo the African's reference to the "recent" introduction of mulberry trees in Zgane, that is, shortly before the beginning of the sixteenth century, is intriguing albeit inconclusive.)[21]

The northern part of the Maghrib was affected by drought and other calamities at various points during the Marīnid period. An invasion of locusts in 679/1280 devastated the countryside, causing the price of wheat to rise to ten dirhams per *ṣāʿ*. Drought struck the country in 683/1284,[22] again in 721/1321 (the first of a five-year drought), and again in 744/1344; from the end of the eighth/fourteenth century to the middle of the ninth/fifteenth century, a series of droughts struck the far Maghrib in general and Fez and its environs in particular.[23] At such times, a downstream settlement might engage in informal negotiations with its upstream neighbors to borrow water – or, if the negotiations proved unsuccessful, it might

18 Al-Wansharīsī, *Miʿyār*, vol. 8, 7, ll. 10, 13 and 20. Many men bearing the name *al-Barīdī* served as administrators at the Marīnid court and Raḥḥū is a common Berber name. On Raḥḥū, see Benmira, "Qaḍāyā al-miyāh," 84–5, where the author observes that a Mārinid general by the name of Abū ʿAlī Raḥḥū led a revolt in Ceuta in the year 709/1310. It may be significant, in this context, that the current Berber inhabitants of Zgane identify themselves as members of the Ait Raḥḥū tribe.

19 On *sāqiyas*, see Lucie Bolens, "L'irrigation en al-Andalus: Une Société en Mutation, Analyse des Sources Juridiques (Les "Nawâzil" d'al-Wansharîsî)," in idem, *L'Andalousie du quotidien au sacré XIe–XIIIe siècles* (Aldershot, Hampshire, UK: Variorum, 1990), chap. III, 75; Francisco Vidal Castro, "El Agua en el Derecho Islámico: Introducción a sus orígenes, propriedad y uso," in *El Agua en la Agricultura de al-Andalus* (Granada: El legado Andalusi, 1995), 99–117, esp. 104; E.W. Lane, *Arabic-English Lexicon* (London: Williams and Norgate, 1863), s.v. s-q-y ("a small channel for the irrigation of land").

20 On the introduction of hydraulic technology to Morocco, see G.S. Colin, "La noria marocaine et les machines hydrauliques dans le monde arabe," *Hespéris*, XIV (1932), 22–60, esp. 38; idem, "L'origine des norias de Fès," *Hespéris*, XVI (1933), 156–7. On al-Andalus, see Bolens, "L'irrigation en al-Andalus," chap. III; Vincent Lagardère, "Moulins d'Occident Musulman au Moyen Age (IXe au XVe siècles): Al-Andalus," in *al-Qanṭara*, XIII (1991), 59–118; Thomas Glick, *Irrigation and Society in Medieval Valencia* (Cambridge: Harvard University Press, 1970). On Ifrīqiyā, see Robert Brunschvig, *La Berbérie Orientale sous les Hafsides*, 2 vols (Paris: Adrien Maisonneuve, 1940–47), vol. 2, 205–16. See also A.M.A. Maktari, *Water Rights and Irrigation Practices in Lahj: A Study of the Application of Customary and Sharīʿah Law in South-West Arabia* (Cambridge: Cambridge University Press, 1971), chap. 4; C. Edmund Bosworth, "Some Remarks on the Terminology of Irrigation Practices and Hydraulic Constructions in the Eastern Arab and Iranian Worlds in the Third-Fifth Centuries AH," in *Journal of Islamic Studies*, 2:1 (1991), 78–85; *EI*[2], s.v. Māʾ.

21 Benmira, "Qaḍāyā al-miyāh," 82–3. The introduction of mulberry trees by the inhabitants of Zgane would have increased their demand for water to irrigate the trees.

22 ʿAbd el-Ḥaqq El-Bâdisî, *El-Maqṣad (Vie des saints du Rîf)*, tr. by G.S. Colin (Paris: Librairie Ancienne Honoré Champion, 1926), 202, note 351 (citing al-Nāṣirī al-Salāwī, *Istiqṣā*, II, 43).

23 Benmira, "Qaḍāyā al-miyāh," 81–2; idem, "al-Nawāzil wa'l-mujtamaʿ," 360 ff.; Ibn Abī Zarʿ, *Roudh el-Kartas. Histoire des souverains du maghreb et annales de la ville de Fes*, tr. A. Beaumier (Paris: L'Imprimerie Impériale, 1860), 564–5.

attempt to steal the water. Alternatively, an upstream community might manipulate the stream by diverting additional quantities of water into its fields or pools, thereby cutting off the flow of water to its downstream neighbors. Disputes over water distribution were settled, variously, through fighting, bargaining or amicable negotiation, or with the assistance of outside authorities – especially *sharīf*s or descendants of the Prophet (see Introduction), and by Sufi *murābiṭ*s, or by appeal to muftīs whose fatwās served as the basis for negotiated settlements.[24]

It is against this historical background that we must attempt to situate the dispute between the residents of Zgane and Mazdgha: the revival of Mālikism; the arrival of the Marīnids and the introduction of the *iqṭāʿ* system; increased investment in hydrology and changing patterns of agricultural production; and the vagaries of climate, especially intermittent drought. The complex interplay among these phenomena may have combined to upset the delicate balance of power between the upstream and downstream communities, which were dependent for their livelihood upon the extraction of water from the wadi, as regulated by private agreements and understandings, local custom (including Berber customary law), and Islamic law. As these forces came to bear upon the two settlements, situated one above the other along the wadi, social tension and conflict no doubt increased, especially in years of reduced rainfall or drought, when there was not enough water to satisfy the needs of both communities.

Islamic Water Law

Water is a fluid and ephemeral element of nature that is in a constant state of change. Thus, it may not be owned in the same way as land, which is stable and fixed.

The major principles and features of Islamic water law were worked out by Muslim jurists between the eighth and the tenth centuries CE on the basis of the Qur'ān, *ḥadīth*, analogy, and consensus. The fully developed doctrine on water

[24] For comparative purposes, see R. Le Tourneau, "Documents sur une contestation relative à la répartition de l'eau dans la medina de Fès," in *Mélanges William Marçais* (Paris, 1950), 191–204; Clifford Geertz, Hildred Geertz, and Lawrence Rosen, *Meaning and Order in Moroccan Society: Three essays in cultural analysis* (Cambridge: Cambridge University Press, 1979), Annex A: "Irrigation in the Oasis of Sefrou and the Lower Aggai River," 113–22; Abdellah Hammoudi, "Substance and Relation: Water Rights and Water Distribution in the Ḍrā Valley," in *Property, Social Structure, and Law in the Modern Middle East*, ed. Ann Elizabeth Mayer (Albany: State University of New York Press, 1985), 27–57; Martha Mundy, "Irrigation and Society in a Yemeni Valley: On the life and death of a bountiful source," in *Yemen Sanaa: Peuples méditerranéens*, 46 (1989), 97–128; Daniel M. Varisco, "Water Sources and Traditional Irrigation in Yemen," *New Arabian Studies*, 3 (1996), 238–57; idem, "*Sayl* and *Ghayl*: The Ecology of Water Allocation in Yemen," *Human Ecology*, 11 (1983), 365–83; David Hart, "Comparative Land Tenure and Division of Irrigation Water in Two Moroccan Berber Societies: The Aith Waryaghar of the Rif and the Ait 'Atta of the Saghru and South-Central Atlas," *Journal of North African Studies*, vol. 4:2 (1999), 172–218.

law can be found in doctrinal lawbooks, in chapters devoted to purity (*ṭahāra*), sale (*bay*ʿ), and the revival of wasteland (*iḥyāʾ al-mawāt*). Despite minor doctrinal differences, the four Sunnī *madhhab*s have similar water doctrines.[25]

Water doctrine may be approached in terms of the type of water source or the legal status that applies to it. We begin with the former. Islamic law distinguishes three types of water source that may be the subject of use (*intifā*ʿ) or ownership (*milk*): (1) large rivers, small rivers, and canals; (2) wells; and (3) springs.[26]

(1) Naturally occurring water is the common property (*mubāḥ*) of all living things and cannot be owned or sold. Thus, if a river is sufficiently large that its water can be used by all, no constraints or limitations may be placed on its use for drinking and irrigation. As for small rivers, two cases must be distinguished: (a) if there is a sufficient amount of water for all users, but it is possible to cause a shortage of water to others, for example, by digging a canal to divert water away from the river, use of the water is determined in consideration of the consequences of such actions; (b) if the river must be dammed and the water allocated at fixed times in order to provide sufficient water for irrigation, the river is generally regarded as the joint property of the cultivators who live along its banks, and the amount of water that may be taken by those living upstream will depend on circumstances such as the season of the year and type of crop irrigated. Canals are treated as the private property of the landowners on whose land they are located; if a canal is held jointly, no landowner may make unilateral changes in the arrangements for sharing the water.

(2) Wells dug for the public benefit are freely available to all, although the excavator has the right of first use; on the other hand, if a person digs a well for his own use, he enjoys first entitlement to the water as long as he continues to live in the vicinity of the well, but he is obligated to give water to persons suffering from thirst.

(3) Natural springs – a critical concern here – are treated as analogous to permanently flowing rivers. If the water supply is limited, the first person to use

[25] On Mālikī water law, see, for example, Saḥnūn (d. 240/854), *al-Mudawwana al-Kubrā*, 16 vols in 4 (Cairo: Maṭbaʿat al-Saʿādah, 1323/1905), vol. 10, 121–3; vol. 11, 70; vol. 14, 130–2, 138–9, 221, 235–7; vol. 15, 189–99; Ibn Abī Zayd al-Qayrawānī (d. 386/996), *Risāla* (Beirut: al-Maktaba al-Thaqāfiyya, n.d.), 35 ff., 495 ff.; Abū al-Walīd Muḥammad b. Aḥmad b. Rushd (d. 595/1198), *Bidāyat al-Mujtahid wa-Nihāyat al-Muqtaṣid*, 2 vols (Cairo: Shirkat al-Maṭbūʿāt al-ʿArabiyya, 1966), vol. 1, 7 ff., vol. 2, 102 ff. [= Ibn Rushd, *The Distinguished Jurist's Primer*, tr. Imran Nyazee and Muhammad Abdul Rauf, 2 vols (Reading, UK: Garnet Publishing, 1996), vol. 1, 1 ff., vol. 2, 153 ff.]; Ibn Juzayy al-Gharnāṭī (d. 741/1340–41), *Qawānīn al-aḥkām al-sharʿiyya wa-masāʾil al-furūʿ al-fiqhiyya* (Beirut: Dār al-ʿIlm li'l-Malāyīn), 44–6, 271 ff., 367–8; Khalīl b. Isḥāq (d. 776/1374), *al-Mukhtaṣar fī al-fiqh ʿalā madhhab al-Imām Mālik* (Paris: L'Imprimerie Nationale, 1272/1855), 7 ff., 122 ff., 183–4. Cf. David Santillana, *Istituzioni di Diritto Musulmano Malichita*, 2 vols (Roma: Istituto per L'Oriente, 1938), vol. 1, 416 ff. On Shāfiʿī water law, see ʿAlī b. Muḥammad al-Mawardī, *al-Ahkam as-Sultaniyyah: The Islamic Laws of Governance*, tr. Dr Asadullah Yate (London: Ta-Ha Publishers, 1996), 252–62. On Ḥanbalī water law, see Michael Norvelle, "Water Use and Ownership According to the Texts of Ḥanbalī Fiqh," Masters thesis, McGill University, 1980.

[26] The following summary relies on *EI*², s.v. Māʾ. See also Vidal Castro, "El Agua en el Derecho Islámico," 99–117; Norvelle, "Water Use and Ownership," 23 (citing Ibn Qudāma).

the water for irrigation has priority; otherwise, the water has to be shared equally. Although the physical entity that constitutes the spring belongs to the owner of the land on which it is located, the water itself is not owned and is common property, because it flows underground to the property and is therefore analogous to the water in a flowing river.

We also may analyze Islamic water law in terms of three legal statuses that may be applied to water. (1) Naturally occurring water is essentially "ownerless" and is therefore the property of all human beings. Such water is appropriated among users on a first-come, first-served basis. (2) Alternatively, water may be the subject of a usufruct (*manfaʿa*) obtainable by holders according to certain specified criteria. Usufructory rights apply to water sources that are inadequate to meet the needs of all competing users (including wells and natural springs) and therefore must be granted according to specific criteria. (3) Finally, water may be the property (*milk*) of a possessor, for example, someone who appropriates water by placing it in a canal, irrigation channel, or container.[27]

In the present case, we are concerned with the status of water in a spring-fed wadi in which numerous diversion dams and canals had been constructed for the purposes of agriculture (irrigation) and industry (milling). On the one hand, the water of the springs and of the wadi was the property of everyone; on the other hand, any water that had been appropriated by means of a canal or an irrigation channel was considered the property (*milk*) of its possessor. How did the users of the system regulate the use of water in such a situation? What happened if the wadi's resources were exhausted by the use of appropriated water by the upstreamers? The conflict we are studying raised questions about the relationship between two interconnected but potentially conflicting legal norms. (1) Islamic law assumes that the person (or settlement) closest to the source is the first to have put it to productive or beneficial use and, accordingly, holds that physical proximity to the source confers priority in use. Thus, the person (or settlement) nearest the source may retain the water until he has irrigated his trees and gardens but must then allow the surplus water to flow down to the next person, and so on. The next beneficial user and all following users are entitled only to the surplus remaining after the person preceding them has met his needs. (2) But upstream communities are frequently offshoots of downstream communities and it is not always the case that the person (or settlement) closest to the source was the first to put it to use. For example, it is possible that a person arrived at a water source and irrigated virgin land; that a second person arrived, upstream, and irrigated his land also; that a third person arrived and irrigated land even further upstream, and so on. In such cases historical precedence in cultivation prevails over physical proximity to the source in determining priority in use.[28]

[27] Norvelle, "Water Use and Ownership," 65.
[28] Ibid., 34 (citing Ibn Qudāma), 74–7.

Stage I: The Fatwās of al-Waryāghlī, al-Walīdī, and al-Ṣughayyir (*ca.* 1280–1320)

The Fatwā of al-Waryāghlī (d. 683/1284–85)[29]

The earliest fatwā relating to our dispute was issued by Abū Ibrāhīm Isḥāq b. Yaḥyā b. Maṭar al-Waryāghlī al-Aʿraj, that is, "the lame", a sobriquet acquired after brigands wounded him while he was studying in a mosque one night. Originally from the Rīf, al-Waryāghlī was attracted to Fez, where he became a distinguished jurist and a revered sufi saint.[30] He remained aloof from members of the Marīnid family and did not hesitate to criticize the Sulṭān Abū Yaʿqūb Yūsuf in public. Al-Waryāghlī wrote a marginal commentary or *Ṭurar* on the *Tahdhīb al-Mudawwana* of al-Barādhiʿī and a short commentary on the *Muwaṭṭaʾ* of Mālik, contributing to the dissemination of Mālikī doctrine throughout the Marīnid realm. He was buried in Fez and his tomb became a popular shrine.[31]

Although we do not know the exact date on which the fatwā was issued, it will be recalled that Morocco was stricken by drought in 683/1284–85, the year in which al-Waryāghlī died. It is tempting to assume that the fatwā was issued in this year or shortly before. Be that as it may, the *istiftāʾ*, or request for a judicial opinion, to which the muftī responded was formulated as follows:

> Know – may God guide you to what is correct – the case of people who have water on which there are mills, gardens, and settlements (*manāzil*) that are of long-standing. It is not known who was first [to establish these entities] because of the length of time and the extinction of the generations. At the present time, those who are at the top (*al-aʿlūn*) have sought to cut off [the water] from those who are at the bottom (*al-asfalīn*).[32]

The question, formulated in general and abstract terms, refers to "people" (*qawm*) without specifying their identity, number, or location; it also suggests that the water in question was used both for milling and irrigation, a point of potential significance to which the muftī does not address himself.[33] The problem was clear. The upstream community was attempting to manipulate the stream in an effort to

[29] On al-Waryāghlī, see El-Bâdisî, *El-Maqṣad*, 105–9, no. 23; Ibn al-Qāḍī (d. 1025/1616), *Durrat al-Ḥijāl fī Asmāʾ al-Rijāl*, ed. Muḥammad al-Aḥmadī Abū al-Nūr (Cairo: Dār al-Turāth, 1390/1970), vol. 1, 207, no. 290; idem, *Jadhwat al-iqtibās fī dhikr man ḥalla min aʿlām madīnat fās* (Rabat: Dār al-Manṣūr li'l-Ṭibāʿa wa'l-Wirāqa, 1973–74), vol. 1, 164–5, no. 116; Aḥmad Bābā al-Tunbuktī (d. 1036/1627), *Nayl al-ibtihāj bi-taṭrīz al-Dībāj* (Cairo, 1351/1932), 100; Muḥammad b. Muḥammad Makhlūf, *Shajarat al-nūr al-zakiyya fī ṭabaqāt al-mālikiyya*, 2 vols in 1 (2nd edn, Beirut: Dār al-Kitāb al-ʿArabī, *ca.* 1975), vol. 1, 202, no. 692; Manūnī, *Waraqāt*, 294. See also Kably, *Société, pouvoir et religion*, 273–6, 314.

[30] Al-Waryāghlī is one of forty-eight saints included in El-Bâdisî, *El-Maqṣad*, 105–9.

[31] For details, see El-Bâdisî, *El-Maqṣad*, 106–7; Kably, *Société, pouvoir et religion*, 275–6, characterizes al-Waryāghlī as "radical," "imprégné de mysticisme," "un savant mystique," and "un sufi."

[32] *Miʿyār*, vol. 8, 10, ll. 6–10.

[33] On mills, see Lagardère, "Moulins d'Occident Musulman au Moyen Age," 59–118.

cut off the water supply to the downstream community, and the fact or issue that was in dispute was that of historical precedence. Which community had been the first to establish its mills, gardens, and settlements? Presumably, the answer to this question would provide the key to the resolution of the dispute. But the communities in question were of great antiquity – they had been established at least as early as the Almohad period and probably before – and the collective memory of their respective inhabitants had not preserved this historical "fact." What was to be done?

Al-Waryāghlī began his response with a pious invocation formulated in terms appropriate to the case at hand, making a connection between natural resources and sacred law: "May God assist us and you in the preservation of His trusts (*wadāʾiʿihi*) and in the recollection of His sacred laws (*sharāʾiʿihi*) that He deposited with us." The muftī explained that in the absence of any evidence regarding its legal status, the water should be treated on the basis of the status quo, according to which – for as long as anyone could remember – it had been shared by the two communities. There is only one circumstance, he added, in which the upstream community legitimately might claim an exclusive right to the water, to wit, if it were able to produce "ancient documents" (*ʿuqūd qadīma*) establishing that it had given the water to the downstream community merely as a gratuitous concession (*irtifāq*) or as a loan for a specified period of time (*ʿāriyya ilā mudda maʿlūma*).[34] If, however, the upstream community had allowed the downstream community to use the water without placing any time constraints on usage, then the loan was unrestricted (*ʿāriyya muṭlaqa*) and should be treated as perpetual, with the result that the downstream community's extended possession (*ḥawz*) of the water – to the point that its original legal status had been forgotten – is of sufficient strength to repel any claim that may be put forward by the upstream community. In this case, the burden of proof would lie upon the upstream community.

As support for his argument, the muftī adduced an historical consideration: the settlements in question had been established prior to the time of the Almohads (524–667/1130–1269), and since their establishment the status quo with respect to use of the water had been maintained without any objection – notwithstanding the availability of legal mechanisms for making such claims. Thus, shared usage of the water was supported by the established tradition of the ancestors of the two communities in question. Anyone who now claims that the situation was once different than it is at present "claims to possess greater knowledge and to be more upright than our ancestors."[35] Such a claim is clearly false and is belied by local custom (*ʿāda*); anyone who holds otherwise has fallen into error. This position, al-Waryāghlī asserted, is in accordance with fatwās issued by earlier, unspecified Mālikī jurists. Finally, at the end of his fatwā al-Waryāghlī raised the linguistic register of his response, moving from a legal to a theological plane and invoking

[34] J. Schacht, *An Introduction to Islamic Law* (Oxford: Clarendon Press, 1964), 157 defines *ʿāriyya* as "putting another temporarily and gratuitously in possession of the use of a thing, the substance of which is not consumed by its use ... The owner may at any time demand the return (*rujūʿ*) of the thing which he has lent." See also Santillana, *Istituzioni*, vol. 1, 354, 455; vol. 2, 183–4.

[35] *Miʿyār*, vol. 8, 10, ll. 17–18.

the powerful rhetoric of the Qur'ān. Implicitly attributing *kufr*, or infidelity, to anyone who might challenge his opinion, the muftī cited Qur'ān 3:83 ("What, do they desire another religion than God's ... ?") and issued a warning that anyone who engages in injustice will be defeated by God, as indicated by the Messenger of God. The fatwā was signed: Isḥāq b. Ibrāhīm (*sic*) al-Waryāghlī.[36]

We must keep in mind one aspect of al-Waryāghlī's fatwā as we continue with our analysis: while situating himself in the chain of juristic tradition, the muftī made no reference to Qur'ānic verses that might be relevant to the case, to prophetic *ḥadīth*, or to Mālikī authorities, but instead placed great emphasis on local custom.

The Fatwā of al-Walīdī (d. ca. *695/1295–96)*

Attached to the fatwā of al-Waryāghlī is a short fatwā issued soon thereafter by Abū al-Faḍl Rāshid b. Abī Rāshid al-Walīdī.

Like al-Waryāghlī, al-Walīdī was a sufi jurist and he too played an instrumental role in the dissemination of Mālikī doctrine throughout the Marīnid realm. The selection of al-Walīdī to consider the dispute was fortuitous, for the muftī had strong links to the countryside and personal knowledge and experience of farming. A member of the clan known as the Banū Walīd (part of the tribe of Ṣanhāja), al-Walīdī remained in contact with his village even after moving to Fez to study law. Indeed, some sources portray him as the quintessential farmer-jurist. It is reported that he regularly returned to his village, where he would participate actively in agricultural activities, cleverly integrating the study of law with the practice of farming by placing the *Jāmiʿ* of Ibn Yūnis at the end of one row that he was plowing, and the *Tabṣira* of al-Lakhmī at the end of another (both texts were commentaries on the *Mudawwana*). Whenever he reached the end of a row, he would read a case from one of the books and work it over in his mind as he was ploughing the next row. As a result of this "methodology," al-Walīdī mastered the *Mudawwana* of Saḥnūn, which he taught in his *fiqh* classes (rather than the shorter and more commonly taught *Tahdhīb* of al-Barādhiʿī). He was the author of a treatise entitled *al-Ḥalāl wa'l-Ḥarām*.[37] He died in Fez and was buried either in Fez or in the village of Banū Walīd, where his tomb is the site of an annual celebration. His descendants in Fez claim to be *sharīfs*.[38]

There is some uncertainty regarding the date of al-Walīdī's death. The biographical dictionaries all state that he died in 675/1276–77. But al-ʿImrānī, the modern

[36] Ibid., vol. 8, 10, ll. 11–23.

[37] *Al-Ḥalāl wa'l-Ḥarām*, ed. ʿAbd al-Raḥmān al-ʿImrānī al-Idrīsī (Rabat: Maṭbaʿat Faḍāla al-Muḥammadiyya, 1410/1990). The editor's introduction (5 ff.) contains an important clarification of the date on which al-Walīdī died.

[38] For biographical details, see Ibn al-Qāḍī, *Jadhwat al-iqtibās*, vol. 1, 196–7, no. 156; al-Tunbuktī, *Nayl al-ibtihāj*, 117; Makhlūf, *Shajarat al-nūr al-zakiyya*, vol. 1, 201, no. 685; and Manūnī, *Waraqāt*, 294, 302; regarding the place of his burial and the sharīfian status of his descendants, see *al-Ḥalāl wa'l-Ḥarām*, 44–8.

editor of *al-Ḥalāl wa'l-Ḥarām*, has recently demonstrated that this date cannot be correct. Based upon a careful examination of manuscripts, he has shown that al-Walidī himself stated in the colophon to an autograph manuscript of *al-Ḥalāl wa'l-Ḥarām* that he began work on the treatise on 1 Shawwāl 681/2 January 1283 and completed it on 5 Rabīʿ II 684/11 June 1285; another manuscript of the same text contains al-Walīdī's signature and is dated 26 Jumādā II 689/6 July 1290. The editor further notes that the *Miʿyār* of al-Wansharīsī contains another fatwā of al-Walīdī, issued on 17 Rabīʿ I 688/10 April 1289. Al-ʿImrānī concludes that al-Walīdī's life definitely extended beyond 675/1276–77, perhaps until 695/1295–96 (he speculates that a copyist may have changed "ninety-five" to "seventy-five").[39]

The detective work performed by al-ʿImrānī is helpful to our investigation, for we know that al-Walīdī's fatwā was issued *after* that of al-Waryāghlī. And we have already speculated that al-Waryāghlī did not issue his fatwā until 683/1284–85, the year of a major drought in the Maghrib. The determination that al-Walīdī did not die until *ca.* 695/1295–96 supports our assumption that al-Waryāghlī's fatwā was issued during the drought year of 683/1284–85.

Be that as it may, al-Walīdī's fatwā was very short, amounting to a footnote to the fatwā of al-Waryāghlī. First, he asserted that the latter's response was legally sound (*ṣaḥīḥ*). Then, taking as indisputable, for reasons not specified, the historical precedence of the downstreamers, al-Walīdī added the following specification: the upstream community is entitled to whatever surplus remains only after the downstream community has irrigated its ancient trees (*ghurūs al-asfaliyyīn al-qadīma*).[40] Like al-Waryāghlī, al-Walīdī cited no authoritative sources.

The Fatwā of al-Ṣughayyir (d. 719/1319)

The next fatwā in our corpus was issued by another sufi jurist Abū al-Ḥasan ʿAlī b. Muḥammad b. ʿAbd al-Ḥaqq al-Yāliṣūṭī al-Zarwīlī, known as al-Ṣughayyir (d. 719/1319), whom we have already encountered in chapter two. As a young man al-Ṣughayyir had studied with both al-Waryāghlī and al-Walīdī, and he went on to become qāḍī of Tāzā and later chief qāḍī of Fez. By the end of his life, he was widely recognized as the outstanding jurist of his generation.[41]

Al-Ṣughayyir's fatwā differs from those of his predecessors in three respects. First, he mentioned the names of the two communities involved in the dispute: Ahl Zgane, the upstream community, and Ahl Mazdgha, the downstream community. Second, he began his response by introducing an issue not raised by either al-Waryāghlī or al-Walīdī: appropriation of the water. And, third, he attempted to establish the legitimacy of his answer by referring to earlier authorities.

[39] *Al-Ḥalāl wa'l-Ḥarām*, 42–51.
[40] *Miʿyār*, vol. 8, 11, ll. 1–3.
[41] For biographical details, see chapter two, note 23.

Al-Ṣughayyir began by identifying an assumption held by al-Waryāghlī and al-Walīdī, namely that the disputed water had been appropriated by (*mutamallakan li-*) the residents of Zgane. Noting that this assumption had not been established by any legal test, al-Ṣughayyir asserted that if this assumption were correct, then the first two responses were legally valid and unambiguous. Certain possibilities had to be taken into consideration, however. If the upstream community had established its fields along the water before the downstream community had done so, or if both communities had established their fields simultaneously (*maʿan*), then the upstream community would enjoy a right or entitlement (*ḥaqq*) in proportion to its needs (*kifāya*),[42] after the satisfaction of which any surplus water should be allowed to descend to the downstream community. As textual authority for this point, the muftī mentioned in passing a *sunna* of the Prophet with regard to a stream along which were located the communities of Mahzūr and Mudhaynīb.[43]

A second consideration was whether the upstream community had established its fields subsequent to those of the downstream community. In that case, the situation would be reversed, and the downstream community would have a right or entitlement to the water in proportion to its needs, after the satisfaction of which any remaining surplus might be used by the upstream community. As support for this point, al-Ṣughayyir referred to a transmission (*samāʿ*) of Muḥammad b. Mālik on the authority of Ibn al-Qāsim[44] in the chapter on diversion dams and rivers in the *ʿUtbiyya* of Abū ʿAbdallāh Muḥammad al-ʿUtbī (d. 255/869)[45] – without, however, repeating the text. Fortuitously, our source preserves a fatwā issued by ʿAbdallāh al-ʿAbdūsī approximately a century later, in the year 824/1421, in which al-ʿAbdūsī specified the text to which al-Ṣughayyir had only alluded.[46] Al-ʿAbdūsī's specification makes it possible to identify the relevant text in the commentary of

42 Presumably, "needs" refers to drinking and irrigation, but not milling.

43 For the correct reading of these toponyms, see *Miʿyār*, vol. 13, additions and corrections. It is narrated that the Prophet decreed concerning the flood water of Mahzūr [viz., a wadi in the Hijaz] that the water should be held back until it reaches the ankles, and that the nearest [to the water] should take it first and then let the water pass through to the one below. See Mālik b. Anas, *al-Muwaṭṭaʾ*, ed. Muḥammad Fuʾād ʿAbd al-Bāqī, 2 vols (Cairo: Dār Iḥyāʾ al-Kutub al-ʿArabī, 1370/1951), vol. 2, 744; no. 28; Abū Dāʾūd, *Sunan*, ed. Muḥammad Muḥyī al-Dīn ʿAbd al-Ḥamīd, 4 vols (2nd edn, Cairo: al-Maktabah al-Tijāriyya al-Kubrā, 1369/1950), vol. 3, 429, no. 3638; Ibn Māja, *Sunan*, ed. Muḥammad Fuʾād ʿAbd al-Bāqī (Cairo: ʿĪsā al-Bābī al-Ḥalabī, 1972), vol. 2, 829, no. 2481.

44 Text: "Muḥammad b. Khālid b. Abī al-Qāsim" (*Miʿyār*, vol. 8, 19, l. 5). Cp. *Miʿyār*, vol. 8, 16, l. 19, where the reading is "Muḥammad b. Mālik on the authority of Ibn al-Qāsim". I follow the latter reading.

45 Al-ʿUtbī was a Cordovan jurist who studied in North Africa under Saḥnūn and Aṣbagh. The *ʿUtbiyya* is available in the commentary of Abū al-Walīd Ibn Rushd, *al-Bayān wa'l-taḥṣīl wa'l-sharḥ wa'l-tawjīh wa'l-taʿlīl fī masāʾil al-mustakhrajah*, ed. Muḥammad Ḥajjī and Aḥmad al-Sharqāwī Iqbāl, 20 vols (2nd edn, Beirut: Dār al-Gharb al-Islāmī, 1408/1988). For biographical details on al-ʿUtbī, see Ibn Farḥūn, *Dībāj*, 238; Makhlūf, *Shajarat al-nūr*, vol. 1, 75, no. 110; Henry Toledano, *Judicial Practice and Family Law in Morocco: The Chapter on Marriage from Sijilmāsī's al-ʿAmal al-Muṭlaq* (Boulder: Social Science Monographs, 1982), 64, note 52; Francisco Vidal Castro, "El *Miʿyār* de al-Wanšarīsī (m. 914/1508). I: Fuentes, manuscritos, ediciones, traducciones," in *Miscelánea de Estudios Árabes y Hebráicos*, vols XLII–XLIII (1993–94), 317–61, esp. 334–5; Ana Fernández Feliz, "Biografias de al faquies: la generación de al-ʿUtbī," in *Estudios onomástico-biográficos de al-Andalus* (Madrid: CSIC, 1996), VIII, 141–75.

46 *Miʿyār*, vol. 8, 19, ll. 5–21.

Ibn Rushd al-Jadd (d. 520/1126)[47] on the *ʿUtbiyya*, entitled *al-Bayān wa'l-taḥṣīl*:

> I [viz., Muḥammad b. Mālik] asked him [viz., Ibn al-Qāsim] about a man who has water with which he irrigates, and of which there is a surplus. Subsequently, some people plant trees (*ghirās*) with the surplus water, on the basis of a gift from him (*bi-ʿaṭiyya minhu*), and they "feed" the trees (*ghars*). Subsequently, the possessor of the water (*ṣāḥib al-māʾ*) wants to deny them [the water]. He [viz., Ibn al-Qāsim] said, "He may not do that unless he has a need for it, in which case, he has a greater right to it than they do."[48]

In his commentary on this text, Ibn Rushd qualified the statement of Ibn al-Qāsim by focusing on the language that the possessor of the water may have used when making the gift:

> Muḥammad Ibn Rushd said: The analogy (*qiyās*) in this case is as follows: the possessor of the water (*ṣāḥib al-māʾ*) does not have the right to deny them his surplus, even if he has a need for it, because he had given it to them [as a gift]. However, the proper understanding of this, in my opinion, is that, if he did not make a public declaration of his gift of the surplus to them, but only said, "Plant with the surplus of my water," or "Take the surplus of my water and plant with it," then he has the right to say, "It was my desire only that he take it in the form of a gratuitous concession (*al-ʿāriyya*), until such time as I have a need for it, or so long as I have no need for it." In that case, he swears an oath to this effect, and he takes it, if and when he needs it. As for the case in which he made a public declaration of the gift (*ʿaṭiyya*) or the present (*hiba*), by saying, "I have given you (*wahabtuka*) the surplus of my water" or "I have given it to you (*aʿṭaytuka*)," he does not have the right to take it from them, even if he needs it. Had he made a public declaration of a gratuitous concession (*ʿāriyya*), he would have the right to take it back, if the period of time stipulated for [the concession] had expired; and [also] if a period of time had expired that one would consider to be the period of the gratuitous concession, if no period of time had been stipulated.
>
> Ibn Abī Zayd [al-Qayrawānī][49] said: His words, "On the basis of a gift" (*bi-ʿaṭiyya*), signify a gratuitous concession (*ʿāriyya*) without transfer of ownership (*tamlīk*), and a gratuitous concession, according to this [interpretation] is perpetual, except if a need for it arises. However, [if] those [people] expended and planted with his knowledge, and they have no other water, it is like a conveyance (*taslīm*). God knows best." This is the opinion of Ibn Abī Zayd.
>
> He [viz., Ibn Rushd] said, "I am familiar with a similar opinion that is attributed to Saḥnūn (d. 240/854). God is the master (*walī*) of success."[50]

Taking for granted his audience's familiarity with these passages, al-Ṣughayyir explained their underlying reasoning (*wajh*), as follows: If the downstream

[47] Abū al-Walīd Muḥammad b. Aḥmad Ibn Rushd, a famous Mālikī jurist of Cordova. His fatwās have been published as *Fatāwā Ibn Rushd* (Beirut: Dār al-Gharb al-Islāmī, 1987). See Ibn al-Qāḍī, *Jadhwat al-iqtibās*, vol. 1, 254–5, no. 259; Ibn Farḥūn, *Dībāj*, 278; Makhlūf, *Shajarat al-nūr*, vol. 1, 129, no. 376; Toledano, *Judicial Practice*, 52, note 3.

[48] Ibn Rushd, *al-Bayān wa'l-taḥṣīl*, vol. 10, 319, ll. 14–17; cp. *Miʿyār*, vol. 8, 19, ll. 5–8.

[49] Ibn Abī Zayd al-Qayrawānī (d. 386/996) was an early Mālikī jurist renowned for his mastery of Mālik's teachings. Of his many writings, the most famous is the *Risāla*, which has been the subject of many commentaries. See Ibn Farḥūn, *Dībāj*, 136–8; Makhlūf, *Shajarat al-nūr*, vol. 1, 96, no. 227; Toledano, *Judicial Practice*, 27, note 66.

[50] Ibn Rushd, *al-Bayān wa'l-taḥṣīl*, vol. 10, 319 (l. 18)–20 (l. 13); cp. *Miʿyār*, vol. 8, 19, ll. 8–22.

community established its fields prior to those of the upstream community, then it established a right to use the water in proportion to its irrigation needs; the upstream community could not come along subsequently and alter the status quo by creating a new situation that would nullify the downstream community's entitlement to the water, as established by its extended possession (*ḥawz*). To this statement of law al-Ṣughayyir added a statement of fact: it had been established (*wa-qad thabata*) that the residents of Mazdgha planted their trees along the wadi in the distant past (*fī sālif al-aḥqāb*) and that they had irrigated their gardens with that water for generations (*fī ajyāl inṣaramat wa-aʿṣār inqaḍat*). Although no one knew which community had been the first to establish its gardens along the wadi, one may postulate that if the residents of Mazdgha had been the first to do so, they would not have allowed this right to be taken away from them on the basis of something doubtful.[51]

Al-Ṣughayyir concluded by emphasizing that the texts that had been cited referred only to water that had been appropriated and not to unappropriated water or to water whose source is unknown.

Stage II Description of the Wadi by Eyewitnesses: (mid-Rabīʿ I 721/9–19 April 1321)

Relations between the residents of Zgane and Mazdgha no doubt deteriorated in the year 721/1321, when the far Maghrib began to suffer from a drought that would last for five years.[52] The closing statement by al-Ṣughayyir regarding appropriation of the water pointed to the need for greater certainty regarding the "facts" of the case – to wit, which community had been the first to appropriate the water by means of different hydraulic devices and to use it for the purposes of irrigation? For this reason, in Rabīʿ I 721/April 1321 the chief qāḍī of Fez sent expert witnesses to survey the disputed area, accompanied by a delegation of residents from Zgane and Lower Mazdgha (*Mazdagha al-suflā*). The expert witnesses walked the wadi from top to bottom, studied its topography and hydrology and produced a detailed micro-level, description of the wadi that transports the modern investigator directly into the disputed area.[53] Their report makes it

[51] Ibid., vol. 8, 11 (l. 23)–12 (l. 5).

[52] For details, see Ibn Abī Zarʿ, *Roudh el-Kartas*, 564–65; Benmira, "Qaḍāyā al-miyāh," 81–2.

[53] *Miʿyār*, vol. 8, 5 (l. 8)–8 (l. 11). The use of expert testimony was common in the fourteenth-century Mālikī legal system, especially in cases involving claims of damage in which it was necessary to distinguish among the possible causal factors those that were ancient (*qadīm*) and those that were recent (*muḥdath*). Experts served as indispensable auxiliaries of the qāḍī. To be decisive, their testimony had to satisfy two conditions: It must have been solicited expressly by the qāḍī himself, and it had to be consigned to writing. For this reason, upon completion of their assignment, the experts would draw up an affidavit and submit it to the qāḍī so that it became part of the court record. Relying on their powers of observation, experts served as the guarantors and mediators of a culture that was rooted in local conditions. Expert knowledge was produced by a hermeneutical process in which eyewitnessing served as the basis for making an inference (*istidlāl*) drawn from physical evidence or "traces" of the past. Experts used their powers of observation to identify,

possible to identify the type of irrigation system that was used in Wadi Zgane, to speculate about long-term technological changes, and to link these changes to the ongoing dispute between the two settlements.

In the preamble to the description, the authors of the report indicated that the wadi begins near the trees (*ghurūs*) of Majshar al-Qalʿ[54] and proceeds downstream past the fortress (*qalʿa*) of Zgane on the left and Umm Tidshāl on the right. Mazdgha was located further downstream in the direction of the Banū Wanghīl. The first field was located a distance of 200 m[55] below the water source and the fields continued along the downslope toward Mazdgha, with most of the trees being ancient (*qadīm*) – a key term with important legal ramifications. The terrain above and below the source was stony and hard (see figure 3.1).[56]

The bulk of the report was devoted to identifying the four main springs whose waters fed the wadi: the spring (*ʿayn*) of Zgane, which flows from above a rock in a pool at the beginning of the wadi and joins with the second and third springs, located to the right of the *aṣl* of the aforementioned rock, as one walks around it, and joins with a fourth spring in an area that is stony, hard, and uncultivated. At the confluence of these four springs, the depth of the water was one *masaḥḥa*.[57]

The water of this stream flowed along the bottom (*baṭn*) of the wadi until being raised by two diversion dams (*saddān*),[58] located to the right and left as the observer descends the wadi,[59] for the purpose of irrigating gardens (*jannāt*). From those dams there emerged canals (*rashūḥāt*) which carried the water further downstream until meeting a second source located 4 m above the wadi. This second source emerged from the lowest part of the gardens of Lamṭa,[60] near the *aṣl*

isolate and correctly interpret physical signs that might serve as "witnesses" in a litigation. Of course, the final decision in the case remained in the hands of the qāḍī. On this topic, see now Jean-Pierre van Staevel, "Savoir voir et le faire savoir: des relations entre qāḍī/s et experts en construction, d'après un auteur tunisois du VIIleme siècle," paper presented at the II Joseph Schacht Conference on Islamic Law, Granada, December 1997.

[54] A *majshar* is a privately owned, large estate. See Thomas F. Glick, *From Muslim Fortress to Christian Castle: Social and cultural change in medieval Spain* (Manchester and New York: Manchester University Press, 1995), 25.

[55] In the Arabic text, distances are measured in *bāʿ* (also known as *qāma*), which is equivalent to 4 canonical *els* = 199.5 cm or approximately 2 m. See Hinz, *Islamische masse und Gewichte*, 54.

[56] *Miʿyār*, vol. 8, 5, ll. 11–16.

[57] The term *masaḥḥa* is apparently a measurement of the depth of water, although I have been unable to identify it. See R.P.A. Dozy, *Supplément aux dictionnaires arabes*, 2 vols (Leiden: E.J. Brill, 1881), vol. 1, 634, s.v. s-ḥ-ḥ.

[58] The purpose of a diversion dam was, first, to slow down water, and, second, to raise it to a level suitable for diversion into an individual plot for the purpose of irrigation. On this term, see Glick, *Irrigation and Society in Medieval Valencia*, index, s.v. *açut*.

[59] Text: *al-hābiṭ*, literally, "the one who descends." I owe this understanding of the Arabic text to Qāḍī Aḥmad Nāṭūr.

[60] Lamṭa is the name of a southern Berber tribe that occupied the area around Sijilmāsa, some members of which had migrated to the Wadi Sebou, near Fez, in the time of al-Idrīsī (d. *ca.* 560/1165. Lamṭa is a branch of the Ṣanhāja tribe, known as Ṣanhājat al-Jabal, that is, Ṣanhāja of the Middle Atlas mountains. At least two of the jurists involved in the present dispute belonged to this tribe. See Abū ʿAbdallāh Muḥammad al-Idrīsī, *Nuzhat al-mushtāq fī ikhtirāq al-āfāq*, partial translation by R.P.A. Dozy and M.J. de Goeje, *Description de l'Afrique et de l'Espagne par Edrisi* (Leiden: E.J. Brill, 1866; reprinted, 1968), 56–60, 70, 81 (Arabic).

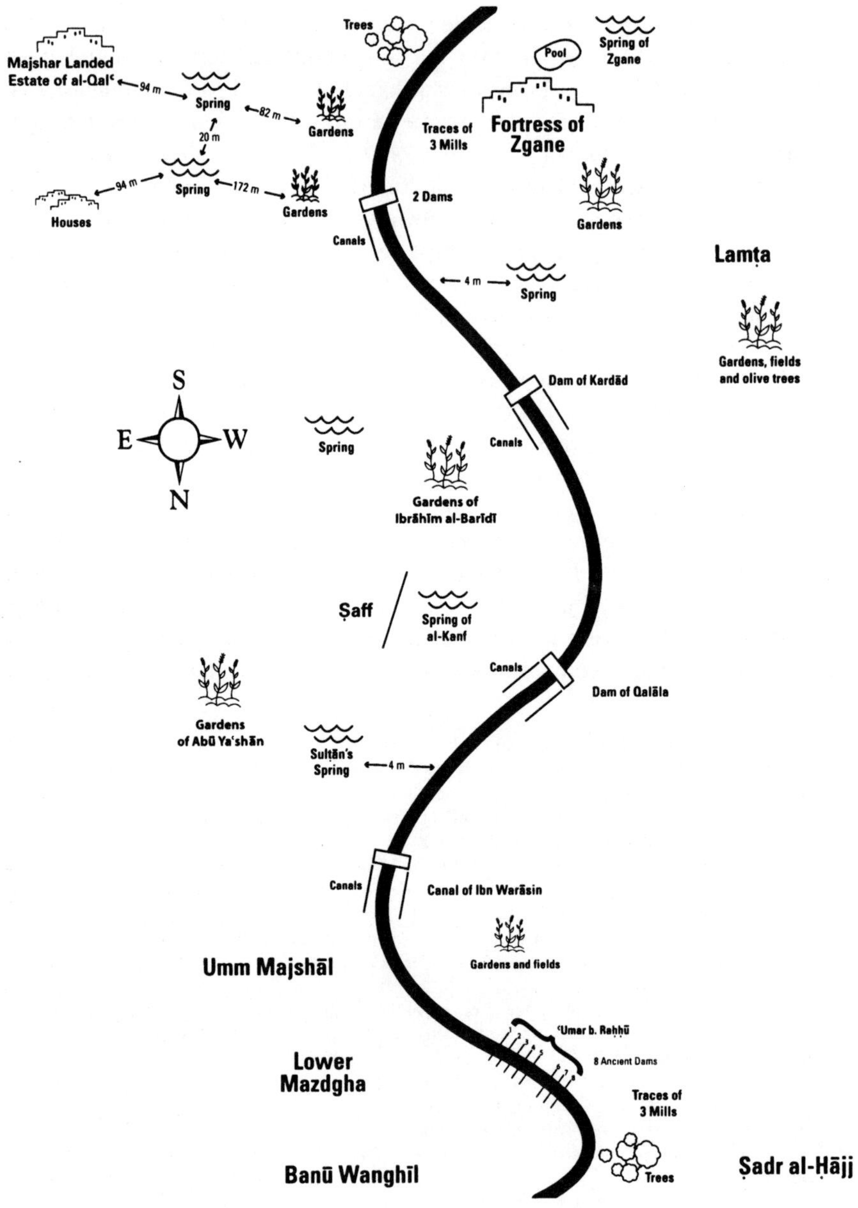

Figure 3.2 Diagram of Wadi Zgane

of one of its trees, in an area that is not suitable for irrigation. At this point the water was one-quarter of a *masaḥḥa* deep. The aforementioned canals joined with the second source and the water flowed downstream until being raised by the diversion dam of Kardād, which provided the fortress of Zgane with water to irrigate gardens, feddans, and olive groves. From the diversion dam of Kardād there emerged additional canals that flowed along the bottom of the wadi until joining with still more canals.[61]

The second and third sources, which were 20 m apart, were located in fertile land under a river bluff in Majshar al-Qalʿ. Of these two sources, the upper was one-quarter as deep as the lower, and together their waters were more than one *masaḥḥa* deep. The water of these two sources was used to irrigate gardens. The distance between the upper source and the gardens that it irrigated was approximately 82 m, while the distance between the lower source and the gardens that it irrigated was approximately 172 m. Also, the lower source was approximately 94 m from the nearest of the houses adjacent to Majshar al-Qalʿ. The water of these two sources came together in the wadi where they were raised by a diversion dam for the purpose of irrigating gardens and feddans. From this diversion dam there emerged canals that flowed along the bottom of the wadi until joining with the two canals that descended from the diversion dam of Kardād (see above). From this point, the three sources flowed together along the bottom of the wadi until reaching ʿAyn al-Kanf. Although the water here was more than one *masaḥḥa* deep, it could not be used to irrigate "that which emerges from its *aṣl*."[62]

The three sources continued to flow collectively until being raised by the diversion dam of Qalāla – here the text specifies that the irrigation channel [*sāqiya*] of this diversion dam passed by Majshar [al-Qalʿ] in the vicinity of the fortress [of Zgane], beyond Īmkūdān – for the purpose of irrigating gardens, feddans, and olive groves. From the diversion dam of Qalāla there emerged canals that flowed along the bottom of the wadi until joining the waters of ʿAyn al-Sulṭān, which were approximately 4 m above the bottom of the wadi, at a point where the water was one *masaḥḥa* deep. This source emerged from below the gardens of Abū Yaʿshān in an area that was not suitable for irrigation. From ʿAyn al-Sulṭān the waters flowed along the bottom of the wadi until reaching the irrigation channel (*sāqiya*) of Ibn Warāsin (which was divided into smaller irrigation channels for the purpose of irrigating gardens and numerous feddans). At this point the water was one *masaḥḥa* deep and it flowed along the bottom of the wadi until being raised by eight diversion dams located to the right and left of the observer who descends the wadi, near Umm Majshāl.[63] All eight of these dams were used for irrigation. Of the eight dams, five were owned by ʿUmar b. Raḥḥū,[64] and the other three were located between, on the one hand, properties belonging to him and, on

[61] *Miʿyār*, vol. 8, 5 (l. 16)–6 (l. 14).
[62] Ibid., vol. 8, 7, l. 2.
[63] Cp. ibid., vol. 8, 5, l. 12, where the text reads "Tidshāl."
[64] See Lagardère, *Histoire et Société*, 334, no. 179, where the reading is "Bardaḥ."

the other, Mazdgha. Finally at the bottom of the wadi, near the first fields of Mazdgha, there was a small amount of water that was "cut off in its course."[65]

At this point in the report, the expert witnesses specified that they had observed, to the right and to the left of the fields of Mazdgha, a total of twelve diversion dams – all of them "ancient" (*qadīma*) – that were used to raise water from the bottom of the wadi. Of these twelve dams, nine were used for irrigation and three were used to operate mills (*arḥā*), traces (*āthār*) of which were visible to the naked eye.[66]

Finally, the experts mentioned a fourth source, a youthful spring (*ʿayn yāfiʿa*),[67] located to the left as the observer descends the wadi, between Majshar al-Qalʿ and the diversion dam of Qalāla, located on an estate (*amlāk*) on which the gardens of Ibrāhīm al-Barīdī were located.[68] The water here was several *masaḥḥas* deep and was used to irrigate gardens (*jinān* and *jannāt*). Regarding the water here the experts specified that "the most that it can do is to irrigate those gardens when they are in need of irrigation; but when there is no need to irrigate, it has no outlet (*mawqiʿ*), except the bottom of the aforementioned wadi."[69]

After completing their topographical description, the witnesses turned their attention specifically to the hydraulic devices and the fields. With regard to the devices, they specified that during their examination of the wadi they had observed the traces (*āthār*) of three ancient mills located near the fields of Mazdgha and the traces of three mills near the fortress of Zgane. But they did not find, apart from the water, anything else that could be utilized, nor did they find, as they seem to have expected, any trace of an irrigation channel (*sāqiya*) that enters the aforementioned wadi, with the exception of traces of a few more recent channels coming from the direction of Ṣadr al-Ḥājj, below the fields of Mazdgha. And, again apparently contrary to their expectations, they found no trace of a very ancient irrigation channel (remaining signs apparently had been obliterated and the channel's lines effaced) coming from above Mazdgha, to the right of the depression (*khandaq*) that surrounds the settlement, until the channel supposedly fell into the depression, in the midst of the fields of Mazdgha.[70]

As for orchards, the experts specified that, except for a small number of trees between Zgane, Umm Majshāl (*sic*), and Mazdgha, they had observed a continuous line of trees planted in the wadi.[71]

The expert witnesses concluded by verifying that everything that was recorded in the document was in accordance with their description of what they had observed and with what they knew about it. The document is dated the middle decade (that is, ten days) of Rabīʿ I 721/9–19 April 1321.[72]

From this report we learn that certain individuals who owned land in Wadi Zgane had invested substantial capital, resources, and energy in the construction

[65] *Miʿyār*, vol. 8, 6 (l. 14)–7 (l. 15). [66] Ibid., vol. 8, 7, ll. 15–18.
[67] I owe this understanding of the Arabic text to Qāḍī Aḥmad Nāṭūr.
[68] See above, note 18. [69] *Miʿyār*, vol. 8, 7, ll. 19–23.
[70] Ibid., vol. 8, 7 (l. 23)–8 (l. 7). [71] Ibid., vol. 8, 8, ll. 7–9.
[72] Ibid., vol. 8, 8, ll. 9–11.

not only of diversion dams but also of hydraulic devices that were designed to maximize the productivity and profitability of the water. The description also mentions several water-raising devices. And an extensive system of canals had been constructed to appropriate the water of the various springs and channel it into agricultural fields, before it spilled into the wadi. As noted, according to Islamic law, free-flowing water is essentially ownerless and the common property of all human beings, whereas water that has been appropriated by being placed in a canal, irrigation channel, or container, is considered to be owned by the person or persons who built the device. Thus, the wadi in question raised important legal questions about the intersection or points of contact between water that was owned or appropriated and water that was ownerless.

Interlude: Irrigation and the Castle/Village Complex

We must remark on the type of irrigation system that is reflected in our documentation. Geographers have identified three scales of irrigation systems common in the Mediterranean region: in macro-scale systems large irrigation works cover an area of 50 to 100 sq. km; meso-scale systems, found in mountain villages and hamlets, draw water from springs or small rivers and cover an area of 15 to 125 ha; and micro-scale irrigation is practiced in small terraced parcels (around 1 ha in area), using tanks or cisterns to store water from minor springs.[73] The irrigation system of Wadi Zgane is clearly a meso-scale system.

Meso-scale irrigation systems in the Mediterranean typically are associated with what historians and archaeologists have identified as a "castle/village complex". Such a complex is composed of three structural elements, all present in the Wadi Zgane irrigation system: a castle (*ḥiṣn* or *qalʿa*), one or more villages, and irrigation. The castle overlooks the complex and the village is located at the edge of the irrigated area, at the point of contact with unirrigated fields.[74] In al-Andalus, there was a further correlation between meso-scale irrigation systems, castle/village complexes, and social organization: villages in Andalusian meso-scale irrigation systems generally were established by Berbers from the Maghrib and were organized along tribal lines according to patterns of segmentary social organization.[75] Residents of a particular village were members of the same tribal segment, were dependent for protection on the castle and its occupant, and made common use of the irrigation system. In this manner, the residents constituted not

[73] See Glick, *Muslim Fortress*, 65, citing Karl W. Butzer et al., "Irrigation Agrosystems in Eastern Spain: Roman or Islamic Origins?", *Annals of the Association of American Geographers*, 75 (1985), 479–509, esp. 486–99.

[74] Glick, *Muslim Fortress*, 84 (drawing on the scholarship of P. Guichard, A. Bazzana, and P. Cressier). Note: according to Glick, the castle/village complex was notably absent in Morocco (ibid., 29). The evidence of the present investigation serves as a counter-example. Indeed, the Almoravids are known to have built castles in an effort to control the Middle Atlas mountains.

[75] Ibid., 13–29, 176–7.

only a tribal but also a political solidarity. The organization of the irrigation system was directly related to the segmentary social organization of its users.[76] All of this was no doubt true of the Zgane castle/village complex.

In a typical Andalusian meso-scale irrigation system, villages had terraced fields irrigated by one or more springs, and one finds many hydraulic devices in combination: cisterns, *shadufs*, norias and clepsydras.[77] An intricate system of canals, arranged in distinct sectors, provided irrigation water to individual tribal segments or clans. The local community controlled the operation of the system. Conflicts were regulated at the local level according to Berber customary law, which, significantly, accords *absolute priority* to upstream irrigators over downstream irrigators; the settlement whose canal is located furthest upstream might divert the entire debit of the river at that point. Indeed, according to Berber law, the upstream irrigator is not required to return unused water to the stream for the use of those further downstream. On this point, Berber law diverges sharply from Islamic law (see above). Local agreements were often ratified by the qāḍī or the sulṭān.[78]

If more than one village drew water from the same watercourse, some form of political organization was required in order to negotiate agreements among the villages. Even when villages were linked in this manner, the irrigation system continued to be administered according to the norms of tribal segmentary society. Although the hydraulic devices of the system might be simple, their design, internal distribution arrangements, and measurement systems, were complex. Even the smallest irrigation system was part of a complex regional arrangement.[79]

The people who controlled these castle/village complexes were resourceful. They had ideas about water and its use and possessed the technological knowledge and skills to design irrigation systems that were appropriate for their own form of social organization. And the villagers knew how to pursue their own interests by using the legal system to resist technological changes that threatened the status quo.[80]

Technological change may be one key to understanding the dispute between the residents of Zgane and Mazdgha. Irrigation systems typically display hyperstability, that is, the appearance of immutability and permanence.[81] Over time, however, change and innovation do in fact occur. The experts sent by the qāḍī to provide an eyewitness description of the wadi we are studying were interested in evidence of initial development and in signs of change. Thus, they noted the existence of "traces" (*āthār*) of three ancient mills located near the fields of Mazdgha and of three mills near the fortress of Zgane. The mills in question presumably were simple horizontal mills like those typically found massed along small streams, not the expensive, geared vertical mills found along large rivers.[82]

[76] Ibid., 67–9. [77] Ibid., 76, citing Butzer, "Irrigation Agrosystems," 491–6.

[78] Glick, *Muslim Fortress*, 75 and 81, citing Vincent Lagardère, *Campagnes et paysans d'Al-Andalus (VIIIe–XVe s.)* (Paris: Maisonneuve et Larose, 1993), 285. See also Abdellah Herzenni, "Derechos de agua de riego en Marruecos. Ley musulmana, normas consuetudinarias y legislacion moderna," in *El agua. Mitos, ritos y realidades*, ed. Jose A. Gonzalez Alcantud and Antonio Malpica Cuello (Barcelona, Anthropos, 1995), 401–40. I am grateful to Professor Thomas Glick for bringing this source to my attention.

[79] Glick, *Muslim Fortress*, 85. [80] Ibid., 91. [81] Ibid., 76. [82] Ibid., 117.

Milling and irrigation may operate at cross-purposes in a small-scale irrigation system in which the volume of available water is finite and limited. There are at least two ways to regulate the relationship between these two activities: one is to regulate the placement of the mill in the irrigation system. Different societies do this differently. In medieval Europe, where feudal rents were demanded in grain, irrigation was subsidiary to milling: thus, the mill was generally located at the top of the water diversion system so that the first canal in the system delivered water to the mill. In the Islamic world, by contrast, milling was subsidiary to irrigation, and the mill was located at the bottom, or tail, of the system so that the last canal in the system delivered water to the mill. Over time, the balance between irrigation and milling may be upset by the construction of one or more new mills further upstream.

A second way to regulate the relationship between milling and irrigation is through the establishment of priorities. Thus, local custom may dictate that the use of water for irrigation takes priority over the use of water for milling activities, or vice versa.[83]

Constructed during the Almohad period, if not before, the Wadi Zgane irrigation system appears to have been originally designed as a tail-ender. However, during the early Marīnid period, landowners in the vicinity of Zgane added three new mills further upstream, with the result that there was not always a sufficient volume of water to operate the downstream mills. Over time, the downstream mills went out of use and, by 721/1321, were apparent only as "traces." Clearly, the upstream community had established itself as the more efficient user of the water.

Stage III: The Qāḍī as Notary (738–39/1338–39)

Seventeen years after the expert testimony had been recorded in the dispute between the residents of Zgane and Mazdgha, there was a flurry of judicial activity relating to the documentation. One of the parties to the conflict requested that a copy be made of the original eyewitness description of the wadi. A scribe executed this request and submitted the copy to the chief qāḍī of Fez, ʿAbdallāh b. Aḥmad b. Muḥammad al-Azdī,[84] who compared the copy to the original for exactness. After verifying that the original was authentic and that the copy was identical to it, al-Azdī summoned witnesses to attest to the legal validity of the copy. This took place "in the seat of his jurisdiction and the court of his ruling" in Fez during the middle ten days of Dhū al-Qaʿda 738/31 May–9 June 1338.[85]

It will be recalled that some time prior to his death in *ca.* 695/1295–96, al-Walīdī had issued a short fatwā in which he held that the downstream community enjoyed priority with regard to use of the water to irrigate its "ancient planted trees" and

[83] Ibid., 70–1; cf. David Guillet, "Rethinking Legal Pluralism: Local Law and State Law in the Evolution of Water Property Rights in Northwestern Spain," *Comparative Studies in Society and History* (1998), 42–65.

[84] I am unable to identify this qāḍī.

[85] *Miʿyār*, vol. 8, 8, ll. 13–17.

that the upstream community was entitled only to whatever surplus remained after that. Now, more than forty years later, one of the parties to the dispute – no doubt the current residents of the downstream community of Mazdgha – brought forward al-Walīdī's fatwā and requested that it be certified and copied. On 25 Ramaḍān 739/6 April 1339, two witnesses gave testimony regarding al-Walīdī's death and verified that the handwriting of the fatwā attributed to him was in fact his, "without any doubt or uncertainty being attached to that."[86] Then, after a scribe had produced a copy of the fatwā, the legal validity of the copy was certified by al-Azdī. This, too, took place in the court of his jurisdiction and the seat of his judgment in Fez, at the end of the month of Ramaḍān 739/mid-April 1339.[87]

In addition, a copy was made of al-Ṣughayyir's longer fatwā after witnesses had examined the original and determined that it was in his handwriting. The copy was compared to the original for exactness and its legal validity was certified in the court of the chief qāḍī at the end of the month of Ramaḍān 739/mid-April 1339.[88]

This information indicates that one function of the qāḍī's court was to serve as a clearinghouse for the notarization of legal documents.

Stage IV: Additional Judicial Activity and Two Fatwās (*ca.* 744–50/1343–50)

On the strength of the fatwās issued by al-Ṣughayyir and al-Walīdī and subsequently certified by the chief qāḍī of Fez, al-Azdī, the residents of the downstream community of Mazdgha continued to use the water as they had in the past. In Muḥarram 744/May–June 1343, however, the residents of Zgane apparently manipulated the stream in such a manner as to cut off the supply of water to Mazdgha. Several months later, the northern part of the far Maghrib was afflicted by drought, and, in 746/1345, when the situation became intolerable for the residents of Mazdgha, they appeared in court armed with a *rasm istirʿā'*, which, as we have seen, is a document containing the testimony of professional witnesses regarding a certain fact or facts – here, the continuous use of water by the residents of Mazdgha – that might be produced in an hour of need.[89] This document reads as follows:

> The witnesses whose names are mentioned following its date testify that the water that descends from the springs of Zgane to the Wadi of Mazdgha b. Ḥandūsh,[90] which belongs to the jurisdiction (*naẓar*) of Sefrou and to the regions (*aḥwāz*) of Fez al-Maḥrūsa [viz., protected by God], has been utilized continuously by the residents of the aforementioned Mazdgha, by night and by day, during the entirety of the period of time during which they have been alive (*adrakūhu bi-aʿmārihim*) and understood with their

[86] Ibid., vol. 8, 11, ll. 5–6. The witnesses are identified as Yūsuf b. Isḥāq b. Ibrāhīm al-Ṣanhājī and ʿAbd al-Samīʿ b. Abī Zayd al-Walīdī (perhaps a relative of the muftī).
[87] Ibid., vol. 8, 11, ll. 9–11. [88] Ibid., vol. 8, 12, ll. 10–16.
[89] On *rasm istirʿā'*, see chapter one, note 35. [90] I have been unable to identify Ibn Ḥandūsh.

> intelligences (*fahimū fīhi bi-ʿuqūlihim*). They use the aforementioned water to irrigate their gardens, olive [groves,] and fruit [trees], and they also use [it] to operate their mills [which are located] along the course of the aforementioned wadi, across the length of the entire aforementioned wadi, by night and by day. [This was the situation] until the residents of the aforementioned Zgane cut off the aforementioned water (*qaṭaʿū al-māʾ al-madhkūr*) from the residents of the aforementioned Mazdgha approximately two years prior to the date [of this document.] This [is from] those who have knowledge of this, in its entirety, in accordance with what is stipulated in writing, and the essence of what was described was verified.[91]

This document, dated the middle ten days of Muḥarram 746/14–24 March 1345, establishes that, for as long as anyone could remember, the residents of Mazdgha had made continuous use of the waters of the wadi to irrigate their gardens, olive groves, and fruit trees and to operate mills belonging to them which were located along the course of the wadi.[92]

The residents of Zgane continued to deny water to Mazdgha, and, in late Jumādā I 748/early September 1347, residents of the downstream settlement took their case to the court of the chief qāḍī of Fez, Muḥammad b. ʿAbd al-Razzāq al-Jazūlī (d. 758/1357).[93] They were careful to bring all supporting documentation and any witnesses who were alive and available, including those connected to the aforementioned *rasm istirʿāʾ*. The chief qāḍī summoned additional witnesses, and all present testified as follows:

> They recorded [the water] on their behalf (*ʿayyanū lahum*), at the time of their taking possession of it (*ʿinda ḥiyāzatihim lahu*), and their recording of it on their behalf (*taʿayyunuhum iyyāhu*) – [namely,] that water that we took possession of on your (pl.) behalf (*ḥaznāhu lakum*), we specified it (*ʿayyannāhu*) in your minutes (*maḥḍar*) – this is [the water] about which we testified in that which is included in the aforementioned document, and we gave our testimony with regard to that, being sound [of mind and body,] voluntarily, legally [capable of conducting our affairs,] and he identified them.[94]

The testimony of these witnesses was certified in the court of al-Jazūlī during the last ten days of Jumādā I 748/29 August–7 September 1347.

Approximately one month later, on 24 Jumādā II 748/1 October 1347, al-Jazūlī summoned witnesses to attest to the legal validity of the *rasm istirʿāʾ*, dated Muḥarram 746/March 1345, and to the "sufficiency" (*iktifāʾ*) of the second document, dated Jumādā I 748/August–September 1347.[95]

[91] *Miʿyār*, vol. 8, 8 (l. 24)–9 (l. 6). [92] Ibid., vol. 8, 9, ll. 6–8.

[93] For biographical details, see Ibn Qunfudh, *Sharaf al-Ṭālib*, in *Alf sana min al-wafayāt fī thalātha kutub*, ed. M. Ḥajjī and M. Ḥajjī (Rabat: Dār al-Maghrib li'l-Ta'līf, 1396/1976), 82; Wansharīsī, *Wafayāt*, 122, Ibn al-Qāḍī al-Miknāsī, *Laqṭ al-farāʾid min lufāẓat ḥuqaq al-fawāʾid*, in *Alf sana min al-wafayāt fī thalātha kutub*, ed. M. Ḥajjī and M. Ḥajjī (Rabat: Dār al-Maghrib li'l-Ta'līf, 1396/1976), 209; idem, *Durrat al-Ḥijāl*, vol. 2, 266, no. 767; idem, *Jadhwat al-iqtibās*, vol. 1, 216–17, no. 183; Makhlūf, *Shajarat al-nūr*, vol. 1, 233, no. 833.

[94] *Miʿyār*, vol. 8, 9, ll. 10–16. The *maḥḍar* and the *sijill* are the two elements that make up the qāḍī's *dīwān*. The *maḥḍar* here appears to refer to a statement made by witnesses to the effect that someone had taken possession of water. See Wael B. Hallaq, "The Qāḍī's Dīwān (*sijill*) before the Ottomans," *Bulletin of the School of Oriental and African Studies*, 61:3 (1998), 415–36.

[95] *Miʿyār*, vol. 8, 9, ll. 16–18.

Subsequently, the qāḍī ʿAbdallāh b. ʿAbd al-Raḥmān b. Aḥmad al-Ṣanhājī[96] put into effect (*aʿmaltuhu*) the document specifying the assignment of the water to the residents of Mazdgha – after verifying the handwriting of the first and the third witnesses, who had died in the meantime, and declaring its authenticity (*istiqlāl).*[97]

These efforts by the residents of Mazdgha to establish their entitlement to the surplus water were apparently unsuccessful. Undeterred, they approached a qāḍī whose name is not specified in our source – in all likelihood al-Jazūlī, the chief qāḍī of Fez – and asked him to intervene on their behalf. After examining the evidence, the qāḍī formulated an *istiftāʾ* which he addressed to two muftīs, Muḥammad b. Miṣbāḥ b. Muḥammad b. ʿAbdallāh al-Yāliṣūtī (one of the most famous students of al-Ṣughayyir, who also bore the *nisba* al-Yāliṣūtī) and Abū Rabīʿ Sulaymān al-Sarīfī (not to be confused with Abū Isḥāq Ibrāhīm al-Sarīfī, a key figure in chapter two). Unfortunately, the fatwās are undated, but since the *istiftāʾ* refers to the fact that the upstream community already had cut off the supply of water to the downstream community, they probably were issued some time after Muḥarram 744/May–June 1343 and before 750/1349–50, the year in which both muftīs died. These two fatwās, which no doubt were issued at or about the same time, mark a dramatic shift in the ongoing struggle between the two settlements.

In his capacity as a *mustaftī*, the qāḍī who requested the fatwā began by identifying the two parties to the dispute: the residents of Zgane and the residents of Lower Mazdgha. After briefly describing the wadi and its sources, the *mustaftī* explained that, after passing through Zgane and Majshar al-Qalʿ, the water was utilized by the residents of Majshar Umm Majshāl (*sic*) by means of a system of diversion dams and canals to irrigate their fields, after which any remaining surplus descended to the residents of Mazdgha. The problem was as follows:

> At the present time, however, the residents of Zgane have raised the water in their diversion dams, in the manner that we have described, and nothing remains in the aforementioned wadi, except for a small amount that does not satisfy [the needs] of the residents of Mazdgha for [the irrigation of] their planted trees (*ghurūs*).[98]

In response to this action, the residents of Mazdgha demanded that the residents of Zgane release to them an amount of water that would be sufficient to irrigate their fields. However, the residents of Zgane refused, putting forward as evidence the fact that the water emerged from their land – as specified by the *mustaftī* in the question – and therefore belonged to them (*milkuhum*).

To the claim of ownership, the residents of Mazdgha responded by invoking the principle of historical priority: many years ago they had established their fields along

[96] Although I have been unable to identify this jurist in the biographical dictionaries, he is mentioned at ibid., vol. 7, 197, where he issued a judicial decision in late Rabīʿ II 792/early April 1390 in his capacity as the chief qāḍī of Fez.

[97] Ibid., vol. 8, 9 (l. 24)–10 (l. 1). On the terms *istaqalla* and *istiqlāl*, see Le Tourneau, "Documents sur une contestation relatives à la répartition de l'eau dans la medina de Fès," where we find: *istiqlāl*, "en possession de toutes ses facultés" (197); *istaqalla qābiluhā bi aṣlihā fa-māthaltuhu*, "Ensuite, le destinaire de cet acte en a gardé l'original et l'a reproduit (ibid.); and *bi-istiqlāl*, "il en possède de plein droit l'original ... " (198).

[98] *Miʿyār*, vol. 8, 13, ll. 5–6.

the banks of the wadi – obviously, using water from above – and these fields now contained mature trees. The residents of Zgane countered this objection by specifying the circumstances in which they had "allowed" their downstream neighbors to use the water: in former years, there had been a large supply of water that was more than sufficient for their irrigation needs. Having no need for the surplus – and not having the means to retain it – they had allowed it to descend to the residents of Mazdgha, who used the surplus to establish their fields and irrigate their trees.[99]

With respect to this factual situation, the *mustaftī* posed two questions. The first question was substantive: which claim (*ḥujja*) was stronger, the claim of historical precedence advanced by the residents of Mazdgha or the claim of ownership (*milk*) advanced by the residents of Zgane?[100] The second question was procedural: according to Mālikī judicial procedure, a defendant must be present in court so that the qāḍī can offer him an opportunity to present evidence on his own behalf (*iʿdhār*) before issuing a judgment.[101] In the present case, the two parties to the dispute – the residents of Zgane and those of Mazdgha – were numerous; indeed, their exact number was unknown. For this reason, it was impossible to determine who was present and who was absent, who was an adult and who was a minor. Further, some of the adult residents of the two settlements were subject to the authority of a guardian while others were not. Still others were women who were either married or widowed, that is, subject to the authority of a husband or guardian. In these circumstances, how was it possible for the qāḍī to know exactly who the defendants were so that he might offer them the opportunity to present evidence? How could he issue *any* judgment in such a case? In light of these procedural problems, the *mustaftī* made a critical observation, asking if it was appropriate to treat the present case like one in which the facts are equivocal and no decisive legal proof exists; in such instances, the qāḍī charges the litigants to conclude a *ṣulḥ*, or amicable settlement.[102] Only if they refuse to do so does the qāḍī intervene to impose a solution, after consulting with a distinguished jurist.[103]

[99] Ibid., vol. 8, 13, ll. 7–13.

[100] Ibid., vol. 8, 13, ll. 13–16.

[101] On the *iʿdhār*, see chapter one, note 46; cf. Farhat J. Ziadeh, "Compelling Defendant's Appearance at Court in Islamic Law," *Islamic Law and Society*, 3:3 (1996), 305–15.

[102] *Ṣulḥ* is defined by Ibn ʿArafa (d. 803/1400) as "the renunciation of a right or a claim in return for the cancellation of a litigation or to prevent its occurrence" (*intiqāl ʿan ḥaqq aw daʿwā bi-ʿiwaḍ li-rafʿ nizāʿ aw khawfi wuqūʿihi*). See Abū ʿAbdallāh Muḥammad al-Anṣārī (d. 894/1489), *Kitāb sharḥ ḥudūd al-Imām al-akbar al-baraka al-qudwa al-anwar Abī ʿAbdallāh b. ʿArafa* (Rabat: Wizārat al-Awqāf, 1412/1992), 439; cf. Santillana, *Istituzioni*, vol. 2, 210; on this institution, see further ibid., vol. 1, 105, 368; vol. 2, 209 ff.; see also Ibn Rushd, *Bidāyat al-Mujtahid*, vol. 2, 318–19 [= Ibn Rushd, *The Distinguished Jurist's Primer*, vol. 2, 353–4]; Schacht, *Introduction*, 148; Scholze, *Malikitisches Verfahrensrecht* (Frankfurt: Peter Lang), 440 ff.; Aharon Layish, *Divorce in the Libyan family: a study based on the* sijills *of the* sharīʿa *courts of Ajdābiyya and Kufra* (New York: New York University Press, 1991), 188. For a nineteenth-century water dispute from Fez in which a *ṣulḥ* was envisaged, see R. Le Tourneau, "Documents sur une contestation relatives à la répartition de l'eau dans la medina de Fès," 202, l. -2.

[103] *Miʿyār*, vol. 8, 13, ll. 16–24. Note: the *mustaftī* does not seem to have envisaged the possibility that the residents of each of the two communities might be represented by a *wakīl*, or legal agent.

After summarizing the dispute and formulating his questions, the *mustaftī* asked the two muftīs to respond, point-by-point, on the basis of the contents of earlier responses (*taḍmīn al-jawābāt*).[104]

The Fatwā of Miṣbāḥ al-Yāliṣūtī (d. 750/1349–50)[105]

Al-Yāliṣūtī obviously regarded the case as justiciable, for he completely ignored the second, procedural question (which is odd) and focused his attention entirely on the substantive issue raised by the *mustaftī*. As is typical of the fatwā genre, the muftī began with the proviso that his response was valid only if the facts of the case were as described by the *mustaftī*. The fatwā itself was short and to the point. After studying the matter, al-Yāliṣūtī identified as the critical issue the "fact" that the water emerged from land belonging to the residents of Zgane and therefore was owned by them, whereas the residents of Mazdgha had merely appropriated surplus water through the construction of canals. Adopting a position diametrically opposed to that of the three muftīs whose opinions we have already considered, al-Yāliṣūtī held strongly in favor of the residents of Zgane; in his view, the fact that the water was owned by the residents of Zgane entailed that it should be awarded (*yuqḍā*) to them. As for the residents of Mazdgha, their entitlement was limited to any remaining surplus, even if the volume of available water decreased to the point that it was sufficient only for the (unspecified) irrigation needs of the residents of Zgane. Moreover, the muftī continued, the residents of Zgane had the right to alter the status quo so that, if the water were plentiful, they could establish new fields and gardens, thereby increasing their demand for water; their entitlement to the amount of water required to satisfy the newly created demand was greater than the entitlement of the residents of Mazdgha to the original surplus needed to irrigate their fields.[106]

As textual support for this position, al-Yāliṣūtī invoked the authority of Ibn al-Qāsim and Ibn Rushd – the two authorities cited by al-Ṣughayyir but to different effect. A statement attributed to Ibn al-Qāsim, as transmitted by Muḥammad b. Mālik, appears to provide unequivocal support for al-Yāliṣūtī's holding: A man used surplus water belonging to someone else in order to plant something. Subsequently, the owner of the water needed the surplus for his own needs, and Ibn al-Qāsim held that he was entitled to the surplus.[107] Ibn Rushd, in his *Sharḥ*,[108]

104 Ibid., vol. 8, 14, ll. 1–3.
105 Some sources give this name as al-Yāṣlūtī. For biographical details see al-Wansharīsī, *Wafayāt*, 119; Ibn al-Qāḍī, *Laqṭ*, 203; idem, *Durrat al-Ḥijāl*, vol. 3, 17, no. 910; idem, *Jadhwat al-iqtibās*, vol. 1, 46, note 81; al-Tunbuktī, *Nayl*, 344. For other fatwās issued by this jurist, see *Mi'yār*, vol. 8, 14, 49–50; 9, 241–2, etc.
106 Ibid., vol. 8, 14, ll. 4–10.
107 Ibid., vol. 8, 14, ll. 11–12. Note the editor's correction of *mā'* to *rabb al-mā'*.
108 Probably a reference to Ibn Rushd's commentary on the *Mudawwana* entitled, *al-Muqaddimāt al-mumahhidāt li-bayān mā iqtaḍathu rusūm al-Mudawwana min al-aḥkām*.

affirmed Ibn al-Qāsim's opinion by articulating the only circumstances which would render the right of surplus to the planter instead of the owner:

> Unless the planter had acquired ownership (*malaka*) of that [water] by virtue of a gift from the possessor of the surplus (*rabb al-faḍl*), in which case the possessor of the water (*rabb al-māʾ*) may not prevent [him] from [using] that surplus – even if he is in need of it, because the other person has acquired ownership of it (*malakahu*) by virtue of the gift, in contradistinction to [the case in which] he plants something along [the water], and the possessor of the surplus remains silent.[109]

That is to say, if the residents of Zgane had explicitly gifted the surplus water to their downstream neighbors, then they might not subsequently deny them that water, whereas if they merely had been silent with respect to their downstream neighbors' usage of the water, they might subsequently deny them use of the surplus. No gift was established.

At this point, the fatwā ends abruptly, albeit with typical rhetorical flourish: "Success resides in the exalted God. Signed: Muḥammad b. Miṣbāḥ b. Muḥammad b. ʿAbdallāh al-Yāliṣūtī. May the most complete peace be upon you, and the mercy and blessings of the Exalted God."[110]

The Fatwā of al-Sarīfī (d. 750/1349–50)[111]

A second response to the same questions[112] was issued by Abū al-Rabīʿ Sulaymān b. ʿAbdūn al-Sarīfī, who based his response on two factual assumptions: first, that the residents of Zgane had established that the source (*aṣl*) of the water appropriated by them (*al-mutamallak*) was located on their land; and, second, that the only legal claim (*daʿwā*) entered by the residents of Mazdgha was that they had established their fields along the wadi many years earlier and had utilized (*intifāʿ*)[113] the water during the intervening period to irrigate their trees. If this were the case, al-Sarīfī reasoned, then there was no legal basis (*ḥujja*) to the argument put forward by the residents of Mazdgha because the mere act of taking possession (*ḥiyāza*) of water by someone who does not own it does not create an entitlement to it.[114] As support for this conclusion, al-Sarīfī invoked the authority of Ibn Rushd without any further specification.[115]

109 *Miʿyār*, vol. 8, 14, ll. 12–15.
110 Ibid., vol. 8, 14, ll. 16–17.
111 Biographical details on al-Sarīfī (alternatively, "al-Surayfī" or "al-Sharīfī"), also known as al-Lujāʾī, are limited. He is mentioned in the sources as the teacher of al-Wānghīlī al-Ḍarīr (d. 779/1377–78). On the latter, see Ibn al-Qunfudh, *Sharaf al-Ṭālib*, 86; Ibn al-Qāḍī, *Laqṭ*, 214; idem, *Jadhwat al-Iqtibās*, vol. 2, 424, no. 446. Al-Sarīfī reportedly introduced the *Mukhtaṣar* of Ibn al-Ḥājib into the Maghrib. His son, Abū Zayd ʿAbd al-Raḥmān, died in 773/1371–72.
112 *Miʿyār*, vol. 8, 14 (l. 19)–15 (l. 7).
113 On *intifāʿ* see Santillana, *Istituzioni*, vol. 1, 197, 404, 435, 458; vol. 2, 376 n. 17.
114 On *ḥiyāza* see ibid., vol. 1, 326, 330; vol. 2, 402, 432.
115 *Miʿyār*, vol. 8, 14, ll. 20–3.

Before concluding his response, al-Sarīfī drew attention to, and expanded upon, the issue of silence and its legal effects. In the final analysis, the case may be reduced to the silence (*sukūt*) of the residents of Zgane. However, the muftī explained, the legal effect of silence is disputed by Mālikī jurists. According to some, silence constitutes the granting of permission (*idhn*) to use; according to others, it does not. Following the former view, the silence of the residents of Zgane with regard to the use of the water by the residents of Mazdgha is equivalent to the granting of permission. Now the question arises, are the residents of Zgane entitled to revoke a grant of permission that resulted from their silence? The founding generation of Mālikī jurists gave different answers to this question: According to Mālik in the *Mudawwana*, the person who granted the permission is entitled to revoke it even if he does not establish a need for it, whereas according to Ibn al-Qāsim, the person who granted the permission may not revoke it unless he can establish a need for it. And, al-Sarīfī added, other – unspecified – opinions had been issued on this question.[116]

On the other hand, if one holds that silence does not constitute the granting of permission, then the owner of the water may take it after having sworn an oath to the effect that his silence did not constitute consent.[117]

Al-Sarīfī left his audience to draw the appropriate conclusions in the case at hand: According to the view that silence constitutes the granting of permission, the residents of Zgane are entitled to revoke the permission even if they do not have a need for it (following Mālik) or after having established a need for it (following Ibn al-Qāsim). According to the view that silence does not constitute the granting of permission, the residents of Zgane may take the water after swearing an oath. In a worst-case scenario the residents of Zgane must either establish their need for the water or swear an oath that their silence over the years did not constitute the granting of permission.

Stage V: Two Final Fatwās and an Implementation (*Iʿmāl*) (824/1421)

The Fatwā of al-ʿAbdūsī

We may assume that the residents of Zgane continued to exercise control over the wadi and its water, first satisfying their own irrigation needs and then allowing any surplus to pass downstream to the residents of Mazdgha. Any increase in the volume of water used by the residents of Zgane for irrigation or milling and/or any decrease in the level of rainfall would have had adverse consequences on the ability of the residents of Mazdgha to irrigate their trees.

116 Ibid., vol. 8, 15, ll. 1–5. On *sukūt* see Santillana, *Istituzioni*, vol. 1, 36.

117 *Miʿyār*, vol. 8, 15, ll. 5–6.

Our source contains no evidence of any further litigation for nearly seventy-five years following the issuance of the fatwās by al-Yāliṣūṭī and al-Sarīfī. This period, roughly the second half of Marīnid rule, was marked by a breakdown of central authority and a reported loss of central control over the countryside.[118] We know that the residents of the two communities were brought into conflict once again in the year 824/1421, at which time the documentary record resumes. We also know that from the end of the eighth/fourteenth century until the middle of the ninth/fifteenth century, the Maghrib, in general, and Fez and its surrounding countryside, in particular, suffered from a series of droughts.

It will be recalled that, among the fatwās that had been issued previously, the fatwā of al-Ṣughayyir held that if it were legally certified that the downstream community had established its fields prior to those of the upstream community, then the downstream community would enjoy an entitlement to the water in proportion to its needs. It will further be recalled that in support of his opinion al-Ṣughayyir had referred in passing to the *ʿUtbiyya* and to a fatwā of Ibn Rushd – without however citing either text.

Seeking to make the record as complete as possible, someone – we must assume it was the residents of Mazdgha – approached the muftī ʿAbdallāh b. Muḥammad b. Mūsā b. Muʿṭī al-ʿAbdūsī (d. Jumādā II 858/May–June 1454 or in 843/1439–40)[119] and apparently asked him to specify and fully cite the texts to which al-Ṣughayyir had only alluded, that is the *Kitāb al-Bayān wa'l-Taḥṣīl* of Ibn Rushd and the *ʿUtbiyya*. In compliance with this request, al-ʿAbdūsī made a copy in his own hand of the fatwā issued previously by Abū al-Ḍiyāʾ Sīdī Miṣbāḥ, that is, al-Yāliṣūtī, in which al-Yāliṣūtī cited the *Sharḥ* of Ibn Rushd. Al-ʿAbdūsī indicated that he considered al-Yāliṣūtī's fatwā to be legally valid and effective, and he made an exact copy of the wording of the texts to which al-Ṣughayyir had made only passing reference (see above).[120] Thus, it was the residents not of Zgane but of Mazdgha who benefited from al-ʿAbdūsī's fatwā.

On 24 Rabīʿ I 824/29 March 1421, al-ʿAbdūsī summoned two witnesses to testify that the response that he had issued was indeed in his handwriting, that he was in agreement with the response issued by Abū al-Ḍiyāʾ Miṣbāḥ, viz., al-Yāliṣūtī, and that, in his words, there was complete agreement among contemporary jurists with regard to this case. The witnesses attached their signatures to this certification.[121]

[118] *EI*[2], s.v. Marīnids.

[119] For biographical details, see al-Wansharīsī, *Wafayāt*, 143; Ibn al-Qāḍī, *Laqṭ*, 251; idem, *Durrat al-Ḥijāl*, vol. 3, 53, no. 959; idem, *Jadhwat al-iqtibās*, vol. 2, 425, no. 450; Badr al-Dīn al-Qarāfī, *Tawshīḥ al-dībāj wa'l-ḥilya al-ibtihāj* (Beirut: Dār al-Gharb al-Islāmī, 1403/1983), 114, no. 97; al-Tunbuktī, *Nayl*, 157–8.

[120] *Miʿyār*, vol. 8, 18 (l. 24)–19 (l. 23).

[121] Ibid., vol. 8, 19 (l. 24)–20 (l. 9). The witnesses' names were Muḥammad b. ʿAlī b. Muḥammad al-Malīlī and Muḥammad b. Muḥammad b. ʿAbdallāh.

The Fatwā of al-Tāzaghdrī

At the beginning of the month of Jumāda I 824/May 1421, the residents of Mazdgha and Zgane approached the chief qāḍī of Fez, Muḥammad b. Muḥammad al-Ṣanhājī,[122] and placed before him all of the documentation that had accumulated over the course of nearly a century and a half with regard to the dispute between the two settlements – the description of the wadi, fatwās, judicial certifications, a *rasm istirʿāʾ*, and one *iʿmāl*. Faced with this documentation, the chief qāḍī was understandably reluctant to issue a judgment on his own authority, and he conveyed the documentation to a distinguished Fāsī jurist, muftī, and preacher by the name of Abū al-Qāsim Muḥammad b. ʿAbd al-ʿAzīz al-Tāzaghdrī (d. 831/1427–28),[123] to whom he made the following short and simple charge:

> Praise be to God. My Lord – may God be pleased with you and may He cause your life to be a source of pleasure for the Muslims. Scrutinize the documents and the responses that are transcribed above and consider what judicial action (*ʿamal*) should be taken in this matter with regard to them. Do the residents of Mazdgha have a right to the water together with the residents of Zgane? Or [do they] not, and they have no right to it – except for the surplus? Respond to this – may you be rewarded and thanked. Farewell – and may the mercy of the Exalted God and His blessings be upon you.[124]

Al-Tāzaghdrī carefully studied the documentation for approximately two weeks and then, on 19 Jumāda I 824/22 May 1421, issued his response. The resulting fatwā is of special interest because the muftī not only stated his opinion regarding entitlement to the water but also attempted to identify the key jurisprudential and factual issues that had been raised by his predecessors and to explain the complex interaction between these issues. His fatwā thus constitutes a summing up of a legal discussion that had unfolded over the course of a century and a half with respect to a discrete and narrowly circumscribed dispute.

It is through performance that al-Tāzaghdrī teaches us what it meant for a muftī to "scrutinize" a legal document. He began with a clear statement of his legal holding:

> The response – and God is the one who guides to success in His benevolence – is that the residents of Zgane should be given priority over the residents of Mazdgha in the irrigation of their crops and gardens, and the residents of Mazdgha are entitled only to the remaining surplus.[125]

[122] I have been unable to identify this particular Ṣanhājī.

[123] Al-Tāzaghdrī, who was born in the countryside near Tangier, was the author of a commentary on the *Sharḥ al-Mudawwana* of Abū al-Ḥasan al-Ṣughayyir. He was slain in 831/1427–28 by an assailant who was never identified. See further al-Wansharīsī, *Wafayāt*, 140; al-Tunbuktī, *Nayl*, 290–1; Ibn al-Qāḍī, *Laqṭ*, 245 (where a death date of 833/1429–30 is specified); idem, *Durrat al-Ḥijāl*, vol. 3, 281, no. 1349; idem, *Jadhwat al-iqtibās*, vol. 1, 239, no. 220 (where a death date of 833/1429–30 is specified); Makhlūf, *Shajarat al-Nūr*, vol. 1, 252, no. 915.

[124] *Miʿyār*, vol. 8, 15, ll. 8–12.

[125] Ibid., vol. 8, 15, ll. 14–16.

Having stated his general conclusion, the muftī proceeded to give a detailed explanation of the process of legal reasoning whereby he had arrived at it. There are, he said, two possibilities that must be considered: that the residents of Zgane had appropriated (*mutamallakan li*) the water or that they had not. In either case, the entitlement of the upstream community is greater than that of the downstream community.[126]

As for the first possibility, if the water had been appropriated by the residents of Zgane, then they clearly have the greatest right to the water for the purpose not only of irrigation but also manufacture, such as grinding wheat in mills. Further, they may withhold any surplus from the residents of Mazdgha and use it as they see fit. However, there are exceptions to this rule: the residents of Zgane may not withhold the remaining surplus, even if they are in need of it, if the residents of Mazdgha can legally establish that their upstream neighbors previously had given them the surplus as an outright gift (*ʿaṭiyya ṣarīḥa*). Similarly, the residents of Mazdgha are entitled to any remaining surplus – on the condition that they have a need for it – if either of the following contingencies holds: (a) the residents of Zgane gave the water to the residents of Mazdgha as a gratuitous transfer of usufruct (*ʿāriyya*) for a specified period of time which has now expired; or for an unspecified period of time, the customary period for which (*mithluhu*) has now expired; (b) the residents of Mazdgha established their fields – with or without the knowledge (*ʿilm*) of the residents of Zgane – who were silent with regard to their usage of the water.[127]

As for the second possibility, namely, that the water had not been appropriated by (*ghayr mutamallak*) the residents of Zgane but merely passes through their land before descending to the residents of Mazdgha, al-Tāzaghdrī opined that in this case the relative entitlement of the two communities is determined by their respective locations: because the residents of Zgane live upstream, they have a greater right to the water than the residents of Mazdgha, who live downstream; the entitlement of the downstream community is limited to any remaining surplus. In support of this view, al-Tāzaghdrī invoked the precedent established by the Prophet with respect to the communities of Mahzūr and Mudhaynīb (see above), which establishes that people living upstream have priority in entitlement over people living downstream. Here, the citation of a prophetic *ḥadīth* points to an important shift in this 150-year-long case from reliance on local custom and *ijtihād* to reliance on the *sunna* of the prophet.

There is, however, al-Tāzaghdrī added, one exception to this general principle: the downstream community will have a greater right to the water if it can legally establish that it introduced its fields prior to those of the upstream community. Al-Tāzaghdrī explained that his view was based on the authority of Ibn al-Qāsim,

126 Ibid., vol. 8, 15, ll. 16–18.

127 Ibid., vol. 8, 15, ll. 19–23. Al-Tāzaghdrī indicated that there was another possibility that should be taken into consideration, namely, that the residents of Mazdgha did not have a need for the water. He did not explore this possibility.

which, he admitted, was disputed by Aṣbagh in the *Wāḍiḥa*.[128] Then al-Tāzaghdrī made an important distinction between milling and irrigation, the first such distinction made by any of the jurists handling this case. The priority of the downstream community in this exceptional case, he stated, applies exclusively to water used for the purpose of irrigation. It does not apply to water that is needed for the purpose of grinding wheat in mills. If the water is needed for both purposes, then priority is given to the needs of irrigation over those of grinding wheat, regardless of the location of the fields to be irrigated (upstream v. downstream) or of temporal precedence (earlier v. later). As support for this distinction, al-Tāzaghdrī referred without specification to a statement by Ibn Rushd in his *Nawāzil*.[129]

Al-Tāzaghdrī's conclusion was at variance with two documents and three fatwās issued previously, and, before completing his response, he felt an obligation to sort out and clarify the legal issues that jurists had debated for nearly a century and a half. He began by considering the document of mid-Rabīʿ I 721/9–19 April 1321, in which eyewitnesses described the topography of the wadi. On the strength of the testimony contained in this document regarding the "antiquity" of their dams, the residents of Mazdgha had claimed a right to the source (*aṣl*) of the water. This argument was now rejected by al-Tāzaghdrī on the grounds that, if the residents of Mazdgha had in fact been entitled to the *aṣl* of the water, they would have denied the residents of Zgane the right to raise the water by means of their diversion dams. Apparently, however, the residents of Mazdgha had never done so.[130]

Al-Tāzaghdrī turned next to the *rasm istirʿāʾ* drawn up in Muḥarram 746/ March 1345, two years after the residents of Zgane had cut off the water supply to Mazdgha. In this document the residents of Mazdgha attempted to establish their continuous use of the water. The muftī rejected their claim on the grounds that water may not be acquired (*lā yuḥāz*) on the basis of usage (*intifāʿ*) in the absence of entitlement to its source (*aṣl*), invoking as support for this position a statement by ʿĪsā b. Dīnār (d. 212/827) in his *Nawāzil*,[131] as quoted in the chapter on diversion dams and rivers in the *ʿUtbiyya*.[132]

Having disposed of these two documents, al-Tāzaghdrī embarked upon a critique of the earlier fatwās that had been issued in the case, beginning with that of al-Waryāghlī (d. 683/1284–85), who, it will be remembered, had held in favor of the residents of Mazdgha. Al-Tāzaghdrī focused his attention on two statements made by al-Waryāghlī. The first statement, "As for an unrestricted loan (*ʿāriyya*

[128] An exposition of Mālikī doctrine composed by Abū Marwān ʿAbd al-Malik Ibn Ḥabīb, one of the early Mālikī jurists in Andalusia. On this jurist, see Ibn Farḥūn, *Dībāj*, 154–6; Makhlūf, *Shajara*, vol. 1, 74, no. 109; Toledano, *Judicial Practice*, 55, note 5. For additional references, see Vidal Castro, "El *Miʿyār* ... I," 335–6.

[129] *Miʿyār*, vol. 8, 15 (l. 23)–16 (l. 8).

[130] Ibid., vol. 8, 16, ll. 9–12.

[131] Abū Muḥammad ʿĪsā b. Dīnār b. Wahb, an early Mālikī jurist of Cordova who is credited with spreading Mālikī doctrine in al-Andalus. See Ibn Farḥūn, *Dībāj*, 178; Makhlūf, *Shajarat al-nūr*, vol. 1, 64, no. 47; Toledano, *Judicial Practice*, 52, note 5.

[132] *Miʿyār*, vol. 8, 16, ll. 12–15. On al-ʿUtbī, see above, note 45.

muṭlaqa), it is, in this case, perpetual," suggested that a lender (here, the residents of Zgane) may not revoke his loan even if he has a need for its object. This conclusion, al-Tāzaghdrī explained, is contradicted by the opinion of Ibn al-Qāsim in the case of a man who had given surplus water to people who used it to plant crops next to the water source and to irrigate their crops. Subsequently, the owner wanted to cut off their water. According to Ibn al-Qāsim, he could do so only if he had a need for it. This position was subsequently clarified by Ibn Rushd, who explained that the owner of the water had not made an *explicit* declaration of a gift, but had said merely, "Plant with surplus water," or "Take surplus water and plant with it." For this reason, he might subsequently claim that it had been his intention that the recipient of the water would take it in the form of a gratuitous concession (*ʿāriyya*) until such time as he himself had a need for it. The implication for the present case, al-Tāzaghdrī said, was that the residents of Zgane might revoke their gratuitous concession of water to the residents of Mazdgha if they could establish a need for it.[133]

The second problematic statement by al-Waryāghlī was his assertion regarding the passage of time since the period of the Almohads and the subsequent ability of people to make claims regarding their rights.[134] This assertion, al-Tāzaghdrī argued, had no legal basis (*lā ḥujja lahu*), because the upstream community may have been silent with regard to its rights because it had no need for the surplus water during the period in question, and, he repeated, entitlement to water is not acquired on the basis of usage.[135]

Al-Tāzaghdrī now took up the short fatwā of al-Walīdī (d. *ca.* 695/1295–96), who had reasoned that if the residents of Mazdgha were able to prove that they had established their fields before the residents of Zgane had established theirs, then the downstream community would enjoy the first claim on the water and the upstream community would be entitled only to the surplus ("those living upstream are entitled only to the surplus of the ancient plantings of those living downstream"). Al-Tāzaghdrī had no quarrel with this statement as an assertion of a principle of law, and he acknowledged that it was legally valid and grounded in the authority of a statement attributed to Ibn al-Qāsim. In the case at hand, however, it was not the law but the facts that were in question. Before any qāḍī or other judicial authority issued a judgment in favor of the residents of Mazdgha, it was his obligation to legally establish the historical precedence of their fields. The eyewitness description of the wadi formulated in the year 721/1321 does not, al-Tāzaghdrī observed, conclusively establish this fact. Rather the witnesses merely established that most of the fields that were *above* Mazdgha were "ancient" (*qadīm*) whereas only a few of those that were *within* the borders of Mazdgha were "ancient." Further, the expert witnesses attested to having seen "the trace of an ancient irrigation channel"[136] (*sāqiya*) located above Mazdgha which then falls

[133] Ibid., vol. 8, 16, ll. 15–23.

[134] On the relationship between the Almohads and Mālikism, see now Fierro, "The Legal Policies of the Almohad Caliphs," 226–48.

[135] *Miʿyār*, vol. 8, 16 (l. 23)–17 (l. 1).

[136] Ibid., vol. 8, 17, ll. 6–7 (cp. vol. 8, 8, ll. 5–7).

in the depression (*khandaq*) in the midst of the fields of Mazdgha. This testimony suggested to al-Tāzaghdrī the possibility that the fields of Mazdgha had been established in two stages: in a first stage, the "ancient" fields of Mazdgha "drank" from an irrigation channel (*sāqiya*) that subsequently went out of use. In a second stage, the residents of Mazdgha established additional plantings, drawing on the surplus water of Zgane. If this were correct, then there would be no legal basis to the claim of the residents of Mazdgha that their fields were planted before those of the residents of Zgane.[137]

Finally, al-Tāzaghdrī turned his attention to the fatwā of al-Ṣughayyir (d. 719/1319–20), who, like al-Walīdī, held in favor of the residents of Mazdgha. It will be recalled that al-Ṣughayyir had stated, with regard to water that is owned, that if the downstream community established that it had introduced its fields prior to those of the upstream community, then it would have priority over the upstream community and would be entitled to use of the water in proportion to its needs. Taking account of the impossibility of determining with absolute certainty which community first irrigated its land (the reader will recall that there were ancient traces of mills near both settlements), al-Ṣughayyir said that the residents of Mazdgha had established that their fields were ancient and that they had been using the water continuously for the purpose of irrigation. He continued:

> But since it is not known (*wa-lammā lam yuʿlam*) who first established the gardens alongside the aforementioned water, and it is conceivable (*wa-iḥtamala*) that [the first to do so were] the residents of Mazdgha, one should not remove from their possession that to which they have established a claim – namely, a sufficient [amount of water] for their gardens – on the basis of something doubtful (*al-shakk*).[138]

Al-Tazghadrī found this statement problematic for three reasons. First, it contradicts a *sunna* of the Prophet Muḥammad, who, in similar circumstances, had given priority to an upstream community over a downstream community. Second, al-Ṣughayyir's argument regarding the possibility that the residents of Mazdgha were the first to establish their fields cuts both ways. In the absence of certain knowledge, one could as well assume that it was the residents of *Zgane* who had been the first to establish their fields. This assumption would lead one to the conclusion that the upstream community should not be denied an entitlement that is supported by a *sunna* of the Prophet. Third, in cases of this type, the granting of priority to an upstream community on the strength of the *sunna* is a matter on which there is general agreement (*maḥall ittifāq*), whereas the granting of priority to a downstream community on the ground of precedence in planting is something that is done only on the basis of *ijtihād* or independent reasoning – which is a source of disagreement (*maḥall ikhtilāf*). Clearly, for al-Tāzaghdrī, the status of *ijtihād* as the basis of a legal argument was inferior to the status of a prophetic *sunna*.

As support for his argument, al-Tāzaghdrī cited Ibn Rushd's comment on a case discussed by Aṣbagh, as transmitted in the *Wāḍiḥa*: "No irrigation rights are

[137] Ibid., vol. 8, 17, ll. 1–10. [138] Ibid., vol. 8, 17, ll. 11–13 (cp. vol. 8, 12, ll. 3–5).

attributed to the lower, earlier [walled garden,] in accordance with the plain meaning of the statement of the Prophet – may God bless him and grant him peace, 'Those living upstream retain [the water] until it reaches the ankles; then they send [it down].'" According to Ibn Rushd, this prophetic statement has general application and was not intended to apply exclusively to a particular case (*ʿamma wa-lam yakhuṣṣ*).[139] This principle stems from the fact that water is not private property but rather common property, and it therefore must be treated in accordance with the general presumption that upstream communities are established prior to downstream communities. In cases of doubt, one must search, as Ibn al-Qāsim reportedly had, for an indicator of priority, as, for example, the testimonial declaration of notary witnesses establishing the right of the downstream community to use the water for the purpose of irrigation.[140]

Referring to the case discussed by Ibn al-Qāsim, al-Tāzaghdrī concluded his fatwā, saying, "This is the situation in our case, and this is clear – and God is the source of success, in His benevolence." His signature followed.[141]

On the day on which he issued the fatwā – 19 Jumāda I 824/22 May 1421 – al-Tāzaghdrī summoned three witnesses who gave the following testimony regarding his response:

> The *futyā* in which he issued his response in accordance with the case that is recorded in the aforementioned documents, with respect to the objection and the litigation that is recorded there – the response begins [with the words], "Praise be to God – and God is the one who guides to success in His benevolence. The residents of Zgane ...", and it ends with [the citation from Ibn Rushd in the chapter on] diversion dams, "and in the course of [his discussion]." [The fatwā] is sound, being nineteen and one-half lines long – and it is his response, in his handwriting, to the aforementioned case, to which he gave his consent, and this is established school doctrine (*taqallada al-futyā bihi*), and he signed it (*wa-amḍāhu*), after exerting the efforts of his [mental] faculties in the examination of the aforementioned case regarding the rights and obligations of those who are involved in it.[142]

Following the certification of the fatwās of al-Tāzaghdrī and of al-ʿAbdūsī, the qāḍī Muḥammad b. Muḥammad al-Awrabī[143] added, "[The document] is authentic, and he made public announcement of its authenticity" (*istaqalla wa-aʿlama bi'stiqlālihi*).[144]

139 Ibid., vol. 8, 17, ll. 14–22.
140 Ibid., vol. 8, 17 (l. 22)–18 (l. 3).
141 Ibid., vol. 8, 18, ll. 3–5.
142 Ibid., vol. 8, 18, ll. 13–19. The witnesses are identified as Muḥammad [b.] ʿAlī b. Muḥammad al-Miṣbāḥ, Muḥammad b. Muḥammad [b.] ʿAbd al-Raḥmān al-Kinānī, and Aḥmad b. Muḥammad [b.] ʿAlī b. Muḥammad al-Ṣabbāgh (who was perhaps the son of the first witness).
143 I have been unable to identify this jurist in the biographical dictionaries. He no doubt was related to ʿAbdallāh b. Muḥammad b. ʿAbdallāh al-Awrabī al-Fāsī (d. 16 Dhū al-Qaʿda 782/10 February 1381), who was serving as chief qāḍī of Fez on Jumāda I 778/September 1376. On the latter, see Aḥmad Bāba, *Nayl*, 149; Ibn al-Qāḍī, *Jadwat al-iqtibās*, vol. 2, 424, no. 447; *Miʿyār*, vol. 7, 192–3, 488.
144 Ibid., 8, 18, ll. 22–3 (cf. vol. 8, 20, l. 9 where the same phrase recurs). On the terms *istaqalla* and *istiqlāl*, see above, note 97.

The response of al-Tāzaghdrī was arguably the best documented and most persuasive of all the fatwās issued in connection with the dispute. The muftī addressed the problem thoroughly and systematically, examined various contingencies, and reviewed the opinions of his predecessors before critiquing their reasoning. Most important, however, he grounded his argument in specific references to prophetic authority and scholarly precedent, citing the *sunna* of the Prophet, Ibn al-Qāsim, ʿĪsā b. Dīnār – as quoted in the *ʿUtbiyya*, and Ibn Rushd. In his fatwā the movement from local custom and *ijtihād* to *sunna* becomes explicit. By modern standards, his opinion would be respected as a thorough examination of the facts.

Muḥammad b. Muḥammad al-Ṣanhājī's Implementation of al-Tāzaghdrī's Fatwā (late Jumādā I 824/late May or early June 1421)

Finally, in late Jumādā I 824/late May or early June 1421, the chief qāḍī of Fez, Muḥammad b. Muḥammad al-Ṣanhājī, summoned witnesses to testify to his implementation of the implementation of an earlier decision by another qāḍī, his namesake (and, possibly, one of his ancestors): ʿAbdallāh b. ʿAbd al-Raḥmān b. Aḥmad al-Ṣanhājī (see above):

> The chief qāḍī in the city of Fez al-Maḥrūsa – may the Exalted God preserve it – Muḥammad b. Muḥammad al-Ṣanhājī – may the Exalted God fortify him and protect it – summoned witnesses [to testify] to the implementation (*iʿmāl*) of the implementation that is recorded above, because of its legal validity, in his opinion, and its authenticity, in his view, as incumbent upon him. That [occurred] in the court of his jurisdiction and judgment, in the place that they mentioned, [at] the end of Jumādā I of the year eight hundred and twenty-four [late May or early June, 1421].[145]

At this point our documentation of the dispute ends. The fatwā of al-Tāzaghdrī, together with the attached documentation, was preserved in the *sijill* of the chief qāḍī of Fez,[146] and nearly half a century later, al-Wansharīsī made a copy of al-Tāzaghdrī's fatwā, specifying that it was in the latter's own handwriting.[147]

[145] Ibid., vol. 8, 8, ll. 17–21. Editor's note: "This is how the text reads in the original. The correct reading may be: 'seven hundred' ", that is, "at the end of Jumādā I of the year seven hundred and twenty-four," which corresponds to late May, 1324. Cp. ibid., vol. 8, 10, l. 5, where the editor again notes two variants of the year, "seven hundred" and "eight hundred".

[146] As noted at ibid., vol. 8, 18, l. 6. See Hallaq, "The qāḍī's diwan (*sijill*) before the Ottomans," 415–36.

[147] *Miʿyār*, vol. 8, 15, l. 14.

Analysis

Qāḍīs, Muftīs and Conflict Resolution

The case that we have examined here no doubt extended further back in history than our documentation permits us to follow and, in all likelihood, continued after the date at which our documentation ends. The case is important for the purposes of historical investigation because it allows us to look closely at the "traces" of social, economic, and political changes in Wadi Zgane over a period of approximately 150 years. Our documentation begins *ca.* 683/1285, just after the Marīnids had seized control of northern Morocco and began to exploit the resources of the countryside by granting land to soldiers and *amīr*s. The landowners mentioned in the eyewitness description of the wadi, ʿUmar b. Raḥḥū, Ibrāhīm al-Barīdī, and Ibn Warāsin, may have received their lands in the form of *iqṭāʿ*s. All three invested significant resources in the Wadi Zgane irrigation system, building numerous diversion dams, canals and sub-channels in an effort to increase the area of land under cultivation, thereby placing an increasing burden on available water resources. The outbreak of drought in 721–25/1321–25 and its recurrence over the course of the eighth/fourteenth century made the situation intolerable for the residents of Mazdgha, who took their case to the judicial authorities in Fez and attempted to have the dispute re-opened on the strength of new arguments. Finally, toward the end of the eighth/fourteenth century or the beginning of the ninth/fifteenth, the residents of Zgane built new mills for the grinding of wheat (and they may have introduced the cultivation of mulberry trees), placing additional burdens on the water supply. These new elements had the effect of again increasing tension between the residents of Zgane and Mazdgha.

The documentary record of the dispute we have studied is tantalizingly incomplete. On the one hand, our source transports the modern investigator directly into the disputed area, where one can almost see the springs that spill into the wadi, the diversion dams, the water-raising devices, and the mills – indeed, even the traces of ancient mills – that made life possible in this rustic, rugged and remote environment. We can follow residents of the upstream and downstream communities in and out of the qāḍī courts as they sought to resolve their differences regarding the use and distribution of water over a period of a century and a half. And we can analyze the judicial opinions written by a series of muftīs in connection with these disputes. On the other hand, we do not know anything about the specific terms of the resolution of those disputes or the nature of any agreements between these two communities. Our source points toward certain outcomes but leaves the exact nature of those outcomes to the imagination of the reader.

This very absence of specificity is, in my view, evidence of an unstated fact: that the judicial authorities were reluctant to respond to the dispute by issuing a *ḥukm*, or binding judgment. We are conditioned to expect a *ḥukm* by the vigor of the case and by our own experience of how a judicial system operates, but our source contains no reference whatsoever to one. Despite their attempts to bring the dispute to resolution, the qāḍīs, for the most part, confined themselves to establishing evidence, authenticating witness testimony and documents, and confirming the validity of fatwās. In 738/1338 al-Azdī registered the testimony of witnesses who attested to the legal validity of the eyewitness description of the wadi; in 748/1347 al-Jazūlī summoned witnesses to testify to the complete legal validity of the *rasm istirʿāʾ* and to the sufficiency (*iktifāʾ*) of a second document; in 824/1421 al-Awrabī certified the response of al-ʿAbdūsī; and in the same year Muḥammad al-Ṣanhājī summoned witnesses to attest to an earlier implementation (*iʿmāl*).[148]

Indeed, the very length of the case tells us that an absolute and binding resolution was not imposed on Zgane and Mazdgha, perhaps in part because the litigants were not fixed in number and did not have an opportunity to present their case in court (*iʿdhār*). Considering this state of affairs, the unidentified qāḍī cum *mustaftī* who requested a judicial opinion from al-Yāliṣūtī reasoned that it would be difficult for him to provide either group an adequate opportunity to do so and that, because Mālikī legal doctrine required that a qāḍī not give judgment against an absent party, the dispute should be resolved, if possible, by means of a *ṣulḥ*, or amicable settlement. If the parties refused to submit to arbitration, then the qāḍī should refer the case to a muftī whose considered legal opinion might serve as the basis of an imposed resolution.[149]

One may argue that the incompleteness of our record may hide the fact that a *ḥukm* was issued. Our documentation comes entirely from a single source, the *Miʿyār* of al-Wansharīsī, who was interested primarily in fatwās, not *ḥukm*s. It is possible, of course, that al-Wansharīsī had access to one or more *ḥukm*s connected to the dispute but that he chose not to transcribe them; alternatively, it is possible that one or more *ḥukm*s relating to the dispute were issued but that al-Wansharīsī did not have access to them. Let us suppose, for the sake of argument, that a *ḥukm* was issued by al-Azdī in 738/1338 in favor of the downstream community, and let us suppose further that ʿAbdallāh al-Ṣanhājī issued a *ḥukm* in 792/1390 in favor of

148 See ibid., vol. 8, 8, ll. 13–21; 9 (l. 20)–10 (l. 5); 19 (l. 24)–20 (l. 9).

149 On *ṣulḥ*, see note 102 above. The second question addressed to al-Yāliṣūtī was formulated as follows: "Also, is it appropriate for the judicial magistrate (*al-ḥākim*) who issues the judgment for the two parties to issue a judgment (*ḥukm*) in this case, or not – because a judgment may be handed down only with regard to someone who is given a final opportunity to present evidence on his behalf (*iʿdhār*)? But neither of the two parties to the dispute is limited [in number] and it is not possible to offer a final opportunity to present evidence, because neither of the two parties to the dispute can be enumerated, and none of them can be treated as present or absent, adult or minor; [futher,] the adults among them include those who are subject to [someone's] authority and others who are not subject to [someone's] authority; and they include women who are married and [others] who are widows. Thus, how is it appropriate for the judge to issue a judgment affecting those who are of this status?

"Or should this [case] be treated like one in which the facts are ambiguous, as a result of which the judge charges the two parties [to conclude] an amicable settlement (*ṣulḥ*), to the extent that he is able to do so. But if they refuse, the correct solution is sought, following study [of the case] by a scholar whose status is satisfactory, so that whatever he and they regard as correct [should serve as the basis of an agreement], in the manner in which judgments were decided in ancient times?" See ibid., 8:13 (l. 16)–14 (l. 1).

the upstream community. If both assumptions are correct, then the judgment of al-Ṣanhājī necessarily reversed the earlier judgment of al-Azdī. But on what grounds would it have done so? Mālikī law teaches that a judicial decision is subject to reversal by the issuing judge himself, by one of his contemporaries, or by a successor judge – but *only* if the issuing judge lacked proper jurisdictional authority, engaged in the improper use of independent reasoning (*ijtihād*), or misconstrued the judicial consensus. That is to say, the grounds for reconsideration are limited to questions of law and exclude questions of fact.[150] However, our source contains no evidence whatsoever indicating that any of the qāḍīs involved in the case lacked jurisdictional authority or committed a judicial error in the application of the law.

It is useful to consider the point that anthropologist Lawrence Rosen makes, writing about twentieth-century Moroccan judges. Rosen argues that the primary function of the judge is to put the litigants into a position in which they can negotiate the terms of their relationships.[151] In the present case we see that the qāḍī played an important role in the resolution of the dispute by offering his services as a mediator between the two parties: he listened to the litigants' arguments, translated those arguments into the language of the law, authorized his agents to gather additional information relating to the dispute, and, when all of these tasks had been completed, attempted to persuade the parties to agree to a *ṣulḥ*. They seem to have refused, whereupon he formulated a request for a considered legal opinion which he conveyed to a distinguished muftī.

After receiving the *istiftāʾ*, the muftī studied the case and then issued his fatwā, a detailed statement of the law, grounded in authoritative legal sources. By its very nature, the jurist's application of the modes of reasoning that were his stock-in-trade to the cluster of legal concepts associated with disputes (for example, *milk*, *manfaʿa*, *ḥaqq*, *sukūt*) afforded flexibility to the system. This flexibility was implicit in the conviction that the Islamically correct solution to any and every problem could be reached through legal reasoning based on the two primary sources of the law, the Qurʾān and the *sunna* of the Prophet Muḥammad, which serve as a kind of ethical template or storehouse of Islamic norms and values. The results of such reasoning were contested by Muslim jurists as early as the first two centuries AH, as evidenced by fundamental disagreements among, first, the founders of the four Sunnī *madhhab*s and, later, among their respective disciples. The body of legal doctrine that developed over the course of the succeeding centuries was so wide ranging and open-ended that each new generation of Muslim jurists had a broad range of authoritative precedents upon which to base their opinions.

[150] See David S. Powers, "On Judicial Review in Islamic Law," *Law & Society Review*, 26:2 (1992), 315–41, esp. 322–4.

[151] Lawrence Rosen, *The Anthropology of Justice: Law as Culture in Islamic Society* (Cambridge: Cambridge University Press, 1989). Cf. R.H. Coase, *The Firm, the Market, and the Law* (Chicago: University of Chicago Press, 1988).

The muftī sent the fatwā to the *mustaftī* – who was in fact a qāḍī. Finding the fatwā to be persuasive, the qāḍī "executed" or "implemented" (*aʿmala*, v.n. *iʿmāl*) it and entered a copy in the *sijill*, or judicial record of his court.[152]

The qāḍī's implementation (*iʿmāl*) of the fatwā, and the record that he entered in the *sijill*, served as the moral and legal basis of whatever agreement the two parties reached. Had the qāḍī issued a judgment in favor of one of the disputing parties, the matter would have been settled once and for all, because a judgment is binding; similarly a *ṣulḥ*, while a mutual decision, is endorsed by a qāḍī and would have been final and binding on the two parties. However, because there was no binding resolution, the matter remained open to further discussion, and the parties to the dispute were thus free to return to the qāḍī, or to one of his successors, before whom they might adduce new arguments relating to the dispute or claim that circumstances had changed. It was thus that the process remained open and flexible for a century and a half.[153]

Law and Economy

The need to regulate the usage of water by upstream and downstream communities is a universal problem that every legal system must address in one way or another. Our concern here is to understand how Mālikī jurists in the far Maghrib dealt with this problem in the Marīnid period.

The inhabitants of Wadi Zgane used their wealth and technological skills to construct and install a complex system of dams and canals that made it possible to irrigate crops and to run mills. And they used their social skills to work out an equitable system for the distribution of the water. The downstream community of Mazdgha may have been the first to install hydraulic devices in Wadi Zgane. However, by the beginning of the Marīnid period if not before, upstreamers in and around Zgane added new dams and mills, thereby increasing the demand for water and creating a certain amount of "crowding" along the banks of the wadi. So long

[152] *Miʿyār*, 8:18, l. 6.

[153] One finds a similar case in Muḥammad b. ʿIyāḍ (d. 575/1179), *Madhāhib al-ḥukkām fī nawāzil al-aḥkām*, ed. M. Bencherifa (Beirut, 1989), 243–4: Qāḍī Iyāḍ was asked about a village in which the waters of a stream were used to run a mill and irrigate an orchard. It was not known which was the first to have been established. When a dispute arose regarding the use of the water, several qāḍīs persuaded the litigants to accept an amicable settlement. The situation remained stable for many years, until a drought broke out, whereupon the owner of the orchard sought to re-negotiate the earlier agreement. This case is cited in Delfina Serrano, "Legal practice in an Andalusī-Maghribī Source from the Twelfth Century CE: The *Madhāhib al-Ḥukkām fī nawāzil al-aḥkām*," *Islamic Law and Society*, 7:2 (2000), 187–234, at 218. And we also find qāḍīs serving as arbitrators in seventeenth-century Morocco. See Jacques Berque, *Ulémas, fondateurs, insurgés du Maghreb, xviie siècle* (Paris: Sindbad, 1982), 227 ("Son rôle aura été, non de dire le droit, mais d'activer, sous le signe et dans le langage du droit, les forces sociales en présence dans le litige. La judicature maghrébine a toujours affectionné ce genre de magistrat."). See now also Christian Müller, "Litigations without judgment: the importance of a *ḥukm* for qāḍī cases in Mamlūk Jerusalem" (forthcoming).

as the supply of water was plentiful, everyone might benefit from the system. But expectations of bountiful resources were dashed intermittently by outbreaks of drought, which severely reduced the volume of available water. Increasing demands for water were frustrated by a decrease in supply, leading to intense competition for the available resources.

By 683/1285, the upstream community of Zgane appears to have established itself as a more efficient user of the water than the downstreamers. When resources became scarce, the residents of Zgane had to engage in some form of rational bargaining with the residents of Mazdgha for the re-allocation of "ancient rights." On those occasions in which these negotiations proved unsuccessful, the upstreamers resorted to the use of force, manipulating the water supply so as to reduce the flow to the downstreamers or cut it off entirely. At this point, the only option available to the downstreamers – apart from violence – was to bring the dispute to the legal establishment in Fez.[154]

Once the dispute entered the Mālikī court system, jurists translated social, economic, and political issues into the language of the law. The process of translation made it possible for the jurists to identify the relevant legal principles that might be used to resolve the dispute: historical precedence, location, ownership, gift, loan, and silence. All other factors being equal, upstreamers have priority over downstreamers, although they must allow any surplus to pass downstream. In addition, the law gives preference to domestic and agricultural uses (drinking and irrigation, respectively) over manufacturing uses such as milling. These principles are superseded, however, in the event that a downstream community can establish its historical precedence and prior appropriation of the water.

These principles can be used to resolve a wide range of legal problems. In order to do so, however, it is first necessary to establish certain basic facts, in the present instance: which community had been the first to appropriate the water, when, and with whose knowledge and acquiescence? As we have seen, the courts went to great lengths in an effort to establish these facts, eventually sending expert witnesses to survey the wadi and describe its topography and hydraulic devices. In the end, however, the relevant legal facts proved to be indeterminate, that is to say, the downstream community could not conclusively establish either historical precedence or the acquiescence of the upstreamers in the use of surplus water. Once this became clear, the legal presumption shifted in favor of the upstream community.

The Mālikī jurists who issued judicial opinions relating to this dispute were bound to their school doctrine by the principle of *taqlīd*, that is, they were obligated to follow and apply established school doctrine and they did not have the power

[154] According to Ronald Coase, the assignment of property rights may be analyzed in terms of "transaction costs." If transaction costs are low, the goal of economic efficiency will encourage parties to exchange rights in a manner that best suits them, irrespective of the manner in which those rights were assigned at an earlier stage. But if transaction costs are high, efficiency will be sacrificed to the initial assignment of property rights. See Coase, *The Firm, the Market, and the Law*.

to change the law through the exercise of *ijtihād.* Although the law was fixed, stable and unchanging, the jurists were skilled legal technicians who were capable of using their skills in a creative manner to respond to changing social and economic conditions. The dramatic shift in the juristic treatment of the dispute that occurred *ca.* 750/1349–50 suggests to me that the inhabitants of Zgane succeeded in persuading the jurists that they had become more efficient users of water resources than their downstream neighbors; and that, beginning in 750/1349–50, a series of muftīs was able to work, in subtle ways, to adapt the law to changing patterns of economic efficiency.

FOUR

Conflicting Conceptions of Property in Fez, 741–826/1340–1423

Do not spend two consecutive nights without your last will and testament being written and placed underneath your pillow. (prophetic *ḥadīth*)

The words of the founder [of an endowment] are like the words of the Divine Lawgiver. (Moroccan jurist)

In this chapter we will examine a case in which two families living in Fez became embroiled in a dispute over a familial endowment created a generation after the appearance of the Black Death. The dispute raised the question of how it was possible to know the intent of the founder of the endowment many years after he or she had died. The qāḍī hearing the case sought the advice of two distinguished muftīs. Frustrated by their line of reasoning, the plaintiff, himself a jurist, used his knowledge of the law to exploit an irregularity in the witnessing clause of the original endowment deed. In this manner, the case was reduced to two contradictory claims that were resolved through the imposition of an oath. In this instance, the oath appears to have been an effective means for eliciting the truth and resolving the dispute.

The Black Death

Originating in Central Asia in 739/1338–39, the Black Death raced across Eurasia, in the next two years reaching the Middle East, North Africa, and Europe. The epidemic followed established trade routes. Borne on merchant ships and trade caravans, it jumped from one urban center to the next. In 748/1347 it reached Cairo and from there spread to Sicily and Tunisia in 749/1348. From Tunisia, it cut a path across North Africa in a westerly direction, reaching Oran, Tlemcen, Taza, and, finally, Salé on the Atlantic coast. As many as a thousand people per day died in major urban centers of the Maghrib. Great and small, rich and poor, old and young were struck down – although it should be noted that mortality rates among children aged one to six were especially high. In 749/1348 the plague forced the Marīnid Sulṭān, Abū al-Ḥasan, to withdraw his army from Tunis. In the same year Ibn Baṭṭūṭa witnessed the outbreak of plague in Damascus and, in 750/1349, he learned that his mother had succcumbed to the disease in Taza. Ibn Khaldūn's father, mother, and several of his teachers were victims of the plague in Tunis.[1] Although the epidemic eventually subsided, recurrences in Fez, Tlemcen, and other urban centers of the far Maghrib are recorded for the years 761/1359, 765/1363–64, 817–18/1414–15, 871/1466–67, and 905–06/1499.[2]

The Black Death had a profound impact on Muslim society. It retarded population growth (according to some estimates the population of major urban centers declined by as much as 25 percent), depopulated town and countryside, and decimated powerful armies. It led to inflated prices, increasing the cost of labor, disrupting the system of land tenure, and sending commerce into general decline.[3]

The Black Death also interfered with established Islamic mechanisms for the intergenerational transmission of property. Sudden mortality caused inheritances to pass in rapid succession from one family member to another, making it difficult to keep track of who owned what shares of familial property. If a person died leaving no heirs, the Public Treasury was entitled to confiscate his estate. One way to avoid the progressive fractionalization and fragmentation of familial property or its confiscation by the state was to leave a last will and testament (*waṣiyya* or *ʿahd*). Many property owners, however, were caught unprepared by the Black Death or were frustrated in their attempts to make plans for the future by the sudden death of family members young and old. Consider the case of the Fāsī jurist and mosque preacher ʿAbd al-Raḥmān b. Masūna, who, on the morning of 30 Muḥarram 750/20 April 1349, took out a pen and a piece of paper and drafted a last will and testament. Later that day, Ibn Masūna revoked this legal instrument and drafted a second one. It is likely that one or more of the legatees nominated in the first will had died.

Ibn Masūna began his second last will and testament by stating that he had undertaken this action

> in preparation for meeting God the Exalted, in the hope of receiving His forgiveness and mercy, and in preparation for death – fearing that death would occur suddenly and unexpectedly; [and] in accordance with the admonition of the Messenger of God – may God bless him and grant him peace – to leave a legacy (*waṣiyya*).[4]

Ibn Masūna then stipulated that upon his death – "from which there is no escape and which no living creature can avoid"[5] – three actions should be taken with respect to the bequeathable third of his estate: (1) 35 *wasq*s of wheat and 50 *wasq*s of barley should be distributed among the poor and indigent in the city of Fez;[6] (2) two slaves should be purchased and manumitted;[7] (3) and whatever remained of the bequeathable third should be given "in its entirety to the male sons of his male sons and to any male sons who will be born to his male sons in the future."[8]

[1] Michael W. Dols, *The Black Death in the Middle East* (Princeton: Princeton University Press, 1977), 63–7, 143 ff. [2] Ibid., 63–7, 305 ff. [3] Ibid., 255 ff. [4] *Miʿyār*, vol. 7, 25, ll. 2–4.

[5] Ibid., vol. 7, 25, ll. 4–5.

[6] Ibid., vol. 7, 25, ll. 8–11. A *wasq* is a measure of capacity used in the Hijaz in the days of Muḥammad, equal to 60 *mudd*s. See *EI*², s.v. Makāyil.

[7] *Miʿyār*, vol. 7, 25, l. 11. [8] Ibid., vol. 7, 25, ll. 5–8.

Ibn Masūna regarded all three of these actions as acts of piety by means of which he "sought the face of God the Exalted, His significant recompense, and the next world."[9] To emphasize the underlying pious motivation of the bequest, the testator cited Qur'ān 18:30: "Surely we leave not to waste the wage of him who does good works."[10] After completing the last will and testament, Ibn Masūna summoned two witnesses to attest to the fact that he understood its import and was of sound mind. Unfortunately, only one of the witnesses arrived before Ibn Masūna himself succumbed, no doubt a victim of the Black Death; the second witness could do no more than verify the testator's handwriting.[11]

Other Muslims also responded to the Black Death by drawing up their last wills and testament. Some devised new and creative strategies for the intergenerational transmission of property.[12] In the present chapter, we will examine in detail the case of a Berber family, the Ibn Khannūsas, that experienced the plague and its recurrences. The heads of the family devised an unusual legal strategy to ensure the continuation of the patrimony. But the strategy generated controversy and the familial estate became the subject of a bitter litigation. Before turning to the details of the dispute, I will survey briefly the contours of what I refer to as the Islamic inheritance system.

The Islamic Inheritance System

Islamic inheritance law (*ʿilm al-farāʾiḍ*) places substantial constraints upon the freedom of a person contemplating death to determine the devolution of his (or her) property: bequests may not exceed one-third of an estate and may not be made in favor of any person who qualifies as a legal heir. Compulsory inheritance rules have their basis in Qur'ānic verses that traditionally have been understood as recognizing two classes of heirs: "sharers," that is, those persons for whom the Qur'ān specifies a fractional share of the estate (one or more daughters [in the absence of a son], a father, mother, or spouse – and, in the absence of children, one or more siblings), and agnates, arranged in a series of hierarchical classes, that is, descendants, ascendants, descendants of the father, etc. In the presence of a son, a daughter is treated as an agnate and her share of the estate is reduced to half that of her brother. The division of an estate proceeds as follows: the qualifying "sharers" take their Qur'ānic entitlements, and the closest surviving male agnate inherits whatever remains.[13]

[9] Ibid., vol. 7, 25, ll. 12–13. [10] Ibid., vol. 7, 25, l. 13. [11] Ibid., vol. 7, 25, ll. 14–19.

[12] Ibid., vol. 7, 191, 267, 269, 272.

[13] On the operation of the Islamic inheritance rules, see Joseph Schacht, *An Introduction to Islamic Law* (Oxford, 1964), 169–74; Noel J. Coulson, *Succession in the Muslim Family* (Cambridge, 1971). On the historical development of the inheritance rules, see David S. Powers, *Studies in Qur'ān and Ḥadīth: The Formation of the Islamic Law of Inheritance* (Berkeley: University of California Press, 1986); idem, "Islamic Inheritance Law: A Socio-Historical Approach," in *Islamic Family Law and the State*, ed. Chibli Mallat and Jane Connors (London: Graham and Trotman, 1990), 11–29.

During the first centuries of Islamic history, Muslim jurists taught that the inheritance rules take effect only on property owned by the deceased at the moment he or she enters his or her deathbed illness and that a proprietor is free to dispose of his or her property in any way he or she wishes prior to that moment. There are no restrictions on the amount of property that a person may alienate *during* his or her lifetime, whether in favor of potential heirs or anyone else, and a Muslim proprietor may therefore shift assets to his or her desired heirs by means of a sale, gift, or acknowledgement of a debt – on the condition that these transactions conform to the requisite legal formalities.[14] The distinction between *inter vivos* and *post mortem* transactions had the effect of situating the compulsory Islamic inheritance *rules* within a larger and more flexible Islamic inheritance *system*, a system that restored a measure of the individual's freedom to control the intergenerational transmission of property.

An important component of the Islamic inheritance system was the familial endowment (*waqf ahlī*, known in the Maghrib as *ḥabūs*; Fr. *habous*), a post-Qur'ānic institution that allows a proprietor to transform immovable property, such as a house or shop or a field, into a perpetual endowment for one or more beneficiaries and subsequent generations of lineal descendants; the property thereafter may not be bought, sold, or transmitted through inheritance. A familial endowment created between two living beings (*inter vivos*) takes effect immediately, cannot be revoked by the founder, and is not subject to any restriction with regard to its size. A testamentary endowment, by contrast, takes effect only upon the founder's death, may be revoked by the founder at any time prior to that occurrence, and is subject to the normal constraints on Muslim wills (that is, it may not exceed one-third of a person's net assets and may not be made in favor of a legal heir without the consent of the other heirs).[15]

Whereas inheritance law imposes compulsory rules for the division of property among a wide group of male and female heirs, each of whom receives a fractional share of the estate as private property that subsequently may be bought, sold, or recycled through further inheritance, endowment law removes all or part of a patrimony from the effects of the inheritance rules, reducing the amount of property available as an inheritance to those of the founder's potential heirs who do not qualify as beneficiaries of the endowment. A founder who establishes a familial endowment for his children and their lineal descendants effectively "disinherits" his spouse, siblings, cousins, uncles, nephews and other potential heirs. Having been disinherited, these "outsiders" have an obvious material interest in challenging the validity of the endowment, for a successful challenge may result in the property's redesignation as inheritable property.[16]

14 Many proprietors paid lip service to these formalities while designing transactions that created a merely nominal transfer of ownership. On such behavior, see chapter six.

15 See *EI*², s.v., Waḳf; and Peter Charles Hennigan, "The Birth of a Legal Institution: The Formation of the Waqf in Third Century A.H. Ḥanafī Legal Discourse", PhD. dissertation, Cornell University, 1999.

16 See David S. Powers, "The Maliki Family Endowment: Legal Norms and Social Practices," *International Journal of Middle East Studies* 25 (1993), 379–406.

The Endowment of Fāṭima al-Zarhūnī and her Son Abū Zayd

Family Background

Abū Faḍl al-Zarhūnī[17] was a jurist whose daughter, Fāṭima, married Abū ʿAbdallāh Muḥammad b. Khannūsa[18] some time between the years 741/1340 and 746/1345. Our source provides little information about the couple except for the names of their children and grandchildren (see figure 4.1).

Abū ʿAbdallāh Muḥammad pre-deceased Fāṭima at an unspecified date prior to 791/1389, leaving two children: a son, Abū Zayd ʿAbd al-Raḥmān, and a daughter whose name is not mentioned in our source. Both children lived to adulthood, married, and reproduced. Abū Zayd fathered two children, a son, Muḥammad (named after his grandfather), and a daughter, ʿĀ'isha. As for Abū Zayd's unnamed sister, she married out of the Banū Khannūsa clan to a certain Abū al-ʿAbbās Aḥmad b. Rāshid, thereby creating an alliance between the Banū Khannūsa and the Banū Rāshid.[19] The couple had two children, a son, Abū ʿAbdallāh Muḥammad (whose name echoes that of his maternal grandfather), and a daughter, Raḥma. These four individuals – the unnamed sister, Abū Zayd, and the latter's two children – were all agnatic lineal descendants of Muḥammad b. Khannūsa, whereas the unnamed sister's son, Muḥammad, and daughter, Raḥma, were his cognatic lineal descendants. With the exception of Muḥammad b. Khannūsa himself, all of the above-mentioned individuals were alive in the year 791/1389.

Fāṭima accumulated substantial economic resources during her lifetime. Some of these she may have inherited from her father or from other members of her family; others she may have acquired at the time of her marriage, either as a gift (*niḥla*)[20] from her parents or as dower from her husband; and when her husband died, she presumably inherited one-eighth of his estate. By the year 791/1389 Fāṭima's assets included, at a minimum, an unspecified number of shares of an olive grove that were her exclusive property; a second olive grove owned jointly with her son, Abū Zayd

[17] The Bayt Banī al-Zarhūnī were Berbers of Jabal Zarhūn, an area located approximately one-half day's journey from Fez. The clan reportedly included many jurists and pious men. See Ismāʿīl b. al-Aḥmar, *Buyūtāt fās al-kubrā* (Rabat: Dār al-Manṣūr, 1972), 22.

[18] The Bayt Banī Khannūsa were of the tribe of Maṣmūda, from Sūs. One member of the clan was appointed chief qāḍī of Fez in the year 563/1167–68. The clan possessed a street (*darb*) in Fez known as "the street of Khalūf." See *Buyūtāt fās al-kubrā*, 40.

[19] I have been unable to identify the Banū Rāshid.

[20] On *niḥla* and other forms of pre-mortem inheritance, see Amalia Zomeño, "Transferencias matrimoniales en el Occidente islamico medieval: las joyas como regalo de boda," *Revista de Dialectologia y Tradiciones Populaires* LI (1996), 79–95; idem, "Donaciones matrimoniales y transmissión de propriedades inmuebles: estudio del contenido de la *siyāqa* y la *niḥla* en al-Andalus," in *Urbanisme musulman*, ed. P. Cressier, M. Fierro et J.-P. Van Staëvel (Madrid, CSIC, 2000), 75–99; Annelies Moors, "Gender, Relations and Inheritance: Person, Power and Property in Palestine," in *Gendering the Middle East: Emerging Perspectives*, ed. Deniz Kandiyoti (London and New York: I.B. Tauris, 1996), 69–84.

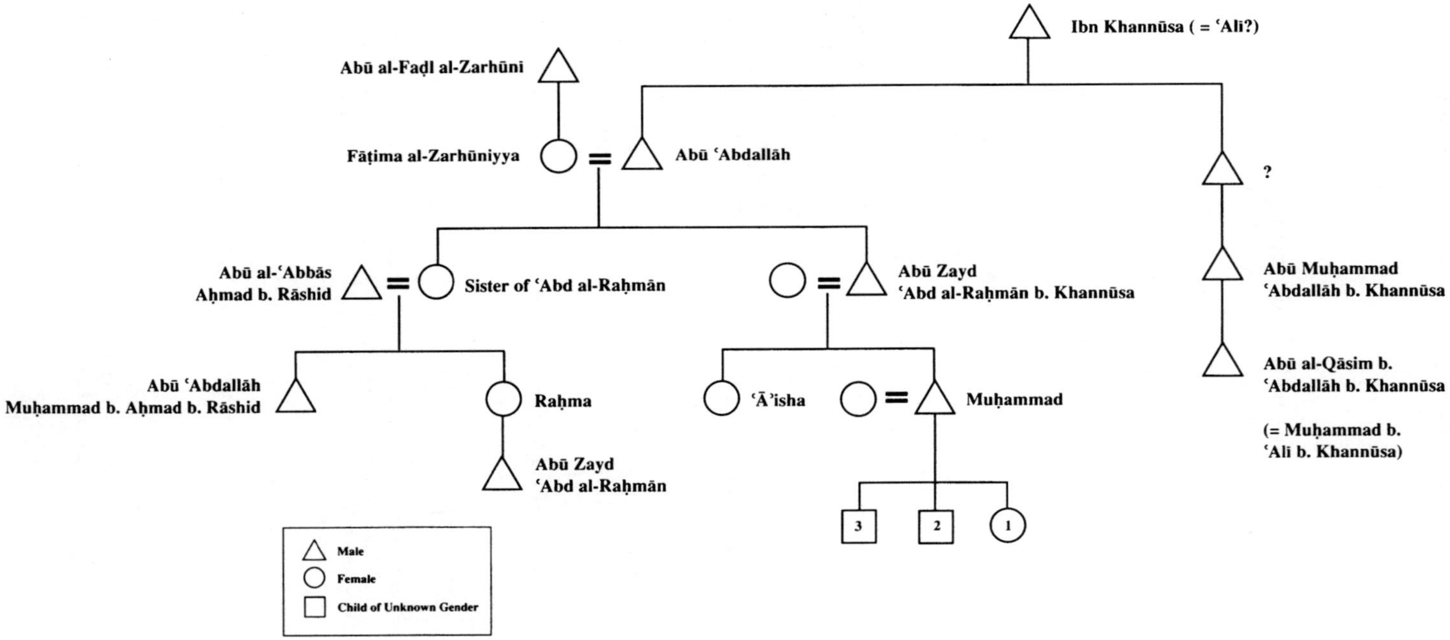

Figure 4.1 Genealogical reconstruction of the Banū Khannūsa and the Banū Rāshid

ʿAbd al-Raḥmān; and an unspecified number of shares of *sājilīn* (a term that I have been unable to define),[21] also owned jointly with her son.[22]

Our source indicates that Fāṭima was middle-aged in the year 791/1389, using a term, *naṣaf*, that signifies a person between the ages of forty-five and fifty (the date of her marriage [see above] suggests that she may have been closer to sixty). Although Fāṭima was a survivor of the Black Death, several members of her family may have succumbed to the plague. Be that as it may, as she contemplated her own mortality, Fāṭima may have asked herself about the best manner in which to transmit her accumulated assets to the next generation.

Creation of the Endowment: 791/1389

As the daughter of a jurist, Fāṭima surely understood that the operation of the Islamic inheritance rules would result not only in the fragmentation of her estate but also in its partial transfer to another clan. Upon her death, one-third of her estate would pass as an inheritance to her daughter, who had married into the Banū Rāshid, leaving her son, Abū Zayd ʿAbd al-Raḥmān, with the remaining two-thirds. Were she not a Muslim, Fāṭima might have circumvented this outcome by drawing up a last will and testament in which she bequeathed her entire estate to her son. As noted, however, Islamic inheritance law places substantial restrictions on the power of testation. According to the compulsory inheritance rules, the two-thirds of his mother's estate that Abū Zayd ʿAbd al-Raḥmān stood to inherit was the maximum that he might receive; depending upon the constellation of surviving heirs, he might receive less.

Abū Zayd ʿAbd al-Raḥmān, who held two of the properties in co-ownership with his mother, stood to lose the most from the operation of the inheritance rules, which would not only reduce his interest in the jointly-owned properties by one-third but also bring him into co-ownership with his sister – and, in effect, with the latter's husband, Aḥmad b. Rāshid, Abū Zayd's brother-in-law, also a jurist. Abū Zayd no doubt viewed both of these results as undesirable. I imagine that he accompanied his mother to a document specialist (*muwaththiq*) who operated in the vicinity of the Friday Mosque in Fez, before whom he laid out their situation.[23] In response, the document specialist suggested a complex and unconventional strategy composed of two elements. First, Fāṭima and Abū Zayd were to

21 Perhaps a corruption of *ma'jal* or *mājil*, which means cistern? On this term see Robert Brunschvig, *La Berbérie Orientale sous les Ḥafṣides*, 2 vols (Paris: Adrien-Maisonneuve, 1940–47), vol. 2, 210.

22 On the ability of Muslim women to accumulate property, see Maya Shatzmiller, "Women and Property Rights in al-Andalus and the Maghrib: Social Patterns and Legal Discourse," *Islamic Law and Society*, vol. 2 (1995), 219–57.

23 On document specialists, see Brinkley Messick, "Literacy and the Law: Documents and Document Specialists in Yemen," in *Law and Islam in the Middle East*, ed. Daisy Hilse Dwyer (New York: Bergin & Garvey Publishers, 1990), 61–76.

consolidate their shared and unshared assets and, second, they were to transform the consolidated assets into a familial endowment to be created by means of a testamentary instrument (as such, the proposed endowment would be limited to one-third of the co-founders' net assets). By creating such an endowment, Fāṭima and Abū Zayd defined the meaning of family for their lineal descendants and insured the physical integrity of their resources in perpetuity.

There were technical obstacles to the successful implementation of this strategy. As a testamentary instrument, the proposed endowment might not be made in favor of any person who stood to inherit a fractional share of Fāṭima's estate. For this reason, Fāṭima could not designate her son Abū Zayd as the initial beneficiary of the endowment, for that would constitute a bequest to an heir. It will be remembered, however, that Abū Zayd was the father of two children, Muḥammad and ʿĀʾisha, both of whom reportedly were minors in the year 791/1389. As long as their father was alive, these two children were disqualified from inheriting from their grandmother, but might receive a bequest from her. Thus, Fāṭima could achieve her desired objective by designating her two agnatic grandchildren as the initial beneficiaries of the endowment. But this solution was still inadequate, for the proposed testamentary endowment was to consist of resources belonging to both Fāṭima *and* her son, Abū Zayd. Although Muḥammad and ʿĀʾisha legitimately might receive a bequest from their grandmother, they were not entitled to receive one from their father. Were the testamentary instrument to be created for their benefit, the endowment would be open to challenge. To prevent such a challenge, the document specialist advised his clients to create the endowment for an as yet unborn grandchild of Abū Zayd ʿAbd al-Raḥmān who legitimately might receive a bequest from its grandfather.[24] Formulated in this manner, the legal instrument would be immune from challenge on the ground that it constituted a bequest to an heir. This solution had a further advantage for Abū Zayd ʿAbd al-Raḥmān. The present legal minority of his children meant that the prospective grandchild could not come into existence for many years. In the meantime, Abū Zayd would exercise *de facto* control of the endowment revenues in his capacity as his children's legal guardian (*walī*) and he might continue to do so even after the birth of a grandchild.[25]

Before drafting a fair copy of the testamentary instrument, the document specialist had to clarify several issues. In addition to designating the initial line of beneficiaries, a founder customarily identifies secondary and tertiary branches of beneficiaries who will enter the endowment in the event that an earlier branch fails. And to insure the perpetuity of the endowment, it was customary to designate a religious institution – whose continuous existence could be taken for granted –

[24] It is a general rule that the legatee must be alive in fact or in law at the time of the testator's decease, except according to the Mālikī school and certain Shāfiʿī authorities, who allow bequests in favor of members of a restricted class or group who may come into existence after the death of the testator. See Coulson, *Succession in the Muslim Family*, 227–8.

[25] For examples of the use of patriarchal authority for such purposes, see Powers, "The Maliki Family Endowment," 396–8; idem, "Parents and their Minor Children: Familial Politics in the Middle Maghrib in the Eighth/Fourteenth Century," *Continuity and Change*, 16:2 (2001), 177–200.

as the ultimate beneficiary. Having specified the unborn grandchild and the latter's male and female descendants as the first branch of beneficiaries, the co-founders had to envisage the possibility either that the grandchild would not come into existence or that it would not reproduce. There were options. For example, the co-founders might have sought to keep the endowment property within the Banū Khannūsa clan by designating Abū Zayd ʿAbd al-Raḥmān's closest surviving agnate and the latter's descendants as the endowment's secondary beneficiaries. This was a common choice among founders of endowments. Instead they chose to designate Abū Zayd's unnamed sister's children, Muḥammad and Raḥma, and their male descendants, as the second branch of beneficiaries. This choice was significant because it opened the door for cognatic descendants of the male co-founder to enter the endowment at a later stage of its history. To insure the ultimate perpetuity of the endowment, the co-founders stipulated that if the second branch of beneficiaries came to an end, the endowment would revert to the Congregational Mosque of Fez, specifying that the revenues were to be used for the purchase of olive oil and carpets and for the repair of the mosque itself, and that any surplus was to be used to feed the poor (viz., Ṣūfīs) and Murābiṭs who frequented the institution.

There remained one final issue. Fāṭima previously had formulated a bequest whose nature is unspecified in our source. Before the document specialist could draft a fair copy of the testamentary endowment (and collect his fee), Fāṭima had to revoke the earlier bequest – an action that no doubt would have negative consequences for one or more members of the family. She complied, whereupon the scribe drafted a fair copy of the document on 5 Rajab 791/30 June 1389. The terms of the resulting legal instrument were read aloud in the presence of two professional witnesses (*ʿudūl*) who had been summoned for that purpose: Abū Yaḥyā b. ʿAbd al-Raḥmān b. Ṣāliḥ and Muḥammad b. ʿAbd al-Raḥmān [b.] Yaskun al-Kinānī.[26] The witnessing clause specifies that both witnesses were acquainted with the co-founders, but this assertion is qualified at the very end of the document, immediately following the witnesses' names, where, significantly, the scribe indicated that the testimony of the first witness did *not* include acquaintance with Fāṭima, whereas that of the second witness did, a point to which I shall return.

To the best of my knowledge, the original copy of the testamentary endowment is not extant. What has survived is a summary transcription of the endowment deed composed in the year 825/1422 in connection with a dispute over its interpretation. This transcription was included in a fatwā that subsequently came into the hands of al-Wansharīsī, who copied it into the *Miʿyār*. As best I can determine, the transcription reproduced by al-Wansharīsī is faithful to the original, except for the omission of certain details such as the identity of the properties, their boundaries and the number of shares owned by Fāṭima and Abū Zayd ʿAbd al-Raḥmān.

[26] Al-Kinānī is identified as a witness to several documents preserved elsewhere in the *Miʿyār*. See Wansharīsī, *Miʿyār*, vol. 7, 497 (bottom), 498, ll. 17–18 and 25 (where the text specifies *Yaskur* instead of *Yaskun*). The documents in which this individual's name appears are translated and analyzed in David S. Powers, "A Court Case from Fourteenth Century North Africa," *Journal of the American Oriental Society* 110.2 (1990), 229–54, at 252.

The endowment deed begins by identifying the names of the co-founders, the nature of the property, and the identity of the initial beneficiary:

> The most eminent and excellent shaykh, Abū Zayd ʿAbd al-Raḥmān, son of the late, blessed, most venerable shaykh, Abū ʿAbdallāh Muḥammad b. Khannūsa, and his chaste[27] mother, Fāṭima, daughter of the late, most venerable jurist, the shaykh Abū al-Faḍl al-Zarhūnī, stipulated in writing that upon the occurrence of the event of their death, from which there is no escape and which no living creature can avoid, one-third of their entire estate – the entirety of the olive grove situated at so-and-so; and the share [of the groves] belonging exclusively to Fāṭima, to his exclusion, known as such-and-such; and all of the *sājilīn*[28] owned jointly by the two of them in such-and-such a place – all of the above – should be excluded, in their name, after their death, from one-third of their estate, in its entirety, both immovables and movables. All of that shall be given to the first child (*walad*) born alive to the two children of the aforementioned ʿAbd al-Raḥmān, the aforementioned legator, [namely] Muḥammad and ʿĀʾisha, who are minors at the present time, whether the child is a male or a female, equally and impartially among the two children [*sic*] of the two aforementioned children. This will be an endowment for the two of them [*sic*] and for their [dual] descendants (*aʿqābihimā*), so long as they continue to propagate and their branches extend, to be divided equally and impartially among them.[29]

The deed continues by specifying who would enter the endowment in the event that the first branch failed:

> If the two aforementioned full siblings, Muḥammad and ʿĀʾisha, die without any descendant, [the endowment] reverts to the two children of the sister of the aforementioned ʿAbd al-Raḥmān, who are the maternal grandchildren of the aforementioned Fāṭima, [namely] Muḥammad and Raḥma, the two children (*ibnā*) of the most eminent shaykh, the revered pilgrim, Abū al-ʿAbbās Aḥmad b. Rāshid, [to be divided] equally and impartially among them, and also for their [dual] male descendants, so long as they continue to propagate and their branches extend, males to the exclusion of females.[30]

The deed then identifies the ultimate beneficiary of the endowment and specifies the purposes for which the revenues are to be used:

> If they die out and their descendants die out, [the property] reverts as an eternal and perpetual endowment for the Jāmiʿ al-Ṣābirīn, of Ūzqūr,[31] inside Bāb al-Futūḥ,[32] one of the gates of Fez al-Maḥrūsa, for the purchase of olive oil for lighting the aforementioned Friday Mosque and for carpets; and for the repair of anything that has become worn out

27 Text: *al-maṣūna*. On this term see Huda Lutfi, "A Study of Six Fourteenth-Century *Iqrārs* from al-Quds Relating to Muslim Women," *Journal of the Social and Economic History of the Orient* 26 (1983), 246–94, esp. 262–3 and 278–9.

28 On this term, see note 21, above.

29 Wansharīsī, *Miʿyār*, vol. 7, 311, ll. 9–20.

30 Ibid., vol. 7, 311, ll. 20–5.

31 Text: *min Ūzqūr*. Perhaps: "For the Jāmiʿ of the Ṣābirīn from Ūzqūr." I have been unable to identify Ūzqūr. Vincent Lagardère, *Histoire et Société en Occident Musulman au Moyen Âge: Analyse du Miʿyār d'al-Wanṣarīsī* (Madrid: CSIC, 1995), 227 gives the vocalization, *Ūzaqqūr*.

32 Bāb al-Futūḥ is one of the main gates of Fez. See Roger Le Tourneau, *Fez in the Age of the Marinides* (Norman: University of Oklahoma Press, 1961), 20–1, 68; idem, *Fès avant le protectorat: étude économique et sociale d'une ville de l'occident musulman* (Casablanca: Société Marocaine de Librairie et d'Edition, 1949), index, s.v., Bab Ftouh.

> in the aforementioned Friday Mosque. Any surplus revenue shall be used to purchase food to feed the poor [Ṣūfīs] and the Murābiṭs who come to the aforementioned mosque and attend it faithfully[33] – after expending, in the service of that [mosque], on whatever will cause the aforementioned endowment to endure, and on its repair, with those proceeds, and its material appurtenances and all of its abstract rights,[34] both inside and outside of [the Friday Mosque], that are known [to belong to it] and are attributed to it.[35]

The endowment deed concludes with a pious formality; the witnessing clause; the dating clause (which includes a description of Fāṭima and the specification that she had revoked all previous bequests); and, finally, the names of the witnesses (including the aforementioned qualification of their testimony):

> [This is] a valid, complete legacy by means of which they [dual] intended the face of Glorious God – may He be Exalted – His weighty merit, and the next world. "Surely God (*sic*) does not leave to waste the wage of him who does good works."[36] He (*sic*) understood the import of that, and [the witnesses whose names appear below] bore witness with regard to this on behalf of the two of them, being in a state of soundness [of mind and body], voluntarily, legally capable [of conducting their affairs; [they also] identified the two of them. This occurred on the evening of Tuesday 5 Rajab 791/30 June 1389, after the aforementioned Fāṭima had retracted, on the date of [this legacy], every legacy that she had made prior to this date. Among the physical features of the woman are middle age, fine figure, wheat-colored countenance and cheeks, and a straight nose (*wa-min naʿat al-marʾa naṣaf ḥasanat al-qadd qamḥiyyat baljāʾ wa-janāʾ qawīmat al-anf*). [Witnessed by] Abū Yaḥyā b. ʿAbd al-Raḥmān b. Ṣāliḥ, except for the identification of the woman; and Muḥammad b. ʿAbd al-Raḥmān [b.] Yaskun al-Kinānī, who identified the aforementioned woman.[37]

The scribe no doubt drafted two copies of the endowment deed, one of which was placed in the qāḍī's register, while the other was given to the co-founders for deposit in their family archive, together with other important documents.[38] Since the endowment would not become effective immediately, Fāṭima and Abū Zayd resumed their affairs and awaited the birth of Abū Zayd's first grandchild.

The First Generation: 791–825/1389–1422

A recurrence of plague ravaged Fez in 817–18/1414–15, killing an estimated 36,000 people, not including foreigners and the poor.[39] It is possible that the

[33] Text: *al-multazimīn bihā*.

[34] Text: *bi-manāfiʿ dhālika wa-marāfiqihi wa-kāfat ḥuqūqihi kullihā*. On such accessory clauses, see Jeanette Wakin, *The Function of Documents in Islamic Law* (Albany: State University of New York Press, 1972), 49–53.

[35] Wansharīsī, *Miʿyār*, vol. 7, 311 (l. 25)–12 (l. 7).

[36] Qurʾān 18:30. Note: the scribe has substituted "God does not leave" for "We do not leave".

[37] Wansharīsī, *Miʿyār*, vol. 7, 312, ll. 7–14.

[38] On family archives, see Powers, "Maliki Family Endowment," 389–91.

[39] Dols, *The Black Death*, 175, 309.

co-founders of the endowment and one or more of its beneficiaries were victims of this outbreak of the plague.

Be that as it may, we know that by 825/1422 both Fāṭima al-Zarhūniyya and Abū Zayd ʿAbd al-Raḥmān were dead. As for Abū Zayd's children, we do not know whether or not ʿĀʾisha lived to adulthood or married; she reportedly died without leaving any descendants. Her brother, Muḥammad, on the other hand, married and fathered a daughter to whom he gave the name of Fāṭima, no doubt in honor of the girl's great-grandmother, the female co-founder of the endowment. Fāṭima bt. Muḥammad arguably was "the first child born to Muḥammad and (*sic*) ʿĀʾisha" and, according to this reading of the endowment deed, she qualified as the initial beneficiary of the endowment. Fāṭima reportedly established her claim to the endowment, but predeceased her father, Muḥammad, without leaving any children. Significantly, upon her death, control of the endowment properties reverted to her father, Muḥammad. The latter fathered additional children (whose gender is not specified), but these did not qualify as beneficiaries of the endowment because none of them was the *first* child born to him. It is possible that both ʿĀʾisha and Fāṭima were victims of the plague epidemic of 817–18/1414–15.

Muḥammad b. ʿAbd al-Raḥmān followed ʿĀʾisha and Fāṭima to their graves, thereby bringing to an end the initial line of beneficiaries specified by the co-founders. It was at this critical juncture, in 825/1422, that the Ibn Khannūsa clan intervened to prevent transmission of the endowment to the second line of beneficiaries (who were cognates), that is, to Muḥammad b. Aḥmad b. Rāshid and his sister (the latter had given birth to a son, Abū Zayd ʿAbd al-Raḥmān b. Rāshid, whose agnomen [*kunyā*] and personal name recall that of the co-founder, Abū Zayd ʿAbd al-Raḥmān b. Khannūsa). Upon the death of Muḥammad b. ʿAbd al-Raḥmān, an uncle or cousin of the male co-founder by the name of Abū Muḥammad ʿAbdallāh b. Khannūsa seized control of the endowment properties on the grounds that he was the senior member of the Banū Khannūsa and Muḥammad b. ʿAbd al-Raḥmān's closest surviving agnatic relative.[40]

Abū Muḥammad ʿAbdallāh b. Khannūsa's seizure of the property triggered the dispute. Subsequent to this action, Muḥammad b. Rāshid filed a complaint with an unnamed Fāsī qāḍī (perhaps Abū al-Faḍl ʿAbd al-ʿAzīz b. Abī Jamāʿa al-Tujībī, who is mentioned in a later document) who then summoned the two men to appear in his court to put forward their respective claims to the property. The dispute set one jurist against another. Abū Muḥammad ʿAbdallāh b. Khannūsa claimed that he was entitled to the endowment revenues in his capacity as Abū Zayd ʿAbd al-Raḥmān b. Khannūsa's closest surviving agnatic relative. Muḥammad b. Rāshid responded that his adversary's appeal to kinship was irrelevant, because the transmission of entitlement to the endowment revenues was governed by the specific descent strategy defined by the co-founders. In support of this claim, Muḥammad b. Rāshid brought forward the endowment deed and contended that the plain meaning of the founders' words required that entitlement to the revenues should pass to him and his sister.

[40] Wansharīsī, *Miʿyār*, vol. 7, 312 (l. 21)–13 (l. 2).

The Istiftā'

Before rendering his decision, the qāḍī decided to request a fatwā from two judicial experts (it will be recalled that the technical term for the person who requests such an opinion is *mustaftī*, and for the request itself, *istiftā'*). He wrote a long and detailed letter[41] to two distinguished muftīs of Tlemcen who were experts in the interpretation of legal texts, Muḥammad b. Marzūq (d. 842/1439)[42] and Qāsim al-ʿUqbānī (d. 854/1450).[43] By referring the case to jurists who were unlikely to have close ties to either of the litigants, the qāḍī may have sought to insure the impartiality of the judicial process. In his letter, the qāḍī cum *mustaftī* provided a summary transcription of the endowment, re-presented the arguments of the two litigants (beginning with that of ʿAbdallāh b. Khannūsa – one point, and continuing with that of Muḥammad b. Rāshid – six points), and sought clarification of the relevant issues.

The descent strategy formulated by the co-founders had been designed to regulate the smooth and continuous functioning of the endowment, and the document specialist who drafted the deed presumably had acted with great care. But the inherently equivocal and ambiguous nature of language made it possible for ʿAbdallāh b. Khannūsa to argue his case in a court of law, where the resolution of the dispute revolved around the key notion of the co-founders' *intent*. Who exactly did the co-founders have in mind as primary, secondary, and tertiary beneficiaries when they created the endowment in 791/1389?[44] This question, in turn, raised the

[41] Ibid., vol. 7, 314 (bottom)–17 (l. 21).

[42] Abū ʿAbdallāh Muḥammad b. Aḥmad b. Muḥammad b. Muḥammad b. Abī Bakr b. Marzūq al-ʿUjaysī al-Tilimsānī, known as Ibn Marzūq the grandson, was born on 13 Rabīʿ I 766/1 December 1364. A polymath who wrote on a wide variety of subjects, including the Qur'ān, law, grammar and Sufism, he was a contemporary of Saʿīd al-ʿUqbānī, with whom he studied and whose fatwā on the subject of sufi practices he refuted. Ibn Marzūq performed the pilgrimage to Mecca on two occasions, first in 790/1388 and again in 819/1416–17. He died in Cairo on Thursday evening of 14 Shaʿbān 842/30 January 1439. The Mamlūk Sulṭān and lesser dignitaries are reported to have attended his funeral. See Aḥmad al-Wansharīsī, *Wafayāt*, in *Alf sana min al-wafayāt fī thalātha kutub*, ed. M. Ḥajjī (Rabat: Dār al-Maghrib li'l-ta'līf, 1396/1976), 141; Ibn al-Qāḍī al-Miknāsī, *Laqṭ al-farā'id min lufāẓat ḥuqaq al-fawā'id, in Alf sana min al-wafayāt fī thalātha kutub*, 248; Aḥmad Bābā al-Tunbuktī, *Kitāb nayl al-ibtihāj bi-taṭrīz al-dībāj* (Cairo: n.p., 1932), 293–9; Badr al-Dīn al-Qarāfī, *Tawshīḥ al-dībāj wa'l-ḥilya al-ibtihāj* (Beirut: Dār al-Gharb al-Islāmī, 1983), 171, no. 170; Muḥammad b. Muḥammad Makhlūf, *Shajarat al-nūr al-zakiyya fī ṭabaqāt al-mālikiyya*, 2 vols (2nd edn, Beirut: Dār al-Kitāb al-ʿArabī, 1975), vol. 1, 252, no. 918. See also al-Maqqarī al-Tilimsānī, *Nafḥ al-ṭīb min ghuṣn al-Andalus al-raṭīb*, 7 vols (Beirut: Dār Ṣādir, 1388/1968), vol. 5, 420–33.

[43] Abū al-Faḍl Qāsim b. Saʿīd b. Muḥammad b. Muḥammad al-ʿUqbānī was born in 768/1367. A jurist and Qur'ān commentator, he also served as chief qāḍī of Tlemcen. He performed the pilgrimage in 830/1427 and died in Dhū al-Qaʿda 854/December 1450. See al-Wansharīsī, *Wafayāt*, 144; Ibn al-Qāḍī al-Miknāsī, *Laqṭ al-farā'id*, 253; Qarāfī, *Tawshīḥ*, 99, note 3; Makhlūf, *Shajara*, vol. 1, 255, no. 925.

[44] This question is compounded by the fact that the testamentary instrument was created jointly by two people. Were Fāṭima's objectives the same as her son's? If they were not, whose intent should be privileged? If they were, how does one determine their collective intent? These issues, ignored here because they were never raised in conjunction with the dispute, deserve further attention.

epistemological issue of how one can know or discover the intent of a founder – now long dead – at the time of the endowment's creation.

As a jurist trained in the interpretation of legal texts, ʿAbdallāh b. Khannūsa understood that he would have to support his claim with a persuasive reading of the endowment deed. To this end Ibn Khannūsa identified, isolated and highlighted several key words in the deed, specifically, the clause that stipulates, "If the two aforementioned full siblings, Muḥammad and ʿĀʾisha, die without any descendant …" According to Ibn Khannūsa, the operative phrase here was the expression "without any descendant," which he interpreted in a general, unrestricted manner (*ʿalā wajh al-ʿumūm*): entitlement was to pass from the first line of beneficiaries to the second only in the event that Muḥammad and ʿĀʾisha died "without *any* descendant" (emphasis added). This contingency, he argued, had yet to materialize, for Muḥammad died leaving his second and third children and several agnatic collaterals (including himself). For this reason, control of the endowment should remain with the Banū Khannūsa because Muḥammad had died leaving descendants.[45]

Muḥammad b. Rāshid, also a jurist, told his story as persuasively as he could in the language of the law. In support of his claim that the endowment should revert to himself and to his sister, he advanced the following six arguments:

1 Ibn Rāshid argued that ʿAbdallāh b. Khannūsa did not qualify as a beneficiary of the endowment. He reasoned that if the testators had intended to include the agnates as beneficiaries, they would have mentioned the agnates in the deed. But the two testators did not mention them, nor did they specify that the second and third child born to Muḥammad or ʿĀʾisha would qualify as beneficiaries of the endowment. They did, on the other hand, identify the children of Muḥammad or Raḥma as potential beneficiaries of the endowment, specifying the manner in which the endowment revenues were to be divided among these beneficiaries.[46]

2 Ibn Rāshid rejected Ibn Khannūsa's interpretation of the endowment deed on the grounds that his adversary had taken the phrase "without any descendant" out of its proper context. Ibn Rāshid argued that when the testators used the word *descendant* in the phrase "without any descendant," they were referring specifically to a *descendant who was entitled to the legacy*. Although the second and third children admittedly were the testators' descendants, they did not qualify as beneficiaries. In the specific context in which the phrase was used, the existence of the second and third children was legally irrelevant[47] – a point which, Ibn Rāshid observed, explains why those children never demanded inclusion in the endowment. Therefore, the "descendant" specified in the endowment deed must be someone other than the second and third children born to Muḥammad (it will be recalled that ʿĀʾisha had no children). The document leaves no room for doubt as to the identity of this beneficiary, for the

[45] Wansharīsī, *Miʿyār*, vol. 7, 315, ll. 1–11.
[46] Ibid., vol. 7, 315, ll. 12–17.
[47] Text: *maʿdūm* (perhaps: "non-existent").

testators stipulated that the endowment was for "the first child born alive to ... Muḥammad and ʿĀʾisha." Thus, they did not use the word *descendant* in a general, unrestricted manner (as, for example, in the phrase, "for the descendants of Muḥammad and ʿĀʾisha") – as Ibn Khannūsa claimed, but rather restricted the semantic range of the word *descendant*. This explanation addressed the major thrust of ʿAbdallāh b. Khannūsa's argument.[48]

3 Having argued that the endowment deed does not envisage the inclusion of ʿAbdallāh b. Khannūsa, Ibn Rāshid proceeded to make the positive argument for his own entitlement, invoking a sophisticated logical consideration. He noted that the existence of some of the beneficiaries and potential beneficiaries was contingent, while that of others was not.[49] The contingent beneficiaries were those persons whose existence depended upon the fulfillment of the condition of birth (that is, the unborn children), while the non-contingent beneficiaries were those persons whose existence did not depend on the fulfillment of such a condition (that is, Muḥammad and ʿĀʾisha). The latter, Ibn Rāshid argued, have a stronger claim on the endowment than the former. It was therefore significant, in his view, that the testators had designated him as the person to whom the endowment was to revert if the first set of non-contingent beneficiaries became extinct. *Ad minorum ad majorum*, his entitlement was even stronger in the case of the extinction of persons whose entitlement to the endowment was merely contingent. "It is most proper," Ibn Rāshid asserted, "that I take the legacy."[50]

4 Drawing upon his training in the rhetoric of legal argumentation, Ibn Rāshid observed that whereas his adversary, ʿAbdallāh b. Khannūsa, based his claim to the endowment on an external linguistic sign (*lafẓ*), he based his entitlement on the sign's underlying signification (*maʿnā*).[51] The latter, in his view, was of greater import because people who leave a legacy customarily intend "what is most certain" (*al-ākid fa'l-ākid*). In the present instance, the certainty of the endowment was assured, firstly, by Muḥammad and ʿĀʾisha; secondly, by Muḥammad b. Rāshid and his sister; and thirdly, by the Friday Mosque. In further support of this point, Ibn Rāshid observed that the testators had inserted the copula "and" (*wāw*) between the primary and secondary beneficiaries, rather than the conjunction "then" (*thumma*). (In the technical language of the

[48] Ibid., vol. 7, 315, ll. 17–24.

[49] Note: Muḥammad b. Rāshid does not use the abstract concepts of *contingency* and *non-contingency*.

[50] Ibid., vol. 7, 315 (l. 24)–16 (l. 4).

[51] On the distinction between *lafẓ* and *maʿnā*, see *EI*², s.v. *maʿnā*; Bernard Weiss, "Exotericism and Objectivity in Islamic Jurisprudence," in *Islamic Law and Jurisprudence: Studies in Honor of Farhat J. Ziadeh*, ed. Nicholas Heer (Seattle and London: University of Washington Press, 1990), 53–72; idem, "Language and Law: The Linguistic Premises of Islamic Legal Science," in *In Quest of Islamic Humanism: Arabic and Islamic Studies in Memory of Mohamed al-Nowaihi*, ed. Arnold Green (Cairo: American University Press, 1984), 15–21; Wolfhart Heinrichs, "*Lafẓ/maʿnā* in rhetorics," in *Arabische Dichtung und griechische Poetik* (Wiesbaden: F. Steiner, 1969), 62–82; Muhsin Mahdi, "*Lafẓ/maʿnā* in the debate between logic and grammar," in *Logic in Classical Islamic Culture*, ed. G.E. von Grunebaum (Wiesbaden: O. Harrassowitz, 1970), 51–83.

law, the copula "and" signifies a bridge that joins two entities, whereas the conjunction "then" signifies a barrier that separates two entities).[52] It was as if the testators had foreseen the inevitable extinction of the first line of beneficiaries and, having utmost in their minds the welfare of Ibn Rāshid, designated him and his male descendants as the second line of beneficiaries.[53]

5 Ibn Rāshid drew attention to the testators' concern for the Friday Mosque. Like the first line of beneficiaries, the second line also might die out. The testators therefore designated the Friday Mosque – an institution that arguably would never cease to exist – as the ultimate beneficiary of the endowment. Their concern for the mosque was a manifestation of the pious and charitable purpose of the endowment, as reflected in the testators' specific stipulations regarding the use of the endowment revenues: the purchase of olive oil and carpets; maintenance; and the purchase of food for the poor Ṣūfīs and Murābiṭs who frequent the mosque. Any interpretation of the deed that ignored the rights of the Friday Mosque, Ibn Rāshid contended, "constitutes a diversion of the legacy from its intended purpose and an alteration of the endowment."[54] By emphasizing the status of the Friday Mosque as the ultimate beneficiary of the endowment, Ibn Rāshid reinforced his own entitlement as an endowment beneficiary. "To the extent that my statement confirms the mosque's interest," he asserted, "I am prior in rank to it."[55]

In support of his fifth point, Ibn Rāshid posed a hypothetical question designed to elicit the co-founders' state of mind at the moment of the endowment's creation: suppose someone had asked the two testators, before they died, whether it was their intention – upon their deaths and in the event that Muḥammad and ʿĀʾisha left no descendants – that the endowment would revert to the agnates, to the exclusion of both Ibn Rāshid and the Friday Mosque? No reasonable person who examined the legacy, Ibn Rāshid asserted, would come to that conclusion.[56] (Although his conclusion sounds reasonable, it glosses over the epistemological problem of how he could possibly know what he claimed to know.)

6 Finally, Ibn Rāshid adduced two legal precedents. Citing an opinion attributed to Mālik b. Anas (d. 179/795) in the case of a person who had designated his house as an endowment without specifying the beneficiary, Ibn Rāshid observed that Mālik allowed the *imām* (ruler) to determine the identity of the beneficiary on the basis of his independent reasoning and knowledge of custom. Inasmuch as it was customary for people to establish endowments for pious purposes, the *imām* ruled that the endowment should revert to the poor and the indigent. Ibn

[52] On the legal function of the particles *thumma* and *wāw*, see Wansharīsī, *Miʿyār*, vol. 7, 440–1; Aharon Layish, "The Mālikī Family *waqf* according to Wills and *Waqfiyyāt*," *Bulletin of the School of Oriental and African Studies* 46:1 (1983), 1–32, esp. 13–14.

[53] Wansharīsī, *Miʿyār*, vol. 7, 316, ll. 4–11.

[54] Ibid., vol. 7, 316, ll. 18–19.

[55] Ibid., vol. 7, 316, l. 19.

[56] Ibid., vol. 7, 316, ll. 11–25.

Rāshid also cited an opinion attributed to the Cordoban jurist Ibn Rushd al-Jadd (d. 520/1126)[57] in the case of a woman who left a last will and testament in which she referred to the object of the legacy in vague and ambiguous terms ("Whatever is in my house is for my client"). In such a case, Ibn Rushd opined, one must refer to the obvious, apparent, and most likely meaning, as manifested in the testator's intention or what is most likely to have been her intention (again, begging the question of whether there is such a thing as "plain meaning," and, if there is, how one can know it). These two cases supported Ibn Rāshid's contention that the intended meaning – that is, the meaning attributed to the testator's words by a presumably objective third party – should prevail over the literal meaning of the words used in the endowment deed.[58]

After completing his summary of the litigants' respective arguments, the *mustaftī* asked the two muftīs to answer three questions: First, he asked whether the legacy should revert to Muḥammad b. Rāshid, to the agnates, or to the Friday Mosque. Second, he asked the muftī to clarify the significance of certain omissions and imprecisions in the deed and of certain deficiencies in the scribe's knowledge of the Arabic language. Third, he asked whether the underlying meaning of the phrase "without any descendant" should prevail over its external linguistic formulation, thereby allowing the conclusion that the legacy should revert to a person or institution intended by the testator – but not specifically mentioned?[59] The first and third questions were two sides of the same coin, whereas the second question related to an apparently extraneous issue.

The Judicial Opinions

The response of Muḥammad b. Marzūq

Ibn Marzūq began his response with the customary disclaimer that what he was about to say was merely his personal opinion and that God alone knows what is correct, thereby emphasizing his humility and subordination to the Divinity and acknowledging the limitations of human knowledge. Following the disclaimer, the muftī announced his support for Muḥammad b. Rāshid. Upon the extinction of the descendant (*sic*) of the first child born to Muḥammad or ʿĀʾisha, he explained, the endowment reverts to Muḥammad b. Rāshid and his sister, Raḥma. After the latter two siblings and their (male) descendants die out, the endowment should revert to the Jāmiʿ al-Ṣābirīn. Neither the agnates nor any person other than the first child born to Muḥammad or ʿĀʾisha is entitled to the endowment.[60]

[57] For biographical references, see chapter one, note 73.
[58] Wansharīsī, *Miʿyār*, vol. 7, 316 (bottom)–17, l. 10.
[59] Ibid., vol. 7, 317, ll. 11–21.
[60] Ibid., vol. 7, 317 (l. 22)–18 (l. 3).

Ibn Marzūq rejected ʿAbdallāh b. Khannūsa's interpretation of the deed, for two reasons. First, the latter's contention that the word *descendant* in the phrase "without any descendant" should be construed in a general, unrestricted manner has no force, on two grounds, both relating to Arabic syntax: (a) as an indefinite noun that occurs in the context of an affirmative statement, the word *descendant* is qualified or restricted; and (b) there is no contextual qualifier that would transform the word into a general expression.[61] Even if one assumed, for the sake of argument, that the phrase was used in a general sense, on the grounds that an indefinite noun that occurs in the context of a conditional statement may be considered to have a general significance, the phrase "the first child born to the two aforementioned persons" nevertheless serves as a contextual qualifier that specifies the general statement. In further support of this hypothetical case, the muftī drew an analogy to the determination of whether an appointment of agency is restricted or unrestricted, as discussed by Ibn Rushd in his *Muqaddimāt*.[62]

Second, the muftī rejected ʿAbdallāh b. Khannūsa's argument that Muḥammad b. ʿAbd al-Raḥmān had died leaving a descendant, again on two grounds: (a) the word *descendant* in the legacy does not refer to descendants in general, but rather is used restrictively in the sense of *the descendant of the first child born to either of them*; however, the first child born to Muḥammad did not leave a descendant and (b) if it is conceded that no one other than the first child born to either Muḥammad and (*sic*) ʿĀʾisha enters the endowment, it follows that each of them died without leaving any descendant who qualified as a beneficiary of the endowment.[63] These two counter-arguments undermined the substance of Ibn Khannūsa's position.

Having discharged his primary obligation, Ibn Marzūq devoted the remainder of his response to the *mustaftī*'s second question regarding the drafting of the document. The muftī identified two problems with the endowment deed, neither of which, he stated, was germane to his conclusion. The first problem relates to the testators' statement, "the first child born alive to the two children of ... ʿAbd al-Raḥmān, the ... legator, [namely], Muḥammad *and* ʿĀʾisha" (emphasis added). This formulation, the muftī observed, may be interpreted as indicating that the first child born to Muḥammad *and* the first child born to ʿĀʾisha would qualify as beneficiaries of the endowment (as the document specialist who drafted the deed apparently assumed). In fact, the muftī clarified, the context requires that only the first child born to *either* of the two siblings would qualify as the beneficiary. The point was moot because ʿĀʾisha had no children.[64]

The second problem relates to the testators' statement, "If [Muḥammad or Raḥma] die out, *or* if their descendants die out" (emphasis added).[65] On the

[61] On the legal significance of a contextual qualifier (*qarīna*), see Wael Hallaq, "Notes on the Term *qarīna* in Islamic Legal Discourse," *Journal of the American Oriental Society* 108:3 (1988), 475–80.
[62] Wansharīsī, *Miʿyār*, vol. 7, 318, ll. 3–14.
[63] Ibid., vol. 7, 318 (l. 21)–19 (l. 2).
[64] Ibid., vol. 7, 319, ll. 2–9.
[65] Note, however, that the transcribed version of the deed preserved in our source has "and" in place of "or". Ibid., vol. 7, 311, l. 25.

surface, the testators' use of the disjunctive particle "or" (*aw*) seemingly requires that the condition be interpreted alternately, not inclusively. Viewed in this manner, the endowment would revert to the Friday Mosque if any one of three contingencies materialized: if either Muḥammad or Raḥma died; if both Muḥammad and Raḥma died, the existence of their descendants notwithstanding; or if their descendants died, the existence of Muḥammad and Raḥma notwithstanding. Ibn Marzūq rejected this interpretation (which posed a clear threat to the interests of the Ibn Rāshids)[66] on the ground that several contextual qualifiers indicate that the conjunctive particle "and" (*wāw*) should have been used; he suggested that the problematic phrase should be treated as if such a particle in fact had been used. That is to say, he interpolated the text to accommodate its wording and interpretation to his understanding of the co-founders' intent![67] That this issue was raised by the *mustaftī* suggests that someone may have asserted a claim to the endowment on behalf of the Friday Mosque.

Ibn Marzūq concluded by addressing the standards to be upheld in drafting legal documents. The examples that have just been discussed suggested to him that legal documents were being drafted by people who did not possess the standards of their craft. To counter this decline in standards, the muftī recommended that the writing of documents be limited to religious scholars so that "the drafting of legal formularies and documents would be undertaken exclusively by those who are knowledgeable in these matters, so long as there is a need for such a matter."[68]

Attached to the fatwā itself is a judicial certification (*ishhād*), dated late Ṣafar 825/February 1422, in which two professional witnesses – Muḥammad b. ʿĪsā al-Baṭṭūʾī (or: al-Baṭṭīwī)[69] and Muḥammad b. ʿAbdallāh b. Aḥmad – certified that the response was that of Ibn Marzūq and was in his handwriting.[70]

The response of Qāsim al-ʿUqbānī

In a response issued on the same day as that of Ibn Marzūq, the distinguished jurist, Qāsim al-ʿUqbānī, reached the same conclusion as his colleague, to wit, the endowment reverts to Muḥammad b. Rāshid and his sister, Raḥma. Al-ʿUqbānī directed his attention to the distinction between form and substance, between the literal and underlying meaning of the co-founders' words. The muftī observed that when interpreting oaths and other legal formulations, some jurists take into consideration the external linguistic sign, to the exclusion of its underlying meaning – even when the linguistic sign is accompanied by an external qualifier that might suggest another, different, signification. Al-ʿUqbānī rejected this approach, arguing

[66] Representatives of the Friday mosque might have invoked this argument to advance the mosque's claim to the endowment revenues.

[67] Ibid., vol. 7, 319, ll. 10–19. [68] Ibid., vol. 7, 320, ll. 3–5.

[69] Muḥammad b. ʿĪsā al-Baṭṭīwī is perhaps the brother of Aḥmad b. ʿĪsā al-Baṭṭīwī, whom we will encounter in chapter five.

[70] Ibid., vol. 7, 320, ll. 5–12.

that the testators' initial mention of the word *descendants* ("for their descendants") refers to the first child born to either Muḥammad or ʿĀʾisha, and not to the first child born to each of them. Therefore, the word *descendant* in the statement, "If Muḥammad and ʿĀʾisha die without any descendant," should be interpreted restrictively as referring to the descendant *as previously specified*. Furthermore, the testators' specification of "the first child born to Muḥammad" entails that Muḥammad's second child and any subsequent children do not qualify as beneficiaries.[71]

Attached to al-ʿUqbānī's fatwā is a judicial certification issued on the same date as that of Ibn Marzūq and certified by the same two professional witnesses.[72] This certification is followed by Qāsim al-ʿUqbānī's formal declaration that the two fatwās were authentic.[73]

Subsequent Developments

Deposition of Abū al-Qāsim b. Khannūsa: 17 Muḥarram 826/31 December 1422

The next document in our source is dated 17 Muḥarram 826/31 December 1422. I can only speculate about what transpired in the ten months between this date and the issuance of the two fatwās in late Ṣafar 825/February 1422.

The fatwās presumably were conveyed to the *mustaftī*/qāḍī. Although a fatwā is not binding, the concurring opinions of two distinguished jurists, arrived at independently, provided the qāḍī with authoritative support for a judgment (*ḥukm*) in favor of Muḥammad b. Rāshid and his sister, Raḥma. But the qāḍī apparently refrained from issuing a judgment, perhaps in the hope that the two parties would reach a *ṣulḥ*, or amicable settlement.[74] When ʿAbdallāh b. Khannūsa refused to relinquish control of the endowment, however, Muḥammad b. Rāshid and his sister had no choice but to return to the qāḍī and request a formal judgment confirming their entitlement to the endowment revenues. Before issuing such a

[71] Ibid., vol. 7, 320 (l. 13)–1 (l. 1). In further support of his restrictive reading of the word *descendant*, al-ʿUqbānī adduced an analogous case that occurs later in the same document (ibid., vol. 7, 321, ll. 1–8). The testators specified the *male* descendants of Muḥammad and Raḥma as subsequent beneficiaries: "for their male descendants, so long as they continue to propagate and their branches extend, males to the exclusion of females." The very next sentence reads, "If [Muḥammad and Raḥma] die out, or if their *descendants* die out ... " Here, the word *descendant* is not qualified; if it were interpreted in an unrestricted manner, male *and* female descendants might demand inclusion in the endowment on the strength of this sentence. Clearly, however, the meaning of the word *descendant* here is conditioned by the qualification contained in the previous sentence. In other words, once a term has been qualified, it is not necessary to repeat the qualification every time that the term is used subsequently.

[72] Ibid., vol. 7, 321, ll. 13–17.

[73] Ibid., vol. 7, 321, ll. 17–19. Text: *aʿlama bi-istiqlālihi*. On the terms *istaqalla* and *istiqlāl*, see chapter three, note 97.

[74] On *ṣulḥ*, see chapter three, note 102.

decision, the qāḍī summoned Ibn Khannūsa and asked him to explain the grounds on which he continued to exercise control over the property.

It is at this moment that our documentation resumes. Either unable or unwilling to appear in court himself, ʿAbdallāh b. Khannūsa designated his son, Abū al-Qāsim (yet another jurist), to serve as his legal representative (*wakīl*).[75] On 17 Muḥarram 826/31 December 1422, ten months after the two fatwās had been issued, Abū al-Qāsim presented himself to the qāḍī, who read the endowment deed to him and asked him to interpret the document. Abū al-Qāsim's response indicates a dramatic shift in legal strategy that was facilitated by a seemingly insignificant detail in the endowment deed. Recall, first, that the endowment deed included a physical description of Fāṭima al-Zarhūniyya and, second, that only one of the two witnesses had identified the woman. ʿAbdallāh b. Khannūsa now contended, through his son and legal agent, that the endowment had been created under fraudulent circumstances and was therefore null and void. In his deposition, Abū al-Qāsim acknowledged the validity of the testamentary endowment only insofar as it pertained to Abū Zayd ʿAbd al-Raḥmān b. Khannūsa. He asserted that the physical features attributed to the female co-founder in the witnessing clause were *not* those of Fāṭima al-Zarhūniyya, who therefore could not have been Abū Zayd ʿAbd al-Raḥmān's mother, as claimed.[76] If this were the case, the endowment would be null and void, the endowment properties would be transformed into private property, and ʿAbdallāh b. Khannūsa would *inherit* those properties in his capacity as Abū Zayd ʿAbd al-Raḥmān's closest surviving heir.[77] That is to say, ʿAbdallāh b. Khannūsa sought to override the specific terms of the endowment by appealing to the Islamic inheritance rules, according to which, as the closest surviving relative of the deceased, he was entitled to inherit the latter's entire estate. But the success of this strategy was dependent upon his ability to demonstrate that the endowment was null and void.

Appeal to the Sulṭān: 22 Muḥarram 826/5 January 1423

The dispute had now reached an impasse. On the one hand, ʿAbdallāh b. Khannūsa had physical control of the property and claimed that the endowment should be declared null and void because it had been created under fraudulent circumstances and that it should revert to him in full ownership in accordance with the Islamic inheritance rules. On the other hand, Muḥammad b. Rāshid pointed to the fatwās issued by Ibn Marzūq and by Qāsim al-ʿUqbānī, respectively, both of which provided unequivocal support for his claim to the endowment. A resolution to the

[75] On legal representation (*wakāla*), see Schacht, *Introduction*, 119–20; Tyan, "Judicial Organization," in *Law in the Middle East: Origin and Development of Islamic Law*, ed. M. Khadduri and H.J. Liebesny (Washington DC: Middle East Institute, 1955), 257–9.

[76] For a similar allegation of fraud, see Wansharīsī, *Miʿyār*, vol. 10, 267.

[77] Ibid., vol. 7, 312 (l. 18)–13 (l. 21).

impasse was sought by taking the case to the highest authority in the land, the Marīnid Sulṭān, who held a weekly council (*majlis*) at which he and the leading jurists of the capital city considered difficult legal cases and disputes.[78] (In the year 826/1423, the Sulṭān, ʿAbd al-Ḥaqq, was a young boy of only seven years, having acceded to the throne as an infant following the assassination of his father, Abū Saʿīd III, in 823/1420. The real power was the former governor of Salé, the Waṭṭāsid, Abū Zakariyāʾ Yaḥyā, who had installed ʿAbd al-Ḥaqq and was acting as his regent.)[79]

Shortly after Abū al-Qāsim's deposition of 826/1422 he and Muḥammad b. Rāshid appeared at the Sulṭān's *majlis*, where they presented their respective cases. On 22 Muḥarram 826/5 January 1423, six days after Abū al-Qāsim's deposition, an imperial decree (*amr*) was issued in the name of the Sulṭān, charging the qāḍī Abū al-Faḍl ʿAbd al-ʿAzīz b. Abī Jamāʿa al-Tujībī[80] with the task of resolving the dispute. The decree began with a clause referring to the Sulṭān as the Servant of God, the one who is aided by God (*al-muntaṣar billāh*), Muḥammad, and then tracing his descent back nearly two centuries to the third Marīnid Sulṭān, Abū Yūsuf b. ʿAbd al-Ḥaqq (r. 656–85/1258–86).[81] After affirming his intent and readiness to uphold the *sharīʿa*, or Sacred Law, the Sulṭān charged the qāḍī, Ibn Abī Jamāʿa, to resolve the case and execute a judicial decision "in accordance with the requirements of the Sacred Law."[82] He instructed the qāḍī to base his decision on the opinions of contemporary jurists, either muftīs or non-muftīs (perhaps suggesting that the qāḍī was not obligated to rely upon the fatwās of Ibn Marzūq and Qāsim al-ʿUqbānī). The decree stated that the decision of the qāḍī would be final, immune from further criticism, and irreversible. Following a summary of the contents of the endowment deed, the decree concluded with the request that the qāḍī "address himself to this [deed] in the manner of the distinguished qāḍīs who are his models, and exercise his independent reasoning (*ijtihād*) regarding it in the manner of those Muslim scholars who possess insight and discernment."[83]

Imposition of the oath: *ca.* Muḥarram 826/January 1423

A dispute that began as a question of law had now been transformed into a question of fact: On 5 Rajab 791/30 June 1389, a woman who claimed to be

[78] *Majlis al-sulṭān*. For details on the role played by the sulṭān in the Islamic legal system, see Hiroyuki Yanagihashi, "The Judicial Functions of the *Sulṭān* in Civil Cases according to the Mālikīs up to the Sixth/Twelfth Century," *Islamic Law and Society*, vol. 3 (1996), 41–74.

[79] See Mohamed Kably, *Société, pouvoir et réligion au Maroc à la fin du Moyen Age (XIVe – XVe siècle)* (Paris: Maisonneuve & Larose, 1986), 207, 217; Jamil Abun-Nasr, *A History of the Maghrib in the Islamic Period* (Cambridge: Cambridge University Press, 1987), 114.

[80] I have not been able to identify this qāḍī. He may have been a descendant of ʿAlam al-Dīn Abū al-Qāsim b. Yūsuf al-Balansī al-Sabtī al-Tujībī (d. *ca.* 730/1329), a *ḥadīth* scholar and author of *al-Targhīb fīʾl jihād*, dedicated to the Marīnid Sulṭān Abū Saʿīd ʿUthmān, and other works. On him see *EI*², s.v. al-Tudjībī (Maribel Fierro).

[81] Wansharīsī, *Miʿyār*, vol. 7, 313 (l. 22)–14 (l. 2). Note: the text omits ʿAbd al-Ḥaqq's father and grandfather.

[82] Ibid., vol. 7, 314, ll. 2–10. [83] Ibid., vol. 7, 314, ll. 10–24.

Fāṭima al-Zarhūniyya had summoned two witnesses to attest to a testamentary endowment that she had created together with her son, Abū Zayd. One of the witnesses, Muḥammad al-Kinānī, specified that he was familiar with the woman; the other witness said that he was not. Thirty-five years later, in 826/1423, ʿAbdallāh b. Khannūsa denied that the woman who had created the endowment was in fact Fāṭima al-Zarhūniyya. Thus, the dispute between the two families had been reduced to two contradictory claims. Did al-Kinānī lie? Or was ʿAbdallāh b. Khannūsa the prevaricator? Who was to be believed and how would the truth come out?

According to the rules of procedure, the burden of proof falls on the party that affirms or claims (*al-muddaʿī*); in the absence of proof, the presumption operates in favor of the party that denies (*al-muddaʿā ʿalayhi*), to whom the qāḍī offers the decisory oath (*yamīn*), sworn "in the name of God, other than Whom there is no God." If that party accepts the oath, the case is decided in its favor; if not, the oath is offered to the other party.[84]

In the present instance, ʿAbdallāh b. Khannūsa and his son Abū al-Qāsim sought to change the existing state of affairs by claiming that the witness had lied, whereas Ibn Rāshid sought to preserve the existing state of affairs by denying that claim. In the absence of proof, the dispute would have to be resolved by resort to the oath. Surely, all indicators suggested that the qāḍī Ibn Abī Jamāʿa would offer the oath to Ibn Rāshid. Surprisingly, however, some time after 22 Muḥarram 826/5 January 1423, the qāḍī offered the oath to Abū al-Qāsim b. Khannūsa (still serving as his father's legal representative), thereby providing him with an opportunity to end the dispute in his favor. In view of the great lengths to which his father had gone in his effort to gain access to the property, it is remarkable that Abū al-Qasim refused to swear, deterred perhaps by fear of punishment in the next world or by damage to his reputation in this one. Be that as it may, Abū al-Qāsim's refusal to swear exposed as a ruse his family's claim regarding the fraudulent identity of the female co-founder.

Following Abū al-Qāsim's refusal, the qāḍī offered the oath to Muḥammad b. Rāshid and his nephew (Raḥma's son), Abū Zayd ʿAbd al-Raḥmān. The two men "swore a complete, binding, legally valid oath" in which they affirmed that Muḥammad b. ʿAbd al-Raḥmān b. Yaskun al-Kinānī, the witness who had identified Fāṭima, had borne witness to the truth, to wit, that Fāṭima al-Zarhūniyya was the woman about whom testimony had been given in the legacy. The qāḍī accepted the oath from the two men, noting Abū al-Qāsim b. Khannūsa's earlier refusal to swear. The swearing of the oath, its acceptance by the qāḍī, and Abū al-Qāsim's refusal to swear were duly witnessed and certified.[85] At this point, our documentation comes to an end.

[84] On the oath, see, for example, Muḥammad b. Aḥmad b. Rushd, *Bidāyat al-mujtahid wa-nihāyat al-muqtaṣid*, 2 vols (Cairo: Maktabat al-Kulliyāt al-Azhariyya, 1389/1969), vol. 2, 502–5 [= Ibn Rushd, *The Distinguished Jurist's Primer*, vol. 2, 560–67]; Schacht, *Introduction*, 159; Peter Scholz, *Malikitisches Verfahrensrecht: Eine Studie zu Inhalt und Methodik der Scharia mit rechtshistorischen und rechtsvergleichenden Anmerkungen am Beispiel des malikitischen Verfahrensrechts bis zum 12. Jahrhundert* (Frankfurt: Peter Lang, 1997), 285 ff.

[85] Wansharīsī, *Miʿyār*, vol. 7, 313, ll. 4–22.

Conclusion

Unlike the anthropologist who studies contemporary disputes, the historian's vision of a past dispute is limited by the nature and boundaries of his source, and he is not in a position to question the litigants regarding the dispute's underlying issues. In the present case, we know that the Banū al-Zarhūnī and the Banū Khannūsa were Berbers who had settled in Fez; that several of the men involved in the dispute were jurists; that the men and women who belonged to these families possessed substantial economic resources; and that they had lived through the plague of 749/1348 and the epidemic of 817–18/1414–15. However, we do not know anything about the marriage and residence patterns of these individuals, the order of their births and deaths, and/or their mutual affective relations.

The fatwā that has served as the basis of our reconstruction of the case is a complex text composed of several discrete documents: the *istiftāʾ*, the transcription of the endowment deed, the responses of the two jurists, a deposition, and an oath. These documents, precious artifacts of the society we seek to understand, shed light on common strategies for the intergenerational transmission of property, on the ideology of kinship, and on the apparatus of justice under the Marīnids.

The very creation of the endowment points to the desire to keep property intact and to circumvent the Islamic inheritance rules. The descent strategy specified by the two co-founders, which defined the meaning of *family* for future generations of descendants, manifested greater concern for biological reproduction than it did for any principle or rule of agnation. Recall that the co-founders specified as the first line of beneficiaries "the first child born alive to Muḥammad and (*sic*) ʿĀʾisha", despite the fact that the first child born to ʿĀʾisha would have been a *cognatic* descendant of the male co-founder. The co-founders further specified that if the first line of beneficiaries failed, entitlement to the endowment revenues was to pass to the two children of the male co-founder's sister, both of whom were related to him cognatically. What is striking about this strategy is the systematic exclusion from the endowment of the surviving agnates, the Ibn Khannūsas, which suggests that agnation was not an exclusive norm within this community of urban notables. (Presumably, the choices made were conditioned by factors about which our source is silent, for example, patterns of marriage, residence, and landholding; or emotional forces such as hostility or feud.)

In Muslim societies, endowment rules and inheritance rules represent alternative, overlapping, and competing legal norms. Inheritance rules award fractional shares of the estate to different members of the family, including daughters, sisters, and wives, thereby undermining the cultural norm of agnation, fragmenting property and diverting it from the patrimony when women marry out of the family. Endowment rules serve as a corrective to inheritance rules by funneling property downwards within a lineal descent group that generally is agnatic (in this regard, the present case is exceptional) and by keeping property intact. The interplay between competing cultural norms (agnation and cognation) and legal norms (inheritance rules and endowment rules), coupled with changing demographic realities – births, marriages, and deaths – created structural tensions between *heirs* and *beneficiaries* and between *insiders* and *outsiders*. In such a situation, individuals who knew the law and were skilled in its manipulation were in a position to maximize their material interests. Knowledge was power.

The complex interplay between these competing cultural and legal norms made disagreements over the intergenerational transmission of property inevitable. Unfortunately, our source sheds no light on the informal mechanisms that may have been used to resolve such disagreements. It does, however, elucidate the formal mechanisms of dispute resolution that were available, pointing to three distinct loci of judicial authority within the Marīnid realm: the qāḍī, the muftī, and the sulṭān (see Introduction). Once the dispute entered the apparatus of justice, it wended its way through the qāḍī's court, the muftī's study and the sulṭān's *majlis*, before returning to the qāḍī for final settlement.

As the case passed through the apparatus of justice, its underlying socio-economic and emotional basis was transformed into a question of textual analysis, that is, to the relationship between law and language. Charged to determine the intent of the founders at the moment of the endowment's creation, the qāḍī and the two muftīs drew upon a theory of language and textual interpretation that will be familiar to jurists in other legal systems: the intent of the founder is identical to the words that he used in the endowment deed.[86] These words are comparable to God's words as preserved in the Qur'ān. As one Maghribī jurist put it, "The words of the founder [of an endowment] are like the words of the Divine Lawgiver (*al-shāriʿ*). They must be carefully adhered to and their legal effects must be faithfully executed."[87]

The analogy is instructive. In seeking to determine the intent of the founder of an endowment, Muslim jurists had at their disposal a vast repertoire of hermeneutical methods and rhetorical strategies that had been developed by Muslim commentators in their efforts to explicate the Qur'ān. This repertoire included conventions of argumentation, considerations of context, logic, and the tools and categories of rhetoric. In the present case, ʿAbdallāh b. Khannūsa sought to give new meaning to the endowment deed by focusing attention on the external form or literal meaning (*lafẓ*) of the word *descendant*, whereas Muḥammad b. Rāshid sought to focus attention on the word's spirit or underlying meaning (*maʿnā*). The dichotomy between external form and underlying meaning was reinforced by the perceived difference between the legal signification of words and their signification in non-legal forms of discourse. *Pace* Rosen, Muslim jurists did attribute special meaning to ordinary language; indeed the technical meanings

[86] For purposes of comparison, see *Interpreting Law and Literature: A Hermeneutic Reader*, ed. Sanford Levinson and Steven Mailloux (Evanston: Northwestern University Press, 1988); Stanley Fish, *Doing What Comes Naturally: Change, Rhetoric, and the Practice of Theory in Literary and Legal Studies* (Durham: Duke University Press, 1989); *Legal Hermeneutics*, ed. Gregory Leyh (Berkeley: University of California Press, 1992).

[87] Wansharīsī, *Miʿyār*, vol. 7, 280, ll. 16–18; cf. ibid., vol. 7, 285, ll. 1–2.

attributed even to commonplace particles and conjunctions often played a key role in the resolution of disputes.[88]

That Muḥammad b. Rāshid prevailed in the end was due, in part, to the fact that the rhetorical and linguistic arguments that he adduced on his own behalf conformed more closely than those of his adversary to the conventions of textual analysis and to the theory of language adhered to by contemporary Muslim jurists. By translating social, economic and political phenomena into the language of legal discourse, Muslim jurists performed an important role as mediators of social conflict. The two muftīs who were called upon to examine this case presented themselves as experts on law and language. They understood their task as the application of a theory of language to a legal instrument and the integration of the results of their linguistic analysis to the facts of the case.

But Muḥammad b. Rāshid also prevailed because the oath worked as an effective mechanism for discovering the truth. By instituting the oath, the qāḍī did in fact return the resolution of the dispute to the parties. Abū al-Qāsim b. Khannūsa's refusal to swear amounted to a concession that he and his father had been wrong. Perhaps this was enough to make it possible for the two clans to bury the hatchet and to renegotiate the terms of their relationship. Perhaps not.

[88] Cp. Rosen, *The Anthropology of Justice*, 39, 57, 61, 71.

FIVE

Preserving the Prophet's Honor: Sharīfism, Sufism, and Mālikism in Tlemcen, 843/1439

God loves not the public utterance of evil speech. (Q. 4:148)

Truly the noblest among you in God's eyes is he who is most Godfearing. (Q. 49:13)

O people, I have left among you that which, if you hold fast to it, you will not go astray: the Book of God and my descendants, the people of my house. (prophetic *ḥadīth*)

[be] securers of justice, witnesses for God, even though it be against yourselves or your parents and kinsmen". (Q. 4:134)

Based upon his observations of the court of Sefrou in the 1960s and 1970s, Rosen has argued that the primary function of the qāḍī was to place litigants back in a position in which they could negotiate the terms of their relationship. Rosen's observation is an important one, albeit overstated. The interest of Muslim jurists in restoring social harmony cannot be viewed in isolation from their mandate to apply the law. The relationship between law and social harmony manifests itself dramatically in the case to be examined in the present chapter: a father and son living in Tlemcen in the middle of the ninth/fifteenth century were accused of slandering several distinguished *sharīfs* and defaming the Prophet Muḥammad. In his artful and carefully crafted opinion, the jurist who was called upon to resolve the dispute defused a potentially explosive situation by seeking a middle position between the "extremists of the hour." Lacing his opinion with citations from the Qur'ān and *ḥadīth* that make repeated references to love, forgiveness, repentance, and humility, the muftī transformed a case that might easily have yielded the death penalty into a statement about how *sharīfs* and non-*sharīfs* should relate to one another.

The Facts of the Case

On 6 Rabīʿ I 843/17 August 1439, an argument broke out among three distinguished residents of Tlemcen, in the presence of two witnesses. The dispute involved the white-haired Berber scholar Aḥmad b. ʿĪsā al-Baṭṭīwī,[1] who was a jurist, qāḍī, writer of legal documents and professional witness;[2] al-Baṭṭīwī's son, curiously also referred to as Aḥmad, and who apparently had attained the age of legal majority (although his age is not specified in our source);[3] and a certain Abū al-Faraj b. Abī Yaḥyā, a jurist and a *sharīf*, or descendant of the Prophet Muḥammad. About the argument itself we know only that it related to the inheritance of a certain Abū ʿAbdallāh, the father in-law (*ḥamū*) of Abū al-Faraj's brother.

As tempers flared and angry words were exchanged, Abū al-Faraj, alluding to his status as a descendant of the Prophet, taunted Ibn ʿĪsā the father, saying, "Do you want the truth? By God, you have no superiority (*faḍl*)." Our source says that Ibn ʿĪsā's face turned red, and he asked, "What shall I say to you in response to this?" At no loss for words, Abū al-Faraj directed Ibn ʿĪsā to respond as follows: "[Say:] 'Correct. Indeed, we have no superiority because the likes of us among people have as their predominant quality the separation from goodness.' " Oddly, Ibn ʿĪsā motioned toward his son, standing behind him, and said, "I am not the one whose response is appropriate; rather, the correct one (*al-qayyim bihi*) is that dog!" Abū al-Faraj remained focused on the elder Ibn ʿĪsā, asking with disdain, "What makes you too great to confront me?" To this Ibn ʿĪsā retorted, "Verily, you do not have the stature for this thing." Abū al-Faraj now raised the stakes. Referring to Ibn ʿĪsā in the third person, he used Ibn ʿĪsā's own invective: "He has spoken well – by God – the dog, the son of the dog." Enraged, Ibn ʿĪsā shouted at

[1] Abū al-ʿAbbās Aḥmad b. ʿĪsā al-Baṭṭīwī, alternatively, "al-Baṭṭūʾī." It is tempting to identify this otherwise unknown figure with the better-known jurist, Abū al-ʿAbbās Aḥmad b. Muḥammad al-Mawāsī al-Baṭṭīwī, father of Abū Mahdī ʿĪsā b. Aḥmad b. Muḥammad al-Baṭṭīwī. But al-Mawāsī al-Baṭṭīwī reportedly died in Fez in the year 842/1438–39, while Aḥmad b. ʿĪsā al-Baṭṭīwī was still alive in the year 843/1438–39. Indeed, the biographer al-Tunbuktī specifies that Aḥmad b. ʿĪsā al-Baṭṭīwī was *not* the father of Abū Mahdī. See Aḥmad Bāba al-Tunbuktī, *Nayl al-ibtihāj bi-taṭrīz al-dībāj*, on the margin of Ibn Farḥūn, *Kitāb al-Dībāj* (Cairo: Dār al-Turāth, 1351/1952), 78; cf. Ibn Maryam, *al-Bustān fī dhikr al-awliyāʾ wa'l-ʿulamāʾ bi-Tilimsān* (Algiers, 1326/1908), 51 [= *El Bostan ou Jardin des biographies des saints et savants de Tlemcen*, tr. F. Provenzali (Alger: Imprimerie Orientale Fontana Frères, 1910), 56]. On Abū Mahdī, who died in 911/1505–06, see Aḥmad Ibn al-Qāḍī (d. 1025/1616), *Durrat al-ḥijāl fī asmāʾ al-rijāl*, ed. Muḥammad al-Aḥmadī Abū al-Nūr, 3 vols (Cairo: Dār al-Turāth, 1390/1970), vol. 1, 91, no. 128; al-Tunbuktī, *Nayl al-Ibtihāj*, 194; Ibn Maryam, *Bustān*, 51; al-Ḥafnāwī, *Taʿrīf al-khalaf bi-rijāl al-salaf*, 2 vols in 1 (Tunis: Muʾassasat al-Risāla, 1402/1982), vol. 2, 74; see also Houari Touati, "En relisant les *Nawâzil* Mazouna: Marabouts et chorfa au maghreb central au xve siècle," *Studia Islamica*, 69 (1989), 75–94, esp. 78; G.S. Colin and H.P.J. Renaud, "Note sur le "*muwaqqit*" marocain Abû Muqriʿ – ou mieux Abû Miqraʿ – al-Baṭṭīwī," *Hespéris*, XXV (1938), 94–6. Note: a man by the name of Muḥammad b. ʿĪsā al-Baṭṭīwī appears as a professional witness in the testimonial certification (*ishhād*) of a fatwā of Ibn Marzūq dated late Ṣafar 825/February 1422. This Muḥammad may have been the brother of Aḥmad al-Baṭṭīwī. See *Miʿyār*, vol. 7, 320.

[2] Al-Baṭṭīwī's *nisba* points to his membership in the Zanātā tribe of Baṭṭūya, originally settled between Nakkūr (Nkur) and the Malwīya river. The status of this tribe increased significantly during the Marīnid period, when members of the family served as generals and *wazīr*s in the service of different Marīnid sulṭāns. For further details, see Fernando R. Mediano, *Familias de Fez (ss. xv–xvii)* (Madrid: Consejo Superior de Investigaciones Cientificas, 1995), 140–2.

[3] The text of the *Miʿyār* (vol. 2, 542, ll. 10–11) reads: *man muqaṣṣir fī dhālika ḥattā kāda lā yūjibu ʿalā al-shābb ḥaddan wa-lā taʿzīran*. "*Al-shābb*" here is a scribal error. Read in its place *al-sābb*, as in ms. D6691, 154, verso, in the Bibliothèque Générale in Rabat.

Abū al-Faraj, "Your father is the dog, the son of the dog, the disgrace (*al-ʿār*), the son of the disgrace – and the father of your father." To this his son Aḥmad added, from the apparent safety of his position behind his father, "May God curse the accursed one, the first father of your grandfather (*abū jaddika al-awwal*)."[4]

In another time and place, this exchange might have been dismissed as ordinary utterances made in the heat of argument, of little or no import. In ninth/fifteenth-century Tlemcen, however, the consequences of seeming to defame the Prophet in public were grave – indeed, potentially fatal. Although our source does not specify what happened next, it is clear that someone brought the incident to the attention of the judicial authorities in Tlemcen. We do know that the chief qāḍī of that city in the year 843/1439 was Abū al-Faḍl Qāsim al-ʿUqbānī, whom we have already encountered in chapter four. Al-ʿUqbānī had been appointed chief qāḍī of Tlemcen at a young age and continued to serve in that position until his death in 851/1450. A distinguished scholar who had mastered both the rational and transmitted sciences, al-ʿUqbānī was one of only a handful of jurists in the Maghrib at this time who were regarded as having attained the level of *ijtihād*; he reportedly was not averse to transcending the boundaries of the Mālikī *madhhab* in his search for the solution to a legal problem. He was also a sufi who taught Ibn ʿAbbād's commentary on the *Ḥikam* of the Suhrawardī mystic Ibn ʿAṭāʾ Allāh and who composed a poem in *rajaz* meter that was recited by sufis at their assemblies. His death in 851/1450 was an occasion for mourning by the entire Muslim community of Tlemcen, including the sulṭān and his court.[5]

Surely it was to al-ʿUqbānī that the incident was reported. Upon receiving the report and examining the evidence, the chief qāḍī apparently was persuaded that one or both of the Ibn ʿĪsās had violated the sacred honor (*ḥurma*) of the Prophet, an offense for which the penalty is death by stoning. Before implementing any penalty, however, al-ʿUqbānī decided to seek the advice of a distinguished muftī. The resulting fatwā, which is the object of study in the present chapter, was an occasion for thought and argument, a moment when the law was made real. Before analyzing this fatwā, however, we must first consider the identity of Abū al-Faraj, and then examine Mālikī legal doctrine on slanderous accusations, in general, and slander of the Prophet, in particular.

Abū al-Faraj and Sharīfism

Sharīfism was one of three powerful religio-political forces that had come to dominate the Maghrib by the ninth/fifteenth century (see Introduction). Only two years prior to the argument between Abū al-Faraj and the two Ibn ʿĪsās, a family of *sharīf*s had played a key role in repelling the Portuguese siege of Tangier, and

[4] *Miʿyār*, vol. 2, 541, ll. 1–9.
[5] Ibn Maryam, *El Bostan*, 161–3; Tunbuktī, *Nayl*, 223–4; Makhlūf, *Shajara*, vol. 1, 255, no. 925.

the tomb of Idrīs II had been "discovered" at the mosque of the *sharīf*s in Fez. A quarter of a century later, a family of *sharīfs* would seize political power and establish the first of two sharīfian dynasties that would control the Maghrib for the next 500 years. Clearly, this was a decisive and pivotal moment in the history of the Maghrib.

One of the groups recognized as legitimate *shurafā'* was a family of jurists known as ʿAlawids,[6] who lived in Tlemcen, capital of the ʿAbd al-Wādid sulṭāns. In 753/1353, the Marīnid prince Abū ʿInān captured Tlemcen, and, in an effort to bolster his religious prestige, brought back to Fez the famous jurist, Abū ʿAbdallāh Muḥammad b. Aḥmad al-Sharīf al-ʿAlawī (710–71/1310–70), known as al-Sharīf al-Tilimsānī, who traced his descent, through Idrīs, back to al-Ḥasan b. ʿAlī.[7] Figure 5.1 shows his genealogy.

A *mujtahid* who was arguably the greatest scholar of his age and a man of great influence and authority, al-Sharīf al-Tilimsānī had studied a wide range of subjects in the traditional and rational sciences, including law, jurisprudence, theology, philosophy, mathematics, and astronomy. In addition to his mastery of these subjects, he was a sufi who transmitted his profound knowledge of mysticism to his disciples. In Fez he served as a member of the academic council of the sulṭān (*al-majlis al-ʿilmī*) and as the tutor of the royal family, children of nobility, and eminent members of the court. He escaped the Black Death of 749/1348 (see chapter four), which decimated the intellectual élite of the Maghrib. When Abū ʿInān died in 759/1358, the ʿAbd al-Wādid sulṭān Abū Ḥammū II (723–91/1323–89) invited al-Sharīf al-Tilimsānī to return to Tlemcen. After obtaining the approval of the Marīnid *wazīr*, he accepted the invitation and returned to Tlemcen, where his new patron asked for the hand of his daughter in marriage and then designated him as the director of the Madrasa Yaʿqūbiyya, newly founded for his son-in-law and richly endowed with revenue-producing properties.[8]

Al-Sharīf al-Tilimsānī had two sons, Abū Muḥammad Abdallāh (748–92/1347–90), sometimes called "al-Imām," and Abū Yaḥyā ʿAbd al-Raḥmān (757–826/

[6] According to Ibn Khaldūn, the *nisba* al-ʿAlawiyyīn refers to a village (*qarya*) known as al-ʿAlawiyyīn located near Tlemcen. He continues: *wa-kāna ahl baladihi lā yudāfaʿūna fī nasabihim wa-rubbamā yughmaz fīhi baʿḍ al-fajra mimman lā yazaʿuhu dīnahu wa-lā maʿrifatahu bi'l-ansāb fa-yuʿaddu min al-laghū wa-lā yultafatu ilayhi* (Beck, *L'Image d'Idrīs II*, 169, citing *al-Taʿrīf bi-Ibn Khaldūn wa-riḥlatuhu gharban wa sharqan*, ed. Muḥammad b. Tāwit al-Ṭanjī [Cairo, 1370/1951], 62–64 = *Le voyage d'Occident et d'Orient. Autobiographie*, tr. Abdesselam Cheddadi [Paris, 1980], 77–9).

[7] Al-Tunbuktī reports that he saw a document in the handwriting of al-Sharīf al-Tilimsānī's son which specified his genealogy as follows: Muḥammad b. Aḥmad b. ʿAlī b. Yaḥyā b. ʿAlī b. Muḥammad b. al-Qāsim b. Ḥammūd b. Maymūn b. ʿAlī b. ʿAbdallāh b. ʿUmar b. Idrīs b. ʿAbdallāh b. Ḥasan b. al-Ḥasan b. ʿAlī b. Abī Ṭālib. See al-Tunbuktī, *Nayl al-Ibtihāj*, 255–64, at 255; cf. al-Ḥafnāwī, *Taʿrīf al-khalaf*, vol. 1, 110–27, at 110.

[8] Abū ʿAbdallāh Muḥammad b. Aḥmad al-ʿAlawīnī al-Sharīf al-Ḥasanī, known as al-Sharīf al-Tilimsānī: *kāna min aʿlām al-ʿulamā' wa'l-a'imma al-fuḍalā' aʿlam man fī ʿaṣrihi bi-ijmāʿ kāna al-ustādh Ibn Lubb yaʿtarifu bi-faḍlihi*. See *Miʿyār*, vol. 12, 224–5; Ibn Maryam, *Bustān*, 164–84; Ibn al-Qāḍī, *Durrat al-ḥijāl*, vol. 2, 269, no. 773; al-Tunbuktī, *Nayl al-Ibtihāj*, 255–64; al-Ḥafnāwī, *Taʿrīf al-khalaf*, vol. 1, 110–27, vol. 2, 352; Muḥammad b. Muḥammad Makhlūf, *Shajarat al-nūr al-zakiyya fī ṭabaqāt al-mālikiyya*, 2 vols in 1 (2nd edn, Beirut: Dār al-Kitāb al-ʿArabī, *ca*. 1975), vol. 1, 234, no. 840; *EI*², s.v. al-Sharīf al-Tilimsānī, section 1; Beck, *L'Image d'Idrīs II*, 186.

ʿAlī b. Abī Ṭālib
|
al-Ḥasan
|
Ḥasan
|
ʿAbdallāh
|
Idrīs
|
ʿUmar
|
ʿAbdallāh
|
ʿAlī
|
Maymūn
|
Ḥammūd
|
al-Qāsim
|
Muḥammad
|
ʿAlī
|
Yaḥyā
|
ʿAlī
|
Aḥmad
|
Muḥammad

Figure 5.1 The genealogy of al-Sharīf al-Tilimsānī

Source: al-Tunbuktī, *Nayl al-Ibtihāj*, 255–64, as found by al-Tunbuktī in the handwriting of Aḥmad al-Sharīf al-Tilimsānī.

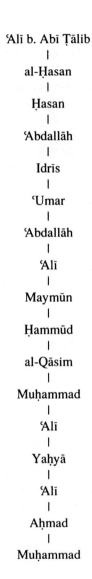

1356–1423). As a young boy, Abū Muḥammad Abdallāh accompanied his father to Fez, where he studied Qur'ān, grammar, logic, law, and jurisprudence with the masters of that city; he also studied philosophy, theology, rhetoric, dialectics, geometry, logic, and Sufism with his father.[9] Upon his father's death in 771/1370, Abū Muḥammad Abdallāh succeeded him as director of the Madrasa Yaʿqūbiyya.

Al-Sharīf al-Tilimsānī's second son, Abū Yaḥyā ʿAbd al-Raḥmān, received his name from two distinguished personages present at his father's home in Fez on the night of his birth: the qāḍī of Fez, Abū Yaḥyā al-Sakkāk and the famous historian ʿAbd al-Raḥmān Ibn Khaldūn. Abū Yaḥyā ʿAbd al-Raḥmān, who followed a curriculum of study similar to that of his older brother, developed a reputation for his skill in Qur'ānic exegesis and in the analysis of the apparent and hidden meanings of texts. Three further aspects of his intellectual biography are of special importance to the present investigation: first, he studied the *Kitāb al-Shifā bi-taʿrīf ḥuqūq al-muṣṭafā* of Qāḍī ʿIyāḍ (d. 544/1149), an important text in which the author defined the obligations of Muslims toward the Prophet and his descendants, thereby contributing to the popularity of the "House of the Prophet" in the Maghrib; second, he taught many eminent students, including Ibn Zāghū, author of the fatwā to be analyzed below; and, third, he wrote a treatise on the forgiveness of sins, entitled *Ta'līf ʿalā al-maghfira*, a passage from which is cited in Ibn Zāghū's fatwā.[10]

Abū Yaḥyā ʿAbd al-Raḥmān had two sons. The older, Abū al-ʿAbbās Aḥmad (d. 895/1490), sometimes called Abū Jaʿfar, served as chief qāḍī of Granada.[11] The younger, Abū al-Faraj (d. 868/1463), was the jurist who had engaged Aḥmad al-Baṭṭīwī and his son in the verbal exchange presented at the outset of this chapter.

Our knowledge about Abū al-Faraj is derived exclusively from his association with Ibn Marzūq VI al-Ḥafīḍ (one of the muftīs who issued a fatwā in the case analyzed in chapter four),[12] scion of a family that had played an important role in the religious, political, and intellectual life of the Maghrib since the end of the fifth/eleventh century. Abū Bakr b. Marzūq had been a trusted servant and agent of the Andalusian mystic Abū Madyan, and several generations of his descendants served as caretakers of the shrine of Abū Madyan just outside of Tlemcen. In the seventh/thirteenth century, members of the Ibn Marzūq family became leaders of the Shādhilī order in the Maghrib. Some members of the family came to be regarded as saints in their own right; others became famous as preachers (*khaṭībs*) and

9 See Ibn Maryam, *al-Bustān*, 117–20; al–Ḥafnāwī, *Taʿrīf al-khalaf*, vol. 2, 245–9; Makhlūf, *Shajara*, vol. 1, 234, no. 841; *EI²*, s.v. al-Sharīf al-Tilimsānī, section 2.

10 On Abū Yaḥyā ʿAbd al-Raḥmān, see Ibn al-Qāḍī, *Durrat al-ḥijāl*, vol. 3, 88–9, no. 1012; al-Tunbuktī, *Nayl al-Ibtihāj*, 170; Ibn Maryam, *al-Bustān*, 42, 127–9; al-Ḥafnāwī, *Taʿrīf al-khalaf*, vol. 2, 208–9; Makhlūf, *Shajara*, vol. 1, 251, no. 911; *EI²*, s.v. al-Sharīf al-Tilimsānī, section 3. His honorifics included *sharīf al-ʿulamā'*, *ʿālim al-shurafā'*, and *khātimat al-mufassirīn wa'l-fuḍalā'*.

11 See Ibn al-Qāḍī, *Durrat al-ḥijāl*, vol. 1, 89, no. 124; al-Tunbuktī, *Nayl al-Ibtihāj*, 80; Ibn Maryam, *al-Bustān*, 44 [= *El Bostan*, 48]; Makhlūf, *Shajara*, vol. 1, 267, no. 985; *EI²*, s.v. al-Sharīf al-Tilimsānī, section 4.

12 The fact that none of the biographical dictionaries that I have consulted includes an independent entry on Abū al-Faraj is not without significance in the context of the present investigation.

religious scholars associated with the mosque-*madrasa* complex that was added to the shrine of Abū Madyan by Abū al-Ḥasan between 737/1339 and 747/1347. Ibn Marzūq VI al-Ḥafīḍ (766–842/1364–1438), a sufi saint (*al-walī al-ṣāliḥ*), was generally regarded as the master of the traditional Islamic sciences in the Islamic West and the greatest intellectual of his age.[13]

Ibn Marzūq VI al-Ḥafīḍ served as a key spiritual and intellectual link between two generations of the family of al-Sharīf al-Tilimsānī. He studied with the two sons of al-Sharīf al-Tilimsānī, Abū Muḥammad ʿAbdallāh and Abū Yaḥyā, and he taught Abū Yaḥyā's two sons, Abū al-ʿAbbās and Abū al-Faraj. In light of the fact that Ibn Marzūq had studied with his father and his uncle and had taught his older brother, it is not surprising that Abū al-Faraj should have sought out Ibn Marzūq as his teacher and spiritual master. In the *Bustān* of Ibn Maryam, Abū al-Faraj is cited as a source on the life of Ibn Marzūq, and from this citation we learn much about Abū al-Faraj's intellectual and spiritual formation.[14] In an extensive quotation, Abū al-Faraj states that he traveled to the *madrasa* attached to the shrine of Abū Madyan at al-ʿUbbād, just outside of Tlemcen, precisely for the purpose of attaching himself to Ibn Marzūq, whom he describes as his "master", the Pivot of the Age, and a man who combined exoteric knowledge of the law with esoteric truth (*ḥaqīqa*). When Abū al-Faraj presented himself to Ibn Marzūq, the scholar-mystic welcomed him as his spiritual son and began to teach to him the Islamic texts that he had received from his masters.[15]

Ibn Marzūq devised a rigorous course of training for Abū al-Faraj. Together, master and disciple read widely in the traditional exoteric sciences. Ibn Marzūq gave Abū al-Faraj an *ijāza*, or license to teach texts in the following areas of Islamic scholarship: (1) the Qurʾān; (2) the major collections of *ḥadīth*, including those of Bukhārī, Muslim, Tirmidhī, and Abū Dāwūd; (3) grammar: the *Muqarrib* of Ibn ʿUṣfūr, *Kitāb* of Sībawayhi, *Alfiyya* of Ibn Mālik, and *Mughnī al-Labīb* of Ibn Hishām al-Naḥwī; (4) Mālikī law: the *Muwaṭṭaʾ* of Mālik b. Anas; *Tahdhīb li-masāʾil al-Mudawwana* of al-Barādhiʿī, *Mukhtaṣar* of Khalīl, *Talqīn* of ʿAbd al-Wahhāb b. ʿAlī, *Matīṭiyya* of al-Kinānī, *Kitāb al-Bayān wa'l-Taḥṣīl* of Ibn Rushd, and *Risāla* of Ibn Abī Zayd al-Qayrawānī; (5) various Shāfiʿī, Ḥanafī, and Ḥanbalī legal texts; (6) jurisprudence: the *Maḥṣūl* of Fakhr al-Dīn al-Rāzī, *Mukhtaṣar al-muntahā fī'l-uṣūl* of Ibn al-Ḥājib, *Kitāb al-Miftāḥ fī uṣūl al-fiqh* of al-Sharīf al-Tilimsānī, *Kitāb al-maṣāliḥ wa'l-mafāsid* of al-Ghazālī, *Tanqīḥ al-fuṣūl fī'l-uṣūl* of al-Qarāfī, and the *Irshād* of al-Āmidī; and (7) dogmatic theology: both the *Muḥaṣṣal* and the *Irshād* of Fakhr al-Dīn al-Rāzī.[16]

Ibn Marzūq also prepared his disciple in the esoteric science of mysticism. Abū al-Faraj informs us that he studied with his master the first three "quarters"

[13] *EI*², s.v. Ibn Marzūḳ.
[14] Ibn Maryam, *al-Bustān*, 201–14, esp. 204–6 [= *El Bostan*, 230–46, esp., 234 ff.].
[15] Ibn Maryam, *El Bostan*, 234–5.
[16] Ibid., 235–6. This appears to have been a standard legal curriculum in Mālikī *madrasas*; see Robert Brunschvig, *La Berbérie Orientale sous les Hafsides*, 2 vols (Paris: Adrien Maisonneuve, 1940–47), vol. 2, 365–6.

of al-Ghazālī's magnum opus, the *Iḥyā' ʿulūm al-dīn*, that is, the sections on (1) cult practices, (2) social customs, and (3) defects of character that lead to perdition. In retrospect, it may be significant that the fourth "quarter", which he did not read with his master, deals with qualities of character that lead to salvation. Be that as it may, when Ibn Marzūq determined that Abū al-Faraj's spiritual and intellectual formation were complete, he invested his disciple with the robe that he himself had received from his father and uncle, thereby solidifying Abū al-Faraj's association with the Mazāriqa and with the Suhrawardī order that they represented.[17]

Abū al-Faraj's juristic identity was composed of prophetic descent (*sharaf*), *ʿilm*-knowledge, and saintly power (*baraka*). We may reasonably assume that when Ibn Marzūq VI al-Ḥafīḍ died on 14 Shaʿbān 842/30 January 1439, his disciple regarded himself as the inheritor of his master's legacy. The dispute presently under consideration occurred just seven months after Ibn Marzūq's death, and it is not difficult to imagine the tension between Abū al-Faraj and the Berber jurist Aḥmad al-Baṭṭīwī, who, with his son insulted Abū al-Faraj and his ancestors and blackened the name of an entire dynasty of saintly scholars who traced their descent back to the Prophet. Indeed, the son's slanderous insults do appear to have targeted the Prophet himself. To better appreciate the significance of this action, we turn now to Mālikī legal doctrine on slander.

Mālikī Legal Doctrine on *Qadhf* and *Sabb al-nabī*

Qadhf

One of five crimes against religion for which *ḥadd* punishments are specified in the Qur'ān, *qadhf* refers to a slanderous accusation of either fornication or illegitimate descent, for which Q. 24:4 specifies a punishment of eighty lashes for a free Muslim.[18] The Shāfiʿīs, Ḥanafīs and Ḥanbalīs regarded as *qadhf* only a direct, unequivocal expression (*taṣrīḥ*), on the ground that equivocality creates *shubha*, or uncertainty, which necessitates averting the *ḥadd* punishment. By contrast, Mālik b. Anas argued that an indirect expresssion (*kināya*) may be raised to the level of an explicit utterance by virtue of linguistic custom and usage (*ʿurf al-ʿāda*); as a result, Mālikī jurists extended the range of *qadhf* to include an accusation expressed through a clear allusion (*taʿrīḍ*). Anyone who has attained puberty and is in possession of his reason, whether slave or free, Muslim or non-Muslim, may be punished for committing *qadhf*. The majority view holds that if a person slanders several people by means of a single expression, only one *ḥadd*

[17] See Ibn Maryam, *al-Bustān*, 204–6, 209–10 [= *El Bostan*, 236]; *EI*², s.v. al-Sharīf al-Tilimsānī, section 5.

[18] In Arabic, the verb *qadhafa* signifies to cast or throw, for example, stones and, by metonymy, to reproach, upbraid, vilify, or defame; it is synonymous with *farā, shatama, and ṭaʿana*. See E.W. Lane, *Arabic–English Lexicon* (London: Williams and Norgate, 1877), s.v. q-dh-f.

punishment should be applied. As for the possibility of forgiveness, two views are attributed to Mālik. On one occasion, he reportedly held that it is permissible for the person who has been slandered to waive the punishment in return for an apology (*'afw*) from the slanderer, whether or not the matter has already reached the ruler (*imām*) – who, by general agreeement, is responsible for execution of the punishment. On another occasion, however, Mālik reportedly held that a waiver of punishment in return for an apology is permissible only if the matter has not reached the ruler; otherwise, an apology results in waiver of punishment only if the victim desires to forgive the slanderer.[19]

Sabb al-nabī

Sabb al-nabī, or slander of the Prophet, is not mentioned in the Qur'ān, although by the second/eighth century, if not before, the act of insulting the Prophet was regarded as a religious offense that should be punished by execution.[20] By the beginning of the fourth/tenth century, a consensus had developed among Muslim jurists that someone who insults the Prophet – or, by extension, one of his Companions – has apostatized and committed an act of infidelity (*kufr*), for which he or she should be executed.[21] Henceforth, blasphemy against the Prophet regularly was treated in the Mālikī legal manuals in the chapters on apostasy (*ridda*). According to Ibn 'Abd al-Barr al-Qurṭubī (d. 463/1070–71), the penalty to be imposed on anyone who vilifies (*shatama*) God, the Prophet Muḥammad, or any other prophet, is death by execution. Further, most Mālikī jurists differed from

[19] On *qadhf*, see *al-Mudawwana al-kubrā li-Mālik b. Anas al-Aṣbaḥī: riwāyat Saḥnūn b. Sa'īd al-Tunūkhī*, 16 vols in 7 (Cairo: Maṭba'at al-Sa'āda, 1323/1905; repr. Beirut: Dār Ṣādir), vol. 16, 2–34; Ibn 'Abd al-Barr (d. 463/1070), *Kitāb al-kāfī fī fiqh ahl al-Madīna al-mālikī* (Beirut: Dār al-Kutub al-'Ilmiyya, 1407/1987), 575 ff.; Ibn Rushd (d. 520/1126), *Bidāyat al-mujtahid wa-nihāyat al-muqtaṣid*, 2 vols (Cairo: Maktabat al-Kulliyāt al-Azhariyya, 1389/1969), vol. 2, 475 ff. = Ibn Rushd, *The Distinguished Jurist's Primer*, tr. Imran Ahsan Khan Nyazee and Muhammad Abdul Rauf, 2 vols (Reading, UK: Garnet Publishing, 1996), vol. 2, 531–4; Ibn 'Abd al-Rafī' (d. 733/1332), *Mu'īn al-ḥukkām 'alā al-qaḍāyā wa'l-aḥkām*, 2 vols (Beirut: Dār al-Gharb al-Islāmī, 1989), vol. 2, 881 ff.; Ibn Juzayy al-Gharnāṭī (d. 741/1340–41), *Qawānīn al-aḥkām al-shar'iyya wa-masā'il al-furū' al-fiqhiyya* (Cairo: 'Alam al-Fikr, 1405–06/1985), 377 ff.; Khalīl b. Isḥāq (d. 776/1374), *al-Mukhtaṣar fī al-fiqh 'alā madhhab al-imām Mālik b. Anas* (Paris: L'Imprimerie Nationale: 1272/1855), 211–12; Khalil Ibn-Ishak, *Précis de Jurisprudence Musulmane*, tr. M. Perron, 6 vols (Paris: Imprimerie Nationale, 1848–52), vol. 6, 35 ff.; *EI*[2], s.v. Ḳadhf; Peter Scholz, *Malikitisches Verfahrensrecht* (Frankfurt: Peter Lang, 1996), 513 ff.; Mohammad Hashim Kamali, *Freedom of Expression in Islam* (Kuala Lumpur: Berita Publishing, 1994), 165–69.

[20] On *sabb al-nabī*, see Kamali, *Freedom of Expression in Islam*, 206–42; Lutz Wiederhold, "Blasphemy against the Prophet Muḥammad and his Companions (*sabb al-rasūl, sabb al-saḥābah*): The Introduction of the Topic into the Shāfi'ī Legal Literature and its Relevance for Legal Practice under Mamluk Rule," *Journal of Semitic Studies*, 42:1 (1997), 39–70; cf. Bercher, "L'apostasie, le blasphème et la rébellion en droit musulman malékite," *Revue Tunisienne*, 1923, 115–30; Isabel Fierro, "Andalusian 'Fatāwā' on Blasphemy," *Annales Islamologiques*, 25 (1990), 103–17; *EI*[2], s.v.v. Ḥadd, Ḳatl.

[21] Ibn al-Mundhir, *al-Ijmā'*, ed. Fu'ād 'Abd al-Mu'min Aḥmad (Qaṭar, 1402 AH), 122.

their counterparts in other schools of law by maintaining that the offender should *not* be given the opportunity to repent, although the point was disputed within the school.[22] Nearly three centuries later, the school doctrine, as articulated by Ibn Juzayy al-Gharnāṭī (d. 741/1340–41), remained essentially unchanged: anyone who insults God, the Prophet Muḥammad, or one of the angels or other prophets, should be executed without being given the opportunity to repent; a minority view held that the blasphemer should be asked to repent.[23] The view of Ibn Juzayy was reiterated, one generation later, by Khalīl b. Isḥāq (d. 776/1374).[24]

It will be recalled that during the exchange between Abū al-Faraj and the two Ibn ʿĪsās, the elder Ibn ʿĪsā referred to the father of Abū al-Faraj as "the dog, the son of the dog," thereby impugning the legitimate descent of Abū al-Faraj, his father Abū Yaḥyā ʿAbd al-Raḥmān, and his grandfather Abū ʿAbdallāh Muḥammad. This constituted *qadhf*, and, as noted, the penalty for slanderous accusation of illegitimate descent is eighty lashes. But the offense committed by Ibn ʿĪsā the father was vastly exceeded by that of Ibn ʿĪsā the son, for the witnesses to the exchange understood his curse ("May God curse the accursed one, the first father of your grandfather") as referring to the Prophet Muḥammad, whose good name, honor, and reputation are inviolable according to Islamic legal doctrine. The penalty for *sabb al-nabī* is death by stoning.

The Request for a Fatwā

Almost immediately after the confrontation between Abū al-Faraj and the two Ibn ʿĪsās, an unidentified party brought the matter to the chief qāḍī of Tlemcen, whom we have tentatively identified as Qāsim al-ʿUqbānī. Upon learning of the incident, al-ʿUqbānī summoned to his court, and questioned, the eyewitnesses to the dispute. The number of witnesses is not specified, but it seems to have been two, the minimum required by law, a point to which we shall return. The eyewitnesses related the verbal exchange to the qāḍī, word-for-word, and these words were recorded by the qāḍī or, perhaps, by his scribe. At the end of the resulting document, the qāḍī certified that the transcription was a complete statement and valid reiteration of the confrontation "as heard by the ear and remembered by the heart, without any doubt whatsoever."[25] He also specified that the eyewitnesses were sound of mind and body, had acted of their own free will, and were legally competent to testify; the certification is dated 7 Rabīʿ I 843/18 August 1439, one

[22] See M. Muranyi, *ʿAbd Allāh b. Wahb (125/743–197/812). Leben und Werk. Al-Muwaṭṭaʾ. Kitāb al-muḥāraba* (Wiesbaden, 1992), 287–8; al-ʿUtbī (al-Qurṭubī) (d. 255/869), *al-ʿUtbiyyah*, on the margin of Ibn Rushd, *al-Bayān wa'l-taḥṣīl* (Beirut: Dār al-Gharb al-Islāmī, 1988), vol. 16, 420 (al-ʿUtbī specifies that a Christian, unlike a Muslim, should be given an opportunity to repent); Ibn ʿAbd al-Barr al-Qurṭubī, *al-Kāfī*, 585. Cp. Ibn Rushd, *Bidāyat al-mujtahid*, vol. 2, 480–1 (= *The Distinguished Jurist's Primer*, vol. 2, 552 where the chapter on *al-murtadd* makes no reference to *sabb al-nabī*).

[23] Ibn Juzayy al-Gharnāṭī, *Qawānīn al-aḥkām al-sharʿiyya*, 387–9.

[24] Khalīl b. Isḥāq, *Mukhtaṣar*, 208–9.

[25] *Miʿyār*, vol. 2, 541, l. 9.

day after the argument.[26] Soon, certain elements within the population of the city began to call for implementation of the stoning penalty, as required by Mālikī legal doctrine.

The testimonial evidence seemingly established that the elder Ibn ʿĪsā had slandered the good name of three distinguished *sharīfs* and that the younger Ibn ʿĪsā had violated the sacred honor of the Prophet; if this were true, then the father had committed *qadhf* and should be flogged, and the son had committed *sabb al-nabī* and should be executed. Some argued that the elder Ibn ʿĪsā also had committed *sabb al-nabī*, either because his own utterances could be interpreted as referring to the Prophet or because he bore ultimate legal responsibility for his son's actions and utterances. Those who defended the two Ibn ʿĪsās argued that the curse uttered by the son did not explicitly mention the Prophet and, further, that it was Abū al-Faraj who was responsible for the insults because he had taunted the elder Ibn ʿĪsā.

Given the gravity of the case and the difficulty of untangling the various threads of which it was composed, al-ʿUqbānī proceeded with caution by seeking the advice of a distinguished muftī before issuing his judgment. After careful consideration of the available candidates, his choice fell upon the Berber jurist Ibn Zāghū. A native of Tlemcen, Ibn Zāghū would have been about sixty-one years old in 843/1439 and at the peak of his intellectual powers. His intellectual and spiritual mentors included al-ʿUqbānī's father, Abū ʿUthmān Saʿīd, and Abū al-Faraj's father, Abū Yaḥyā al-Sharīf, with whom he studied the *Kitāb al-Maghfira*, or *Treatise on the Forgiveness of Sins*. Ibn Zāghū eventually became a professor at the Madrasa Yaʿqūbiyya, where he was esteemed as a scholar, author, and teacher. His students included al-Qalaṣādī (who praises him in his *Riḥla*), al-Māzūnī, Ibn Zakrī, and, possibly, the dream visionary al-Zawāwī.[27]

Like his colleague Ibn Marzūq, Ibn Zāghū had mastered both the exoteric and the esoteric sciences. His biographers describe him as a "friend of God who was devoted to Sufism and asceticism." At the Madrasa Yaʿqūbiyya he reserved two days of each week for the teaching of sufi texts, including the *Iḥyāʾ ʿulūm al-Dīn* of al-Ghazālī and Abū Yaḥyā's *Treatise on the Forgiveness of Sins*. He reportedly renounced the material things of this world, with the exception of fine clothes, and was fond of silent contemplation and seclusion. He was a popular figure with both laymen and the élite. He succumbed to the plague on the afternoon of Thursday Rabīʿ I 845/3 August 1441, and the entire population of the city is reported to have attended his funeral.[28]

[26] For this document, see ibid., vol. 2, 540 (l. 22)–541 (l. 12).

[27] On the possibility of Ibn Zāghū's link to al-Zawāwī, see Jonathan G. Katz, *Dreams, Sufism and Sainthood: The Visionary Career of Muḥammad al-Zawâwî* (Leiden: E.J. Brill, 1996), 4, note 11.

[28] Ibn Zāghū's full name is Abū al-ʿAbbās Aḥmad b. Muḥammad b. ʿAbd al-Raḥmān al-Maghrāwī al-Khazrī. For biographical details, see al-Tunbuktī, *Nayl al-Ibtihāj*, on the margin of Ibn Farḥūn, *Dībāj*, 78–9; Ibn Maryam, *al-Bustān*, 41–3 [= *Bostan*, 45–7]; al-Ḥafnāwī, *Taʿrīf al-khalaf*, vol. 1, 46–8; Makhlūf, *Shajarat al-Nūr*, 254, no. 921; ʿUmar Riḍā Kaḥḥāla, *Muʿjam al-muʾallifīn*, 4 vols (Beirut: Muʾassasat al-Risāla, 1414/1993), vol. 1, 272, no. 1983; Qalṣādī, *Riḥla*, ed. Boulajfan (Tunis, 1978), 102; *EI*², s.v., al-Sharīf al-Tilimsānī. For other fatwās by this muftī, see *Miʿyār*, vol. 13 (index), s.v. Ibn Zāghū.

Al-ʿUqbānī sent Ibn Zāghū a request for a judicial opinion (*istiftāʾ*) in which he presented a concise summary of the relevant judicial issues. He attached to the *istiftāʾ* the verbatim transcript of the argument between Abū al-Faraj and the two Ibn ʿĪsās.[29] The chief qāḍī began the *istiftāʾ* with a pious invocation that had been carefully formulated for its relevance to the case at hand:

> Praise be to God who chose as His Prophet our Lord and our Master Muḥammad – may God bless him and grant him peace – who protected him and preserved his noble reputation, purified him and all of the members of his House, eliminated any impurity from them and from the scholars of his Ḥanīfī religion who followed him, and obligated all [members] of his Community to honor and glorify him.[30]

Thus, at the very outset, the *mustaftī* signaled the importance of respecting the sanctity of the Prophet.

Al-ʿUqbānī continued by making it clear that in his view the two Ibn ʿĪsās had committed a crime against God (*ḥaqq ilāhī*) and His Prophet and were guilty as charged, "since the two of them dishonored his [viz., the Prophet's] sanctity (*hatakā ḥurmatahu*) – may God bless him and grant him peace – by cursing his offspring and those who trace their descent to his noble house and his perfect prophetic status (*sharafihi al-ʿamīm*)." He characterized the exchange among the three men as "swearing, obscene speech, and falsehood." The only question would appear to be what punishment the two men should receive.[31]

The Response of Ibn Zāghū

Introduction

According to the norms of fatwā-giving, a muftī is expected to limit himself to providing a legal assessment of the facts of the case, as delineated by the *mustaftī*. The present case, however, was exceptional. The dispute, which involved a distinguished family of *sharīf*s, had torn the fabric of communal harmony in Tlemcen. "Minds have become confused and opinions have become split," the muftī observed at the outset of his statement.[32] Moreover, the fracas no doubt posed a threat to the ʿAbd al-Wādid rulers, for, by calling into question the legitimate descent of the *sharīf*s of Tlemcen, the incident undermined a main source of the religious authority and legitimacy of these Berber rulers. Although there is no evidence that the ʿAbd al-Wādid sulṭān was directly involved in the litigation, he would have followed the proceedings with great care and interest.

[29] Al-Wansharīsī specifies that he copied the text of the answer of Ibn Zāghū in the latter's own handwriting. He refers to Ibn Zāghū as "our Master and the leader of our Shaykhs." *Miʿyār*, vol. 2, 541, ll. 22–3.

[30] Ibid., vol. 2, 541, ll. 13–16.

[31] Ibid., vol. 2, 541, ll. 16–21.

[32] Ibid., vol. 2, 542, ll. 2–3.

Ibn Zāghū felt that it was incumbent upon himself to transcend the conventions of fatwā-giving. With conscious attention to his art, the muftī explained that his fatwā would deviate from the standard conventions of fatwā-giving in three respects: first, it would contain a preface dealing with issues that would serve as the basis for his legal assessment. Second, it would contain certain supplementary considerations, and, at the end of the fatwā, an appendix. Third, it would contain numerous citations from the Qur'ān and the *sunna* of the Prophet Muḥammad – as immediately exemplified by his citation of Qur'ān 51:55, "And remind; the Reminder profits the believers."[33]

For Ibn Zāghū, the discovery of juristic truth was dependent upon divine assistance, and the muftī was careful to situate his response in a sacred context.[34] He began, "In the name of God the Merciful the Compassionate. May God bless our Master Muḥammad, his family, and his Companions, and [may He] grant them peace." Next, in an effort to establish his authority to deal with the case, he quotes Qur'ān 17:80: "My Lord, lead me in with a just ingoing, and lead me out with a just outgoing; grant me authority from Thee, to help me." Like the Prophet Muḥammad, the muftī seeks divine authority for his assessment of the case, and he sends a signal to his audience that his response will be issued within the parameters of divine law and prophetic precedent. The introductory clause concludes with additional pious rhetoric: "Praise be to God, Lord of the Universe. The ultimate reward is for those who fear [God]."[35]

The imbroglio had divided the residents of Tlemcen into two factions. On one side were members of the community who held up as their supreme value the honor of the Prophet and demanded implementation of the death penalty. On the other side were members of the community who held up as their supreme value the notion that blood should not be shed unnecessarily and argued that Ibn ʿĪsā and his son should be spared the death penalty; indeed, they apparently argued that the two men should not be punished at all. Ibn Zāghū categorized the two positions as extremes of excess and neglect, respectively: the former because its adherents sought to impose a punishment that was too harsh; the latter because its adherents sought to forgo punishment altogether. According to the muftī, both extremes were reprehensible and pointed to the pursuit of personal inclinations and material interests (*hawan*). Without explicitly saying so, Ibn Zāghū clearly sought to occupy the middle ground between these two extremes.[36]

The audience addressed by Ibn Zāghū no doubt was aware of the fact that the muftī had studied with Abū al-Faraj's father, Abū Yaḥyā al-Sharīf.[37] Sensitive to the accusation of possible judicial bias, Ibn Zāghū stated that anyone who

[33] Ibid., vol. 2, 542, ll. 3–7.

[34] The same was true of writers of *consilia* in fourteenth- and fifteenth-century Italy. See Julius Kirshner, "*Consilia* as Authority in Late Medieval Italy: The Case of Florence," in *Legal Consulting in the Civil Law Tradition*," ed. Mario Ascheri, Ingrid Baumgärtner, and Julius Kirshner (Berkeley: The Robbins Collection, 1999), 107–40, esp. 121–3.

[35] *Miʿyār*, vol. 2, 541 (l. 23)–542, l. 8.

[36] Ibid., vol. 2, 542, ll. 7–13; cf. 552, ll. 23–4, quoting ʿIyāḍ.

[37] See above, note 10.

ventured to consider this case or any case – in his capacity as either a witness, judge, muftī, member of the qāḍī's consilium, or arbitrator – must fear God, act justly, and

> ... [be] securers of justice, witnesses for God, even though it be against yourselves, or your parents and kinsmen, whether the man be rich or poor; God stands closest to either. Then follow not caprice, so as to swerve; for if you twist or turn, God is aware of the things you do (Qur'ān 4:134).[38]

It is here, in my view, that the muftī signals the character that he will attempt to establish for himself in the resulting judicial opinion: a securer of justice. (What it meant to be a securer of justice will emerge from the fatwā itself.) The muftī sent a clear message to anyone related to the litigants by ties of blood or affection who might attempt to intervene in the dispute on behalf of one party or the other. The Qur'ānic verse teaches that the obligation of these people to do justice is greater than their obligation to assist a close relative, whether he be a transgressor or one against whom a transgression has been committed. It is only natural, the muftī explained, that if a person's relatives, in-laws, and dear ones became involved in a dispute, that person would attempt to provide them with assistance, whether they were in the right or in the wrong. This natural tendency cannot be overcome, except with the assistance of God. It is also forbidden to dispute on behalf of someone who is known to dispute in vain. Once again, Ibn Zāghū found support for his assertion in the Qur'ān:

> And do not dispute on behalf of those who betray themselves; surely God loves not the guilty traitor. They hide themselves from men, but hide not themselves from God; for He is with them while they meditate at night discourse unpleasing to Him; God encompasses the things they do. Ha, there you are; you have disputed on their behalf in the present life; but who will dispute with God on their behalf on the Resurrection Day, or who will be a guardian for them? (Qur'ān 4:106–107).[39]

Ultimately, there is no escape for the "guilty traitor." Even if he escapes punishment in this world, he will not escape it in the next.

The present case, Ibn Zāghū announced, raises two fundamental legal issues. First, the two Ibn ʿĪsās, who regard themselves as "bearers of superiority and majesty,"[40] had the audacity to violate what is sacred by expressing contempt for persons who trace their lineage back to the Prophet Muḥammad, notwithstanding knowing the validity of that relationship. Second, Ibn ʿĪsā the father, perhaps out of envy or hatred, had denied the claim of Abū al-Faraj to be a *sharīf* when he said to him, "Verily, you do not have the stature for this thing."

[38] Ibid., vol. 2, 542, ll. 13–19. [39] Ibid., vol. 2, 542 (l. 20)–543 (l. 1).

[40] Berbers expressed their resistance to Arabs and Arabism in treatises that exalted their noble qualities and praised their race. Ethnic tension was strong, and the *mafākhir al-barbar* theme became prominent in historical chronicles produced in the eighth/fourteenth century. See, for example, E. Lévi-Provençal, *Fragments historiques sur les Berbères au Moyen-Age: Extraits inédits d'un receuil anonyme compilé en 712/1312 et intitulé Mafākhir al-Barbar* (Rabat, 1934); Maya Shatzmiller, *The Berbers and the Islamic State: The Marīnid Experience in Pre-Protectorate Morocco* (Princeton: Markus Wiener Publishers, 2000), 31–2.

As Ibn Zāghū had indicated at the outset of his response, this was not a normal case and his would not be a standard fatwā. He could not address the narrow legal issues raised by the dispute without first addressing the broader, underlying societal and cultural issues. He therefore launched into a preliminary discourse in which he expounded upon the notion of the *ḥurma*, or sanctity, of the Prophet and his offspring, on the obligation of Muslims to respect that sanctity, and on the exceptional nature of the lineage of the Prophet.[41]

The Sanctity of the Prophet

The sanctity of the Prophet (*ḥurmat al-nabī*), Ibn Zāghū explained, is a notion that is of the utmost magnitude (*ʿaẓīma*) in the eyes of God and every Muslim. Muslims are enjoined to respect and preserve the sanctity of the Prophet both in this world and in all other worlds, and are forbidden to violate or dishonor his sanctity. How could it be otherwise, Ibn Zāghū asked rhetorically, when Muḥammad was the most beloved of God's creation?[42] And how do Muslims know that Muḥammad was the most beloved of God's creation? Ibn Zāghū weaves Islamic tradition into his discourse by citing a *ḥadīth* reportedly transmitted by ʿUmar b. al-Khaṭṭāb on the authority of the Prophet:

> When Ādam committed the sin, he asked, "O Master, I ask you in the name of Muḥammad, 'Why have you not forgiven me?'" God responded, "O Ādam, how do you know Muḥammad when I have not yet created him?" [Ādam] replied, "O Master, when you created me with your hand and infused your spirit in me, I raised my head and behold, I saw it written on the pillars of the [heavenly] throne, 'There is no God but God [and] Muḥammad is the Messenger of God.' I knew that You would not bring into connection with Your name anyone other than Your most beloved creation." The Exalted God replied, "You are right, O Ādam, that he is My most beloved creation. Because you have asked me in his name, I have forgiven you. But were it not for Muḥammad, I would not have forgiven you and would not have created you."[43]

The *ḥadīth*, which emphasizes Muḥammad's special status among God's creatures, also introduces a subject to which the muftī will return later in his discourse, that of forgiveness. It is possible that Ibn Zāghū was sending a subtle signal to his audience. If God forgave Adam, should not the people of Tlemcen forgive Ibn ʿĪsā and his son?

The special status of sacred things is acknowledged in Qurʾān 22:30, where God urges the believers to magnify his "sacred things" ("All that; and whosoever venerates the sacred things of God (*ḥurumāt allāh*), it shall be better for him with his Lord") and in Qurʾān 22:32 ("All that; and whosoever venerates God's

[41] *Miʿyār*, vol. 2, 543, ll. 3–13.
[42] Ibid., vol. 2, 543, ll. 13–17.
[43] Ibid., vol. 2, 543, ll. 17–23; the *ḥadīth* may be found in al-Ḥākim al-Nīsābūrī, *al-Mustadrak*, 4 vols (Riyad: Maṭbaʿa wa-Maṭābiʿ al-Naṣr al-Ḥadītha, n.d.), vol. 2, 615.

waymarks (*shaʿāʾir allāh*), that is of the godliness of the hearts").[44] The question of what things are sacred thus arises, a subject about which Muslim scholars had written extensively before this case. Drawing selectively on the *Kitāb al-Shifā* of Qāḍī ʿIyāḍ (d. 544/1149)[45] and *al-Durr al-munaẓẓam* of al-Azafī (d. 633/1256),[46] Ibn Zāghū presented the following list of the sacred things (*ḥurumāt*) associated with the Prophet: (1) his sublime essence and his noble appearance; (2) his sacred law and his *sunna* (citing Qurʾān 53:30); (3) his Companions, including ʿAlī, al-Ḥasan, al-Ḥusayn, Fāṭima, and the members of his family; (4) his virtuous wives, his relatives by marriage, his servants, his clients, and any believer who, for any reason, was attached to his family; (5) the scholars of his community (*ʿulamāʾ*) who uphold his sacred law, revive his *sunna*, propagate it, cling fast to its rope, and act in accordance with their knowledge – such men as would not sell God's verses and their knowledge in exchange for even a trifling sum; (6) the rest of his community who believe in him, adhere to what he brought, follow his path and imitate his example; these are brothers in faith, and every brother must respect with regard to the other the rights (*ḥaqq*) associated with this sanctity (citing Qurʾān 49:10 and 3:110); and, finally, (7) the Prophet's good virtuous descendants (*dhurriyyatuhu*).[47]

The list is comprehensive, including not only the Prophet's relatives and descendants, but also the *ʿulamāʾ* and "the rest of his community." At this point in his response, Ibn Zāghū focused his attention and that of his audience on the seventh item in the list, the descendants of the Prophet, although it is important to keep in mind that he would later return to the sixth item, "the rest of the community."

The sanctity of Muḥammad's descendants, Ibn Zāghū asserted, must be respected, honored, revered, and venerated, and its obligatory duty performed. To prove this point, the muftī drew attention to a cult of the Prophet that had become widespread among both the élite and the masses, to the point that Muslims had begun to magnify and revere physical objects or relics (*āthār*) associated with Muḥammad.[48] In Egypt, he explained, there exists a shrine known as "The Traces" (*al-āthār*), similar to a *khānaqāh*, or sufi lodge, which possesses *awqāf*, or revenue-producing properties dedicated to it, and a manager who supervises its

[44] *Miʿyār*, vol. 2, 543, ll. 24–6.

[45] ʿIyāḍ, who was the outstanding *ḥadīth* scholar of the late Almoravid period, served as chief qāḍī of Granada and Ceuta. See *EI*², s.v., ʿIyāḍ b. Mūsā; Makhlūf, *Shajara*, vol. 1, 140–1, no. 411.

[46] The full title of the text is *al-Durr al-munaẓẓam fī mawlid al-nabī al-muʿaẓẓam*; the author was Abū al-ʿAbbās Muḥammad b. ʿAbdallāh al-Lakhmī al-ʿAzafī al-Sabtī. The text was written in support of the celebration of *mawlid al-nabī*, the Prophet's birthday, which some regarded as an innovation. See Brockelmann, *Geschichte der Arabischen Litteratur* (Leiden: E.J. Brill, 1937), S I, 626; F. de la Granja, "Fiestas cristianas en al-Andalus (Materiales para su estudio). I: *al-Durr al-munaẓẓam* de al-ʿAzafī," *al-Andalus*, 34 (1969), 1–53.

[47] *Miʿyār*, vol. 2, 543 (bottom)–5 (l. 5).

[48] On relics see generally, David Margoliouth, "The Relics of the Prophet Mohammed," *The Moslem World*, 27:1 (1937), 20–7; R. Basset, "Les empreintes merveilleuses," *Revue des Traditions Populaires*, 9 (1894), 689; Brannon Wheeler, "From Dar al-Hijra to Dar al-Islam: The Islamic Utopia," in *The Concept of Territory in Islamic Law and Thought*, ed. Hiroyuki Yanagihashi (London: Kegan Paul International, 2000), 3–36. On relics in the Maghrib, see Jacques Berque, *Ulémas, fondateurs, Insurgés du Maghrib, xvii*ᵉ *siècle* (Paris: Sindbad, 1982), 239.

affairs. The shrine contained relics of the Prophet, including one of his *qiṭʿas*, a section of his *ʿithra*, his toothpick, and the awl with which he used to repair his noble sandal.[49] The Muslims of Egypt were in the habit of visiting the shrine in order to receive *baraka*, or sacred power, by putting the relics in their hands and rubbing them against their bodies. Similarly, in the Arabian peninsula, shrines reportedly had been constructed over the places where Muḥammad had entered and exited and over the resting-spots of his feet in al-Ḥaramayn al-Sharīfayn.[50]

These references to the cult of the Prophet were part of the muftī's overall strategy, for they allowed him to make an argument *ad minorum ad majorum*, from inanimate objects to human beings. If Muslims magnify and revere lifeless and inanimate physical objects associated with the Prophet, how much more appropriate it is for them to magnify persons who trace their lineage to him![51] Indeed, the special status of Muḥammad's offspring is confirmed by three prophetic *ḥadīth*: (1) "Fāṭima is part of me; what disquiets me disquiets her;"[52] (2) "Al-Ḥasan and al-Ḥusayn are the masters of the youth residing in the Garden;"[53] and (3) "Knowledge of the family of Muḥammad frees one from the Fire; love of the family of Muḥammad [merits] permission [to cross the bridge known as] al-Ṣirāṭ; and a relationship of clientage with the family of the Prophet [merits] security from punishment."[54]

[49] The Ayyūbid Sulṭān al-Ashraf (r. 626–35/1228–37) reportedly purchased a sandal said to have belonged to the Prophet so that he might wear it around his neck and derive *baraka* or sacred power from it. But the jurists of Damascus persuaded him to establish the Dār al-Ḥadīth al-Ashrafiyya and to deposit the object there. See Sibṭ Ibn al-Jawzī, *Mirʾāt al-zamān fī tārīkh al-aʿyān* (Hyderabad, 1370/1952), vol. 8, 713; and Yūnīnī, *Dhayl mirʾāt al-zamān*, 4 vols (Hyderabad, 1374–80/1954–61), vol. 2, 45–6 – both texts cited in Michael Chamberlain, *Knowledge and Social Practice in Medieval Damascus, 1190–1350* (Cambridge: Cambridge University Press, 1994), 49. The Ṭāhirid Siqillīs are also reported to have had the sandals of the Prophet; see Abdelahad Sebti, "Au Maroc: Sharifisme Citadin, Charisme et Historiographie," *Annales ESC* (1986), 433–57, at 448.

[50] *Miʿyār*, vol. 2, 545, ll. 5–14.

[51] Ibid., vol. 2, 545, ll. 14–17. It is interesting to note that Ibn Zāghū expresses no overt disapproval of the cult of the Prophet, although he surely was familiar with treatises by Ibn Waḍḍāḥ and al-Ṭurṭūshī in which these authors attacked the cult of the Prophet (*ittibāʿ āthār al-nabī*) (with specific reference to the Egyptian cult mentioned by Ibn Zāghū). See Muḥammad b. Waḍḍāḥ, *Kitāb al-bidaʿ*, ed. Ma. Isabel Fierro (Madrid: Consejo Superior de Investigaciones Cientificas, 1988); Muḥammad b. al-Walīd al-Turtūshī, *Kitāb al-Ḥawādith wa'l-bidaʿ*, ed. ʿAbd al-Majīd Turkī (Beirut: Dār al-Gharb al-Islāmī, 1990); tr. by Maribel Fierro as *El Libro de las novedades y las innovaciones* (Madrid: Consejo Superior de Investigaciones Cientificas, 1993).

[52] *Miʿyār*, vol. 2, 545, l. 18. See Bukhārī, *Ṣaḥīḥ*, ed. Krehl, 4 vols (Leiden: E.J. Brill, 1862), vol. 3, 453, no. 109 (nikāḥ); Abū Dāʾūd, *Sunan*, ed. Muḥammad Muḥyī al-Dīn ʿAbd al-Ḥamīd, 4 vols (Cairo: al-Maktaba al-Tijāriyya al-Kubrā, 1369/1950), vol. 2, 226, no. 2071 (nikāḥ); Tirmidhī, *Ṣaḥīḥ bi sharḥ Ibn al-ʿArabī al-Mālikī*, ed. ʿAbd al-Wāḥid Muḥammad al-Tāzī, 13 vols (Cairo: Maṭbaʿat al-Ṣāwī, 1353/1934), vol. 13, 247–8 (manāqib); Ibn Ḥanbal, *Musnad* (Beirut: al-Maktaba al-Islāmiyya, 1398/1978), vol. 4, 328; Ismāʿīl b. Muḥammad al-ʿAjlūnī al-Jarrāḥī (d. 1162/1748–49), *Kashf al-khafāʾ wa-muzīl al-ilbās ʿammā ashara min al-aḥādīth ʿalā alsinat al-nās*, 2 vols in 1 (Beirut: Dār Iḥyāʾ al-Turāth al-ʿArabī, 1351–52/1932–33; repr. Beirut: Dār al-Kutub al-ʿIlmiyyah, 1408/1988), vol. 2, 86–7, no. 1231.

[53] *Miʿyār*, vol. 2, 545, ll. 19–20. See Tirmidhī, *Ṣaḥīḥ*, vol. 13, 191–2 (manāqib); Ibn Ḥanbal, *Musnad*, vol. 1, 80; vol. 3, 3, 62, 64, 82; vol. 5, 391, 392; al-ʿAjlūnī al-Jarrāḥī, *Kashf al-khafāʾ*, vol. 1, 358, no. 1139.

[54] *Miʿyār*, vol. 2, 545, ll. 21–2.

To these *ḥadīth*s, the muftī added the following citation from Qur'ān 42:23 ("Say: 'I do not ask of you a wage for this, except love for the kinsfolk [*al-qurbā*]' "), glossing the phrase "love for the kinsfolk" as "that you love me through my relatives" (*qarābatī*). Having previously established that the Prophet's *dhurriyya*, or descendants, are included among his sacred things (the seventh item in the list of sacred things associated with the Prophet, see above), Ibn Zāghū now linked this "fact" to the present situation by stating that the Prophet's descendants are the closest of his relatives (*wa'l-dhurriyya aqrab al-qarāba*).

This assertion posed a problem. The word *dhurriyya* in Arabic customarily refers to a person's agnatic descendants.[55] The Prophet, however, did not have a son, and anyone who claims to be a descendant of the Prophet must base that claim on descent from Muḥammad's daughter, Fāṭima, through one of her two sons, al-Ḥasan or al-Ḥusayn.[56] In his effort to prove that it is obligatory for Muslims to respect those members of the Muslim community who trace their lineage directly to the Prophet, Ibn Zāghū had worked his way to the crux of a major scholarly debate regarding the articulation of the *sharīfī* genealogical system. Indeed, the very notion that it is in fact possible to trace one's descent back to the Prophet through Fāṭima had been contested. How is it possible to reconcile the transmission of prophetic descent through the female line with the principle of agnatic descent that prevailed in Muslim society? Can *sharaf* be transmitted through females?

These questions were of more than academic interest. It will be recalled that Abū Ḥammū II (d. 791/1389) had married the daughter of al-Sharīf al-Tilimsānī and no doubt considered his offspring by this woman to be descendants of the Prophet. It is thus no coincidence that the ability of a *sharīfa* to transmit her status to her children became a subject of intense debate in the Maghrib and Ifrīqiyā. Ibn ʿAbd al-Rafīʿ (d. 733/1332) had issued a fatwā in which he held that prophetic descent may be transmitted through the female line.[57] In response to this fatwā, al-Bijā'ī (d. 754/1353–54) composed a treatise in which he refuted the view of Ibn ʿAbd al-Rafīʿ.[58] Some time later, Ibn Qunfudh al-Qusanṭīnī (d. 810/1407–08), the qāḍī of Constantine,[59] wrote a treatise entitled *Tuḥfat al-wārid fī ikhtiṣāṣ al-sharaf min qibal al-wālid*.[60] And Ibn Marzūq VI al-Ḥafīḍ wrote a treatise entitled *Ismāʿ*

[55] See Ibn Manẓūr, *Lisān al-ʿArab*, 15 vols (Beirut: Dār Ṣādir li'l-Ṭibāʿa wa'l-Nashr, 1375/1955), vol. 4, 304; Lane, *Lexicon*, s.v. dh-r-r.

[56] *Miʿyār*, vol. 2, 545, ll. 23–5.

[57] Abū Isḥāq Ibrāhīm b. Ḥasan b. ʿAbd al-Rafīʿ al-Tunsī (d. Ramaḍān 733/May–June 1333). See Makhlūf, *Shajara*, vol. 1, 207, no. 719.

[58] Abū ʿAlī al-Ḥasan b. Ḥusayn al-Bijā'ī. See ibid., vol. 1, 232, no. 831.

[59] Abū al-ʿAbbās Aḥmad b. al-Ḥusayn b. ʿAlī, known as Ibn al-Qunfudh. See Ibn al-Qāḍī, *Jadhwat al-Iqtibās*, vol. 1, 154–5; idem, *Durrat al-ḥijāl*, vol. 1, 121–3, no. 150; al-Tunbuktī, *Nayl al-Ibtihāj*, 75; al-Ḥifnāwī, *Taʿrīf al-khalaf*, vol. 1, 32–7; Makhlūf, *Shajara*, vol. 1, 250, no. 903; E. Lévi-Provençal, *Les Historiens des Chorfa* (Paris: Larose, 1922), 98, note 2; Ben Cheneb, "La *Fârisiya* ou les débuts de la dynastie Ḥafside par Ibn Qonfod de Constantine (1)," *Hespéris*, 8 (1928), 37–41.

[60] A microfilmed mss. of this treatise is located in the Bibliothèque Nationale, Rabat, no. 187; mentioned in Sebti, "Au Maroc: Sharifisme Citadin, Charisme et Historiographie," 455, note 54; and Benchekroun, *La vie intellectuelle marocaine*, 363.

al-ṣamm fī ithbāt al-sharaf min qibal al-umm.[61] Generally speaking, the jurists of Bougie, Tlemcen, and Fez held that, although descent normally passes through males, an exception is made in the case of prophetic descent, which may be transmitted through Fāṭima. This view became the dominant doctrine of the Mālikī West.[62]

Ibn Zāghū made only passing reference to this debate, however. As support for the prevailing position, he cited a Qur'ānic text which, in his view, indicated that the word *dhurriyya* could indeed be applied to the sons of daughters (*awlād al-banāt*): "And Noah We guided before; and of his seed (*dhurriyya*) David and Solomon, Job and Joseph, Moses and Aaron – even so We recompense the good-doers – Zachariah and John, Jesus and Elias" (Qur'ān 6:84–85). Qur'ān commentators had understood this verse as establishing that Jesus was a descendant of Noah and Abraham through Maryam (the daughter of ʿImrān), from which they concluded that prophetic descent can be transmitted through the female line.[63] This was the doctrine of Ibn Zāghū's masters in Tlemcen and the masters of his masters. He concluded:

> Thus, sanctity and rights are confirmed by virtue of descent [through a female] in the same way [as they are confirmed] for descendants of the Prophet [by virtue of descent] through the male line. This is because descendants of the Prophet through the male line must by necessity trace their prophetic descent to a *sharīf* in the female line; because their link to the Prophet – may God bless him and grant him peace – is exclusively through Fāṭima – may God be pleased with her.[64]

Having established that descent from the Prophet may be transmitted through the female line, Ibn Zāghū returned to the primary subject of his discourse, the obligation to venerate Muḥammad's family and descendants. As evidence for this obligation, he cited the following five *ḥadīth*s:

> (1) On the authority of Jābir b. ʿAbdallāh: "I saw the Messenger of God – may God bless him and grant him peace – during his pilgrimage, on the Day of ʿArafa, while he was addressing [the people, sitting] on his she-camel. I heard him say, 'O people, I have left among you that which, if you hold fast to it, you will not go astray: the Book of God and my descendants (*ʿitratī*), the people of my house.'"[65]
> (2) On the authority of Zayd b. Arqam: The Messenger of God – may God bless him and grant him peace – said, "I have left among you that which, if you hold fast to it, you shall not go astray. One of the two is greater than the other – the Book of God is a rope

[61] Ibn Maryam, *al-Bustān*, 211 = *El Bostan*, 243.
[62] See Houari Touati, "Prestige ancestral et système symbolique šarifien dans le Maghreb central du XVIIe siècle," *Arabica*, XXXIX (1992), 1–24. The debate on this subject can be followed in *Miʿyār* vol. 12, 193–233, where one can find fatwās issued by Ibn Marzūq (ibid., 193–207); the jurists of Tlemcen (ibid., 207–21); the jurists of Bougie (ibid., 221–4); Ibn ʿArafa (ibid., 225–6); Nāṣir al-Dīn al-Mishdālī (ibid., 227–31); Ibn ʿAṭiyya al-Wansharīsī (ibid., 231–3). Al-Wansharīsī ends vol. 12 of the *Miʿyār* with a second fatwā issued by al-Mishdālī with regard to the question of whether *sharaf* can be transmitted through a female (ibid., 385–94).
[63] See, for example, *Tafsīr al-Imāmayn al-Jalālayn* (Beirut: Dār Iḥyā' al-Turāth al-ʿArabī, n.d.), 182.
[64] *Miʿyār*, vol. 2, 546, ll. 1–7.
[65] Tirmidhī, *Ṣaḥīḥ*, vol. 13, 199–200 (manāqib).

extended from the sky to the earth; and my descendants (*ʿitratī*), the people of my house. The two shall not be divided until they arrive at the pond (*al-ḥawḍ*).[66] Therefore, consider the manner in which you determine my succession in them."[67]
(3) Upon being asked which of his relatives Muslims are obligated to love, the Prophet said, "ʿAlī, Fāṭima, and their sons."[68]
(4) The Prophet said: "Whoever dies loving the family of Muḥammad dies forgiven; verily, whoever dies loving the family of Muḥammad dies a Believer whose faith is complete; verily, whoever dies loving the family of Muḥammad will be given good tidings of the Garden by the Angel of Death and subsequently by [the angels] Munkar and Nakīr; verily, whoever dies loving the family of Muḥammad will be conducted to the Garden in the manner of a bride who is conducted to her husband's house; verily, whoever dies loving the family of Muḥammad will have two doors opened in his grave [so that he may look] at the Garden; verily, whoever dies loving the family of Muḥammad, God will designate his grave as a shrine for the Angels of Mercy; verily, whoever dies loving the family of Muḥammad dies in conformity with the *sunna* and the community; verily, whoever dies loathing the family of Muḥammad will arrive on the Day of Resurrection [with the words] 'despairing the mercy of God' written between his eyes; verily, whoever dies loathing the family of Muḥammad will not smell the fragrance of the Garden."[69]
(5) The Prophet said: "Every lineage, [blood] relationship, and relationship by marriage will be severed on the Day of Resurrection – except for my lineage, my [blood] relationship, and my relationship by marriage."[70]

Commenting on these *ḥadīth*s, Ibn Zāghū observed that the merits of prophetic descent are so clear that anyone who seeks additional indicators in support of the matter does nothing but bring shame upon himself and his descendants. As an unidentified poet stated,

How can a thing be sound in the minds
When daylight is in need of an indicator?[71]

Ibn Zāghū now brings his discussion of sacred history back to the present case, thereby closing the circle that links the sacred with the mundane. Having established that the preservation of the Prophet's sanctity is obligatory, he concludes that anyone who has the audacity to violate this sanctity is deserving of punishment in proportion to the magnitude of his audacity and the seriousness of his crime.[72] Significantly, however, the muftī did not specify here the punishment to be meted out to Ibn ʿĪsā and his son.

[66] That is, the basin or pond at which Muḥammad will meet the Believers on the Day of Judgment. For details, see Jane Idleman Smith and Yvonne Haddad, *The Islamic Understanding of Death and Resurrection* (Albany: State University of New York Press, 1981), 80 ff.
[67] See Tirmidhī, *Ṣaḥīḥ*, vol. 13, 200–1 (manāqib); Muslim, *Ṣaḥīḥ*, ed. Muḥammad Fu'ād ʿAbd al-Bāqī, 5 vols (Cairo: Dār Iḥyā' al-Kutub al-ʿArabiyya, 1375/1955), vol. 4, 1874, no. 37 (faḍā'il al-ṣaḥāba); cf. Ibn Ḥanbal, *Musnad*, vol. 3, 14, 26, 59; vol. 5, 182.
[68] *al-Muʿjam al-mufahras li-alfāẓ aḥādith Biḥār al-anwār*, 14 vols (Qum: Qism al-Muʿjam, 1413-18/1993-97), s.v. mawaddatihim.
[69] Ibid., s.v. mustakmil. I thank Michael Cook for this and the previous reference.
[70] *Miʿyār*, vol. 2, 546, ll. 7–26; cf. al-Ḥākim al-Nīsābūrī, *al-Mustadrak*, vol. 3, 142.
[71] *Miʿyār*, vol. 2, 547, ll. 1–3. [72] Ibid., vol. 2, 547, ll. 4–5.

Proving One's Status as a Sharīf

Epistemology

Ibn Zāghū turned next to the second fundamental issue raised by the dispute, to wit, the fact that Ibn ʿĪsā the father apparently had denied Abū al-Faraj's claim to be a *sharīf* when he said to him, "Verily, you do not have the stature for this thing." Before addressing this issue, the muftī first had to discuss the epistemological question of how one establishes one's descent from the Prophet. To do so, he posits the following hypothetical situation. Suppose, for the sake of argument, that Abū al-Faraj was indeed a descendant of the Prophet, but that the elder Ibn ʿĪsā – and perhaps others in the community – were unaware of that fact. Should Ibn ʿĪsā the father nevertheless be punished for denying something about which he had no knowledge? Of course not, Ibn Zāghū explained. Rather, before any punishment is meted out, the person who denies should be given a temporary reprieve so that he might be informed of his violation, and, if he chooses to act upon this new knowledge, he may retract his denial.[73]

This contingency pointed to a larger issue. How could anyone prove that he was a descendant of the Prophet, especially at a time when the temptation to fabricate such a genealogy was great (see Introduction)? To this question, Ibn Zāghū responded as follows: a person who claims to be a descendant of the Prophet may establish his status as a *sharīf* on the basis of a widespread rumor (*al-samāʿ al-fāshī*), his testimony relating to his descent, and the fact that people refer to him as a *sharīf* in his presence (*duʿā al-nās ladayhi*). Such evidence is strengthened and reinforced if it is confirmed in writing by Muslim authorities, as apparently was the case with many claimants of *sharīfī* status who possessed ancient documents that had been certified by numerous individuals and signed by outstanding imāms, jurists, and qāḍīs. By means of such documents, some *sharīf*s were able to trace their lineage backwards approximately 290 *hijrī* years to *ca.* 553/1158–59, that is, shortly after the beginning of the Almohad period.[74] These documents, which may have included marriage contracts, estate divisions, contracts of sale, and genealogical trees,[75] had been signed by outstanding scholars, including

[73] Ibid., vol. 2, 547, ll. 7–10; cf. *EI*², s.v. Sharīf.

[74] The fact that the documentary record reaches back only to the beginning of the Almohad period is not coincidental. Ibn Tūmart himself adopted (or was given) an Arab genealogy that linked him to the Prophet Muḥammad; it was under the Almohads that the cult of the Prophet began to flourish in the Maghrib; and it was at this time that *sharīfī* genealogies began to proliferate.

[75] Touati, "Prestige ancestral et système symbolique šarifien," 15, cites the following text from an unpublished ms., the *Kitāb al-tawthīq* of Ḥasan b. Muḥammad al-ʿAṭṭār al-Jazāʾirī: "Attestation de *šaraf*: les témoins qui ont permis de l'établir connaissent parfaitement le requérant X et témoignent qu'ils ont publiquement entendu de gens connus pour leur honorabilité et d'autres (dont ils peuvent confirmer l'honorabilité) que X mentionné ci-dessus est *šarīf* et connu comme tel et qu'avant lui ses pères et grands-pères ont possédé cette généreuse généalogie et l'ont mentionnée dans leurs actes de mariage, d'achat et de transactions (*sic*) et qu'ils ne connaissent personne qui la leur conteste." Cf. Beck, *L'Image d'Idrīs II*, 192–3; according to Munson, "royal decrees attesting to descent from the

members of the Banū Ibn Ṣāḥib al-Ṣalāt,[76] and, most recently, Abū ʿUthmān Saʿīd al-ʿUqbānī (d. 811/1408–09), the father of Qāsim al-ʿUqbānī and one of Ibn Zāghū's teachers.[77]

Documentary evidence of this sort, although desirable, is not required to establish prophetic descent, because, as Ibn Zāghū explained, if certain knowledge (*ʿilm*) were stipulated as a requirement to confirm prophetic lineage, then it would be impossible to establish that anyone was a descendant of the Prophet. This is absurd, he continued, for it is known that Muslim scholars have stipulated that paternity (*nasab*) may be established on the basis of a widespread rumor (*al-samāʿ al-fāshī*).[78] In support of this point, the muftī cited the following anecdote. Someone asked Ibn al-Qāsim (d. 191/806): if someone is not familiar with your father and knows that you are the son of al-Qāsim only on the basis of hearsay, can that person give testimony to the effect that you are in fact the son of (Ibn) al-Qāsim? To which Ibn al-Qāsim responded that hearsay testimony is sufficent to establish his lineage. If this is true with regard to a lineage that is not of special interest to those who bear it, Ibn Zāghū observed, then it follows that this conclusion holds even more with regard to a prophetic lineage, the bearers of which are known to be mindful of it and who possess valid documents containing numerous attestations that have been confirmed by qāḍīs.[79]

Refutation of those who criticize claims of prophetic descent

Having determined that prophetic descent may be established merely on the basis of widespread rumor, Ibn Zāghū turns his attention to the objection of certain contemporary critics who had called into question the validity of claims to prophetic descent and asserted that "prophetic descent after the 700s [AH] and even more so after the 800s [AH] is weak."[80]

Prophet ... were already common by the late fourteenth century." See Henry Munson Jr, *Religion and Power in Morocco* (New Haven: Yale University Press, 1993), 21.

76 Perhaps a reference to descendants of Abū Marwān ʿAbd al-Malik b. Muḥammad al-Bājī, Ibn Ṣāḥib al-Ṣalāt, an Andalusian author of a history of the Almohads entitled *al-Mann bi'l-imāma ʿalā 'l-mustaḍʿafīn bi-an jaʿalahum allāh al-aʾimma wa-jaʿalahum al-wārithīn*. He was still living in 594/1198. Several other men bear the same name. See *EI*², s.v. Ibn Ṣāḥib al-Ṣalāt.

77 Abū ʿUthmān Saʿīd b. Muḥammad al-ʿUqbānī al-Tilimsānī al-Tujībī, a distinguished scholar and jurist who served as chief qāḍī of Bougie, Tlemcen, Salé, and Marrakesh for a period of forty *hijrī* years. Abū Yaḥyā al-Sharīf also studied with him. See Makhlūf, *Shajara*, vol. 1, 250, no. 904.

78 On *al-samāʿ al-fāshī* in connection with paternity, see chapter 1, note 38.

79 *Miʿyār*, vol. 2, 547 (l. 10)–8 (l. 3).

80 This may be a reference to al-Maqqarī (d. 795/1392), about whom the following anecdote is told: "When the *mizwār* of the *sharīfs* in Fez entered the *majlis* of the Sulṭān Abū ʿInān Fāris al-Marīnī (r. 749–59/1348–58), the Sulṭān and those who were present arose out of respect for him, except for the shaykh al-Maqqarī, who remained in his seat. When the *mizwār* noticed this, he complained about al-Maqqarī to the Sulṭān. The Sulṭān said, 'That man has just arrived here. Let us leave him as he is, until he leaves.' Subsequently, the *mizwār* once again entered the *majlis*. The Sulṭān and the members of the *majlis* arose out of respect for him, as was their custom. The *mizwār* looked at al-Maqqarī and said to him, 'O jurist, why is it that you do not stand up as does the Sulṭān – may

This assertion, Ibn Zāghū responded, finds no support among the ancient authorities. Indeed, he explained, the only instance in which it might be construed as a valid statement would be that of specific individuals who, prior to the eighth century AH, were not known to be *sharīfs* but who suddenly claimed to be *sharīfs* during the ninth century AH. Otherwise, he continued, the statement is null and void, and anyone who acts on the strength of it with regard to someone whose prophetic lineage is renowned, having been inherited from his ancestors, builds a castle in the sand; likewise, anyone who treats this assertion as a pretext for discrediting the sacred lineage in question thereby perpetrates "an awesome calamity and a great conceit."[81] Indeed, anyone who invokes this assertion in an attempt to reject a valid claim to prophetic descent thereby nullifies a right after the claim has been confirmed and erroneously refutes a truth after its validity has been established.

Ibn Zāghū posited the following hypothetical case: suppose that a man's prophetic descent was confirmed in the seventh century AH on the strength of his renown and valid, authentic documents. Suppose further that the soundness and legal validity of his lineage continued to be confirmed into the eighth and ninth centuries AH among his descendants, but that in the ninth century someone arose and asserted, "Prophetic descent after the 700s [AH] and even more so after the 800s [AH] is weak." Can this statement be used to invalidate a truth that had been established in the seventh century AH? That is to say, is the mere passage of time sufficient to falsify something that was once true? Of course not, and if one were to act in this manner with regard to prophetic lineages, it would be necessary to discredit other, less important lineages of equal or greater antiquity, the documentation of which is comparatively weak. Apart from *sharīfs*, many people living in Tlemcen in the ninth/fifteenth century traced their lineage back to people who were alive at the time of the Prophet, while others traced their lineage back to the tribes of Quraysh, Qays, and Tamīm, that is, to the *jāhiliyya*, or age of ignorance that preceded the rise of Islam. The members of these three distinguished tribes lived prior to the revelation of the *sharīʿa*, which, for the first time in history, imposed the obligation to be truthful in transmitting information; the only moral force in the universe of these groups was tribal custom. No one, however, had questioned the validity of these lineages, and it was obvious to Ibn Zāghū that it would be incorrect to do so. It followed, by necessity, that the assertion in question was null and void.[82]

God grant him victory – and the members of the *majlis*, in honor of my ancestor (*jaddī*) and my nobility (*sharafī*)? Who are you that you do not arise out of respect for me?' Al-Maqqarī looked at him and said, 'As for my honor (*sharaf*), it is guaranteed by the knowledge that I disseminate. No one can doubt it. As for your nobility, it is subject to doubt (*maẓnūn*). Who can assure us of its soundness after more than 700 years? If it were the case that I possessed apodictic knowledge regarding your nobility, I would make him get up – pointing to the Sulṭān Abū ʿInān Fāris – and I would place you on his seat.' At that, the *mizwār* was silent." See al-Tunbuktī, *Nayl*, 253; Ibn Maryam, *Bustān*, 162 [= *El Bostan*, 179–80]; the anecdote is cited and discussed in Beck, *L'Image d'Idrīs II*, 180 ff. and Mohamed Kably, *Société, pouvoir et religion au Maroc à la fin du Moyen-Age* (Paris: Maisonneuve et Larose, 1986), 321.

[81] *Miʿyār*, vol. 2, 548, ll. 4–14.

[82] Ibid., vol. 2, 548 (l. 14)–9 (l. 2).

Punishment

Legal Doctrine

Having resolved the relevant epistemological issues, Ibn Zāghū now turned to the question of punishment. He wrote that anyone who knowingly slanders the lineage of a person whose noble lineage is a matter of renown thereby commits the Qur'ānic crime of *qadhf*, or false accusation of illegitimate descent, for which he merits the *ḥadd* punishment of eighty lashes. The muftī cited the following statement attributed to the fourth/tenth century Tunisian jurist al-Barādhiʿī in the latter's *Tahdhīb*:[83] "Whoever says to an Arab, 'You are not from the Banū So-And-So,' the tribe to which he belongs is entitled to mete out the *ḥadd* punishment."[84]

If it is the case that the honor of Arabs is protected, the same must hold for descendants of the Prophet who trace their descent back to al-Ḥasan and al-Ḥusayn, the two sons of ʿAlī b. Abī Ṭālib. Thus, anyone who reproaches a *sharīf*, saying, "You are not a *sharīf*," thereby slanders his noble Arab descent. As further support for this assertion, Ibn Zāghū again cited al-Barādhiʿī, regarding someone who said to one of the sons of ʿUmar b. al-Khaṭṭāb, "You are not the son of al-Khaṭṭāb;" this person, al-Barādhiʿī argued, denied the legitimate descent of the son in question and therefore merited the *ḥadd* punishment. Al-Barādhiʿī added that the *ḥadd* punishment should be inflicted even if the speech in question were equivocal, as, for example, in the following case: one man said to another, "You are not a descendant of So-and-So (referring to his reputed grandfather)." Now, this statement might be understood as signifying that the addressee was not the son of the man who he claimed was his father. The person who uttered the statement subsequently clarified his intention, explaining that what he meant was, "You are not his direct descendant (literally: the son of his loins), because you have a different father."[85]

This conclusion was important for Ibn Zāghū, who drew the attention of his audience to the fact that al-Barādhiʿī called for imposition of the *ḥadd* punishment in this case despite the fact that the utterance was open to interpretation in the manner suggested by the speaker. The reason for this, Ibn Zāghū continued, is that the sacred law treats *all* lineages as a *ḥimā*, or entity that must be protected against encroachment, and it provides comprehensive protection for such lineages, to the extent that the *ḥadd* punishment is obligatory on the strength of a mere insinuation (*taʿrīḍ*).[86] If this is true with regard to ordinary lineages, how much more so with regard to those persons who trace their descent back to the most noble of all

[83] Abū Saʿīd Khalaf al-Barādhiʿī (d. 386/996), a Mālikī jurist from Qayrawān who was the author of the *Kitāb al-tahdhīb li-masā'il al-Mudawwana*. See Ibn Farḥūn, *Dībāj*, 112; Makhlūf, *Shajara*, vol. 1, 105, no. 270; Henry Toledano, *Judicial Practice and Family Law in Morocco: The Chapter on Marriage from Sijilmāsī's* al-ʿAmal al-Muṭlaq (Boulder, CO: Social Science Monographs, 1981), 148, note 33.

[84] *Miʿyār*, vol. 2, 549, ll. 2–5.

[85] Ibid., vol. 2, 549, ll. 6–11.

[86] For references, see note 19, above.

lineages, that of the Prophet. To demonstrate that this was established Mālikī doctrine, Ibn Zāghū cited a statement made by the Andalusian jurist Ibn ʿAbd al-Barr (d. 463/1070) in his *Kitāb al-Kāfī*,[87] as mentioned in the *Mufīd* of al-Azdī (d. 606/1209):[88] The *ḥadd* punishment for *qadhf* is obligatory in two cases: if someone impugns (*qaṭaʿa*) the descent of a Muslim whose lineage is widely known, or if someone falsely accuses someone of committing fornication.[89]

Application of Mālikī legal doctrine to the present case

Ibn Zāghū now attempted to apply Mālikī legal doctrine to the present case, beginning with the two Ibn ʿĪsās, after which he turns to Abū al-Faraj. Proceeding with caution, he stated that *if* the reports regarding the utterances of Aḥmad b. ʿĪsā and his son were legally valid and accurate, then both father and son had violated the boundaries of permissible speech by uttering forbidden words that are to be avoided at all costs.[90]

The muftī explained that in order to determine the appropriate punishment in such a circumstance, two possibilities must be taken into consideration. If the two Ibn ʿĪsās were aware of and acknowledged Abū Faraj's status as a *sharīf*, then they knowingly violated the sanctity of the Prophet. In that case, God would "distance the two of them [viz., the father and his son] from the good things of this world and the next and bring them near to the evil things of this world and the next. They would deserve the hatred of God – may He be magnified and exalted – and of the rest of the Community."[91] This conclusion follows from Qur'ān 33:57, which reads, "Those who hurt God and His Messenger – them God has cursed in the present world and the world to come, and has prepared for them a humbling chastisement."[92] But what did this mean? How should the divine pronouncement be translated into mundane terms? Should Ibn ʿĪsā and his son be put to death? Or does a "humbling chastisement" await them only in the next world? Ibn Zāghū did not commit himself to a specific punishment, leaving its determination to the *mustaftī*, who, we have surmised, was Qāsim al-ʿUqbānī.

If, on the other hand, Ibn ʿĪsā and his son were unaware of Abū Faraj's status as a *sharīf*, then they had committed a lesser offense, slanderous accusation of illegitimate descent (*qadhf*), for which they deserved the corresponding *ḥadd* punishment of eighty stripes.[93]

[87] The *Kitāb al-Kāfī* is a systematic treatise on Islamic law by the Andalusian Mālikī jurist, Ibn ʿAbd al–Barr. See Ibn Farḥūn, *Dībāj*, 357; Makhlūf, *Shajara*, vol. 1, 119, no. 337; Toledano, *Judicial Practice*, 81, note 132.

[88] That is, Abū al-Walīd Hishām b. ʿAbdallāh al-Azdī (d. 606/1209). The full title of the work is *Kitāb al-Mufīd li'l-ḥukkām fī-mā yaʿriḍu lahum min nawāzil al-aḥkām*. See Brockelmann, *Geschichte*, i, 384, *S*, 664; Toledano, *Judicial Practice*, 123, note 24; A. Carmona González, "Ibn Hišām al-Qurṭubī y su *Mufīd li-l-ḥukkām*," *Quaderni di Studi Arabi*, 5–6 (1987–88), 120–30.

[89] *Miʿyār*, vol. 2, 549, ll. 12–17. Cf. Ibn ʿAbd al-Barr, *al-Kāfī*, 576.

[90] *Miʿyār*, vol. 2, 549, ll. 19–20.

[91] Ibid., vol. 2, 549, ll. 20–3.

[92] Ibid., vol. 2, 549, ll. 24–5.

[93] Ibid., vol. 2, 549 (l. 20)–50 (l. 1).

Next, the muftī directed his attention to Abū al-Faraj, who had initiated the slanderous exchange by taunting Ibn ʿĪsā with the statement, "You have no superiority." This surely was improper and inappropriate behavior, and the *sharīf* should have been deterred from making such a statement by his knowledge that anyone who initiates a curse exposes not only himself but also his fathers to verbal retaliation equal to or greater than the initial attack. Once again the muftī posits a hypothetical scenario. If one assumes, for the sake of argument, that Ibn ʿĪsā the father had *not* responded to Abū al-Faraj, then the latter would have deserved, in theory, a discretionary punishment for having initiated the exchange. This punishment should be determined by the ruler, who might choose either to apply a discretionary punishment to Abū al-Faraj for his having instigated the cursing, or to pardon him on account of his being a person of elevated status. This is a distinctive feature of Islamic penal law – not uncommon in other legal systems – according to which, the higher a person's social status, the milder his punishment.[94] Thus if a member of the lower class commits a crime, the ruler might decide to imprison him, whereas if a member of the élite class were to commit the same offense, the ruler might punish him by either shunning or rebuking him.[95]

But the elder Ibn ʿĪsā did in fact respond to the verbal attack. Having been insulted, Ibn ʿĪsā would have been within his rights to respond in kind, as suggested by Qurʾān 16:126: "And if you chastise, chastise even as you have been chastised."[96] However, Ibn ʿĪsā had raised the level of verbal abuse by cursing Abū al-Faraj's father and grandfather, both models of piety, good action, and religious knowledge. In this manner, Ibn ʿĪsā had slandered not only Abū al-Faraj – who may have deserved a rebuke – but also two of the latter's ancestors, the *sharīfs* Abū Yaḥyā – who had been one of the muftī's teachers – and Abū ʿAbdallāh Muḥammad, the venerable al-Sharīf al-Tilimsānī. The cursing of any one of these men would have constituted a serious offense that merited severe punishment; the cursing of all three deepened the violation and, perhaps, the nature of an appropriate punishment.[97]

[94] "The correction inflicted on respectable persons of the noble class is lighter than that inflicted on the meaner and lower classes based on the saying of the Prophet, may the peace and blessings of God be upon him: 'Pardon the faults of those who command respect.' " *Al-Ahkam as-Sultaniyyah: The Laws of Governance*, by Abu'l Hasan al-Mawardi, tr. Asadullah Yate (London: Ta-Ha Publishers, 1996), 332; Al-Mawardī, *Les statuts gouvernementaux ou règles de droit public et administratif*, trad. d'E. Fagnan, réimpr., Paris, 1982, 504. Ibn ʿAbdūn writes: "Le *ṣāḥib al-madīna* n'absoudra personne pour un délit contre la loi religieuse, sauf s'il s'agit des gens de haut rang, qui seront absous selon le *ḥadīth*: 'pardonnez les fautes des gens de condition' [*dhawī l-hayʾāt*]; pour eux, la répréhension est plus douloureuse que le châtiment physique" (*Risālat Ibn ʿAbdūn fī l-quḍāt wa-l-ḥisba*, ed. E. Lévi-Provençal, in *Trois traités hispaniques de hisba*, Le Caire, 1955, 17. See also E. García Gómez, "Sobre la diferencia en el castigo de plebeyos y nobles," *al-Andalus*, 36:1 (1971), 71–80; Irene Schneider, "Imprisonment in pre-classical and classical Islamic law," *Islamic Law and Society*, 2:2 (1995), 157–73, esp. 163–4.

[95] *Al-Ahkam as-Sultaniyyah: The Laws of Governance*, 332.

[96] The verse ends: "But if you show patience, that is indeed the best [course] for those who are patient" (*wa-la-in ṣabartum la-huwa khayrun li'l-ṣābirīn*).

[97] *Miʿyār*, vol. 2, 550, ll. 1–19.

Surely, the elder Ibn ʿĪsā deserved to be punished for having insulted three descendants of the Prophet. Ibn Zāghū again took care to support this line of reasoning with citations from Mālikī legal doctrine. Qāḍī ʿIyāḍ said in *al-Shifā*, "To curse the family of his house, his wives, and his Companions – peace be upon him – and to insult them is a forbidden thing whose perpetrator is accursed."[98] ʿIyāḍ also stipulated that a painful punishment should be administered to anyone who utters a repugnant statement to a man who is one of the descendants (*dhurriyya*) of the Prophet – may God bless him and grant him peace – with regard to his fathers, his lineal descendants (*nasl*), or his children – despite his knowledge that the person in question is one of his descendants – may God bless him and grant him peace.[99] Finally, Ibn Zāghū noted that Khalīl b. Isḥāq (d. 776/1374) had made a similar stipulation in his *Mukhtaṣar*,[100] as confirmed by his later commentators.[101] It followed that once Ibn ʿĪsā the father had responded in the manner in which he did, the calculus of culpability shifted in his direction and away from Abū al-Faraj.

Sentencing: father and sons

Exactly what punishment should be meted out? And what distinction, if any, should be made between the crime committed by Ibn ʿĪsā the father and that committed by his son?

The incident, as noted, had divided the Muslims of Tlemcen into two factions. Apparently, it was generally accepted that the younger Ibn ʿĪsā had blasphemed the Prophet ("May God curse the accursed one, the first father of your grandfather"), for which he deserved to be executed. In addition, some people apparently held that the earlier utterance of Ibn ʿĪsā the father ("Your father is the dog, the son of the dog, the disgrace, the son of the disgrace – and the father of your father") *also* constituted slander of the Prophet for which he too merited capital punishment. This claim was based upon a subtle linguistic argument. The phrase "the father of your father" represents a common Arabic linguistic structure known as an *iḍāfa*, or construct state.[102] Because the first term of this particular *iḍāfa* is a generic noun ("father"), one may argue that the word *father* here refers to all fathers, beginning with Adam (and including Muḥammad).

[98] See Ibn Ḥanbal, vol. 4, 87; vol. 5, 54–5, 57; Tirmidhī, *Sunan* (Manāqib), 58.
[99] See Qāḍī ʿIyāḍ, *Kitāb al-shifā bi-taʿrīf ḥuqūq al-muṣṭafā*. 2 vols, ed. Saʿīd ʿAbd al-Fattāḥ ([Saudi Arabia]: Hishām ʿAlī Ḥāfiẓ, 1416/1995), vol. 2, 337.
[100] Khalīl b. Isḥāq, a great Mālikī jurist and author of many works, the most celebrated of which is his *Mukhtaṣar*. See Makhlūf, *Shajara*, vol. 1, 223, no. 794; Toledano, *Judicial Practice*, 26, note 65.
[101] *Miʿyār*, vol. 2, 550 (l. 19)–1 (l. 2).
[102] On the *iḍāfa*, or construct state, see *A Grammar of the Arabic Language*, tr. and ed. W. Wright, 2 vols (3d edn. Cambridge: Cambridge University Press, 1955), vol. 2, 198 ff.

This argument was categorically rejected by Ibn Zāghū. Displaying his skills as an accomplished linguist, he argued as follows: if, in the phrase "the father of your father," one treats the first "father" as an abstract noun referring to all fathers, he explained, then the same should hold for the word "father" in the phrase "your father" (literally: "the father of you") in which the word "father" also functions as a generic noun in a construct state. Ibn Zāghū writes that it is well known that people frequently say, "May God curse the father of so-and-so." Sons often say this to their own fathers, and fathers say this to their sons and slaves. If one were to treat the word "father" in this curse as a generic noun referring to all fathers, then anyone who uttered this curse would thereby slander the Prophet and, accordingly, should be executed. From this it would follow, in theory, that large numbers of people should be executed, for this curse is commonly heard flowing from the lips of men. However, Ibn Zāghū observed that he was unaware of a single jurist who is reported to have called for the execution of someone who had uttered such a curse and that he had not seen any stipulation to that effect in a legal text. In all of these cases, the muftī argued, the person who utters the curse has in mind, and is referring to, a single, specific person. The same holds for the phrase, "the father of your father."[103]

Others argued that Ibn ʿĪsā the father should be executed on the grounds that he was responsible for the slanderous curse uttered by his son, for he had said to Abū al-Faraj, "I am not the one whose response is appropriate; rather, the correct one (*al-qayyim bihi*) is that dog!" – referring to his son, Aḥmad. Proponents of this view argued that Ibn ʿĪsā's prompting of his son to respond to Abū al-Faraj constituted consent on his part to any words that might emanate from his son's mouth, including the latter's cursing of "the first father of the grandfather" of Abū al-Faraj. This argument also was rejected categorically by Ibn Zāghū, for two reasons: first, because Ibn ʿĪsā the father plausibly might argue that he had ordered his son to respond to Abū al-Faraj in a manner that was less severe than the words that his son actually had uttered, and second, because if one person plans a crime (*al-mutasabbib*) and another carries it out (*al-mubāshir*), it is the person who actually commits the crime who is liable for punishment.[104] For this reason, Ibn ʿĪsā the father should not be executed.

Ibn Zāghū now turned his attention to Ibn ʿĪsā the son, who had uttered the curse, "May God curse the accursed one, the first father of your grandfather." Continuing the line of linguistic analysis begun earlier, the muftī observed that even if the speaker had not specified "the first" and had mentioned only "the grandfather," he nevertheless would have merited a severe punishment (*ʿuqūba shadīda*), because the word "grandfather" here may refer to the closest or to the most distant grandfather; the obligatory nature of the punishment follows from the

[103] *Miʿyār*, vol. 2, 551, ll. 2–14.

[104] Ibid., vol. 2, 551, ll. 14–24. On the distinction between a person who orders an agent to kill and the person who actually carries out the execution, see Colin Imber, "Why you should poison your husband: A note on liability in Ḥanafī law in the Ottoman period," *Islamic Law and Society*, 1:2 (1994), 206–16.

mere *possibility* that the speaker was referring to the most distant grandfather, to wit, the Prophet. *Ad minorum ad majorum*, the fact that the son specified the "first" grandfather eliminates this ambiguity and entails that the son must have intended the most distant grandfather, to wit, the Prophet. According to linguistic custom, Ibn Zāghū explained, when people use the word "the first" in curses of this nature, they do so in order to increase the severity of the curse and to highlight their contempt for the object of the curse, formulating the curse in such a manner that it will reach the most distant ancestor and the furthest point to which the object of the curse can be linked – either with respect to prophetic descent (*sharaf*) or absolutely (*muṭlaqan*). If one treats the son's reference to "the first grandfather" as applying to prophetic descent, then the object of the curse would have been the Prophet Muḥammad; alternatively, if one treats it as referring to the absolute limit of his grandfathers, then the object of the curse would have been the first human being, Adam, also a prophet.[105]

A procedural loophole

To this point, all of the arguments advanced by Ibn Zāghū pointed in the direction of the execution of Ibn ʿĪsā the son, for, as the muftī observed, according to the consensus of Muslim jurists, both early and late, the punishment for blaspheming one of the prophets is death by stoning.[106] Having prepared his audience for this severe outcome, the muftī now made a radical shift in his argument, divulging information that was not included in the *istiftāʾ*.

Ibn Zāghū revealed that someone had raised a formal, procedural objection to the proceedings, challenging the validity of the testimony of one of the witnesses who had testified against the two Ibn ʿĪsās (a procedure known as *shahādat al-ṭaʿn*).[107] Although he does not specify the author of the objection, I suspect that it was the elder Ibn ʿĪsā, himself a distinguished jurist well-versed in Islamic substantive law and legal procedure. He no doubt sought to disqualify the witness on the ground that he was prejudiced against him and his son and had a desire to inflict damage on them. As I noted at the outset, there apparently had been only two witnesses to the verbal exchange; thus, the disqualification of one witness, for whatever reason, would make it impossible to establish with legal certainty the

[105] *Miʿyār*, vol. 2, 551 (l. 24)–2 (l. 10).
[106] Cp. Wiederhold, "Blasphemy against the Prophet Muḥammad," 44.
[107] On *shahādat al-ṭaʾn*, see Baber Johansen, *Contingency in a Sacred Law: Legal and Ethical Norms in the Muslim Fiqh* (Leiden: E.J. Brill, 1998), 444, note 57 and the references cited there. In cases of blasphemy, it was not uncommon to avert the severe punishment of stoning by disqualifying a witness. See Fierro, "Andalusian "Fatāwā" on Blasphemy," 103–17; idem, *La heterodoxia en al-Andalus durante el periodo omeya* (Madrid: IHAC, 1987); idem, "Accusations of "*Zandaqa*" in al-Andalus," *Quaderni di Studi Arabi*, 5–6 (1987–88), 251–8; idem, "El processo contra Ibn Ḥātim al-Ṭulayṭulī (afios 457/1064–464/1072)," *Estudios onomástico-biográficos de al-Andalus (Homenaje a José M.ª Fórneas)*, VI (Madrid, 1994), 187–215.

veracity of the words attributed to the two Ibn ʿĪsās. And if it could not be legally established that the two Ibn ʿĪsās had uttered the words attributed to them, there were no grounds for applying the *ḥadd* punishment. That no such grounds existed was apparently the conclusion reached by Ibn Zāghū, although he did not state it explicitly, preferring to remind his audience that had it not been for the disqualification of the testimony, it would have been necessary to execute Ibn ʿĪsā the son "because of the repugnance of that statement and the obscenity of that utterance."[108]

This legal subject, the disqualification of a witness in a manner that cast doubt on the veracity of the accusation, had been discussed by earlier jurists. Ibn Zāghū now cited doctrinal support for his decision *not* to apply the *ḥadd* punishment, again citing ʿĪyāḍ:

> ʿIyāḍ said in *al-Shifā* – and Khalīl said more or less the same in *al-Mukhtaṣar*: Al-Qābisī (d. 403/1012)[109] said: "If someone is sentenced to execution, but some obstacle intervenes to cast doubt (*ashkala*) on the carrying out of the execution, it is not appropriate that he be released from prison, [and he should be imprisoned for a long time],[110] even if he has been residing there for as long a time as he can tolerate and has been restrained in bonds to the limit of his tolerance." He [viz., al-Qābisī] said in a similar case, that is, [the case of] someone whose status becomes a matter of doubt (*ushkila*): "He should be restrained in chains and kept straitened in a prison until it is determined what is obligatory with regard to him [viz., a deterrent punishment, execution, or release]." He [viz., al-Qābisī] said with regard to another case [similar to it]:[111] "Blood should not be shed except in a matter that is clear, and to teach someone by means of the whip and prison serves as a deterrent punishment for the insolent, and he should be chastised severely."

The implication here is that the two Ibn ʿĪsās should be put in prison until the sulṭān determined whether or not to apply a discretionary punishment. ʿIyāḍ continued:

> As for [the case in which] only two witnesses testify against him, and he establishes enmity or a desire to wound[112] on their part in a manner that disqualifies them [viz., their testimony], and that [accusation] has not been heard from anyone other than the two of them, verily, his situation is less serious,[113] because the legal judgment (*al-ḥukm*) against him is nullified, and it is as if no testimony against him has been given. An exception is made, however, if he is one of those for whom that is appropriate[114] and the two witnesses are renowned for their integrity, in which case, if he disqualifies them on the grounds of enmity, even if the judgment against him is not carried out[115] on the basis of

[108] *Miʿyār*, vol. 2, 552, ll. 14–15. The text continues: *wa-majj al-asmāʿ wa'l-ṭibāʿ al-aymāniyya li-aḥad al-nabīyyīn …*, which I am unable to translate.
[109] ʿAlī b. Muḥammad b. Khalaf al-Maʿāfirī al-Qābisī, one of the principal representatives of the Mālikī school of Qayrawān, of which he was the leader after the death of Ibn Abī Zayd in 386/996. See *EI²*, s.v. al-Ḳābisī.
[110] Iyāḍ, *al-Shifā*, vol. 2, 366 adds: *wa-yustaṭāla sijnuhu.*
[111] Ibid., vol. 2, 366 adds: *mithlihā.* [112] Ibid., vol. 2, 366 adds: *aw-jarḥatihimā.*
[113] Text: *fa-akhaffu*. Read: *fa-amruhu akhaffu*, following ibid., vol. 2, 366.
[114] Text: *illā an yakūna mimman yalīqu bihi dhālika.*
[115] Text: *fa-huwa in lam yunaffaẓ al-ḥukm ʿalayhi*. Read: *fa-huwa wa-in lam yanfuẓ al-ḥukm [ʿalayhi]*, following ibid., vol. 2, 366.

their [dual] testimony, the suspicion does not repel the veracity [of their testimony],[116] and the magistrate here may apply a deterrent punishment according to his personal discretion (*ijtihād*).[117] God is the master of guidance.[118]

Unless the two Ibn ʿĪsās were renowned for their impiety *and* the two witnesses were renowned for their integrity, determining enmity on the part of one of the witnesses must result in the nullification of the judgment against the two Ibn ʿĪsās. In a worst-case scenario, the magistrate might apply a deterrent punishment, which, as noted above, might be waived out of consideration for the high social status of the accused.

In addition to the formal, procedural argument, a substantive consideration also pointed in the direction of leniency. Ibn Zāghū explained that there was no escape from the fact that the curse uttered by Ibn ʿĪsā the son was equivocal and subject to at least two interpretations, referring *either* to a specific ascendant (however unlikely that may be) *or* to the Prophet.[119] The problem of linguistic ambiguity had been dealt with by Qāḍī ʿIyāḍ in *al-Shifā*, as one of four topics relating to slander of the Prophet. Ibn Zāghū now cited the relevant section of this text, as follows:

> The fourth topic is that someone utters an ambiguous statement (*mujmal*) and an equivocal expresssion[120] that can be understood as referring to the Prophet or to someone else or that can vacillate with regard to what is intended by it with respect to its being free from that which is reprehensible or evil. On this point, there is room for vacillation, confusion of signs, cause (*maẓanna*) for difference of opinion among the *mujtahids*, and the suspension of the indemnity (*istibrāʾ*) of the *muqallids* [who follow them],[121] "that whosoever perished might perish by a clear sign, and by a clear sign he might live who lived" (Qurʾān 8:43). Thus, among them are those who give preponderance to the sanctity of the Prophet – may God bless him and grant him peace – and to protecting the sanctity of his honor, so that they are emboldened to impose a death sentence; and among them are those who attach the utmost importance to the sanctity of blood and the prevention of a canonical punishment as a consequence of the uncertainty (*shubha*) that inheres in the understanding of the statement. Our imāms disagreed with regard to a man whose debtor was vexing him,[122] and he said to him, "Pray for the Prophet Muḥammad" [i.e., in order to relieve your anger]. To which the creditor (*al-ṭālib*) replied, "No. May God pray for whomever He prays for." Someone

[116] Text: *fa-lā yarfaʿu al-ẓannu bihimā*. Read: *fa-lā yadfaʿu al-ẓannu ṣidqahumā*, following ibid., vol. 2, 366.

[117] Text: *wa-li'l-ḥākim maʿnā fī tankīlihi mawāḍiʿ al-ijtihād*. Read: *wa-li'l-ḥākim hunā fī tankīlihi mawḍiʿu ijtihād*, following ibid., vol. 2, 366.

[118] *Miʿyār*, vol. 2, 553, ll. 4–15; cp. ʿIyāḍ, *al-Shifā*, vol. 2, 365–6.

[119] *Miʿyār*, vol. 2, 552, ll. 11–18.

[120] Text: *wa-bi lafẓ min al-qawl mushkil*. Read: *wa-yalfiẓa min al-qawl bi-mushkilin*, following ʿIyāḍ, *al-Shifā*, vol. 2, 335.

[121] Text: *yataraddadu al-naẓar wa-ḥayratu al-ʿayn wa-maẓinnatun li-ikhtilāf al-mujtahidīn wa-waqafahu istibrāʾ al-muqallidīn*. Read: *mutaraddidu al-naẓar wa-ḥayratu al-ʿibar wa-maẓinnatu ikhtilāf al-mujtahidīn wa-waqfati istibrāʾ al-muqallidīn*, following ibid., vol. 2, 335.

[122] Text: *fī rajul aghḍaba gharīmahu*. Read: *fī rajul aghḍabahu gharīmuhu*, following ibid., vol. 2, 335.

> asked Saḥnūn, "Is he like the person who cursed (*shatama*) the Prophet – may God bless him and grant him peace – or [who] cursed the angels who pray for him? [To which Saḥnūn] replied, "No, [not] if he was in the state of anger that you describe, because he had not resolved [in his mind] (*lā muḍmir*) to curse." [...] Then he said: "Al-Ḥārith b. Miskīn al-Qāḍī[123] and someone other than him held for capital punishment in cases of this nature."[124]

Ibn Zāghū explained the relevance of this reference to the present case. The muftī said that although the doubts regarding the meaning of the words uttered by Ibn ʿĪsā the son entailed averting his execution, that did not entail the aversion of a lesser punishment, as, for example, lengthy incarceration or whatever the ruler might consider appropriate.[125] This concludes the fatwā itself, properly speaking.

Excursus

It will be recalled that at the outset of his response Ibn Zāghū had noted that the present case was exceptional and required special treatment. One of the unusual features of his response is an excursus attached to the fatwā in which the muftī engages in an heuristic exercise – reenacting the exchange between the three men, rewriting their conversation to reflect proper Islamic conduct and behavior.

Ibn Zāghū began with Abū al-Faraj. The *sharīf*, he explained, should never have said to Ibn ʿĪsā the father, "You have no superiority." The elder Ibn ʿĪsā, although not a *sharīf*, was a respected member of the community – as evidenced by his hoary head – and a scholar who possessed the qualities associated with the study and teaching of the sacred law (*faḍīla sharʿiyya*). Had Abū al-Faraj taken these qualities into consideration, Ibn Zāghū observed, it would not have been necessary to "plug the gate of this ugly evil" and neither of the two men would have committed any violation of Islamic values. Once again, Ibn Zāghū found models of proper Islamic behavior in the Qur'ān, as in Qur'ān 2:83, which teaches, "And say to the people good things"; and in Qur'ān 41:33, which reads, "Repel with that which is fairer and behold, he between whom and thee there is enmity shall be as if he were a loyal friend."[126]

In an effort to mend the torn fabric of communal harmony, Ibn Zāghū returns to the comprehensive list of sacred things (*ḥurumāt*) associated with the Prophet Muḥammad, presented earlier in his response. The sixth item in the list specified, "the rest of his community who believe in him, adhere to what he brought, follow

[123] Al-Ḥārith b. Miskīn b. Muḥammad b. Yūsuf al-Qāḍī, Abū ʿAmr al-Miṣrī al-Mālikī (d. 250/864–65), *mawlā* of Muḥammad b. Ziyād b. ʿAbd al-ʿAzīz b. Marwān. A well-known Mālikī traditionist, al-Ḥārith was summoned to Baghdad and imprisoned during the *miḥna*, or Inquisition. He was subsequently released by the caliph al-Mutawakkil, who appointed him qāḍī of Egypt, a position that he held until his death. See ʿIyāḍ, *Shifā*, vol. 2, note 1, citing *al-Nujūm al-Zāhira*, vol. 2, 331.

[124] *Miʿyār*, vol. 2, 552 (l. 18)–3 (l. 2); cp. ʿIyāḍ, *al-Shifā*, vol. 2, 335–6.

[125] Ibid., vol. 2, 553, ll. 4–15. Cf. chapter two in this book.

[126] Ibid., vol. 2, 553, ll. 16–23.

his path and imitate his example; these are brothers in faith, and every brother must respect with regard to the other the rights (*ḥaqq*) associated with this sanctity." That is to say, every Muslim *qua* Muslim participates and shares in the sanctity (*ḥurma*) of the Prophet and, therefore, is protected, by law, against slander and mistreatment. For this reason, it is necessary for every *sharīf* to regard the community (*umma*) of the Prophet and every believer with respect (*bi-ʿayn al-iḥtirām*), because faith in, and adherence to, the Prophet in and of themselves are sacred obligations. A *sharīf* should not regard any believer with contempt, nor should he magnify himself when dealing with another believer on account of his prophetic descent.

It will be recalled that Abū Yaḥyā al-Sharīf – who was Abū al-Faraj's father, Ibn Zāghū's master, and one of the three men who were the object of the curses uttered by the two Ibn ʿĪsās – had written a treatise on forgiveness, entitled *Taʾlīf ʿalā al-maghfira*, in which he apparently struggled with the tension between the social hierarchy created by the concept of *sharaf*, on the one hand, and the egalitarianism of Islam, on the other. To emphasize the magnitude of the error committed by Abū al-Faraj, the following statement put forward by his father in the aforementioned treatise was now cited by the muftī:

> Despite whatever prophetic descent and majesty the *sharīfs* possess in relation to the rest of the community, who magnify them, honor them, and regard them through the lens of their being among the offspring of the Prophet – may God bless him and grant him peace, all Muslims nevertheless possess a great sanctity which it behooves the *sharīfs* to protect on their behalf and to acknowledge their due, because the Muslims derive honor from their Prophet – may God bless him and grant him peace – in the same way that his offspring derive honor from him. If the offspring are a degree higher than the Muslims with respect to their relationship [to the Prophet], the Muslims are, with respect to our Prophet Muḥammad – may God bless him and grant him peace, "the best nation ever brought forth to men, bidding to honor and forbidding dishonor, and believing in God" (Qurʾān 3:110). They are the army of the Prophet – may God bless him and grant him peace – his helpers, his followers, and the ones who advocate his cause and cling fast to his Sacred Law. They have the excellence (*faḍīla*) of the attachment of their name to his noble name, since it is said with regard to them, "The Community of Muḥammad (*ummat Muḥammad*) – may God bless him and grant him peace." All of this confers upon them honor, respect, merit and veneration, like the status of the sons of kings among the armies of their fathers. And a king is not pleased when one of two parties injures the other; rather, he is pleased when each of the two parties gives his counterpart his due. The rank of the Prophet – may God bless him and grant him peace – is higher than the status of a king, and his merit and his justice (*ʿadl*) are more sublime and greater than that – may God bless him and grant him peace – as is [his] nobility and munificence. He said – may God bless him and grant him peace: "One believer is to another believer like [one part of] a building [is to another] – one part of it strengthens the other."[127] He bade people to love and respect one another and he forbade them to snub and oppose one another.[128]

[127] See Bukhārī, *Ṣaḥīḥ*, vol. 1, 132, no. 88 (ṣalāt), vol. 2, 99, no. 5 (maẓālim), vol. 4, 120, no. 36 (adab); Muslim, *Ṣaḥīḥ*, vol. 4, 1999, no. 65 (birr); Tirmidhī, *Ṣaḥīḥ*, vol. 8, 115 (birr); Ibn Ḥanbal, *Musnad*, vol. 4, 405. [128] *Miʿyār*, vol. 2, 554, ll. 3–19.

In this statement, Abū Yaḥyā indicates that *sharīfs* as a group were sensitive to the need to respect the essential equality of all Muslims, *sharīfs* and non-*sharīfs*, lest the community become divided and social friction develop between the two groups. By invoking the voice of Abū al-Faraj's father to make this point, Ibn Zāghū no doubt succeeded in bringing home to the *sharīf* the magnitude of his error. The impact on Abū al-Faraj, one imagines, must have been profound, for by inciting Ibn ʿĪsā, he had betrayed the legacy of his father, who had waxed eloquent about the need for *sharīfs* to treat all Muslims with respect.

Turning now to Ibn ʿĪsā the father, Ibn Zāghū explained that he should have tolerated the taunts and instigations of Abū al-Faraj, on account of the latter's being a *sharīf*, a scholar, and a descendant of two great scholar and *sharīfs*, Abū Yaḥyā and Abū ʿAbdallāh. Given the discrepancy in their respective statuses, Ibn ʿĪsā should have exhibited deference and modesty by abstaining from competition and renouncing whatever claim he may have had against a man who was descended from the Prophet. When Abū al-Faraj insulted him, Ibn ʿIsā should have left the matter in the hands of God and his Prophet, who might, ultimately, pardon the *sharīf* for his transgression.[129]

Ibn Zāghū concluded that Ibn ʿĪsā should have taken as his model the figure of Mālik b. Anas, alluding to a well-known incident in the career of the jurist who gave his name to the Mālikī school (see chapter four). In the year 147/763, Mālik was severely flogged by the ʿAbbāsid governor of Medina, Jaʿfar b. Sulaymān, on account of his having lent indirect support to a coup staged by an ʿAlid pretender two years earlier, at which time he had opined in a fatwā that homage paid to the ʿAbbāsid caliph al-Manṣūr (r. 136–58/754–75) was not binding because it had been given under compulsion. Despite the flogging, Mālik later forgave Jaʿfar, exhibited shame by choosing not to take vengeance on a man belonging to "the family of the Prophet" (*āl al-nabī*), and pardoned him.[130] There was no need for Ibn Zāghū to make explicit the moral of the story and its relevance to the case at hand. On this note, Ibn Zāghū ends the excursus.[131]

129 Ibid., vol. 2, 554, ll. 19–26. Cf. al-Shubrāwī (d. 1172/1758), *Itḥāf bi-ḥubb al-ashrāf* (Cairo, 1318/1900), 7, ll. 17 ff., who observes that reverence and respect should always be shown to the *sharīfs*, especially to the pious and learned among them; this is a natural result of reverence for the Prophet. One should be humble in their presence; the man who injures them should be an object of hatred. Unjust treatment from them should be patiently borne, their evil returned with good; and they should be assisted when necessary. One should refrain from mentioning their faults; on the other hand, their virtues should be lauded abroad. One should try to come nearer to God and His Prophet through the prayers of the devout among them (cited in *EI*[2], s.v. Sharīf).

130 *Miʿyār*, vol. 2, 554 (l. 26)–5 (l. 2). On this incident, see Ibn ʿAbd al-Barr al-Qurṭubī (d. 463/1070–71), *al-Intiqā' fī faḍā'il al-thalātha al-a'imma al-fuqahā'* (Cairo: Maktabat al-Qudsī, 1350), 43–4; *EI*[2], s.v. Mālik b. Anas, and the sources cited there.

131 *Miʿyār*, vol. 2, 555, ll. 2–7.

Conclusion

Power and Authority in the Maghrib

The dispute that we have examined in this chapter operates on several levels. It will be recalled that it began as an argument over the inheritance of property (about which we unfortunately know nothing). The disputants were the elder Berber jurist, Ibn ʿĪsā, his son, and the younger jurist, Abū al-Faraj *al-sharīf*. Differences over the inheritance deteriorated into an angry shouting match. Regardless of whether or not Ibn ʿĪsā, father and son, believed Abū al-Faraj to be a descendant of the Prophet, we can clearly see that attitudes about juristic identity were operating. For Ibn ʿĪsā, juristic identity derived from knowledge and achievement (*ḥasab*). He no doubt felt that his achievements compensated for any defect in his genealogy (*nasab*); he may also have felt that Abū al-Faraj's achievements were incommensurate with, and failed to sustain, his genealogy. Abū al-Faraj, on the other hand, based his juristic identity and self-esteem on his special combination of *ʿilm*-knowledge, saintly power and prophetic descent – the latter being a trump card that he was not ashamed to flaunt, despite the fact that he, as a *sharīf*, was obligated to behave differently.

These differences were related, in turn, to larger cultural issues of power and authority. One of the distinctive features of Maghribī society going back to the tenth/sixteenth century has been the identification of political power with Sharīfism, or descent from the Prophet Muḥammad.[132] For nearly 500 years, the far Maghrib has been governed by two dynasties of *sharīfs*, the Saʿdīs (917–1069/1511–1659) and the Filālīs (1064/1631–present). The notion that the right to rule should be exercised *exclusively* by descendants of the Prophet developed over the course of many prior centuries. Idrīs I, founder of the Idrīsid dynasty, was a great-grandson of al-Ḥasan b. ʿAlī, and he based his claim to rule on the concept of ʿAlid legitimacy, a notion that remained important under the Fāṭimids but that subsequently was rejected by the Almoravids. Under the Almohads, the importance of ʿAlid legitimacy appears to have been revived, judging from the fact that Ibn Tūmart gave himself – or was given – an ʿAlid genealogy. It was only under the Marīnids, however, that *sharīfs* began to proliferate in the Maghrib and *sharīfī* status became an important element of cultural, political and symbolic capital.

The rise of *sharīfs* to positions of power and authority, based on a genealogy that many regarded as fabricated, was contested by certain Mālikī jurists (many of whom were Berbers) who did not enjoy this special status and who were being displaced and passed over in favor of the newcomers. These critics sought to check the rise of *sharīfs* by invoking the Islamic ideal of the basic equality of all

[132] See Mercedes Garcia-Arenal, "La Conjonction du soufism et du sharifism au Maroc: le mahdi comme sauveur," *Revue d'études du monde méditerranéen*, 55–6 (1990), 233–56; idem, "Mahdî, murâbiṭ, sharīf: l'avènement de la dynastie saʿdienne," *Studia Islamica*, 70 (1990), 77–114.

believers, as famously expressed in Q. 49:13: "Truly the noblest among you in God's eyes is he who is most Godfearing." Many argued that Muslims are ennnobled through their achievements, as manifested in acts of piety, words, and good deeds, and not through birth. As we know, some maintained that a noble reputation (*ḥasab*) is *superior* to a noble birth (*nasab*).[133]

The white-haired Ibn ʿĪsā, old and distinguished, no doubt was an adherent of the latter position. In the year 843/1439, however, he was fighting a losing battle. As mentioned, only two years earlier, influential *sharīf*s had succeeded in breaking the Portuguese siege of Tangier and, in the same year, the tomb of Idrīs II had been "discovered" in Fez. Clearly, Sharīfism was becoming an increasingly important force in the Maghrib and, with the accession of the Saʿdīs less than a century later, the notion that the right to rule is the exclusive right of *sharīf*s would triumph. The exchange between the two Ibn ʿĪsās and Abū al-Faraj was no mere swearing match, but, rather, evidence of a major historical transformation taking place in the Maghrib. That Sharīfism would prevail we now know to be true, but for Ibn Zāghū, who clearly accepted Sharīfism, the key issue was how its claims would be best integrated into Maghribī society. This issue clearly bore heavily on his mind.

The Art of the Judicial Opinion

The *istiftāʾ* of al-ʿUqbānī and the response of Ibn Zāghū have facilitated the present reconstruction of the case. Once again, the evidence from our source is tantalizingly incomplete, leaving us in suspense about the final outcome of the case, about which we can only speculate.

Ibn Zāghū's response sent a clear message to the chief qāḍī of Tlemcen. On the one hand, the elimination of one of the two witnesses to the verbal exchange meant that it could not be established with legal certainty that either of the two Ibn ʿĪsās had in fact uttered the words attributed to them. Thus, there was no evidentiary basis for any *ḥadd* punishment. On the other hand, the qāḍī might nevertheless apply a deterrent punishment (*taʿzīr*) according to his personal discretion (*ijtihād*). The options before him included flogging, imprisonment, or exile. Whatever decision he took no doubt was influenced not only by his own legal assessment of the case but also by his reading of the historical moment and his sense of the impact any punishment would have on the social harmony of Tlemcen. Perhaps the historical record will one day yield evidence of the actual outcome of the dispute.

Our ignorance regarding the outcome of the dispute does not make the fatwā any less important as a cultural artifact that sheds light on the "legal sensibility"

[133] On the rivalry between *sharīf*s and *ʿulamāʾ* in seventeenth-century Morocco, see Berque, *Ulémas, fondateurs, Insurgés*, 233; cf. Louise Marlow, *Hierarchy and Egalitarianism in Islamic Thought* (Cambridge: Cambridge University Press, 1997).

of Muslim jurists living in Tlemcen in the second quarter of the ninth/fifteenth century. The fatwā of Ibn Zāghū was an occasion for thought and argument that took the form of a literary performance. As such, it can be analyzed in terms of its language, rhetoric, and style: what was the linguistic and cultural milieu within which Ibn Zāghū was operating? What was the art by means of which the muftī sought to reconstitute that culture through the use of language? And what kind of community did he seek to establish with his audience through the experience that he offered them?[134]

Living in Tlemcen nearly 800 years after the death of the Prophet, Ibn Zāghū was a member of a society that regarded itself as being faithful to the norms and values of Islam. One of his primary functions, as a muftī, was to articulate, through language, the norms and values that defined what it meant for his society to be Islamic. To this end, he reached into the past, drawing upon his extensive knowledge of the Islamic literary tradition to select verses of the Qur'ān, sayings of the Prophet, and statements of authoritative jurists which, cumulatively, provided the terms for a truly Islamic resolution of the dispute. By collapsing the chronological gap that separated himself and his contemporaries from the period of revelation, the muftī placed himself and his audience within the framework of a history that was perceived as sacred.

At the outset of the response, the "voice" that we hear is that of the muftī as he seeks to establish himself through performance as a "securer of justice." It is noteworthy, however, that as the response unfolds, the voice of Ibn Zāghū gives way to that of the Islamic past. As the reader works through the response, the voices that are heard are those of God, the Prophet Muḥammad, his Companions and Followers, and the outstanding authorities of the Mālikī school of law. Ibn Zāghū's response was a unique literary performance in which he established his own point of view through the voices of earlier Muslim authorities. By seeking authority for his views outside himself, the muftī formulated a response that was faithful to the past, appropriate for the present, and mindful of the future. In this manner, he reaffirmed the fact that the culture in which he lived was faithful to the norms and values of Islam.

Ibn Zāghū's response was not a mélange of authority statements, but a literary composition that was carefully thought out and arranged so as to have the maximum impact on its audience. And who was that audience? Was it the *mustaftī* and the parties to the dispute? Or was it the community of Tlemcen at large? We must keep in mind that the muftī may well have known, prior to drafting his legal opinion, that one of the two witnesses to the argument had been disqualified on grounds of prejudice. If his audience consisted only of the *mustaftī* and the parties in the dispute, it would not have been necessary for him to write a fatwā that exceeded the usual form and fit of that genre. The fact that he withheld the disqualification of the witness until the end of his response suggests his intention

[134] See James Boyd White, *Justice as Translation: An Essay in Cultural and Legal Criticism* (Chicago, University of Chicago Press, 1990).

to send a didactic message, not only to the three litigants, but also to all of the jurists and *sharīfs* of Tlemcen – indeed, to the entire population of the city.

An especially impressive aspect of the document is the manner in which Ibn Zāghū struggled to find a middle ground between two groups that he regarded as "extremist." One of his talents is his ability simultaneously to uphold the core values of both groups while demonstrating that neither provides a truly just solution to the case. Ibn Zāghū was able to hold the opposing views in mind and to weigh them in the scales of Islamic justice, seeking a position that was balanced, objective, and dispassionate. By doing so, he demonstrated what it meant to be a securer of justice.

Ibn Zāghū seems in the end to have been as interested in restoring the balance and harmony of the religio-social order of Tlemcen as he was in the matter of punishment. It is not insignificant, in my view, that the verses of the Qur'ān and sayings of the Prophet cited by the muftī throughout his response refer repeatedly to love, forgiveness, repentance, and humility. The fatwā ends with the remarkable excursus in which the muftī rewrote the script of the argument in an attempt to instruct the three men in the norms of social etiquette that should govern relations between *sharīfs* and non-*sharīfs* – not a subject normally considered by Muslim judges and jurists.

How are we to explain the seemingly non-legal character of Ibn Zāghū's response? The answer to this question, I believe, has to do with the complex historical relationship between Sharīfism, Mālikism, and Sufism in the Maghrib (see Introduction). These three religio-political forces were uniquely combined in the person of al-Sharīf al-Tilimsānī, who brought together the qualities of noble descent (*sharaf*), exoteric knowledge (*ʿilm*), and esoteric knowledge (*maʿrifa*), a powerful combination that he passed on to his son Abū Yaḥyā and grandson, Abū al-Faraj. Of course, not everyone in Tlemcen possessed all three elements of this cultural and symbolic capital. Some possessed more, some less.

Also relevant to the question is the phenomenon of juridical Sufism, which was the common culture of the *ʿulamāʾ* of the Maghrib in the eighth/fourteenth and ninth/fifteenth centuries. Sufi jurists such as al-Sharīf al-Tilimsānī and his disciples all practiced this juridical Sufism, a characteristic feature of which was its focus on the just equilibrium. Al-Sharīf al-Tilimsānī's understanding of the just equilibrium has been described as follows:

> It is the concern for just equilibrium (*iʿtidāl*), and the feeling that the certainty obtained is only a probable certainty, which leads the jurist, a devout Muslim, subject to the omnipotence of the Legislator (God), to an attitude of moderation (*hayʾat al-tawassuṭ*) and of wisdom (*al-ḥikmah*). Thus, the judge becomes the arbiter, or finds his role in arbitration (since *ḳaḍāʾ* is to settle a dispute, to arbitrate), as is shown by Aristotle's definition of equity (*aequitas*): "Equity seems to be justice which goes beyond the written law" (*Rhetoric*, I, 1374a).[135]

[135] *EI*², s.v. al-Sharīf al-Tilimsānī.

This understanding of the just equilibrium and the role of the judge was transmitted by al-Sharīf al-Tilimsānī to his disciples and to their disciples: Qāsim al-ʿUqbānī, Ibn Marzūq VI al-Ḥafīḍ, Abū Yaḥyā al-Sharīf, and Ibn Zāghū. As a practitioner of juridical Sufism, Ibn Zāghū's ultimate objective in the case at hand was not to apply the strict letter of the law and to punish the parties to the dispute, but to transcend the law in his capacity as a "securer of justice" in order to restore the social equilibrium among the three litigants and within the community at large. The muftī threatened the two Ibn ʿĪsās with severe punishment in the next life; and he confronted Abū al-Faraj *al-sharīf* with the enormity of the gap between his own behavior and the ideals espoused by his father, Abū Yaḥyā. The latter, in his *Ta'līf ʿalā al-maghfira*, had written that *sharīf*s must acknowledge the sanctity of *all* Muslims because God commanded Muslims to love and respect one another, not to snub and oppose one another. Through repentance comes forgiveness. If these three men could be moved to repent, then just as God forgave Adam, as reported in the *ḥadīth* cited by the muftī at the beginning of his fatwā, so too might Abū al-Faraj forgive the two Ibn ʿĪsās, and they him. In emphasizing the point that *sharīf*s bear a special responsibility towards non-*sharīf*s, notwithstanding their special status, Ibn Zāghū, himself a Berber, seems to have had in mind the integration of Sharīfism into Maghribī society.

SIX

On Judicial Style: Two Fatwās on *Tawlīj* (*ca.* 880/1475)

It is better for you to leave your heirs rich than to leave them destitute, begging from others. Any expense that you incur, seeking thereby the face of God, will be rewarded – even the morsel of food that you put into your wife's mouth. (prophetic *ḥadīth*)

Fear God – and treat your children equitably. (prophetic *ḥadīth*)

In a series of essays published since 1989, Rosen has argued that Islamic law and Moroccan culture are best understood as two interlocking domains and that Muslim judges and jurists employ a mode of judicial reasoning that closely resembles the modes of reasoning found in other domains of Moroccan life. When a qāḍī decides a case, Rosen argues, he seeks to determine the consequences that his judgment will have on the "networks of ties that people possess" by making commonplace assumptions about human nature and the meaning of specific acts. Rosen mentions a Moroccan judge with whom he spoke in 1978 who claimed to be familiar with everyone in the town where he served and thus to be able to distinguish good people from bad on the basis of this knowledge. "All you have to do," the judge explained to Rosen, "is look at what a person does in order to determine what is in a person's head. If someone is bad it will show up in the way he acts toward other people, and you cannot hide what you do." According to Rosen, this rudimentary "mode of reasoning" distinguishes Islamic law from most western legal systems. Unlike western judges, he concludes, Moroccan judges do *not* use artificial legal language, do *not* focus on antecedent concepts, do *not* transform ordinary words into terms of art, do *not* make comparisons with other cases, and do *not* draw on earlier legal precedents.[1]

Rosen based his conclusions on his observations of Moroccan judges living in Sefrou in the 1960s and 1970s and serving in a modern legal apparatus. But he writes as if "Islamic law" were a timeless and unchanging phenomenon. Rosen pays scant attention to the historical development of Islamic law and blurs the

[1] Lawrence Rosen, *The Anthropology of Justice* (Cambridge: Cambridge University Press, 1989), 50–2; idem, *The Justice of Islam* (Oxford: Oxford University Press, 2000), 118.

distinction between classical Islamic law and its modern counterparts. Most important, he largely disregards the work of the muftī. As we have seen, however, the work of the muftī complemented that of the qāḍī in the Marīnid judicial system. Whereas the qāḍī was an assessor of fact, the muftī was an assessor of legal doctrine. Any conclusions about the nature of Islamic law that focus on the qāḍī to the exclusion of the muftī, or vice versa, will perforce be truncated, incomplete, and distorted.

In the present chapter I shall analyze two fatwās issued during the second half of the ninth/fifteenth century, with special attention to the modes of reasoning employed by the muftīs who issued each fatwā. In both instances, the fatwā was issued with regard to a father who reportedly attempted to disinherit one or more of his children by engaging in the practice of *tawlīj*, a term of art to be defined below. The first fatwā was issued by al-Wansharīsī himself some time after 880/1475 (it will be recalled that al-Wansharīsī continued his activities as a muftī as he was compiling the *Miʿyār* from 890/1485 to 901/1496). The second fatwā was issued by an unnamed Tunisian muftī at an unspecified date but in all likelihood during the lifetime of al-Wansharīsī. After copying the text of the Tunisian muftī into the manuscript that would become the *Miʿyār*, al-Wansharīsī added a substantial judicial comment of his own in which he questioned the line of reasoning advanced by his colleague.

To better appreciate these two cases, it will be helpful to reiterate the essential features of the Islamic inheritance system (see chapter four) and to briefly summarize the law relating to gifts and guardianship.

Inheritance, Gifts, and Guardians

Islamic inheritance law places substantial constraints upon the freedom of a person contemplating death to determine the ultimate devolution of his (or her) property: bequests may not exceed one-third of an estate and may not be made in favor of any person who qualifies as a legal heir, unless the other heirs give their consent. A minimum of two-thirds of any estate is divided according to compulsory inheritance rules that have their basis in Qurʾān 4:11–12 and 176.[2]

During the first centuries of Islamic history, Muslims living throughout the Near East found themselves subject to these rules of partible inheritance which, to the extent that they were applied, resulted in the progressive fragmentation of wealth and capital. It is perhaps not surprising that Muslim proprietors found numerous ways to circumvent the inheritance rules and that they received important assistance in this regard from Muslim jurists, who, distinguishing between *post mortem* and *inter vivos* transactions, taught that the inheritance rules take

[2] For a standard view of Islamic inheritance law, see Noel J. Coulson, *Succession in the Muslim Family* (Cambridge: Cambridge University Press, 1971).

effect only on property owned by the deceased at the moment he (or she) enters the deathbed illness[3] and that proprietors are essentially free to dispose of their property in any way they wish prior to that moment. Thus, a proprietor may shift assets to his desired heir or heirs by means of a gift, acknowledgement of a debt, sale, or creation of a familial endowment, on the condition that these transactions conform to the requisite legal formalities.[4]

With regard to gifts, there is one apparent restriction on the freedom of a proprietor to dispose of his property, a restriction that is based upon a prophetic injunction to "fear God, and treat your children equitably" (*ittaqū llāha waʿdilū fī awlādikum*).[5] Interpreted by Muslim jurists as signifying that a proprietor should neither gift all of his wealth to one of his children to the exclusion of the others nor give preference to one or more of his children over the others, this restriction nevertheless came to be regarded as merely an ethical recommendation, and a proprietor who, for example, gifted all of his wealth to one of his children performed an action that, although *makhrūh*, or reprehensible, was legally permissible and effective.[6] Early Mālikī sources such as the *Wāḍiḥa* of Ibn Ḥabīb (d. 238/852)[7] and the *Mudawwana* of Saḥnūn (d. 240/854) mention cases in which Muslim proprietors shifted property to one or more of their heirs by means of gifts and other *inter vivos* transactions.[8]

Although the gifting or sale to one child of a certain property, for example, a house, might result in its preservation as an integral physical entity in the hands of

[3] On the historical development of the doctrine of deathbed illness, see Hiroyuki Yanagihashi, "Doctrinal Development of *Maraḍ al-Mawt* in the Formative Period of Islamic Law," *Islamic Law and Society*, 5:3 (1998), 326–58.

[4] For additional details on the Islamic inheritance system, see David S. Powers, "The Islamic Inheritance System: A Socio-Historical Approach," in *Islamic Family Law and the State*, ed. Chibli Mallat and Jane Connors (London: Graham & Trotman, 1990), 11–29.

[5] See, for example, al-Bukhārī, *Ṣaḥīḥ*, ed. Muḥammad Tawfīq ʿAwīḍa, 6 vols (Cairo: Lajnat Iḥyāʾ Kutub al-Sunna, 1390/1970), vol. 4, 320; al-Nasāʾī, *al-Sunan al-kubrā*, 7 vols (Beirut: Dār al-Kutub al-ʿIlmiyya, 1411/1991), vol. 4, 119; and Aḥmad b. Ḥanbal, *Musnad al-Imām Aḥmad b. Ḥanbal*, 6 vols (Cairo: 1895; reprinted Beirut: al-Maktab al-Islāmī li'l-Ṭabāʿa wa'l-Nashr, 1969), vol. 4, 275.

[6] On gift (*hiba*), see Ibn Abī Zayd al-Qayrawānī (d. 386/996), *Risāla* (Beirut: al-Maktaba al-Thaqāfiyya, n.d.), 555; Abū al-Walīd Muḥammad b. Aḥmad b. Rushd (d. 595/1198), *Bidāyat al-Mujtahid wa-Nihāyat al-Muqtaṣid*, 2 vols (Cairo: Shirkat al-Maṭbūʿāt al-ʿArabiyya, 1966), vol. 2, 271–7, esp. 272–3 [= Ibn Rushd, *The Distinguished Jurist's Primer*, 2 vols (Reading, UK: Garnet Publishing, 1996), vol. 2, 397–404]; Ibn Juzayy al-Gharnāṭī (d. 741/1340–41), *Qawānīn al-aḥkām al-sharʿiyya wa-masāʾil al-furūʿ al-fiqhiyya* (Beirut: Dār al-ʿIlm li'l-Malāyīn), 397; Khalīl b. Isḥāq (d. 776/1374), *al-Mukhtaṣar fī al-fiqh ʿalā madhhab al-Imām Mālik* (Paris: L'Imprimerie Nationale, 1272/1855),186–8. Cf. David Santillana, *Istituzioni di Diritto Musulmano Malichita*, 2 vols (Roma: Istituto per L'Oriente, 1938), vol. 2, 397–412.

[7] Abū Marwān ʿAbd al-Malik Ibn Ḥabīb, one of the early Mālikī jurists in Andalusia, best known for his *Wāḍiḥa*, an exposition of Mālikī doctrine, part of which has now been published. For biographical details see Beatrix Ossendorf-Conrad, *Das "K. al-Wāḍiḥa" des ʿAbd al-Malik b. Ḥabīb: Edition und Kommentar zu ms. Qarawiyyīn 809/40 (Abwāb al-Ṭahāra)* (Beirut: Franz Steiner, 1994), 7–50; Ibn Farḥūn, *Kitāb al-Dībāj al-mudhahhab fī maʿrifat aʿyān ʿulamāʾ al-madhhab* (Cairo: Dār al-Turāth, 1932), 154–6; Muḥammad b. Muḥammad Makhlūf, *Shajarat al-nūr al-zakiyya fī ṭabaqāt al-mālikiyya* (2nd edn, Beirut: Dār al-Kitāb al-ʿArabī, 1975), 74, no. 109; Henry Toledano, *Judicial Practice and Family Law in Morocco* (Boulder, CO: Social Science Monographs, 1981), 55, note 5.

[8] These cases are cited in al-Wansharīsī, *al-Miʿyār*, vol. 10, 387 (l. 15)–8 (l. 4) (citing the *Wāḍiḥa* of Ibn Ḥabīb, d. 238/852, and the *Mudawwana* of Saḥnūn, d. 240/854).

the donee, such an act deprived the donor or seller of use of, and control over, that property for the remainder of his lifetime and worked against a proprietor's desire to retain physical possession of his property until his very last breath. Muslim proprietors found partial relief from this disadvantage in the laws pertaining to interdiction and guardianship.[9] As the natural legal guardian (*walī*) of his minor children, a father exercised full control over any assets that might belong to those children. Thus, it was possible for a Muslim proprietor to shift assets to his children during the period of their minority by means of a gift, acknowledgement of a debt, or sale of property, while at the same time exercising full control over the property in question during the children's minority. Technically, a father was required to convey control of the assets in question to his children as they reached the age of puberty and attained legal majority;[10] in practice, many fathers retained possession of, and exercised control over, such assets until their death. In this manner a father might use his position as guardian of his minor children to design a *nominal* transfer of ownership to one or more of his children during his lifetime, although the actual conveyance of the property would not take place until after his death. The practical effect of such a transaction would be equivalent to a bequest in favor of an heir, which is prohibited according to Islamic law.

Mālikī jurists invented a term of art to describe transactions of this nature: *tawlīj* (alternatively, *taʾlīj*), pl., *tawlījāt*, derived from the Form I verb *walaja*, which signifies "to enter" or "to penetrate". As a term of art, *tawlīj* signifies an attempt by a proprietor to circumvent the Islamic inheritance rules by transferring wealth to one or more of his children by means of a gift, sale, or acknowledgement of a debt. The seventh/thirteenth century lexicographer Ibn Manẓūr glossed the expression *wallaja mālahu tawlījan* as "he gave (or transferred) his wealth to one of his children during his lifetime."[11] By extension, the term *tawlīj* came to signify generally a "donation déguisée illégale," that is, an illegal, fictive gift.[12] The desired objective could also be achieved by means of an *iqrār,* or acknowledgement.[13] Juristic usage of the term *tawlīj* was clearly pejorative, as in the collocation, "*tawlīj*, deception, and a bequest to an heir" (*tawlīj wa-khudʿa wa-waṣiyya li-wārith*).[14]

While condemning the practice of *tawlīj*, Mālikī jurists established relatively high standards of evidentiary proof. Generally speaking, a qāḍī or muftī would

[9] On interdiction (*ḥajr*), see Ibn Rushd, *Bidāyat al-Mujtahid*, vol. 2, 231–5 [= *The Distinguished Jurist's Primer*, vol. 2, 334–40]; Ibn Juzayy, *Qawānīn*, 348; Ṣāliḥ ʿAbd al-Samīʿ al-Ābī al-Azharī, *Jawāhir al-Iklīl: Sharḥ Mukhtaṣar al-ʿAllāma Khalīl*, 2 vols (Cairo: Maṭbaʿat Muḥammad b. Shaqrūn, 1370/1951), vol. 1, 97–102, esp. 98–9. Cf. Santillana, *Istituzioni*, vol. 1, 304; Joseph Schacht, *An Introduction to Islamic Law* (Oxford: The Clarendon Press, 1964), 124 ff.; David S. Powers, "Parents and their Minor Children: Familial Politics in the Middle Maghrib in the Eighth/Fourteenth Century," *Continuity and Change*, 16:2 (2001), 177–200.

[10] For a model document in which a father conveys previously gifted property to his children, see *Formulario Notarial Hispano-Árabe por el alfaquí y notario cordobés Ibn al-ʿAṭṭār (s. X)*, ed. P. Chalmeta and F. Corriente (Madrid: Instituto Hispano-Árabe de Cultura, 1983), 214–16.

[11] Ibn Manẓūr, *Lisān al-ʿArab*, 15 vols (Beirut: Dār Ṣādir, 1979), vol. 2, 400.

[12] E. Fagnan, *Additions aux dictionnaires arabes* (Alger: Bastide-Jourdan, 1923), 190.

[13] Santillana, *Istituzioni*, vol. 2, 224 ("*la compra-vendita simulata*").

[14] For a discussion of different categories of *tawlīj*, see *Miʿyār*, vol. 8, 76.

invalidate such a transaction only if the plaintiff were able to establish its illegality on the basis of direct evidence, as, for example, if the witnesses to a transaction subsequently acknowledged its nominal and fictitious nature or if circumstantial evidence pointed directly and unequivocally to its fraudulence. In the absence of such evidence, the transaction was presumed to be valid, and the recipient of the property needed only to swear an oath attesting to its legitimacy. By adopting a benign attitude toward *tawlīj*, Mālikī jurists accorded Muslim proprietors considerable freedom to dispose of their property as they saw fit.[15]

Case I: The Fatwā of al-Wansharīsī (*ca.* 880/1475)

The Facts of the Case

At an unspecified date subsequent to the year 880/1475, a jurist by the name of Abū Zayd ʿAbd al-Raḥmān b. Muḥammad al-Ghaṣāwī wrote to al-Wansharīsī asking him to issue a fatwā. About al-Ghaṣāwī I know only that he belonged to the tribe of Banū Burṭāl.

Al-Ghaṣāwī wrote his *istiftāʾ*, or request for a fatwā, at the bottom of a legal document that refers to a sale transacted between two men, ʿUthmān b. al-Ḥasan and Abū al-ʿAbbās Aḥmad b. ʿAlī b. Muḥammad al-Nāṣirī. Of the former, we know only that he probably was a religious figure in the town of Banū Kanīkas, where he was known as "[the] Mahdī al-Kanīksī," and that he was a man of wealth and means; of the latter, we know only that he was a jurist. The document provides no indication of the nature of the relationship between the two men (nor does it indicate the number, gender, and age of any children that ʿUthmān b. al-Ḥasan may have had at the time of the sale). From the document we learn that at an unspecified date prior to 880/1475, ʿUthmān b. al-Ḥasan sold to al-Nāṣirī "all his properties" – fields and date-palm orchards in the towns of Banū Kanīkas, Banū Budārmayn, and Jabal Aʿrūṣ and its environs (I am unable to identify these toponyms). Our source mentions no motive for the sale. Be that as it may, for the sale to be valid, the buyer and seller need only have spoken certain prescribed formulas in the presence of two witnesses; no written documentation was required. Subsequently, in Muḥarram 880/June 1475 – while he was still sound of mind and body, and perhaps anticipating a challenge to the validity of the sale – ʿUthmān had the terms of the sale certified by notary-witnesses, in all likelihood in the presence of a qāḍī. The document which resulted from this procedure is known as an *ishhād* or judicial certification.[16]

[15] Ibid., vol. 10, 388, ll. 19–20.

[16] Ibid., vol. 6, 83; on *ishhād*, see Donald Little, *A Catalogue of Islamic Documents from al-Ḥaram al-Šarīf in Jerusalem* (Beirut: Orient-Institut der Deutschen Morgenländischen Gesellschaft, 1984), 224 ff.; Peter Scholz, *Malikitisches Verfahrensrecht* (Frankfurt: Peter Lang, 1996), 281 ff.

The contents of the judicial certification pointed to the suspicious nature of the sale. The notary who drafted the *ishhād* specified that the witnesses summoned by ʿUthmān (clearly not the same individuals who had witnessed the sale itself) "did not know the amount of the price, because the acknowledger [viz., ʿUthmān] did not specify it at that time." Further, the *ishhād* made no reference to the conveyance (*ḥiyāza*) of the property from the seller to the buyer, generally an essential feature of a valid sale. It is therefore conceivable that ʿUthmān b. al-Ḥasan had designed the transaction to make it appear that he had sold his properties to al-Nāṣirī and that the properties no longer belonged to him, while in fact continuing to use the properties and any revenues that they generated as he had done prior to the "sale." (This, of course, is speculation, for the real facts of the case cannot be known to us and may not have been known to al-Wansharīsī).

Although our source contains no direct information regarding subsequent events, these may be partially reconstructed from the *istiftā*ʾ: ʿUthmān b. al-Ḥasan died some time after 880/1475 but before 901/1496 (the year in which al-Wansharīsī completed the *Miʿyār*), leaving as his heirs an unspecified number of sons and daughters. If ʿUthmān did not convey the properties to al-Nāṣirī and did continue to use them until his death, then his children, who may have been minors at the time of the "sale," may have viewed the properties in question as part of their father's patrimony, to be inherited by them – as his heirs – upon his death. Be that as it may, the properties in question apparently were not treated as part of ʿUthmān's estate (which would have comprised only those assets acquired subsequent to the date of the disputed sale). For this reason, at his death, his children protested, alleging that the sale had been undertaken with the intention of disinheriting them in favor of al-Nāṣirī, who was not related to their father by ties of blood. In an attempt to recover what they considered to be rightfully theirs, they approached the aforementioned jurist, al-Ghaṣāwī, presumably the qāḍī of the locale in which they lived. In accordance with the rules of judicial procedure, al-Ghaṣāwī would have summoned al-Nāṣirī, and when both parties to the dispute were present, they would have told their stories to the qāḍī in the language of everyday discourse, of which no record survives, and in terms of the relations that existed between and among them, about which we can speculate: ʿUthmān b. al-Ḥasan's honorific title (al-Mahdī al-Kanīksī) and al-Nāṣirī's status as a jurist suggest that the two men were situated in a network of religio-legal authority (a network that included al-Ghaṣāwī and al-Wansharīsī). As for the relations between ʿUthmān and his children, our source does not indicate whether, at the time of the sale, the children were minors dependent upon their father or adults who were economically secure and self-sufficient, whether ʿUthmān had made any provisions for his children in the form of *pre mortem* transactions, or whether he was known to have displayed any bias in favor of, or against, his children.

After listening to the respective claims and counterclaims, reviewing the documentary evidence, and, no doubt, asking some questions of his own, al-Ghaṣāwī determined that the case raised a difficult point of law, and he decided to consult with a legal expert before issuing his judgment. He therefore sent the above-mentioned *ishhād* to al-Wansharīsī. Written at the bottom of the judicial certification was his undated request for a legal opinion.

The *istiftā'* was carefully formulated, short, and to the point. Conscious of the conventions relating to a request for an advisory legal opinion, al-Ghaṣāwī began and ended his letter with conventional pious invocations, thereby situating the activity of consultation in a proper Islamic framework. Noteworthy is the manner in which he signaled his subordination to al-Wansharīsī, whom he addressed as "My Lord" and to whom he referred in the second-person plural. Also noteworthy is the manner in which the *mustaftī* transformed the names of the litigants and whatever stories they may have told him into the abstract and impersonal language of legal discourse, as required by the conventions of *futyā*: ʿUthmān b. al-Ḥasan, [the] Mahdī al-Kanīksī became "the seller;" the scholar, al-Nāṣirī, became "the buyer;" and ʿUthmān's children became his "heirs" and "the children of his loins." *Pace* Rosen, the translation of the names of the litigants into abstract legal categories had the effect of masking status, gender, and age differences, thereby facilitating al-Ghaṣāwī's adoption of an impartial attitude toward the litigants, as reflected in his alternately taking into account both sides of the dispute.[17]

Al-Ghaṣāwī asked two questions. The first related to the *ishhād* of 880/1475: is the judicial certification a legally effective document upon which a judgment may be based – its alleged defect notwithstanding? Al-Ghaṣāwī subdivided this question into two parts: (a) does the witnesses' ignorance of the sale-price and their failure to observe its receipt invalidate their testimony – and, by implication, the sale? (b) is the seller's acknowledgement regarding the sale-price sufficient to render the sale legally valid? The second question was formulated carefully and with precision. Properly speaking, the sale transaction did not fall into the category of *tawlīj* because it did not involve a parent's shifting of assets from one child to another. But the plaintiffs sought to have the judicial authorities extend the meaning of the term *tawlīj* to include this type of transaction, for it was all the same to them whether their father had disinherited one of them in favor of another or all of them in favor of a total stranger. In this regard, al-Ghaṣāwī asked whether one should accept the children's claim that their father had "sold" the property to al-Nāṣirī in an attempt to disinherit them (*ʿalā wajh al-ta'līj li'l-mubtāʿ*).[18] If so – and in the event that the buyer was unable to establish the sale-price on the basis of eyewitness testimony – should one pass judgment in favor of the children? If not, was the seller's acknowledgement regarding the sale-price sufficient to maintain the sale as valid?

The Fatwā of al-Wansharīsī

Al-Wansharīsī's response, which opens with the customary pious invocations, was addressed specifically to al-Ghaṣāwī and written in a technical idiom that would

[17] *Miʿyār*, vol. 6, 83–4.
[18] On *tawlīj*, see further ibid., vol. 6, 79, 243–5; vol. 8, 76; vol. 9, 488; and vol. 10, 351–2.

have been fully intelligible only to a jurist familiar with legal discourse, the sources of legal authority, and the art of legal reasoning. Significantly, al-Wansharīsī allowed al-Ghaṣāwī to establish the terms of the argument, organizing his response in the order of the questions posed by the *mustaftī*. Confident of his reader's ability to follow the thread of his reasoning, al-Wansharīsī shifted abruptly from one topic to the next without signaling the direction of his argument (that is, without using verbal cues, such as, "in response to your first question," common in other fatwās).[19]

Al-Wansharīsī began the substantive section of his response to al-Ghaṣāwī's query by invoking earlier legal precedents. Without making any reference to either the Qur'ān or the *ḥadīth*, the muftī found textual authority for his response to al-Ghaṣāwī's initial subquestion (that is, is the validity of a sale conditional upon the witnesses' having observed the receipt of the sale-price?) by citing a statement attributed to two jurists who lived in the middle of the eleventh and twelfth centuries CE, respectively: Ibn 'Abd al-Barr (d. 463/1070), the author of *al-Kāfī*, a systematic treatise on Islamic law, and al-Matīṭī (d. 570/1174), the author of a treatise on legal documents. These two authorities held that eyewitnessing is required only in the abnormal circumstance of a buyer's being reputed to engage in "coercion, compulsion, and violation [of the law]." This observation implicitly touches on a potentially relevant issue, namely, the character of al-Nāṣirī, who had been accused of colluding with 'Uthmān b. al-Ḥasan to deprive the latter's children of their lawful inheritance, behavior which, if substantiated, no doubt would qualify as a "violation of the law." Curiously, al-Wansharīsī completely disregarded this issue, passing immediately to the observation (in this case, irrelevant) that some notaries require eyewitnessing of a sale in which one of the parties to the transaction is acting on behalf of a third party – as, for example, a father acting on behalf of his child, an executor, a proxy, or a custodian (clearly, not the case in the sale in question).

Turning next to al-Ghaṣāwī's second question, al-Wansharīsī explained that in order to determine whether the sale should be classified as *tawlīj*, it was necessary to establish whether or not the seller immediately conveyed the fields and the date-palm orchards to the buyer. As noted above, this detail is not specified in the *ishhād*, for which reason al-Wansharīsī considered two alternative scenarios: if the seller did convey the property immediately, then there is no force to the claim of *tawlīj*. But if he did not, that is, if the seller continued to use the property in any way whatsoever, then there may be force to the claim. Al-Wansharīsī found textual authority for this formulation in three antecedent cases mentioned in the *Ṭurar* of Ibn 'Āt al-Shāṭibī (d. 609/1212), itself a commentary on *al-Wathā'iq al-majmū'a* of Ibn Fattūḥ (d. 462/1069). All three cases deal with a father who purchased property from himself in the name of his minor child. In the first case, the witnesses did not observe the sale-price, and the father retained possession of the property until his death; in the second and third cases, it is further specified that the minor on behalf of whom the purchase was made did not have any assets at the

[19] Ibid., vol. 6, 84.

time of the transaction. In all three instances, when the father died, one of his heirs challenged the transaction on the ground that it constituted *tawlīj*. The legal authorities, however, upheld the validity of each transaction. (In the third case, a minority opinion is attributed to Aṣbagh [d. 225/839], who classified the sale as *tawlīj*. Ibn ʿĀt, however, stated that "his opinion is of absolutely no consequence." It may be significant that al-Wansharīsī did not pursue Aṣbagh's line of reasoning, which represents an alternative view.)[20]

Commenting on the statement attributed to Ibn ʿĀt, al-Wansharīsī reasoned that if an argument can be made for the validity of the sales mentioned in these three cases, an even stronger argument can be made for the validity of the sale in the case at hand (an example of an argument *ad minorum ad majorum*). At this point al-Wansharīsī made a subtle but important shift from the formal language of legal discourse to the simpler expression of everyday speech, observing that in the three cases mentioned by Ibn ʿĀt, a father attempted to transfer assets from one child to another, whereas in the present case the buyer and seller were "strangers" who were not related to one another by blood. Al-Wansharīsī now made a key legal presumption, asserting that the absence of a blood-relationship between the buyer and the seller creates a presumption of validity, for, under normal circumstances, there is no reason to suspect that a father would disinherit his children in favor of a stranger. That is, al-Wansharīsī assumed that because he knew who the seller was in relation to both the buyer and to the plaintiffs, he could know with certainty how the seller would behave and what the seller would or would not do. On these grounds, anyone who would argue that the sale in question should be classified as *tawlīj* goes against the normal legal presumption and bears the burden of proof. Such a claim must be substantiated by the explicit testimony of upright witnesses who attest that the buyer and seller colluded with one another and that the sale was intended as a legal fiction. (This may be an example of what Rosen means by the inter-connection of law and culture.)

In the present case, al-Wansharīsī continued, the claim of *tawlīj* was not supported by such evidence. The muftī appears to have arrived at the determination that the claim of *tawlīj* should be rejected because it was not supported by testimonial evidence. Seeking to make his answer as comprehensive as possible, however, he immediately presented a countervailing consideration: an unsubstantiated claim of *tawlīj* may be accepted if circumstantial evidence signals cause for suspicion. Unfortunately, al-Wansharīsī did not specify what this circumstantial evidence might be, although we assume that he had in mind either evidence of antipathy between ʿUthmān b. al-Ḥasan and his children and/or the fact that he was favorably inclined towards al-Nāṣirī. In the event that circumstantial evidence did point toward *tawlīj*, the case would be resolved by having the buyer swear a decisory oath confirming the legitimacy of the sale; only if the buyer refused to

[20] Ibid., vol. 6, 84–5. Al-Wansharīsī's understanding of Aṣbagh's disagreement with the prevailing Mālikī position on this point subsequently was challenged by a jurist from Tlemcen, Abū ʿAbdallāh Muḥammad al-Ḥawdī (d. 910/1504–05).

swear would the presumption shift in favor of the plaintiffs. This procedural strategy would appear to favor al-Nāṣirī, who, by swearing the oath, could render the sale legally valid even if circumstantial evidence suggested that it was fictitious (on the decisory oath, see chapter four).[21]

An additional level of al-Wansharīsī's reasoning incorporates a fatwā issued by the Andalusian jurist Ibn al-Makwī (d. 401/1010) that introduces a distinction between deathbed and *inter vivos* transactions: Ibn al-Makwī was asked about a father who, during his deathbed illness, summoned witnesses to hear him attest that he had sold all his properties to his daughter's husband, that he had received a specific sale-price from the buyer, and that he had no heirs other than his daughter and his wife. When the sale was contested (presumably by his wife), Ibn al-Makwī reasoned that because the statement was uttered by the father on his deathbed, his acknowledgement (*iqrār*) of receipt of the sale-price is legally effective only if the exchange had been observed by the witnesses. The relevance of this case to the case at hand (in which the acknowledgement was not made on the seller's deathbed) was immediately clarified by al-Wansharīsī. Ibn al-Makwī required eyewitnessing of the sale-price only because the sale was acknowledged on the seller's deathbed. Otherwise, al-Wansharīsī observed, the father's acknowledgement of his receipt of the sale-price would have been legally effective *without* eyewitnessing of the exchange (as in the first of the three cases cited above). As further support for this conclusion, al-Wansharīsī referred to another Andalusian fatwā, issued about a century after that of Ibn al-Makwī. During his final deathbed illness, a husband sold his slave-girl to his wife. Although the sale was certified, witnesses did not observe receipt of the sale-price. Subsequently, the sale was contested, and the case was brought before the qāḍī of Cordoba, Ibn Ḥamdīn, who, before issuing his decision, consulted with the muftīs, Ibn al-Ḥājj and Ibn ʿAttāb (both men died in 520/1126). The muftīs advised the qāḍī that the sale was null and void and that the slave-girl should revert to her master's estate. This case also suggests that if the transaction had not been conducted on the man's deathbed, the sale would have been valid, even though the witnesses did not observe the receipt of the sale-price.[22]

Having nearly finished his analysis, al-Wansharīsī tested it by constructing a hypothetical objection to his line of reasoning. He asked his reader to imagine that the following facts had been established in the present case: the seller retained possession of the sale-object until his death and admitted, in his acknowledgement of 880/1475, both that it was his intention *not* to give the properties to the buyer and that his summoning of witnesses was a legal fiction designed to circumvent the legal requirement relating to the conveyance of property. Under these circumstances, one might argue, the sale should be declared null and void. Indeed, this argument finds support in two antecedent cases. The first case occurred in sixth/twelfth-century Andalusia: while in a state of health, a man sold half of his house to either his wife or his *umm walad*. He summoned witnesses to hear him attest

[21] Ibid., vol. 6, 85–6. [22] Ibid., vol. 6, 86.

that the sale-price was 150 *ʿibādī mithqāl*s and that the sale-price had been received. The seller, however, continued to reside in the house until he died. The sale was invalidated by Ibn ʿAttāb, Aṣbagh b. Muḥammad, Ibn al-Ḥājj, and Ibn Rushd,[23] presumably on the ground that the man's failure to convey the house to the buyer served as an indication of *tawlīj*. The second case, related by Ḥusayn b. ʿĀṣim[24] on the authority of Ibn al-Qāsim (d. 191/806),[25] is the source-text upon which the four Andalusian jurists based their decision: while in a state of health, a man summoned witnesses to hear him attest that he had sold a residence belonging to him to his wife, to his son, or to his heir, for a large sum of money. But the witnesses did not see the sale-price, and the residence remained in the seller's possession until his death. The sale was contested, and Ibn al-Qāsim declared it invalid on the ground that it constituted *tawlīj*, a deception, and a bequest to an heir.[26]

Al-Wansharīsī's hypothetical objection was constructed so that it would collapse upon inspection. Drawing on his expert knowledge of Mālikī fatwās, al-Wansharīsī turned the tables on his imagined "opponent" by saying that the latter had failed to convey all of the facts relating to the first supporting case: the plaintiff was the seller's brother, and witnesses attested, after the fact, that the two men were known to have hated one another and that during his lifetime the seller used to say that he would not allow his brother to inherit any property from him.[27] The latter statement, viewed in conjunction with the fact that the "buyer" was the "seller's" wife or *umm walad*, strengthened the presumption that the "seller" was attempting to disinherit his brother. In other words, this case (as well as the source-text related on the authority of Ibn al-Qāsim), constituted a textbook example of *tawlīj*, which explains why the jurists nullified the sale. Indeed, al-Wansharīsī added, the practice of *tawlīj* was widespread in sixth/twelfth-century Andalusia, where Mālikī jurists sought to eradicate it, out of deference to the Medinese jurists whom they regarded as their authorities. In the present case, on the other hand, the facts were different. Because the seller and the buyer were strangers who were not related to one another and the heirs were the seller's children, the sale in question, properly speaking, could not be classified as *tawlīj* or even, as the plaintiffs had argued, as quasi-*tawlīj*. It might still be invalidated – but only if the plaintiffs demonstrated that the seller misappropriated the sale-object by retaining possession of it and freely disposing of it until his death (and if, as al-Wansharīsī failed to mention, the defendant refused to swear an oath attesting to the legitimacy of the transaction).[28]

[23] Abū al-Walīd Muḥammad b. Aḥmad Ibn Rushd of Cordoba, one of the Mālikī jurists held in great esteem, d. 520/1126. His most important works include: *al-Muqaddimāt al-mumahhidāt li-bayān mā iqtaḍathu rusūm al-Mudawwana min al-aḥkām*, a commentary on the *Mudawwana*; and *Kitāb al-bayān wa'l-taḥṣīl wa'l-sharḥ wa'l-tawjīh wa'l-taʿlīl*, a commentary on the *ʿUtbiyya*. See Makhlūf, *Shajara*, vol. I, 129, no. 376; Toledano, *Judicial Practice*, 52, note 3.

[24] Ḥusayn b. ʿĀṣim was a famous Andalusian jurist whose *samāʿ* is preserved in the *ʿUtbiyya*.

[25] Abū ʿAbdallāh ʿAbd al-Raḥmān b. al-Qāsim al-ʿUtāqī, better known as Ibn al-Qāsim, Mālik's most prominent student. See Ibn Farḥūn, *Dībāj*, 146; Makhlūf, *Shajara*, vol. I, 58, no. 64; Toledano, *Judicial Practice*, 52, note 6.

[26] *Miʿyār*, vol. 6, 86–7.

[27] These details can be found in ibid., vol. 6, 79, where the fatwā is cited in full.

[28] Ibid., vol. 6, 87–8.

Al-Wansharīsī signaled the end of his response – and of our documentation – by appending his distinctive and characteristic signature, which emphasizes his subordinate and supplicatory status with respect to the Divinity: "the one who submits to You (pl.) frequently, the servant who asks for forgiveness, the one who is in need of God – praised be He". Presumably, al-Wansharīsī sent the fatwā to al-Ghaṣāwī, who, after studying it and seeking to determine which of the legal issues raised by the muftī were relevant to the case, issued his judgment (*ḥukm*).[29]

Case II: The Fatwā of a Tunisian Muftī (*ca.* 839–901/1435–96)

The Facts of the Case

The second fatwā to be examined here was issued with regard to a property dispute that took place in Tunis at an unspecified date during the second half of the ninth/fifteenth century.[30] About the jurist who issued the fatwā we know only that he was "one of the muftīs of Tunis." Although the fatwā itself is not dated, a reference to "'Uthmānī" dīnārs indicates that it must have been issued some time after the beginning of the reign of the Ḥafṣid Sulṭān Abū 'Amr 'Uthmān (r. 1435–88) and before al-Wansharīsī completed the *Mi'yār* on 28 Shawwāl 901/10 July 1496.[31] Whether the Tunisian muftī's fatwā was issued before or after that of al-Wansharīsī is a fact which I cannot at present establish.

The facts of the second case bear a striking resemblance to those of the first. At an unspecified date approximately eighteen years prior to his death, a man by the name of Abū 'Abdallāh Muḥammad had five children. Three of these children, Aḥmad, 'Abdallāh, and Fāṭima, were minors; the other two, whose names, ages, and gender are not specified in our source, apparently were older than their three minor siblings. We do not know if the children shared the same mother. Curiously, our source suggests that the three minor children possessed at least 1635 gold 'Uthmānī dīnārs, without indicating how they acquired these assets, for example, through an inheritance, as a result of a gift, or in some other manner.

In his capacity as the *walī*, or natural legal guardian, of his three minor children, Abū 'Abdallāh Muḥammad had the power to use any assets belonging to them to buy and sell on their behalf. And, if he is to be believed, he did just that, using these assets to execute two transactions of an unspecified nature, one with a certain Aḥmad b. 'Abd al-Ḥalīm and the other with a certain Abū al-Faḍl Abū al-Qāsim, identified as a *sharīf* or descendant of the Prophet. As a *sharīf*, Abū al-Faḍl's

[29] Ibid., vol. 6, 88.

[30] Ibid., vol. 10, 383–9. For a brief summary of this fatwā, see Lagardère, *Histoire et Société*, 443, no. 88.

[31] On Marinid coinage, see Muḥammad al-Manūnī, *Waraqāt li-ḥaḍārat al-Marīniyyīn* (Rabat: Kulliyat al-Ādāb, 1996), 127 ff.; Lagardère, *Histoire et Société*, 443.

character and integrity were effectively unassailable (see Introduction and chapter five). As a result of these two transactions, Aḥmad b. ʿAbd al-Ḥalīm became indebted to Aḥmad, ʿAbdallāh, and Fāṭima for 360 gold ʿUthmānī dīnārs, and Abū al-Faḍl Abū al-Qāsim became indebted to them for 1275 gold dīnārs of the same type (see figure 6.1).

Against the background of these debt obligations, we must try to understand two later sale transactions involving Abū ʿAbdallāh Muḥammad. In the first transaction, Aḥmad b. ʿAbd al-Ḥalīm sold a house belonging to him to his wife, Amat al-Raḥmān, for 500 gold ʿUthmānī dīnārs. It will be recalled that the seller owed Abū ʿAbdallāh Muḥammad's three minor children, Aḥmad, ʿAbdallāh, and Fāṭima, 360 gold dīnārs. The sale document specified that the seller took advantage of the sale to extinguish his obligation to his three minor creditors by transferring the aforementioned debt to his wife by means of a *ḥawāla*, or transfer of debt.[32] Thus, the sale unfolded in two stages: first, Amat al-Raḥmān paid her husband Aḥmad 140 gold ʿUthmānī dīnārs; second, Aḥmad b. ʿAbd al-Ḥalīm assigned to his wife the debt (*aḥāla bihi ʿalayhā*) of 360 dīnārs – the amount that he owed his three minor creditors – and authorized her to pay this amount to the children's father and legal guardian. Only when this sum had been paid would the sale become complete. To protect his interests as seller, Aḥmad b. ʿAbd al-Ḥalīm empowered Muḥammad to effect conveyance of the house to Amat al-Raḥmān only upon receipt of the unpaid portion of the sale-price, that is, the amount of his debt. The sale transaction was attested by two professional witnesses.[33]

From a second document relating to the sale, we learn that Abū ʿAbdallāh Muḥammad did in fact receive (*qabaḍa*) from Amat al-Raḥmān the unpaid portion of the sale-price, that is, 360 gold ʿUthmānī dīnārs – an amount equivalent to the debt owed to his children – whereupon he gave her a quittance (*barā'a*) with regard to the debt, and, after taking possession of the money on behalf of his three minor children, conveyed the house to her.[34]

In addition, our source mentions, without providing details, three documents drawn up on behalf of the three minor children with regard to the division of the aforementioned 360 dīnārs. In all likelihood the division was carried out either on a per capita basis, in which case each minor child would have received 120 dīnārs, or on the basis of the Qurʾānic principle that a male is entitled to the share of two females, in which case Aḥmad and ʿAbdallāh would have received 144 dīnārs each and Fāṭima would have received 72 dīnārs. The three documents reportedly were attested by professional witnesses.[35]

At an unspecified date, but while the children were still minors, Abū ʿAbdallāh Muḥammad was involved in a second sale transaction in which he purchased a

[32] On *ḥawāla*, see Ibn Rushd, *Bidāya*, vol. 2, 247–9 [= *The Distinguished Jurist's Primer*, vol. 2, 360–2]; Ibn Juzayy, *Qawānīn*, 355; Khalīl b. Isḥāq, *al-Mukhtaṣar*, 152–3; Santillana, *Istituzioni*, vol. 2, 3, 106, 200–7, 351; Schacht, *Introduction*, 148–9.

[33] *Miʿyār*, vol. 10, 383, ll. 12–26.

[34] Ibid., vol. 10, 383 (l. 26)–4 (l. 4).

[35] Ibid., vol. 10, 384, ll. 4–6.

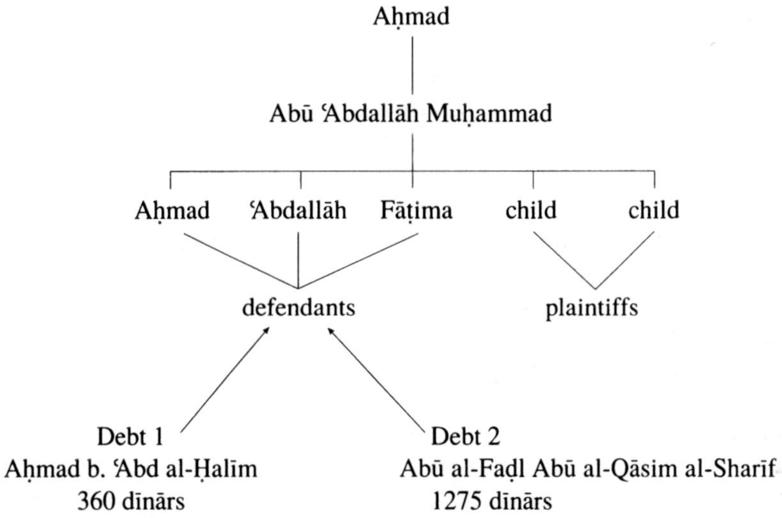

Figure 6.1 Financial transactions involving the children of Abū ʿAbdallāh Muḥammad

bathhouse on his own behalf for 1300 large gold ʿUthmānī dīnārs from Abū al-Faḍl Abū al-Qāsim al-Sharīf, who, as noted, owed the buyer's three children 1275 gold dīnārs as a result of an unspecified earlier transaction that their father had undertaken on their behalf. Because of this debt obligation, the seller reduced (*iqtaʿada*) the sale-price by 1275 gold dīnārs, so that it was necessary for Abū ʿAbdallāh Muḥammad to pay the *sharīf* only 25 gold dīnārs in order to complete the sale. Upon payment of this sum, Abū ʿAbdallāh Muḥammad took possession of the bathhouse and gave a quittance (*barāʾa*) to Abū al-Faḍl Abū al-Qāsim with regard to the latter's debt to the three minors, Aḥmad, ʿAbdallāh, and Fāṭima. As a result of this transaction Abū al-Faḍl Abū al-Qāsim's debt of 1275 gold ʿUthmānī dīnārs to the three minor children was assumed by Abū ʿAbdallāh Muḥammad, who took upon himself responsibility for paying it. This transaction, like the others, was concluded in the presence of two professional witnesses.[36]

With the completion of these two sale transactions, Abū ʿAbdallāh Muḥammad had acquired ownership of the bathhouse but at the same time assumed the debt obligations to his three minor children of 1275 and 360 gold ʿUthmānī dīnārs, for a total of 1635 gold ʿUthmānī dīnārs. In theory, the father should have conveyed the assets to each child as he or she became a major; in fact, however, he retained control of the assets until his death some eighteen years subsequent to the two sale transactions, at which time a dispute arose among his heirs over the division of his estate.

[36] Ibid., vol. 10, 384, ll. 7–19.

At the time of his death, Abū ʿAbdallāh Muḥammad's heirs included not only Aḥmad, ʿAbdallāh, and Fāṭima, now majors, but also an unspecified number of older siblings, also majors. The dispute focused on the status of the two aforementioned debts, totaling 1635 gold ʿUthmānī dīnārs. If this sum were in fact an outstanding debt obligation, then it should be deducted from the deceased's estate and paid to his creditors, Aḥmad, ʿAbdallāh, and Fāṭima; whatever remained after the payment of this debt would then be divided among all of the deceased's legal heirs. However, if this sum were treated as part of Abū ʿAbdallāh Muḥammad's estate, then the estate would be that much larger and the share of each heir would increase proportionally. Much was at stake.

Immediately following their father's death, Aḥmad, ʿAbdallāh, and Fāṭima contended that the assets in question should be excluded from the estate and conveyed to them *prior* to the division of the inheritance among the larger group of qualifying heirs. In support of this contention the three children brought forward: (1) the sale document in which Aḥmad b. ʿAbd al-Ḥalīm acknowledged owing them 360 gold ʿUthmānī dīnārs and (2) the sale document in which Abū al-Faḍl Abū al-Qāsim acknowledged owing them 1275 gold ʿUthmānī dīnārs; these two documents also referred to their father's having taken possession of these sums on their behalf. As noted, both documents had been attested by professional witnesses. These two acknowledgements, the children asserted, together with the fact that their father had taken possession (*qabaḍa*) of the assets on their behalf, created an indefeasible legal obligation that was unaffected by their father's failure to convey the 1635 gold ʿUthmānī dīnārs to them or by the quittances that he had given to both Aḥmad b. ʿAbd al-Ḥalīm and Abū al-Faḍl Abū al-Qāsim, absolving them of any liability for the sum in question.[37]

Abū ʿAbdallāh Muḥammad's other children contested the claim of their three younger siblings. Unable to resolve the dispute amicably among themselves, the two groups turned to a local qāḍī, who listened to their respective claims and counterclaims and examined the submitted documents, after an expert had verified their authenticity on the basis of the witnesses' handwriting.[38] The qāḍī determined that the argument advanced by Aḥmad, ʿAbdallāh, and Fāṭima represented the normal or ordinary position of matters between the two parties (the *aṣl*); and that the claim of the older siblings lacked any ordinary or special presumption in favor of its truth. For this reason, he designated the three younger siblings as the "defendants" (*muddaʿā ʿalayhim*) and the older siblings as the "plaintiffs" (*muddaʿīs*).[39] The burden of proof therefore lay upon the older siblings, whom the

[37] Ibid., vol. 10, 384 (l. 20)–5 (l. 6).

[38] Ibid., vol. 10, 385, ll. 5–7.

[39] On Islamic judicial procedure, see Ibn Abī Zayd, *Risāla*, 604–26; *First Steps in Muslim Jurisprudence*, consisting of excerpts from *Bākūrat al-Saʿd* of Ibn Abū Zayd, tr. Alexander David Russell and Abdullah al-Ma'mūn Suhrawardy (London: Luzac & Co., 1906), 57, 98–103; Ibn Rushd, *Bidāya*, vol. 2, 381–94 [= *The Distinguished Jurist's Primer*, vol. 2, 553–72]; Ibn Juzayy, *Qawānīn*, 327 ff.; Khalīl b. Isḥāq, *al-Mukhtaṣar*, 189–93; Santillana, *Istituzioni*, vol. 2, 580–9; Schacht, *Introduction*, 188 ff.; Scholz, *Malikitisches Verfahrensrecht*, 122 ff.

qāḍī charged to produce evidence that might nullify or offset the testimony of the professional witnesses made on behalf of the defendants.[40]

While conceding that they had no such evidence (*asqaṭū al-ṭaʿn wa'l-maqāl*), the plaintiffs advanced five arguments, no doubt formulated with the assistance of a legal agent.

1 They asserted that neither the seller of the house nor the seller of the bathhouse could possibly have incurred any debt to the three minor children prior to the two sale transactions and that the three children therefore had no claim whatsoever to the 1635 gold ʿUthmānī dīnārs. Rather, these assets were part of their father's estate, to be divided among *all* of his heirs according to the compulsory Islamic inheritance rules.

2 Their father, Abū ʿAbdallāh Muḥammad, had *colluded* with the seller of both the house and the bathhouse, with each seller agreeing to acknowledge a fictitious, non-existent debt owed to the three minor children, and Abū ʿAbdallāh Muḥammad attesting to his having taken possession of the "debt" payment on behalf of his minor children. Presumably, Abū ʿAbdallāh Muḥammad compensated the two "sellers" for their willingness to participate in the scheme, although we are ignorant of the details.[41]

3 In support of the allegation of collusion, the plaintiffs submitted a *rasm istirʿā'* (see chapter one), a document drawn up some time prior to their father's death and in anticipation of that event, containing the testimony of witnesses whom the plaintiffs had summoned to attest to the fact that: (a) Abū ʿAbdallāh Muḥammad was enamored of his three minor children, Aḥmad, ʿAbdallāh, and Fāṭima; (b) that he funneled both visible and hidden assets to them; and that (c), as a result of "the bias and favoritism that were his natural disposition," he was unable to deny them anything that they wanted or requested.[42] This document, in which the plaintiffs asserted that their father loved his three minor children more than he loved them, served as the evidentiary basis for their claim that Abū ʿAbdallāh Muḥammad had designed the sale transactions with the goal of illegally transferring assets to the minors during his lifetime (*tawlījan ilayhim*).[43]

4 The plaintiffs explained that at the time of the two sale transactions, the defendants were minors who did not possess the legal capacity to acquire wealth on their own and, further, were not known to have acquired any wealth through an inheritance or a gift. If they had no assets, how was it possible for Aḥmad b. ʿAbd al-Ḥalīm and Abū al-Faḍl Abū al-Qāsim to owe them money? In this connection, the plaintiffs challenged the defendants to answer the following three questions: (a) how had they acquired the assets allegedly owed them by the two sellers; (b) how, exactly, had these assets come into their possession; and (c) who had served as their legal agent in the transactions that resulted in the alleged debt obligations?[44]

[40] *Miʿyār*, vol. 10, 385, ll. 6–8.
[41] Ibid., vol. 10, 385, ll. 14–15.
[42] Ibid., vol. 10, 385, ll. 22–5.
[43] Ibid., vol. 10, 385, ll. 14–15.
[44] Ibid., vol. 10, 385, ll. 16–20.

5 Finally, the plaintiffs argued that the defendants' silence during the eighteen years between the conclusion of the two sale transactions and the death of their father rendered their claim null and void.[45]

After the qāḍī had examined the evidence and heard the arguments advanced by the plaintiffs, it was his task to determine which claim was supported by preponderating evidence. Should he base his impending judgment on the two acknowledgements (*iqrārs*) which established the debt obligations and the father's receipt (*qabḍ*) of the assets, or should he base his judgment on the plaintiffs' allegation of bias and favoritism on their father's part and on the claim of *tawlīj*, as supported by the *rasm istirʿāʾ*? In weighing the evidence, the qāḍī appears to have been influenced by the fact that the sellers who made the acknowledgements were "strangers," that is, persons who had no blood relation to the defendants and no apparent personal interest in the outcome (it will be remembered that al-Wansharīsī made a similar argument in the first case). Now, whereas the law treats with suspicion the acknowledgement of a debt made by a close relative, "no suspicion attaches to the acknowledgement of a stranger,"[46] which, according to the consensus of scholars, creates its desired legal outcome. At the same time, only indirect evidence, in the form of the *rasm istirʿāʾ*, supported the plaintiffs' allegation that the assets in question belonged to their father's estate and that their father improperly had sought to transfer these assets to his minor children during his lifetime. Was the *rasm istirʿāʾ* of sufficient probative value to impugn the positive acknowledgement of strangers on behalf of the minor children?[47]

These were the facts of the case, and the legal issues that they raised, as articulated by the qāḍī who solicited the fatwā from the unnamed Tunisian jurist.[48]

The Fatwā of the Tunisian Muftī

The unidentified Tunisian muftī began his discussion by addressing the plaintiffs' first argument, namely, that the assets in question belonged to their father, Abū ʿAbdallāh Muḥammad, and should be treated as part of his estate, to be divided up among all his heirs. To this claim the muftī responded by considering a worst-case scenario: he assumed for the sake of argument that no debt obligation existed between the three minor children and the two sellers prior to the two sale transactions and that the 1635 gold ʿUthmānī dīnārs belonged instead to Abū ʿAbdallāh Muḥammad. Even if this were the case, the muftī wrote, the father's assertion that he had taken possession of assets on behalf of his minor children while in a state of health and in his capacity as their legal guardian constituted a legally valid acknowledgement. As support for the argument, the muftī asserted that this was the dominant position of the Mālikī school, as reflected in a statement

[45] Ibid., vol. 10, 385, ll. 20–2.
[46] Ibid., vol. 10, 386, ll. 1–2.
[47] Ibid., vol. 10, 385 (l. 17)–6 (l. 2).
[48] Ibid., vol. 10, 384–6 (top).

of Ibn al-Qāsim[49] and in the judicial practice of qāḍīs. Indeed, the acknowledgement is valid irrespective of whether or not the father provided an explanation for it and, of special relevance to the present case, irrespective of whether or not the children were known to possess any wealth of their own.[50] At this point, the muftī drew a distinction between this hypothetical scenario and the facts of the present case, in which it was not the defendants' father who had acknowledged a debt to his three children but rather "strangers" who did so, a distinction that strengthens the claim of the defendants here. As a result of the two sale transactions, these debts were transferred to their father, Abū ʿAbdallāh Muḥammad, for which reason the claim properly should be directed against him.[51]

Further, Abū ʿAbdallāh Muḥammad's financial liability (*dhimma*) with respect to his children remained in force as long as he was alive. Thus, there was no basis to the plaintiffs' assertion that the defendants' silence for the eighteen years between the date of the sale transactions and their father's death rendered their claim null and void (point 5, above). In support of this point, the muftī invoked the authority of Ibn Rushd (d. 520/1126),[52] who, when asked about an entitlement created twenty-five years previously, replied, "No entitlement may be nullified, even if it is ancient."[53]

As a result of these considerations, the Tunisian muftī already was persuaded that the legal prerequisites for the defendants' claim existed and were supported, positively, by written texts of the Mālikī school, and, negatively, by the plaintiffs' concession that they were unable to produce any testimonial evidence that might impugn the credibility of the professional witnesses who attested the two acknowledgements.

Having dealt with the major issues involved in the case, the muftī moved on to the plaintiffs' claim that the debt acknowledgements made by the two sellers, both of whom were "strangers" or non-relatives, were the product of collusion with Abū ʿAbdallāh Muḥammad (point 2, above). He rejected this argument on the ground that the plaintiffs themselves, as blood relatives of the deceased, were an interested party, for which reason the law presumes that any argument they make is suspect (*mashkūkun fīhi*) and illusory (*mawhūm*). That is to say, the *unsupported* allegation of an interested party was insufficient to impugn the acknowledgement of strangers establishing the defendants' right to the debt. This position, too, reportedly had been discussed by Mālikī jurists, although the muftī did not cite any of the relevant case material.[54]

Next, the muftī addressed the plaintiffs' claim that circumstantial evidence indicated that the true goal of the sale transactions was to serve the interests of the father, Abū ʿAbdallāh Muḥammad, despite his assertions that he was acting on behalf of his three minor children (point 4, above). This evidence was twofold: (a) the *ẓāhir*, or outward appearance of things, that is, the father's continuous possession of, and control over, the assets for eighteen years; and (b) the fact that

[49] On Ibn al-Qāsim, see above, note 25. [50] *Miʿyār*, vol. 10, 386, ll. 3–6.
[51] Ibid., vol. 10, 386, ll. 6–8. [52] On Ibn Rushd, see above, note 23.
[53] *Miʿyār*, vol. 10, 386, ll. 8–11. This case reportedly may be found in Ibn Rushd's *Nawāzil*.
[54] *Miʿyār*, vol. 10, 386, ll. 12–16.

the children were minors at the time of the transactions and therefore legally incapable of acquiring wealth on their own. The muftī rejected this claim on the ground that the outward appearance of things was subject to interpretation and therefore was of insufficient probative value to contradict a *naṣṣ*, or explicit written text, whereas the debt acknowledgements in question had been attested by professional witnesses and therefore had produced legal "certainty." Here the muftī exposed a major driving force behind his legal reasoning, namely, his extreme reluctance to base any judgment on facts that were legally doubtful.[55]

The muftī concluded by returning to his initial point, to wit, the status of an acknowledgement by a father to his minor children. Such an acknowledgement, he explained, should be treated as a unilateral gift (*niḥla*) and a charitable donation (*ṣadaqa*). Again, he supported his assertion by citing earlier legal precedent: the views attributed to Saḥnūn (d. 240/854),[56] Ibn Lubbāba (d. 314/926),[57] Ibn Zarb (d. 381/991),[58] Ibn Abī Zayd al-Qayrawānī (d. 386/996),[59] and Ibn Rushd all corroborate one another on this point.[60] As specific support for this position, the muftī invoked the authority of al-ʿUtbī (d. *ca.* 255/869) and Ibn Rushd, as follows:

> (a) In the second chapter on bequests in the *ʿUtbiyya*,[61] al-ʿUtbī stated, "A man's acknowledgement regarding a specific item that is known to be owned by him to the effect that it is for so-and-so, whether so-and-so is an heir [or a non-relative,] whether in a state of health or during a [final deathbed] illness, is construed in the sense of a gift and a charitable donation and the [object of] the acknowledgement bears the same legal status [as the object of a gift]." In his commentary on the *ʿUtbiyya*, Ibn Rushd stated, "I am not aware of any disagreement on this matter."[62]
> (b) In his *Kitāb al-bayān wa'l-taḥṣīl*, Ibn Rushd commented as follows on a case in which a man made an acknowledgement in favor of his wife, transferring to her ownership of the contents of her apartment: "If it is known that he is the true owner of the property then the acknowledgement constitutes a gift."[63]

Thus there was no doctrinal objection to a man transferring assets to his wife or a father transferring assets to his children by means of an *inter vivos* gift. But,

[55] Ibid., vol. 10, 386, ll. 16–19.
[56] ʿAbd al-Salām Saḥnūn b. Saʿīd b. Ḥabīb al-Tanūkhī, known as Saḥnūn. See Ibn Farḥūn, *Dībāj*, 160; Makhlūf, *Shajara*, vol. I, 69, no. 80; *EI²*, s.v., Saḥnūn; Toledano, *Judicial Practice*, 26, note 64.
[57] Abū ʿAbdallāh Muḥammad b. ʿUmar Ibn Lubbāba of Cordoba. See Ibn Farḥūn, *Dībāj*, 245; Makhlūf, *Shajara*, vol. I, 86, no. 179; Toledano, *Judicial Practice*, 83, note 141.
[58] Abū Bakr Muḥammad b. Baqī Ibn Zarb, chief qāḍī and Imām of Cordoba. See Ibn Farḥūn, *Dībāj*, 269; Makhlūf, *Shajara*, vol. I, 100, no. 249; Toledano, *Judicial Practice*, 67, note 67.
[59] Abū Muḥammad ʿAbdallāh b. Abī Zayd ʿAbd al-Raḥmān al-Nafzī al-Qayrawānī was one of the early Mālikī jurists in Qayrawān. His *Risāla* became a classic of Mālikī law and is the subject of many commentaries. See Ibn Farḥūn, *Dībāj*, 136–8; Makhlūf, *Shajara*, vol. I, 96, no. 227; Toledano, *Judicial Practice*, 27, note 66.
[60] *Miʿyār*, vol. 10, 386, ll. 19–22.
[61] This text, also known as *al-Mustakhraja*, was written by the Cordoban jurist al-ʿUtbī. A commentary on the text was written by Ibn Rushd. See Ibn Farḥūn, *Dībāj*, 238; Makhlūf, *Shajara*, vol. I, 75, no. 110; Toledano, *Judicial Practice*, 64, note 52.
[62] *Miʿyār*, vol. 10, 386, ll. 22–5. According to our muftī, a similar statement by Ibn Rushd may be found in the latter's *Ajwiba*.
[63] *Miʿyār*, vol. 10, 386 (bottom)–7 (l. 1).

our muftī observed, returning to a critical difference between the cases cited in the literature and the case at hand, the doctrine announced by Ibn Rushd applied to property given directly by a man to his children, wife, etc., whereas in the present case, the children's entitlement to the assets in question was based (1) on the acknowledgement of a debt made by the two sellers, who were "strangers" or non-relatives with respect to the creditors, and (2) on their father's having taken possession of the assets in question on their behalf. Reiterating the point made by the qāḍī in his *istiftā'*, the muftī asserted that no suspicion attached to the acknowledgement of a stranger. This acknowledgement, together with their father's having taken possession of the assets in question on behalf of his minor children, as confirmed by professional witnesses, firmly established the defendants' entitlement to those assets.[64]

As for the claim of *tawlīj*, the muftī curtly dismissed the plaintiffs' allegation that their father improperly had sought to divert his assets to some of his children, to the exclusion of others, on the grounds of insufficient evidence.[65]

The Judicial Comment of al-Wansharīsī

As al-Wansharīsī was copying the text of the Tunisian muftī's fatwā into what would become the *Kitāb al-Miʿyār*, he was attracted to his colleague's discussion of *tawlīj* and took the opportunity to comment on his response. (This comment and others by al-Wansharīsī may constitute a sub-genre of the Mālikī legal literature.)

The transition from the end of the Tunisian muftī's fatwā to the comment by al-Wansharīsī is marked concisely by the word *qultu*, "I say." "In my opinion," al-Wansharīsī wrote, shifting from the role of compiler to that of jurist, the judgment (*ḥukm*) in favor of the defendants "requires careful examination" – a polite way of expressing disagreement.[66] Al-Wansharīsī based his view on considerations of legal epistemology. He argued that the documentary evidence submitted by the defendants did *not* contain any reliable knowledge (*maʿrifa*) regarding the nature and source of the debt and the manner in which the two debtors became indebted to them; rather, one found in these documents merely second-hand references (*ḥikāyāt*) to the alleged debts. However, as he read the facts of this case, al-Wansharīsī was less interested in the testimonial evidence submitted by the defendants – its attestation by professional witnesses notwithstanding – than he was in the *underlying circumstances* of the two sale transactions. In his view, these transactions more closely resembled *tawlīj* and a bequest to an heir (both of which are prohibited) than they did legally valid and sound transactions.

Unlike his Tunisian colleague, al-Wansharīsī expressed considerable interest in the *rasm istirʿā'* submitted by the plaintiffs and certified by the qāḍī. He regarded this document as important because of three indicators that it contained: (1) the

[64] Ibid., vol. 10, 387, ll. 1–6. [65] Ibid., vol. 10, 387, ll. 6–7. [66] Ibid., vol. 10, 387, ll. 8–9.

father's bias toward, and favoritism for, his three minor children; (2) the fact that the children were minors who were legally incapable of acquiring wealth on their own; and (3) the fact that the stranger who acknowledged the "debt" reportedly was favorably disposed toward the plaintiffs' father, Abū ʿAbdallāh Muḥammad – a new piece of information that the Tunisian muftī had not mentioned, if he was aware of it. These three indicators, al-Wansharīsī concluded, point clearly toward three phenomena: *tawlīj*, that is, an attempt illegally to divert assets from one heir to another; deception on the part of the father; and an attempt to disinherit a child (or children) with whom one was on bad terms (*al-farār ʿan al-walad al-munāziʿ*).[67]

After this short synoptic analysis of the facts of the case, al-Wansharīsī devoted the rest of his legal note to adducing textual support for his position, as reflected in twelve cases preserved in third/ninth century Mālikī texts such as the *Nawāzil* of Aṣbagh, the *Wāḍiḥa* of Ibn Ḥabīb, the *Mudawwana* of Saḥnūn, and the *Mawwāziyya* of Ibn al-Mawwāz. Al-Wansharīsī cited these cases without any comment, leaving the reader to draw his or her own conclusions regarding their significance to the case at hand.

Conclusion

The two cases examined in this chapter shed light on the reciprocal relationship between the Marīnid qāḍī and muftī. The principal aim of the qāḍī was to establish the facts of a case and to weigh conflicting testimony in the scales of justice according to established rules of procedure and evidence. The principal aim of the muftī was to determine the appropriate legal doctrine that should be applied to these facts.

In both cases, the qāḍī surely had personal knowledge of the litigants and the network of social and economic relations in which they were situated. Once he decided to seek the advice of a muftī, however, he was required to compose a narrative summary of the case, or *istiftāʾ*, in which he transformed the names of the litigants and the testimony of the witnesses into abstract and impersonal categories, for example, buyers, sellers, and heirs. The muftī's response was similarly abstract, composed in a technical legal idiom intelligible only to jurists well versed in Mālikī legal doctrine and the rules of evidence and procedure. The muftī used terms of art such as *tawlīj*. He focused on antecedent concepts, such as *acknowledgement*, *taking possession*, and *silence*. He cited the positions of earlier authorities such as Mālik, Ibn al-Qāsim and Ibn Rushd. He cited antecedent cases, paying careful attention to similarities and differences between those cases and the case at hand. He supported his opinion by engaging in distinctive modes of reasoning, for example, the *argument ad minorum ad majorum* and the *reductio ad absurdum*. And he constructed hypothetical arguments in order to refute potential objections to his line of reasoning. In sum, the modes of reasoning employed by the muftī were complex, arguably as complex as those employed by judges and jurists in other legal systems.

[67] Ibid., vol. 10, 387, ll. 9–15. For another claim of parental bias and favoritism, see ibid., vol. 9, 261 ff.

This conclusion will not surprise readers who are familiar with the texts of classical Islamic law. Rather, what is surprising about the two cases examined here is the apparent contradiction between the mode of reasoning employed by al-Wansharīsī in the first fatwā and that manifested in his judicial comment. Both cases juxtapose two legal norms: a father's obligation (imposed by the Qur'ān and the *sunna*) to provide for his children after his death; and an individual's right (sanctioned by the jurists) to dispose of his property during his lifetime in whatever manner he wishes. In his fatwā, al-Wansharīsī expressed no overt interest in these norms or in the manner in which they relate to one another and he was conspicuously silent with regard to both the Qur'ānic verses that establish the inheritance rights of children and the prophetic *sunna* that establishes the underlying ethos of Islamic inheritance law ("It is better for you to leave your heirs rich ..."). Charged to ascertain the law (not to judge the facts), al-Wansharīsī devoted no overt attention to the human details of the case, specifically, the plaintiffs' allegation that their father, 'Uthmān b. al-Ḥasan, had *colluded* with al-Nāṣirī to deprive them of their lawful inheritance. Rather than consider the character of the buyer and seller and the network of relations in which they were situated, al-Wansharīsī focused his attention on formal, observable, and seemingly objective legal facts: did the transaction take place while the seller was sound of mind and body or while he was on his deathbed? Was the seller legally competent to undertake the transaction? Was he acting on his own behalf or on behalf of a third party? Was the sale-price transferred to the seller, and did the seller immediately convey the property to the buyer? Is the plaintiffs' claim supported by the testimony of upright witnesses or, alternatively, by circumstantial evidence? The mode of reasoning that he adopted in the first case may be described as *formalistic*.

In the second case the Tunisian muftī also adopted a formalistic style of judicial reasoning. Like al-Wansharīsī, he expressed no overt interest in the tension between a father's obligation to treat his children equitably and an individual's right to dispose of his property during his lifetime in whatever manner he wishes. Like al-Wansharīsī, he attended to the form, rather than the viable logic, of the sale transactions. Charged to ascertain the law, the Tunisian muftī was silent about the human elements of the case, specifically, the plaintiffs' assertion that their father was biased in favor of his three minor children and had colluded with the two sellers to deprive them of their lawful inheritance. Rather than consider the details of the sale transactions and the character of the buyers and the sellers, the muftī focused his attention on formal, observable, and seemingly objective legal facts: did any suspicion attach to the debt-acknowledgement of a stranger in favor of the three minor children? Was the claim of collusion supported by direct testimonial evidence? Was there any irregularity in the witnessing of the sale transactions? Having determined that the answer to all three of these questions was "no," the muftī recommended that a judgment be issued in favor of the defendants. Such a judgment, in his view, would be based upon legal certainty, as established by the testimony of professional witnesses whose integrity had been confirmed and certified by a qāḍī.

In his judicial comment, however, al-Wansharīsī sought to pierce the calm surface of the witness-attested sale transactions in an effort to discover their underlying purpose, adopting an *interpretive* judicial style. Unlike the Tunisian muftī who rejected the *rasm istirʿāʾ* on the ground that it contained only second-hand allegations of *tawlīj* and collusion, al-Wansharīsī argued that the *rasm istirʿāʾ* should be attended to with care because it contained three contextual indicators suggesting that there was a solid basis to the plaintiffs' allegations of *tawlīj*: the father had been known to favor his three minor children over his other children; the three children thus favored had been minors who were not known to possess any financial resources; and it had been established that the sellers were favorably inclined toward the father. These three contextual indicators suggested that appropriate conditions had existed for the father to divert resources from his older children to his three minor children. According to al-Wansharīsī, this evidence was of greater probative value than the two acknowledgements, which contained only second-hand knowledge of the nature and origin of the alleged debts.

It is curious that in his *post hoc* judicial comment al-Wansharīsī abandoned the formal judicial style of his fatwā in favor of an interpretive approach. Had he adopted an interpretive approach in his fatwā, the outcome of that case might have been different. How are we to explain the discrepancy between the formal and objective approach adopted by al-Wansharīsī in his fatwā and the interpretive and subjective approach that he adopted in his judicial comment?

It is possible that the differing approaches were conditioned by the cases' differing facts: in the first, a father allegedly sought to disinherit all of his children in favor of a third party who was not a blood relative, an action which, technically, does *not* qualify as *tawlīj*; in the second, a father sought the assistance of two men who were "strangers" in an effort to shift assets from one group of his children to another, an action which, if corroborated, *would* qualify as *tawlīj*.

It is also possible that al-Wansharīsī initially may have perceived the practical utility of *tawlīj* and may have wanted to preserve the status quo, although subsequently opposing *tawlīj*. If he wanted to eliminate or mitigate it, his decision to adopt one judicial style in his fatwā and another in his judicial comment would have been a deliberate strategy designed to achieve a specific policy objective, that is, to discourage the practice of *tawlīj*.

Finally, it is possible that al-Wansharīsī became frustrated with the constraints of the rules of evidence, which prevented him from achieving what he believed to be a just decision. And so, he proposed that the standards of proof should be lowered and that the circumstantial evidence should be allowed to carry the case forward and determine its outcome.

Sometimes the researcher can do no more than pose questions. Whatever the answers to our question may be, it appears that the different modes of reasoning available to muftīs provided them with a degree of flexibility and discretion that had important consequences for judicial outcomes. The systematic study of the modes of reasoning adopted by muftīs in different times and places no doubt will advance our understanding of the nature of Islamic legal culture.[68]

[68] On judicial style see, for example, *Interpreting Law and Literature: A Hermeneutic Reader*, ed. Sanford Levinson and Steven Mailloux (Evanston: Northwestern University Press, 1988); White, *Justice as Translation*; Dennis R. Klinck, *The Word of the Law* (Ottawa: Carleton University Press, 1992).

Conclusion: The Muftī

The cases analyzed in this book cover a rich variety of legal issues: paternity, fornication, water rights, family endowments, slander of the Prophet, and disinheritance of children. These issues are brought to life by the transcribed documents contained in the fatwās, which give us the names of the persons involved in the cases, as well as the dates and locations of legal events. That one or more of the litigants in each case was a prominent member of his community perhaps explains the preservation, length and generally high level of legal argumentation of the fatwās. The Marīnid judicial system from 1300 to 1500 CE is brought into focus as we study them.

The standard mechanism for the resolution of a dispute was a qāḍī judgment issued on the strength of testimonial evidence or a decisory oath, but disputes also were settled through arbitration, and, on occasion, through the direct intervention of the reigning sulṭān. The apparatus of justice was peopled by the sulṭān himself, qāḍīs, muftīs, professional witnesses, notaries, experts, and scribes. Arguably the most important actor within the system was the muftī.

Mālikī law was composed of a body of rules and norms that made it possible for Muslims to make sense of the world and to act in it. It was a cultural form that had its own distinctive language, codes, conventions, presumptions and institutions, its own special qualities, and its own consequences – in a word, its own legal sensibility. The fatwā was a central text in the Islamic legal system, a discursive form in which the muftī articulated and defined the terms of his craft as he used them on a daily basis, sometimes in unforeseen contexts, rendering arguments for which he alone was responsible. Through the *process* of producing the fatwā, the muftī created legal authority. As an authoritative statement of the law, the fatwā conferred legitimacy on the *ḥukm*, or judgment, of a qāḍī.[1]

When a muftī issued a fatwā, he used his knowledge of the multiple layers of the tradition of the school to which he belonged, acquired through long and arduous training, to identify the legal norms, rules, and categories that properly should govern a particular case. Like jurists in other legal cultures, the muftī turned to the

[1] This paragraph draws on James Boyd White, *Justice as Translation: An Essay in Cultural and Legal Criticism* (Chicago: University of Chicago Press, 1990).

legal authority of established sources, first and foremost the Qur'ān and the *sunna* of the Prophet, but also school doctrine as articulated in works on substantive law (*furūʿ*), treatises dealing with legal formularies (*wathāʾiq*), earlier fatwās, and court practice (*ʿamal*). Drawing on his extensive knowledge of these sources, often committed to memory, the muftī articulated the contemporary position of his school (*madhhab*) by selecting from the hundreds of available cases those he considered relevant to the case at hand, carefully arranging them in the narrative that would become his fatwā. The resulting literary performance was the product of a mode of reasoning that frequently involved the unannounced juxtaposition of parallel and contrasting cases. Treating these cases as the relevant sources from which legal rules may be construed, the muftī applied the rules that he identified in earlier cases to the case at hand. Because it was formulated in general terms, the fatwā possessed a timeless quality that accommodated the citation of other cases, formulated in similar terms. In this manner, events that had taken place in eighth-century Medina and twelfth-century Cordoba were brought together in a single fatwā that dealt with yet a third time and place: fourteenth-century Fez. By its very nature, such a literary work displayed a dense intertextuality that was mediated and controlled by the muftī, through whom there emerged a layered voice that *re-presented* the consensus of the jurists of his school as formed over the centuries.

Marīnid jurists operated within a regime of *taqlīd*. A qualified muftī was expected to be familiar with the legal verses of the Qur'ān and the *sunna* of the Prophet. Equally important, however, he was expected to know how Mālik and his disciples had understood and interpreted these legal sources and applied them in actual cases. According to the doctrine of *taqlīd*, in the fourteenth or fifteenth century CE, cases were to be resolved according to the same principles as those that had arisen in preceding centuries. Rare was the jurist who strayed from the well-beaten path and ventured a new and original interpretation of either the Qur'ān or the *sunna*. Only a handful of Marīnid jurists claimed to be *mujtahid*s, and we know little about their modes of judicial reasoning. During our investigation we have met in passing al-Sharīf al-Tilimsānī and Saʿīd al-ʿUqbānī, each of them, arguably, the greatest scholar of his age. And we examined at close range the figure of al-Haskūrī, dubbed the mocking jurist, whose bold pretensions to *ijtihād* were rejected by his colleagues – properly, in my view (recall his novel interpretation of the prophetic *ḥadīth* about the Bedouin who urinated in a mosque).[2] Only occasionally does our source refer to *ijtihād*, and when it does, the term generally signifies modest forms of legal analysis, for example, choosing between basing a judgment about water rights on historical priority or on physical location or reviewing relevant information before applying a discretionary punishment. To the extent that *ijtihād* was applied, it was exercised *within* the school and accounted for the slow but inexorable adaptation of the law to changing conditions.

[2] See Benchekroun, *La vie intellectuelle marocaine sous les Mérinides et les Waṭṭāsides (XIIIe XIVe XVe XVIe siècles)* (Rabat, 1974), 454; Robert Brunschvig, *La Berbérie Orientale sous les Hafsides*, 2 vols (Paris: Adrien-Maisonneuve, 1940–47), vol. 2, 295 ff.

We are now in a position to consider the question posed in the Introduction: was it possible for jurists operating within a regime of *taqlīd* to show legal creativity, and, if so, how? The jurists whom we have studied responded to novel and unforeseen circumstances by manipulating established legal doctrine, and their fatwās display a remarkable discursive vitality. The issuance of a fatwā was a moment when the law was made real, when the principles and rules contained in the Qur'ān and *ḥadīth*, the legal concepts and doctrines set out in treatises on substantive law, and the rules of evidence and procedure, were brought to bear, with greater or lesser force and clarity, upon the facts of an actual dispute. Many of these cases lay at the edges of established legal doctrine and raised issues that no one had foreseen when the earlier texts were produced.[3] If a man has sexual intercourse with a female slave belonging to his daughter, is a child of that union born into slavery or freedom; and if the putative father is dead, what level of proof must be satisfied before a court may pronounce the product of that union to be the legal child of its father? If a man repudiates his wife three times but subsequently acknowledges that he "took her back," does his acknowledgement constitute evidence of sexual intercourse, for which he can be put to death as a fornicator? In a dispute between riparian communities, does circumstantial evidence that the downstreamers were the first to settle in an area confer upon them a greater entitlement to the water than their upstream neighbors; or should entitlement to water be allocated on the basis of physical location? How does one interpret the intention of the founder of an endowment, one or more generations after he or she has died? If a man curses a *sharīf* and his ancestors in the heat of an argument, using the phrase "to the first grandfather," does he thereby slander the Prophet, and, if so, should he be put to death for this offense? Can a man avoid his responsibility to provide for his heirs after death by exercising his right to freely dispose of his property during his lifetime?

In difficult cases of this nature, the legal problem posed by the facts of the case did not lend itself to a solution provided by a pre-existing formula, but rather was an occasion for thought and argument. That this is so contradicts the common assumption that a given verse of the Qur'ān or saying of the Prophet will automatically dispose of a case. At first glance it might appear to do so. But whether it *should* be held to do so, and, if so, to what extent and why, are questions that the muftīs debated. The complex modes of thought and argument by which they examined these questions reveal the legal sensibility of the culture in which they lived. It is the precise nature of the muftī's response to a hard question that made the individual fatwā an interesting literary text – indeed, sometimes a compelling one.

Although the regime of *taqlīd* conferred stability upon the law, the outcome of a particular case was not predictable. Indeed, it would have been difficult if not impossible for a contemporary outside observer to anticipate the outcome of any of the cases that we have analyzed in this book. Who could have predicted that al-Tirjālī would rule in favor of Sālim when ʿAlī b. Abī al-ʿUlā' had not formally

[3] See again, White, *Justice as Translation*.

recognized him as his son during his lifetime; that the Marīnid sulṭān would release al-Haskūrī from prison and send him into exile, notwithstanding al-Sarīfī's insistence that his noxious colleague should be stoned to death for committing fornication; that the upstream community of Zgane would secure its rights to scarce water resources after three muftīs had issued fatwās in favor of the downstream community of Mazdgha; that Ibn Zāghū would dismiss the charges of blasphemy against Ibn ʿĪsā and his son and chastise Abū al-Faraj al-Sharīf for betraying the legacy of his father; or that al-Wansharīsī would argue that circumstantial indicators should be taken into consideration as evidence of *tawlīj* after having argued the opposite in an earlier, similar case?

The very unpredictability of these rulings suggests that the judgment of a qāḍī and the opinion of a muftī were in fact affected by unspecified extra-legal considerations. Qāḍīs and muftīs – like their counterparts in other legal cultures – certainly were concerned about the social, economic, and political consequences of their judgments and opinions. To this extent Weber surely was correct, but only partially so, for whatever his subjective leanings, the qāḍī was required to base his judgment on the facts, as established by testimonial evidence, and in conformity with established legal doctrine. Further, as we have noted, when a qāḍī asked a muftī for advice, he customarily translated the names of the litigants and their stories into the abstract and impersonal language of the law, and the resulting fatwā was equally abstract. Whatever extra-legal factors may have shaped the outcome of a particular case were not explicit – or even apparent. I have attempted in this book to pierce the calm surface of the muftī's opinion (and, in one instance, the qāḍī's judgment), to separate the legal and extra-legal elements, and to demonstrate that judicial outcomes were the product of *combined* legal and extra-legal factors. Given the limitation of our source, this is perhaps the best that we can do. To achieve a better understanding of the underlying nature of a given dispute, the historian must examine additional, especially non-legal, sources that may shed greater light on the litigants' lives and their positions within society.[4]

Whether the fatwā was an intellectual text, as usual, or an ethical or political text, as on occasion, in it the muftī reconstituted the resources of his culture through language, while establishing a relationship with his audience: the qāḍī who solicited the fatwā, the litigants who initiated the dispute, and the larger community of the town or city in which these men and women resided. In effect, the fatwā was part of an ongoing conversation between muftīs and the Muslim community in which adherence to the principles of Islam was ensured. One fatwā led to another, which led to yet another, in a regenerative discussion of legal principles. Some muftīs treated a request for a fatwā as an occasion to display technical legal skill, others as an opportunity to explore a legal problem that required sustained thought and analysis, others as a summons to repair the torn threads of

[4] See, for example, Thomas Kuehn, *Law, Family and Women: Toward a Legal Anthropology of Renaissance Italy* (Chicago: University of Chicago Press, 1991).

communal harmony, and still others as an excuse to promote a particular political or social interest within the community.

To the degree that members of the community were aware of a case (fatwās may have been read aloud and discussed in the congregational mosque or in the *madrasa* in which a muftī taught), the muftī's opinion served to articulate the moral, ethical, and legal norms that were expected to govern the relations of individuals and groups within the community. The activity of issuing fatwās contributed to the creation and consolidation of a public sphere – albeit a limited one – that served as a buffer between the potentially coercive power of the sulṭān, on the one hand, and his subjects, on the other. The collection and dissemination of fatwās reinforced moral, ethical and legal norms among the general public, thereby promoting adherence to, and respect for, the rule of law, and shaping the behavior of subsequent generations of Muslims.

The very existence of fatwās testifies to the importance of reasoned justification of judicial decisions in the Maghrib in the fourteenth and fifteenth centuries CE. They belie the popular image of the Muslim jurist as an unprincipled agent who complacently dispensed justice according to individual expediency, without reference to any settled body of rules or norms. During the period studied in this book, nothing could have been further from the truth.

Bibliography

Primary Sources

Abū Dā'ūd. *Sunan*. Ed. by Muḥammad Muḥyī al-Dīn 'Abd al-Ḥamīd. 4 vols, 2nd edn, Cairo: al-Maktaba al-Tijāriyya al-Kubrā, 1369/1950.

Aḥmad Bābā al-Tunbuktī. *See* al-Tunbuktī, Aḥmad Bābā.

al-'Ajlūnī al-Jarrāḥī, Ismā'īl b. Muḥammad. *Kashf al-khafā' wa-muzīl al-ilbās 'ammā ashhara min al-aḥādīth 'alā alsinat al-nās*. 2 vols in 1, Beirut: Dār Iḥyā' al-Turāth al-'Arabī, 1351–52/1932–33. Reprinted Beirut: Dār al-Kutub al-'Ilmiyyah, 1408/1988.

al-Anṣārī, Abū 'Abdallāh Muḥammad. *Kitāb sharḥ ḥudūd al-Imām al-akbar al-baraka al-qudwa al-anwar Abī 'Abdallāh b. 'Arafa*. Rabat: Wizārat al-Awqāf, 1412/1992.

al-Azharī, Ṣāliḥ 'Abd al-Samī' al-Ābī. *Jawāhir al-iklīl: sharḥ mukhtaṣar al-'allāma al-shaykh Khalīl*. 2 vols, Cairo: 'Īsā al-Bābī al-Ḥalabī, 1913 or 1914. [Maṭba'at Muḥammad b. Shaqrūn, 1370/1951].

El-Bâdisî, 'Abd el-Ḥaqq. *El-Maqṣad (Vie des saints du Rîf)*, tr. by G.S. Colin. Paris: Librairie Ancienne Honoré Champion, 1926 (published in *Archives Marocaines*, vol. XXVI).

al-Bājī, Abū al-Walīd Sulaymān b. Khalaf. *al-Muntaq'a: sharḥ Muwaṭṭa' Imām Dār al-Hijra Sayyidunā Mālik b. Anas*. 6 vols, Cairo: Maṭba'at al-Sa'āda, 1332/1914. Reprinted Dār al-Kitāb al-Islāmī, 1990.

al-Bayhaqī, Abū Bakr Aḥmad b. Ḥusayn. *al-Sunan al-Kubrā*. 10 vols, Hyderabad, AH 1344–57. Reprinted Beirut: Dār Ṣādir, 1968.

al-Bukhārī, Muḥammad b. Ismā'īl. *Ṣaḥīḥ*. Ed. by Krehl. 4 vols, Leiden: E.J. Brill, 1862–98. Also: al-Bukhārī. *Ṣaḥīḥ*. Ed. by Muḥammad Tawfīq 'Awīḍa. 6 vols, Cairo: Lajnat Iḥyā' Kutub al-Sunna, 1390/1970.

al-Dardīr, Abū al-Barakāt Aḥmad. *al-Sharḥ al-ṣaghīr 'alā aqrab al-masālik ilā madhhab al-Imām Mālik*. Ed. by Muṣṭafā Kamāl Waṣfī. 4 vols, Cairo: Dār al-Ma'ārif, 1972–74.

al-Fasawī. *K. al-Ma'rifa wa'l-tārīkh*. Ed. by Akram Ḍiyā' al-'Umarī. 4 vols, 3rd edn, Medina: Maktabat al-Dār, 1410/1989.

al-Fāsī, Muḥammad al-Mahdī. *Kitāb mumti' al-asmā' fī dhikr al-Jazūlī wa'l-tabbā' wa-mā lahumā min al-atbā'*. Fez: lithograph, 1316/1898–99.

Ghazālī's Book of Counsel for Kings (*Naṣīḥat al-Mulūk*). Tr. by F.R.C. Bagley. London: Oxford University Press, 1964.

al-Ḥafnāwī. *Ta'rīf al-khalaf bi-rijāl al-salaf*. 2 vols in 1, Tunis: Mu'assasat al-Risāla, 1402/1982.

Ḥajjī Khalīfa. *Kashf al-ẓunūn ʿan asāmī al-kutub wa'l-funūn*, 2 vols, Istanbul: Maarif Matbaasi, 1941–43.
al-Ḥākim al-Nīsābūrī, Abū ʿAbdallāh Muḥammad. *al-Mustadrak ʿalā al-ṣaḥīḥayn fī'l-ḥadīth*. 4 vols, Riyad: Maṭbaʿa wa-Maṭābiʿ al-Naṣr al-Ḥadītha, 1968.
Ibn ʿAbbād of Ronda: Letters on the Sūfī Path. Tr. by John Renard, SJ. New York: Paulist Press, 1986.
Ibn ʿAbd al-Barr al-Qurṭubī. *al-Intiqāʾ fī faḍāʾil al-thalātha al-aʾimma al-fuqahāʾ*. Cairo: Maktabat al-Qudsī, 1350.
——. *Kitāb al-kāfī fī fiqh ahl al-Madīna al-mālikī*. Beirut: Dār al-Kutub al-ʿIlmiyya, 1407/1987.
Ibn ʿAbd al-Rafīʿ, Ibrāhīm b. Ḥasan. *Muʿīn al-ḥukkām ʿalā al-qaḍāyā wa'l-aḥkām*. 2 vols, Beirut: Dār al-Gharb al-Islāmī, 1989.
Ibn ʿAbdūn, *Risālat Ibn ʿAbdūn fī l-quḍāt wa-l-ḥisba*. Ed. by E. Lévi-Provençal. In *Trois traités hispaniques de hisba*. Le Caire, 1955.
Ibn Abī Zarʿ. *Rawḍ al-Qirṭās*. Tr. by Ambrosio Huici Miranda. 2 vols, 2nd edn, Valencia. n.p., 1964. Tr. by A. Beaumier as *Roudh el-Kartas. Histoire des souverains du maghreb et annales de la ville de Fes*. Paris: L'Imprimerie Impériale, 1860.
Ibn Abī Zayd al-Qayrawānī. *Risāla*. Beirut: al-Maktaba al-Thaqāfiyya, n.d. Partially tr. by Alexander David Russell and Abdullah al-Maʾmūn Suhrawardy as *First Steps in Muslim Jurisprudence*, consisting of excerpts from *Bākūrat al-Saʿd* of Ibn Abū Zayd. London: Luzac & Co., 1906.
Ibn al-Aḥmar, Ismāʿīl. *Buyūtāt Fās al-kubrā*. Rabāṭ: Dār al-Manṣūr li'l-Ṭibāʿa wa'l-Wirāqa, 1972.
Ibn al-ʿAṭṭār. *Formulario Notarial Hispano-Árabe por el alfaquí y notario cordobés Ibn al-ʿAṭṭār (s. X)*. Ed. by P. Chalmeta and F. Corriente. Madrid: Instituto Hispano-Árabe de Cultura, 1983.
Ibn Farḥūn, Ibrāhīm b. ʿAlī. *Kitāb al-Dībāj al-mudhahhab fī maʿrifat aʿyān ʿulamāʾ al-madhhab*. Cairo: Dār al-Turāth, 1351/1932.
——. *Tabṣirat al-ḥukkām fī uṣūl al-aqḍiya wa-manāhij al-aḥkām*. 2 vols, n.p.: 1986.
Ibn Ḥajar al-ʿAsqalānī, Aḥmad b. ʿAlī. *Talkhīṣ al-ḥabīr*. 4 vols, Cairo: Muʾassasat Qurṭubah: Dār al-Mishkāh, 1416/1995.
Ibn Ḥanbal, Aḥmad b. Muḥammad. *Musnad al-Imām Aḥmad b. Ḥanbal*. 6 vols, Cairo, 1895. Reprinted Beirut: al-Maktab al-Islāmī li'l-Ṭibāʿa wa'l-Nashr, 1969. Also: Ibn Ḥanbal. *Musnad*. Ed. by Aḥmad Muḥammad Shākir. 19 vols, Beirut: al-Maktaba al-Islāmiyya, 1398/1978.
Ibn al-Jawzī, Abū al-Faraj ʿAbd al-Raḥmān b. ʿAlī. *Al-Nafīs fī takhrīj aḥādīth Talbīs Iblīs*. Ed. by Yaḥyā b. Khālid b. Tawfīq. Jīzah: Maktabat al-Tarbiyya al-Islāmiyyah, 1994.
Ibn Juzayy al-Gharnāṭī, Muḥammad b. Aḥmad. *Qawānīn al-aḥkām al-sharʿiyya wa-masāʾil al-furūʿ al-fiqhiyya*. Ed. by ʿAbd al-Raḥmān Ḥasan Maḥmūd. Cairo: ʿAlam al-Fikr, 1405–06/1985. Reprinted Beirut: Dār al-ʿIlm li'l-Malāyīn.
Ibn Khaldūn. *al-Taʿrīf bi-Ibn Khaldūn wa-riḥlatuhu gharban wa sharqan*. Ed. by Muḥammad b. Tāwit al-Ṭanjī. Cairo, 1370/1951. Tr. by Abdesselam Cheddadi as *Le voyage d'Occident et d'Orient. Autobiographie*. Paris, 1980.
——. *Kitāb al-ʿIbar*. 7 vols, Beirut: Dār al-Kitāb al-Lubnānī, 1959. Tr. by le Baron de Slane as *Histoire des Berbères et des dynasties musulmanes de l'Afrique Septentrionale*. 4 vols, Paris: P. Geuthner, 1925–56.
——. *The Muqaddimah: An Introduction to History*. Tr. by Franz Rosenthal. 3 vols, Princeton: Princeton University Press, 1958.

Ibn al-Khaṭīb, *al-Iḥāta fī akhbār Gharnāṭa*. Ed. by Muḥammad ʿAbd Allāh ʿInān. 2 vols, 2nd edn, Cairo: Maktabat al-Khānjī, 1393/1973.

Ibn Māja, Abū ʿAbdallāh Muḥammad. *Sunan*. Ed. by Muḥammad Fu'ād ʿAbd al-Bāqī. 2 vols, Cairo: ʿĪsā al-Bābī al-Ḥalabī, 1972.

Ibn Manẓūr, Muḥammad b. Mukarram. *Lisān al-ʿArab*. 15 vols, Beirut: Dār Ṣādir, 1375/1955.

Ibn Maryam. *al-Bustān fī dhikr al-awliyā' wa'l-ʿulamā' bi-Tilimsān*. Algiers, 1326/1908. Tr. by F. Provenzali as *El Bostan ou Jardin des biographies des saints et savants de Tlemcen*. Alger: Imprimerie Orientale Fontana Frères, 1910.

Ibn Marzūq. *El Musnad: Hechos Memorables de Abū L-Ḥasan Sultan de los Benimerines*. Tr. and ed. by Marià J. Viguerra. Madrid: Instituto Hispano-Árabe de Cultura, 1977.

Ibn al-Mundhir al-Naysābūrī, Muḥammad b. Ibrāhīm. *al-Ijmāʿ*. Ed. by Fu'ād ʿAbd al-Munʿim Aḥmad. Qaṭar: Ri'āsat al-Maḥākim al-Sharʿiyya, 1402/1981–82.

Ibn al-Qāḍī al-Miknāsī, Aḥmad. *Durrat al-Ḥijāl fī Asmā' al-Rijāl*. Ed. by Muḥammad al-Aḥmadī Abū al-Nūr. 3 vols, Cairo: Dār al-Turāth, 1390/1970.

——. *Jadhwat al-iqtibās fī dhikr man ḥalla min al-aʿlām madīnata Fās*. 2 vols, al-Ribāṭ: Dār al-Manṣūr li'l-Ṭibāʿa wa'l-Wirāqa, 1973–74.

——. *Laqṭ al-farā'id min lufāẓat ḥuqaq al-fawā'id*. In *Alf sana min al-wafayāt fī thalātha kutub*. Ed. by M. Ḥajjī and M. Ḥajjī. Rabat: Dār al-Maghrib li'l-Ta'līf, 1396/1976.

Ibn Qunfudh. *Sharaf al-Ṭālib*. In *Alf sana min al-wafayāt fī thalātha kutub*. Ed. by M. Ḥajjī and M. Ḥajjī. Rabat: Dār al-Maghrib li'l-Ta'līf, 1396/1976.

Ibn Rushd al-Qurṭubī, Abū al-Walīd Muḥammad b. Aḥmad (d. 595/1198). *Bidāyat al-mujtahid wa-nihāyat al-muqtaṣid*. 2 vols, Cairo: Maktabat al-Kulliyāt al-Azhariyya, 1389/1969. Tr. by Imran Ahsan Khan Nyazee and Muhammad Abdul Rauf as *The Distinguished Jurist's Primer*. 2 vols, Reading, UK: Garnet Publishing, 1996.

——. *Fatāwā Ibn Rushd*. 3 vols, Beirut: Dār al-Gharb al-Islāmī, 1987.

Ibn Rushd, Muḥammad b. Aḥmad. *al-Bayān wa'l-taḥṣīl wa'l-sharḥ wa'l-tawjīh wa'l-taʿlīl fī masā'il al-Mustakhrajah*. Ed. by Muḥammad Ḥajjī and Aḥmad al-Sharqāwī Iqbāl. 20 vols, 2nd edn, Beirut: Dār al-Gharb al-Islāmī, 1408/1988.

Ibn Taymiyyah, ʿAbd al-Salām b. ʿAbdallāh. *al-Ijtimā' wa'l-iftirāq fī'l-ḥilf bi'l-ṭalāq*. Ed. by Muḥammad ʿAbd al-Razzāq. Cairo: al-Manār Press, 1346/1926–27.

Ibn Taymiyyah, Aḥmad b. ʿAbd al-Ḥalīm. *Majmūʿ Fatāwā Shaykh al-Islām Aḥmad Ibn Taymiyyah*. Ed. by ʿAbd al-Raḥmān b. Muḥammad b. Qāsim al-ʿĀṣimī al-Najdī, 35 vols, Riyadh: Maṭābiʿ al-Riyāḍ, 1381–86/1961–67.

Ibn Waḍḍāḥ, Muḥammad. *Kitāb al-bidaʿ*. Ed. by Ma. Isabel Fierro. Madrid: Consejo Superior de Investigaciones Cientificas, 1988.

al-Idrīsī, Abū ʿAbdallāh Muḥammad. *Nuzhat al-mushtāq fī ikhtirāq al-āfāq*. Partial tr. by R.P.A. Dozy and M.J. de Goeje, *Description de l'Afrique et de l'Espagne par Edrisi*. Leiden: E.J. Brill, 1866. Reprinted 1968.

ʿIyāḍ b. Mūsā b. ʿIyāḍ al-Yaḥsubī, Abū al-Faḍl, known as Qāḍī ʿIyāḍ. *Madhāhib al-ḥukkām fī nawāzil al-aḥkām*. Ed. by M. Bencherifa. Beirut: Dār al-Gharb al-Islāmī, 1990.

——. *Kitāb al-shifā bi-taʿrīf ḥuqūq al-muṣṭafā*. Ed. by Saʿīd ʿAbd al-Fattāḥ. 2 vols, [Saudi Arabia]: Hishām ʿAlī Ḥāfiẓ, 1416/1995.

al-Jarīrī, ʿAbd al-Raḥmān. *Kitāb al-Fiqh ʿalā al-madhāhib al-arbaʿ*. 5 vols, Cairo: Dār al-Irshād li'l-Ṭibāʿa wa'l-Nashr, 1980.

Kaḥḥāla, ʿUmar Riḍā. *Muʿjam al-mu'allifīn*. 4 vols, Beirut: Mu'assasat al-Risāla, 1414/1993.

al-Khafīf, ʿAlī. *Furaq al-zawāj fī'l-madhāhib al-islāmiyya*. Cairo, 1958.

Khalīl b. Isḥāq. *al-Mukhtaṣar fī al-fiqh ʿalā madhhab al-Imām Mālik*. Paris: L'Imprimerie Nationale, 1272/1855. Tr. by M. Perron as *Précis de jurisprudence musulmane; ou,*

Principes de législation musulmane civile et religieuse selon le rite mâlékite. 6 vols, Paris: Imprimerie Nationale, 1848–52.

al-Khaṣṣāf, Abū Bakr Aḥmad. *Kitāb adab al-qāḍī*. Ed. by Farhat Ziadeh. Cairo: American University Press, 1978.

al-Khaṭīb al-Baghdādī, Abū Bakr Aḥmad b. ʿAlī. *Taʾrīkh Baghdād*. Cairo: Maṭbaʿat al-Khānjī. Baghdad: al-Maktaba al-ʿArabiyya, 1349/1931.

Leo Africanus. *The History and Description of Africa and of the notable things therein contained*. Tr. by John Pory. Ed. by Robert Brown. 3 vols, London: The Hakluyt Society, 1896. [*see* al-Wazzān]

Leon Africano, Juan. *Descripción de Africa y de las cosas notables que en ella se encuentran*. Tetuan, Imp. Imperio, 1952.

Makhlūf, Muḥammad b. Muḥammad. *Shajarat al-nūr al-zakiyya fī ṭabaqāt al-mālikiyya*. 2 vols in 1, 2nd edn, Beirut: Dār al-Kitāb al-ʿArabī, *ca*. 1975.

Mālik b. Anas. *al-Muwaṭṭaʾ*. Ed. by Muḥammad Fuʾād ʿAbd al-Bāqī. Cairo: ʿĪsā al-Bābī al-Ḥalabī 1370/1951. Tr. by Muhammad Rahimuddin as *Muwaṭṭaʾ Imām Mālik*. Pakistan: Sh. Muhammad Ashraf, 1980. Also *Muwaṭṭaʾ Yaḥyā b. Yaḥyā*. 4 vols, Cairo, 1379/1959.

al-Maqqarī al-Tilimsānī. *Nafḥ al-ṭīb min ghuṣn al-Andalus al-raṭīb*. 7 vols, Beirut: Dār Ṣādir, 1388/1968.

al-Mawardī, ʿAlī b. Muḥammad. *Al-Aḥkām al-sulṭāniyya*. French tr. by E. Fagnan, *Les statuts gouvernementaux ou règles de droit public et administratif*. Reprinted Paris, 1982. English tr. by Asadullah Yate, *Al-Ahkam as-Sultaniyyah: The Laws of Governance, by Abu'l Hasan al-Mawardi*. London: Ta-Ha Publishers, 1996.

al-Mawwāq, Abdallāh Muḥammad b. Yūsuf al-Abdarī. *al-Tāj wa'l-iklīl li-mukhtaṣar Khalīl*. On the margin of al-Ḥaṭṭāb, *Mawāhib al-jalīl li-sharḥ mukhtaṣar Khalīl*. 6 vols, Ṭarābulus, Libya: Maktabat al-Najāḥ, 1978.

al-Muʿjam al-mufahras li-alfāẓ aḥādith Biḥār al-anwār, 14 vols (Qum: Qism al-Muʿjam, 1413–18/1993–97).

al-Mundhirī. *al-Targhīb wa'l-tarhīb min al-aḥādīth al-sharīf*. Ed. by Muṣṭafā Muḥammad ʿUmmāra. Beirut: Dār Iḥyāʾ al-Turāth al-ʿArabī, 1388/1968.

Muslim b. Ḥajjāj. *Ṣaḥīḥ*. Ed. by Muḥammad Fuʾād ʿAbd al-Bāqī. 5 vols, Cairo: Dār Iḥyāʾ al-Kutub al-ʿArabiyya, 1371/1955.

al-Muttaqī al-Hindī, ʿAlī b. ʿAbd al-Mālik. *Kanz al-ʿummāl fī sunan al-aqwāl wa'l-afʿāl*. Beirut: Muʾassasat al-Risāla, 1399/1979.

al-Nasāʾī, Aḥmad b. Shuʿayb. *al-Sunan al-kubrā*. 7 vols, Beirut: Dār al-Kutub al-ʿIlmiyya, 1411/1991. Also: al-Nasāʾī, Aḥmad b. Shuʿayb. *Sunan bi-sharḥ al-Suyūṭī*. Ed. by Ḥasan Muḥammad al-Masʿūdī. 8 vols, Cairo: al-Maktaba al-Tijāriyya al-Kubrā, 1964–65.

al-Nawawī, Abū Zakariyāʾ Yaḥyā. *Adab al-fatwā wa'l-muftī wa'l-mustaftī*. Damascus: Dār al-Fikr, 1988.

Qalṣādī, ʿAlī b. Muḥammad. *Riḥla*. Ed. by Muḥammad Abū al-Ajfan. Tunis: al-Shirkah al-Tūnisiyya li'l-Tawzīʿ, 1978.

al-Qarāfī, Badr al-Dīn. *Tawshīḥ al-dībāj wa-ḥilyat al-ibtihāj*. Beirut: Dār al-Gharb al-Islāmī, 1403/1983.

Saḥnūn b. Saʿīd al-Tanūkhī. *al-Mudawwana al-kubrā li-Mālik b. Anas al-Aṣbaḥī. Riwāyat Saḥnūn b. Saʿīd al-Tunūkhī*. 16 vols in 4. Cairo: Maṭbaʿat al-Saʿāda, 1323/1905a. Reprinted Beirut: Dār Ṣādir, n.d. Also Saḥnūn b. Saʿīd al-Tanūkhī. *al-Mudawwana al-kubrā li-Mālik b. Anas al-Aṣbaḥī. Riwāyat Saḥnūn b. Saʿīd al-Tunūkhī*. 16 vols in 7. Cairo: Maṭbaʿa al-Khayriyya, 1323/1905b.

al-Ṣāwī al-Mālikī, Aḥmad b. Muḥammad. *Bulghat al-sālik li-aqrab al-masālik ilā madhhab al-Imām Mālik.* 3 vols, Cairo: ʿĪsā al-Bābī al-Ḥalabī, 1978.

The Sea of Precious Virtues (Baḥr al-Favāʾid): A Medieval Islamic Mirror for Princes. Tr. by Julie Scott Meisami. Salt Lake City: University of Utah Press, 1991.

al-Shabrāwī, ʿAbd Allāh b. Muḥammad. *Itḥāf bi-ḥubb al-ashrāf.* Cairo: Muṣṭafā al-Bābī al-Ḥalabī, 1318/1900.

al-Shinqīṭī, Muḥammad b. Aḥmad al-Dāh. *al-Fatḥ al-rabbānī: sharḥ ʿalā naẓm risālat Ibn Abī Zayd al-Qayrawānī.* 3 vols in 1. Cairo: Maktabat al-Qāhira, 1969.

Sibṭ Ibn al-Jawzī, Yūsuf b. Qizughlī. *Mirʾāt al-zamān fī tārīkh al-aʿyān.* Hyderabad, 1370/1952.

al-Ṭabarānī, Sulaymān b. Aḥmad. *al-Muʿjam al-Ṣaghīr.* Ed. by ʿAbd al-Raḥmān Muḥammad ʿUthmān. 2 vols, Madina: al-Maktaba al-Salafiyya, 1388/1968.

Tafsīr al-Imāmayn al-Jalālayn. Beirut: Dār Iḥyāʾ al-Turāth al-ʿArabī, 198–.

al-Tirmidhī. *Sunan bi-sharḥ Ibn al-ʿArabī al-Mālikī.* Ed. by ʿAbd al-Wāḥid Muḥammad al-Tāzī. 13 vols, Cairo: al-Maṭbaʿa al-Miṣriyya, 1350/1931.

al-Tunbuktī, Aḥmad Bāba. *Nayl al-ibtihāj bi-taṭrīz al-dībāj.* On the margin of Ibn Farḥūn, *Kitāb al-Dībāj.* Cairo: Dār al-Turāth, 1351/1952.

al-Ṭurṭūshī, Muḥammad b. al-Walīd. *Kitāb al-Ḥawādith wa'l-bidaʿ*, ed. ʿAbd al-Majīd Turkī. Beirut: Dār al-Gharb al-Islāmī, 1990. Tr. by Maribel Fierro as *El Libro de las novedades y las innovaciones.* Madrid: Consejo Superior de Investigaciones Cientificas, 1993.

al-ʿUtbī (al-Qurṭubī). *al-ʿUtbiyyah.* On the margin of Ibn Rushd, *al-Bayān wa'l-taḥṣīl.* 20 vols, Beirut: Dār al-Gharb al-Islāmī, 1988.

al-Walīdī, Abū al-Faḍl Rāshid b. Abī Rāshid. *al-Ḥalāl wa'l-Ḥarām.* Ed. by ʿAbd al-Raḥmān al-ʿUmrānī al-Idrīsī. Rabat: Maṭbaʿat Faḍāla al-Muḥammadiyya, 1410/1990.

al-Wansharīsī, Aḥmad. *Wafayāt.* In *Alf sana min al-wafayāt fī thalātha kutub.* Ed. by M. Ḥajjī. Rabat: Dār al-Maghrib li'l-taʾlīf, 1396/1976.

——. *al-Miʿyār al-Muʿrib wa'l-jāmiʿ al-mughrib ʿan fatāwī ʿulamāʾ Ifrīqiyā wa'l-Andalus wa'l-Maghrib.* Lithograph, 12 vols, Fez, 1314–15/1897–98. Printed edn. 13 vols, Rabat: Ministry of Culture and Religious Affairs, 1401–03/1981–83.

Al-Wazzān al-Fāsī, al-Ḥasan b. Muḥammad. *Waṣf Ifrīqiyā.* 2 vols, Rabat, 1980. [*see* Leo Africanus]

Yūnīnī, Mūsā b. Muḥammad. *Dhayl mirʾāt al-zamān.* 4 vols, Hyderabad, 1374–80/1954–61.

al-Zarrūq, Aḥmad b. Aḥmad. *Qawāʿid al-taṣawwuf.* Ed. by Muḥammad Zuhrī al-Najjār and ʿAlī Muʿbad Farghalī. Beirut: Dār al-Jīl, 1992.

al-Zaylaʿī, ʿAbd Allāh b. Yūsuf. *Naṣb al-rāya li-aḥādīth al-hidāya*, 4 vols, 1st edn [S.l.]: al-Majlis al-ʿIlmī, 1357/1938.

al-Ziriklī, Khayr al-Dīn. *Aʿlām.* 8 vols, 5th edn, Beirut: Dār al-ʿIlm li'l-Malāyin, 1980.

Secondary Sources

Abun-Nasr, Jamil M. *A History of the Maghrib in the Islamic Period.* Cambridge: Cambridge University Press, 1987.

Anderson, J.N.D. "Invalid and Void Marriages in Hanafi Law." *Bulletin of the School of Oriental and African Studies*, 13:2 (1950), 357–66.

Antoun, Richard. *Arab Village: A Social Structural Study of a Transjordanian Peasant Community*. Bloomington: Indiana University Press, 1972.

Arié, Rachel. *L'Espagne musulmane au temps des Naṣrides (1232–1492)*. Paris: Editions E. de Boccard, 1973.

Basset, R. "Les empreintes merveilleuses." *Revue des Traditions Populaires*, vol. 9 (1894), 689.

Beck, Herman L. *L'Image d'Idrīs II, ses descendants de Fās et la politique sharīfienne des sultans Marīnides (656–869/1258–1465)*. Leiden: E.J. Brill, 1989.

Bel, Alfred. *La Religion musulmane en Berbérie: Esquisse d'histoire et de sociologie Religieuses. Tome 1: Etablissement et développement de l'Islam en Berbérie du VIIe au XXe siècle*. Paris: Librairie Orientaliste Paul Geuthner, 1938.

Ben Cheneb, Mohammed. "La *Fârisiya* ou les débuts de la dynastie Ḥafside par Ibn Qonfod de Constantine (1)." *Hespéris*, 8 (1928), 37–41.

Benchekroun, Mohamed b.A. *La vie intellectuelle marocaine sous les Mérinides et les Waṭṭāsides (XIIIe XIVe XVe XVIe siècles)*. Rabat: [s.n.], 1974.

Benmira, Omar. "al-Nawâzil wa'l-mujtamaʿ." PhD dissertation. Kulliyat al-Ādāb bi'l-Rabaṭ, 1989.

——. "Qaḍāyā al-miyāh bi'l-maghrib al-wasīṭ min khilāl adab al-nawāzil." In *al-Taʾrīkh wa-adab al-nawāzil*. Ed. by Muḥammad al-Manṣūr and Muḥammad al-Maghrāwī. Rabat: al-Jamʿiyya al-Maghribiyya li'l-Baḥth al-Taʾrīkhī, 1995, 77–85.

Bercher, Leon. "L'apostasie, le blasphème et la rébellion en droit musulman malékite." *Revue Tunisienne* (1923), 115–30.

Berkey, Jonathan. *The Transmission of Knowledge in Medieval Cairo: A Social History of Islamic Education*. Princeton: Princeton University Press, 1992.

Berque, Jacques. *Ulémas, fondateurs, insurgés du Maghreb, xviie siècle*. Paris: Sindbad, 1982.

Bolens, Lucie. "L'irrigation en al-Andalus: Une Société en Mutation, Analyse des Sources Juridiques (Les 'Nawâzil' d'al-Wansharîsî)." In idem, *L'Andalousie du quotidien au sacré XIe-XIIIe siècles*. Aldershot, Hampshire, Great Britain: Variorum, 1990.

Bosworth, C. Edmund. "Some Remarks on the Terminology of Irrigation Practices and Hydraulic Constructions in the Eastern Arab and Iranian Worlds in the Third–Fifth Centuries AH." *Journal of Islamic Studies*, 2:1 (1991), 78–85.

Bousquet, G.-H. *L'éthique sexuelle de l'Islam*. 2nd edn, Paris: G.P. Maisonneuve et Larose, 1966.

Brockelmann, C. *Geschichte der arabischen Litteratur*. 2 vols plus 3 supplements, Leiden: E.J. Brill, 1937–49.

Brunschvig, Robert. *La Berbérie Orientale sous les Ḥafsides*. 2 vols, Paris: Adrien Maisonneuve, 1940–47.

Bulliet, R.W. *The Patricians of Nishapur: A Study in Medieval Islamic Social History*. Cambridge, MA: Harvard University Press, 1972.

Burton, John. *An Introduction to Hadith*. Edinburgh: Edinburgh University Press, 1994.

Buskens, Leon. *Islamitisch Recht en familiebetrekkingen in Marokko*. Amsterdam Bulaaq, 1999.

Butzer, Karl W., Juan F. Mateu, Elisabeth K. Butzer, and Pavel Kraus. "Irrigation Agrosystems in Eastern Spain: Roman or Islamic Origins?" *Annals of the Association of American Geographers*, 75 (1985), 479–509.

Calhoun, Craig. "Civil Society and the Public Sphere." *Public Culture*, vol. 5 (1993), 267–80.

Carmona González, Alfonso. "Ibn Hišām al-Qurṭubī y su *Mufīd li-l-ḥukkām*." *Quaderni di Studi Arabi*, 5–6 (1987–88), 120–30.

Chamberlain, Michael. *Knowledge and Social Practice in Medieval Damascus, 1190–1350*. Cambridge: Cambridge University Press, 1994.
Chapters on Marriage and Divorce: Responses of Ibn Ḥanbal and Ibn Rāhwayh. Tr. with introduction and notes by Susan A. Spectorsky. Austin: University of Texas Press, 1993.
Coase, R.H. *The Firm, the Market, and the Law*. Chicago: University of Chicago Press, 1988.
Colin, G.S. "La noria marocaine et les machines hydrauliques dans le monde arabe." *Hespéris*, XIV (1932), 22–60.
——. "L'origine des norias de Fès." *Hespéris*, XVI (1933), 156–7.
Colin, G.S., and H.P.J. Renaud. "Note sur le "*muwaqqit*" marocain Abû Muqriʿ – ou mieux Abû Miqraʿ – al-Baṭṭīwī." *Hespéris*, XXV (1938), 94–6.
Cornell, Vincent J. *Realm of the Saint: Power and Authority in Moroccan Sufism*. Austin: University of Texas Press, 1998.
Coulson, Noel J. *Succession in the Muslim Family*. Cambridge: Cambridge University Press, 1971.
Crone, Patricia and Martin Hinds. *God's Caliph: Religious authority in the first centuries of Islam*. Cambridge: Cambridge University Press, 1986.
de la Granja, F. "Fiestas cristianas en al-Andalus (Materiales para su estudio). I: *al-Durr al-munaẓẓam* de al-ʿAzafī." *al-Andalus*, 34 (1969), 1–53.
——. "Fiestas cristianas en al-Andalus (Materiales para su estudio). II: Textos de Ṭurṭūšī, el cadí ʿIyāḍ y Wanšarīšī." *al-Andalus*, 35 (1970), 119–42.
Dictionary of the Middle Ages. 13 vols, New York: Charles Scribner's Sons, 1982–89.
Dols, Michael W. *The Black Death in the Middle East*. Princeton: Princeton University Press, 1977.
——. *Majnūn: The Madman in the Medieval Islamic World*. Oxford: Oxford University Press, 1992.
Dozy, R.P.A. *Supplément aux dictionnaires arabes*. 2 vols, Leiden: E.J. Brill, 1881.
Dufourcq, Charles-Emmanuel. *L'Espagne Catalane et le Maghrib aux XIIIe et XIVe siècles*. Paris: Presses Universitaires de France, 1966.
EI[1], s.v. Zinā.
EI[2], s.v.v. ʿAbd, Abū Madyan, Fas<u>kh</u>, Ḥadd, Ibn Marzūḳ, Ibn Ṣāḥib al-Ṣalāt, Idrīs I, Iḳrār, al-Ḳābisī, Ḳa<u>dh</u>f, Ḳatl, Māʾ, Maʿāfir, Ma<u>dj</u><u>dh</u>ūb, Malāmatīya, Mālik b. Anas, Mālikiyya, Marīnids, Maṣmūda, Mawlid, al-Muwaḥḥidūn, Naḳīb al-A<u>sh</u>rāf, Naṣīḥat al-Mulūk, Naṣrids, Nikāḥ, al-<u>Sh</u>ādhilī, <u>Sh</u>ādhiliyya, <u>Sh</u>āhid, <u>Sh</u>arīf, al-<u>Sh</u>arīf al-Tilimsānī, <u>Sh</u>ubha, Sulṭān, al-Tu<u>dj</u>ībī, Umm al-walad, Waḳf.
EI[2], supplement, s.v. Fuḳahāʾ al-Madīna al-Sabʿa.
Ellickson, Robert C. *Order without Law: How Neighbors Settle Disputes*. Cambridge, MA: Harvard University Press, 1991.
Fagnan, E. (Edmond). *Additions aux dictionnaires arabes*. Alger: Bastide-Jourdan, 1923.
Fernández Feliz, Ana. "Biografías de al faquíes: la generación de al-ʿUtbī." In *Estudios onomástico-biográficos de al-Andalus*, VIII (Madrid: Consejo Superior de Investigaciones Científicas, 1996), 141–75.
Fierro, Maribel. *La heterodoxia en al-Andalus durante el periodo omeya*. Madrid: Instituto Hispano-Árabe de Cultura, 1987.
——. "Accusations of '*Zandaqa*' in al-Andalus." *Quaderni di Studi Arabi*, 5–6 (1987–88), 251–8.
——. "Andalusian 'Fatāwā' on Blasphemy." *Annales Islamologiques*, 25 (1990), 103–17.

——. "El processo contra Ibn Ḥātim al-Ṭulayṭulī (afios 457/1064 – 464/1072)." *Estudios onomástico-biográficos de al-Andalus (Homenaje a José M.ª Fórneas)*, VI (Madrid, 1994), 187–215.

——. "The Legal Policies of the Almohad Caliphs and Ibn Rushd's *Bidāyat al-Mujtahid*." *Journal of Islamic Studies*, 10:3 (1999), 226–48.

Fish, Stanley. *Doing What Comes Naturally: Change, Rhetoric, and the Practice of Theory in Literary and Legal Studies*. Durham: Duke University Press, 1989.

García Gómez, E. "Sobre la diferencia en el castigo de plebeyos y nobles." *al-Andalus*, 36:1 (1971), 71–80.

García-Arenal, Mercedes. "La Conjonction du soufisme et du sharifisme au Maroc: le mahdi comme sauveur." *Revue d'études du monde méditerranéen*, 55–6 (1990), 233–56.

——. "Mahdī, murābiṭ, sharīf: l'avènement de la dynastie saʿdienne." *Studia Islamica*, 70 (1990), 77–114.

Geertz, Clifford. *Local Knowledge: Further Essays in Interpretive Anthropology*. New York: Basic Books, 1983.

Geertz, Clifford, Geertz, Hildred and Rosen, Lawrence. *Meaning and Order in Moroccan Society: Three essays in cultural analysis*. Cambridge: Cambridge University Press, 1979.

Gerber, Haim. *Islamic Law and Culture, 1600–1840*. Leiden: E.J. Brill, 1999.

Getzler, Joshua. "Rules Writ in Water: A Study in Industrialization of the Law." Paper presented to the Law and History forum of the Faculty of Law, Tel Aviv University, 23 December 1998.

Gibb, H.A.R. "Constitutional Organization." In *Law in the Middle East*. Ed. by Majid Khadduri and Herbert Liebesney. Washington, DC: Middle East Institute, 1955, 3–27.

Glick, Thomas F. *Irrigation and Society in Medieval Valencia*. Cambridge: Harvard University Press, 1970.

——. *From Muslim Fortress to Christian Castle: Social and cultural change in medieval Spain*. Manchester and New York: Manchester University Press, 1995.

Gluckman, Max. *The Judicial Process Among the Barotse of Northern Rhodesia*. Manchester: Manchester University Press, 1955.

Goldziher, Ignaz. "Das Prinzip des *Istiṣḥāb* in der Muhammedanischen Gesetzwissenschaft." *Vienna Oriental Journal*, 1 (1887), 228–36.

Graham, William A. "Traditionalism in Islam: An Essay in Interpretation." *Journal of Interdisciplinary History*, 23 (1993), 495–522.

Gribetz, Arthur. *Strange Bedfellows:* mutʿat al-nisāʾ *and* mutʿat al-ḥājj*: a study based on Sunnī and Shīʿī sources of* tafsīr, aḥādīth, *and* fiqh. Berlin: K. Schwarz, 1994.

Guillet, David. "Rethinking Legal Pluralism: Local Law and State Law in the Evolution of Water Property Rights in Northwestern Spain." *Comparative Studies in Society and History* (1998), 42–65.

Habermas, Jürgen. *The Structural Transformation of the Public Sphere*. Cambridge, MA.: MIT Press, 1989.

Hallaq, Wael B. "Was the Gate of *Ijtihād* Closed?" *International Journal of Middle East Studies*, 16 (1984), 3–41.

——. "Notes on the Term *qarīna* in Islamic Legal Discourse." *Journal of the American Oriental Society*, 108:3 (1988), 475–80.

——. "On Inductive Corroboration, Probability, and Certainty in Sunnī Legal Thought." In *Islamic Law and Jurisprudence: Studies in Honor of Farhat J. Ziadeh*. Ed. by Nicholas Heer. Seattle: University of Washington Press, 1990, 3–32.

——. "Ibn Taymiyya on the Existence of God." *Acta Orientalia* (1991): 49–69.

——. "From *Fatwās* to *Furūʿ*: Growth and Change in Islamic Substantive Law." *Islamic Law and Society*, 1:1 (1995), 29–65.

——. *A History of Islamic Legal Theories: An introduction to Sunnī* uṣūl al-Fiqh. Cambridge: Cambridge University Press, 1997.

——. "The Qāḍī's Dīwān (*sijill*) before the Ottomans." *Bulletin of the School of Oriental and African Studies*, 61:3 (1998), 415–36.

Hammoudi, Abdellah. "Substance and Relation: Water Rights and Water Distribution in the Ḍrā Valley." In *Property, Social Structure, and Law in the Modern Middle East*. Ed. by Ann Elizabeth Mayer. Albany: State University of New York Press, 1985, 27–57.

Hart, David. "Comparative Land Tenure and Division of Irrigation Water in Two Moroccan Berber Societies: The Aith Waryaghar of the Rif and the Ait ʿAtta of the Saghru and South-Central Atlas." *Journal of North African Studies*, vol. 4:2 (1999), 172–218.

Heinrichs, Wolfhart. "*Lafẓ/maʿnā* in rhetorics." In *Arabische Dichtung und griechische Poetik*. Wiesbaden: F. Steiner, 1969, 62–82.

Hennigan, Peter Charles. "The Birth of a Legal Institution: The Formation of the Waqf in Third Century AH Ḥanafī Legal Discourse." PhD. dissertation, Cornell University, 1999.

Herzenni, Abdellah. "Derechos de agua de riego en Marruecos. Ley musulmana, normas consuetudinarias y legislacion moderna." In *El agua. Mitos, ritos y realidades*. Ed. by Jose A. Gonzalez Alcantud and Antonio Malpica Cuello. Barcelona: Anthropos, 1995, 401–40.

Hinz, Walther. *Islamische masse und Gewichte: Umgerechnet ins metrische system*. Leiden: E.J. Brill, 1955.

Huici Miranda, Ambrosio. *Historia politica del imperio almohade*. 2 vols, Tetuan: Editora Marroquí, 1956–57.

Idris, Hady R. "Commerce maritime et *qirāḍ* en Berbérie orientale d'après un recueil de *fatwās* médiévales." *Journal of the Economic and Social History of the Orient*, 4 (1961), 225–39.

——. "Le mariage en occident musulman d'après un choix de *fatwās* médiévales extraites du *Miʿyār* d'al-Wanšarīsī." *Studia Islamica* 32 (1970), 157–67.

——. "Le mariage en occident musulman: analyse de *fatwās* médiévales extraites du "*Miʿyār*" d'al Wancharīchī." *Revue de l'Occident Musulman et de la Méditerranée*, 12 (1972), 45–62; 17 (1974), 71–105; and 25 (1978), 119–38.

——. "Les tributaires en Occident musulman médiéval d'après le 'Miyār' d'al Wanşarīsī." In *Mélanges d'Islamologie. Volume dédié à la mémoire de Armand Abel*. 3 vols, Leiden, 1974, vol. 1, 172–96.

Imber, Colin. "Why you should poison your husband: A note on liability in Ḥanafī law in the Ottoman period." *Islamic Law and Society*, 1:2 (1994), 206–16.

Interpreting Law and Literature: A Hermeneutic Reader. Ed. by Sanford Levinson and Steven Mailloux. Evanston: Northwestern University Press, 1988.

Islamic Legal Interpretation: Muftis and Their Fatwas. Ed. by by Muhammad Khalid Masud, Brinkley Messick and David S. Powers. Cambridge, MA: Harvard University Press, 1996.

Johansen, Baber. *Contingency in a Sacred Law: Legal and Ethical Norms in the Muslim Fiqh*. Leiden: E.J. Brill, 1999.

Kably, Mohamed. *Société, pouvoir et religion au Maroc à la fin du Moyen-Age*. Paris: Maisonneuve et Larose, 1986.

Kamali, Mohammad Hashim. *Principles of Islamic Jurisprudence*. Cambridge: Islamic Texts Society, 1991.

——. *Freedom of Expression in Islam*. Kuala Lumpur: Berita Publishing, 1994.

Kaptein, N.J.G. *Muhammad's Birthday Festival*. Leiden: E.J. Brill, 1993.

Karamustafa, Ahmet. *God's Unruly Friends: Dervish groups in the Islamic later middle period, 1200–1550*. Salt Lake City: University of Utah Press, 1994.

Katz, Jonathan G. *Dreams, Sufism and Sainthood: The Visionary Career of Muḥammad al-Zawâwî*. Leiden: E.J. Brill, 1996.

Kilito, Abdelfattah. "Speaking to Princes: Al-Yusi and Mawlay Ismaʿil." In *In the Shadow of the Sultan: Culture, Power, and Politics in Morocco*. Ed. by Rahma Bourqia and Susan Gilson Miller. Cambridge, MA: Harvard University Press.

Kirshner, Julius. "*Consilia* as Authority in Late Medieval Italy: The Case of Florence." In *Legal Consulting in the Civil Law Tradition*." Ed. by Mario Ascheri, Ingrid Baumgärtner, and Julius Kirshner. Berkeley: The Robbins Collection, 1999.

Klinck, Dennis R. *The Word of the Law*. Ottawa: Carleton University Press, 1992.

Kuehn, Thomas. *Law, Family, and Women: Toward a Legal Anthropology of Renaissance Italy*. Chicago: University of Chicago Press, 1991.

Lagardère, Vincent. "Abū l-Walīd b. Rušd qāḍī al-quḍāt de Cordoue." *Revue des Etudes Islamiques*, LIV (1986), 203–24.

——. "La haute judicature a l'époque almoravide en al-Andalus." *Al-Qanṭara* 7 (1986), 135–228.

——. "Droit des eaux et des installations hydrauliques au Maghreb et en Andalus au XIe et XIIe siècles dans le *Miʿyār* d'al-Wanšarīsī." *Les Cahiers de Tunisie*, 37–8 (1988–89), 83–122.

——. "Moulins d'occident musulman au Moyen Âge" (IXe au XVe siècles): al-Andalus." *Al-Qanṭara*, 12:1 (1991), 59–118.

——. "Agriculture et irrigation dans le district (*iqlīm*) de Vélez-Málaga. Droits des eaux et appareils hydrauliques." *Cahiers de Civilisation Médiévale*, 35:3 (1992), 213–25.

——. *Campagnes et paysans d'Al-Andalus (VIIIe-XVe s)*. Paris: Maisonneuve et Larose, 1993.

——. *Histoire et Société en Occident Musulman au Moyen Age: Analyse du Miʿyār d'al-Wanşarīsī*. Madrid: Consejo Superior de Investigaciones Científicas, 1995.

Lambton, A.K.S. "Islamic Mirrors for Princes." *Quaderno dell'Accademia Nazionale dei Lincei*, 160 (1971), 419–42.

Lane, Edward W. *Arabic-English Lexicon*. 8 parts, London: Williams and Norgate, 1863–93. Reprinted Cambridge, UK: The Islamic Texts Society, 1984.

Laoust, Henri. "Une *risāla* d'Ibn Taimīya sur le serment de répudiation." *Bulletin d'études orientales*, 7–8 (1937–38), 215–36.

Laroui, Abdallah. *The History of the Maghrib: An Interpretive Essay*. Tr. by Ralph Mannheim. Princeton: Princeton University Press, 1977.

Layish, Aharon. "The Mālikī Family *waqf* according to Wills and *Waqfiyyāt*." *Bulletin of the School of Oriental and African Studies*, 46:1 (1983), 1–32.

——. *Divorce in the Libyan family: a study based on the* sijills *of the* sharīʿa *courts of Ajdābiyya and Kufra*. New York: New York University Press, 1991.

Le Tourneau, Roger. *Fès avant le protectorat: étude économique et sociale d'une ville de l'occident musulman*. Casablanca: Société Marocaine de Librairie et d'Edition, 1949.

——. "Documents sur une contestation relative à la répartition de l'eau dans la medina de Fès." In *Mélanges William Marçais*. Paris: G.-P. Maisonneuve, 1950, 191–204.

——. *Fez in the Age of the Marinides*. Tr. by Besse Alberta Clement. Norman: University of Oklahoma Press, 1961.

Legal Hermeneutics. Ed. by Gregory Leyh. Berkeley: University of California Press, 1992.

Lévi-Provençal, E. *Les Historiens des Chorfa*. Paris: Larose, 1922.

——. *Fragments historiques sur les Berbères au Moyen-Age: Extraits inédits d'un receuil anonyme compilé en 712/1312 et intitulé Mafākhir al-Barbar*. Rabat, 1934.

Little, Donald. *A Catalogue of Islamic Documents from al-Ḥaram al-Šarīf in Jerusalem*. Beirut: Orient-Institut der Deutschen Morgenländischen Gesellschaft, 1984.

Lutfi, Huda. "A Study of Six Fourteenth-Century *Iqrār*s from al-Quds Relating to Muslim Women." *Journal of the Social and Economic History of the Orient*, 26 (1983), 246–94.

al-Maghrāwī, Muḥammad. "Khiṭṭat qaḍā' al-jamā'a bi-Marākish al-muwaḥḥidīya." Paper presented at the conference, "Marrakesh from its foundation to the end of the Almohad period," April 1988.

Mahdi, Muhsin. "*Lafẓ/ma'nā* in the debate between logic and grammar." In *Logic in Classical Islamic Culture*. Ed. by G.E. von Grunebaum. Wiesbaden: O. Harrassowitz, 1970, 51–83.

Maktari, A.M.A. *Water Rights and Irrigation Practices in Laḥj: A Study of the Application of Customary and Sharī'ah Law in South-West Arabia*. Cambridge: Cambridge University Press, 1971.

Mansour, Mansour H. *The Maliki School of Law: Spread and Domination in North and West Africa 8th to 14th Centuries CE*. San Franciso and London: Austin and Winfield, 1995.

Al-Manūnī, Muḥammad. *Waraqāt 'an al-ḥaḍāra al-Maghribiyya fī 'aṣr Banī Marīn*. Rabat: Kulliyyāt al-Ādāb wa'l-'Ulūm al-Insāniyya, 1979. Reprinted 1996.

Margoliouth, David. "The Relics of the Prophet Mohammed." *The Moslem World*, 27:1 (1937), 20–7.

Marín, Manuela. "*Šūrā* et *ahl al-Šūrā* dans al-Andalus." *Studia Islamica*, 62 (1985), 25–51.

——. *Mujeres en al-Ándalus*. Madrid: Consejo Superior de Investigaciones Científicas, 2000.

Marlow, Louise. *Hierarchy and Egalitarianism in Islamic Thought*. Cambridge: Cambridge University Press, 1997.

Masud, M. Khalid. "*Ādāb al-Muftī*: The Muslim Understanding of Values, Characteristics, and Role of a *Muftī*." In *Moral Conduct and Authority: The Place of Adab in South Asian Islam*. Ed. by Barbara Daly Metcalf. Berkeley: University of California Press, 1984.

Mazīn, Muḥammad. *Fās wa-bādiyatuhā: musāhama fī ta'rīkh al-maghrib al-sa'dī*. 2 vols, Rabat: Manshūrāt Kulliyāt al-'Ulūm al-Insāniyya, 1406/1986.

Mediano, Fernando R. *Familias de Fez (ss. xv–xvii)*. Madrid: Consejo Superior de Investigaciones Científicas, 1995.

Melchert, Christopher. "How Ḥanafism Came to Originate in Kufa and Traditionalism in Medina." *Islamic Law and Society*, 6:3 (1999), 318–47.

Messick, Brinkley. "Literacy and the Law: Documents and Document Specialists in Yemen." In *Law and Islam in the Middle East*. Ed. by Daisy Hilse Dwyer. New York: Bergin and Garvey Publishers, 1990, 61–76.

Moors, Annelies. "Gender, Relations and Inheritance: Person, Power and Property in Palestine." In *Gendering the Middle East: Emerging Perspectives*. Ed. by Deniz Kandiyoti. London and New York: I.B. Tauris, 1996, 69–84.

Motzki, Harald. "Child Marriage in Seventeenth-Century Palestine." In *Islamic Legal Interpretation: Muftis and Their Fatwas*. Ed. by Muhammad Khalid Masud, Brinkley Messick and David S. Powers. Cambridge, MA: Harvard University Press, 1996, 129–40.

Müller, Christian. *Gerichtspraxis im Stadtstaat Córdoba: Zum Recht der Gesellschaft in einer mālikitisch-islamischen Rechtstradition des 5./11. Jahrhunderts*. Leiden: E.J. Brill, 1999.

——. "Judging with God's Law on Earth: Judicial Powers of the *Qāḍī al-jamāʿa* of Cordoba in the Fifth/Eleventh Century." *Islamic Law and Society*, 7:2 (2000), 159–86.

——. "*ṣahāda* und *kitāb al-istirʿāʾ* in der Rechtspraxis: Zur Rolle von Zeugen und Notaren in Gerichtsprozessen des 5./11. Jahrhunderts." In *Tagungsband des XXVII. Deutschen Orientalistentag, Bonn (1998)*. Würzburg: Ergon-Verlag, 2001.

Mundy, Martha. "Irrigation and Society in a Yemeni Valley: On the life and death of a bountiful source." In *Yemen Sanaa: Peuples méditerranéens*, 46 (1989), 97–128.

Munson, Henry Jr. *Religion and Power in Morocco*. New Haven: Yale University Press, 1993.

Muranyi, Miklos. *ʿAbd Allāh b. Wahb (125/743–197/812). Leben und Werk. Al-Muwaṭṭaʾ. Kitāb al-muḥāraba*. Wiesbaden: Harrassowitz, 1992.

Norvelle, Michael. "Water Use and Ownership According to the Texts of Ḥanbalī Fiqh." Masters thesis, McGill University, 1980.

Ossendorf-Conrad, Beatrix. *Das "K. al-Wāḍiḥa" des ʿAbd al-Malik b. Ḥabīb: Edition und Kommentar zu ms. Qarawiyyīn 809/40 (Abwāb al-Ṭahāra)*. Beirut: Franz Steiner, 1994.

Powers, David S. *Studies in Qurʾān and Ḥadīth: The Formation of the Islamic Law of Inheritance*. Berkeley: University of California Press, 1986.

——. "Islamic Inheritance Law: A Socio-Historical Approach." In *Islamic Family Law and the State*. Ed. by Chibli Mallat and Jane Connors. London: Graham and Trotman, 1990, 11–29.

——. "A Court Case from Fourteenth-Century North Africa." *Journal of the American Oriental Society*, 110.2 (1990), 229–54.

——. "*Fatwā*s as Sources for Legal and Social History: A Dispute over Endowment Revenues from Fourteenth-Century Fez." *al-Qanṭara*, 11 (1990), 295–341.

——. "On Judicial Review in Islamic Law." *Law and Society Review*, 26:2 (1992), 315–41.

——. "The Mālikī Family Endowment: Legal Norms and Social Practice." *International Journal of Middle East Studies*, 25:3 (1993), 379–406.

——. "Parents and their Minor Children: Familial Politics in the Middle Maghrib in the Eighth/Fourteenth Century." *Continuity and Change*, 16:2 (2001), 177–200.

Rosen, Lawrence. *The Anthropology of Justice: Law as Culture in Islamic Society*. Cambridge: Cambridge University Press, 1989.

——. *The Justice of Islam*. Oxford: Oxford University Press, 2000.

Rosenthal, Franz. *Knowledge Triumphant*. Leiden: E.J. Brill, 1970.

Santillana, David. *Istituzioni di Diritto Musulmano Malichita con riguardo anche al sistema sciafiita*. 2 vols, Roma: Istituto per l'Oriente, 1925–38.

Schacht, Joseph. *The Origins of Muhammadan Jurisprudence*. Oxford: The Clarendon Press, 1950.

——. *An Introduction to Islamic Law*. Oxford: The Clarendon Press, 1964.

——. "Classicisme, traditionalisme et ankylose dans la loi religieuse de l'Islam." In *Classicisme et déclin culturel dans l'histoire de l'Islam*. Ed. by R. Brunschvig and G. von Grunebaum. Paris: Maisonneuve et Larose, 1977, 141–61.

Schneider, Irene. "Die Merkmale der idealtypischen *qāḍī*-Justiz-Kritische Anmerkungen zu Max Webers Kategorisierung der islamischen Rechtsprechung." *Der Islam*, 70 (1993), 145–59.

——. "Imprisonment in pre-classical and classical Islamic Law." *Islamic Law and Society*, 2 (1995), 157–73.

Scholz, Peter. *Malikitisches Verfahrensrecht: Eine Studie zu Inhalt und Methodik der Scharia mit rechtshistorischen und rechtsvergleichenden Anmerkungen am Beispiel des malikitischen Verfahrensrechts bis zum 12. Jahrhundert.* Frankfurt: Peter Lang, 1997.

Sebti, Abdelahad. "Au Maroc: Sharifisme Citadin, Charisme et Historiographie." *Annales ESC* (1986), 433–57.

Serrano, Delfina. "Legal practice in an Andalusī-Maghribī Source from the Twelfth Century CE: The *Madhāhib al-Ḥukkām fī nawāzil al-aḥkām*." *Islamic Law and Society*, 7:2 (2000), 187–234.

Sezgin, Fuat. *Geschichte des arabischen Schrifttums.* 9 vols, Leiden: E.J. Brill, 1967–.

Shatzmiller, Maya. "Les premiers Mérinides et le milieu religieuse de Fès: l'introduction des médrasas." *Studia Islamica*, 43 (1976), 109–19.

——. "Un texte relatif aux structures politiques mérinides: les cas du *khaṭīb* Abū 'l-Faḍl al-Mazdaghī (746/1345)." *Revue des Etudes Islamiques* (1977), 310–19.

——. "Women and Property Rights in al-Andalus and the Maghrib: Social Patterns and Legal Discourse." *Islamic Law and Society*, 2 (1995), 219–57.

——. *The Berbers and the Islamic State: The Marīnid Experience in Pre-Protectorate Morocco.* Princeton: Markus Wiener Publishers, 2000.

Smith, Jane Idleman and Yvonne Haddad. *The Islamic Understanding of Death and Resurrection.* Albany: State University of New York Press, 1981.

Snouck Hurgronje, C. "De la Nature du droit Musulman," in *Selected Works of C. Snouck Hurgronje*," ed. G.H. Bousquet and J. Schacht. Leiden: E.J. Brill, 1957, 256–63.

"Terminiello v. Chicago". *United States Reports*, 337 (1949), 1–37.

Toledano, Henry. *Judicial Practice and Family Law in Morocco: The Chapter on Marriage from Sijilmāsī's* al-ʿAmal al-Muṭlaq. Boulder, CO: Social Science Monographs, 1981.

Touati, Houari. "En relisant les *Nawâzil* Mazouna: Marabouts et chorfa au maghreb central au xve siècle." *Studia Islamica*, 69 (1989), 75–94.

——. "Prestige ancestral et système symbolique šarifien dans le Maghreb central du XVIIe siècle." *Arabica*, 39 (1992), 1–24.

——. *Entre Dieu et les hommes: Lettrés saints et sorciers au Maghreb (17e siècle).* Paris: L'école des hautes études en sciences sociales, 1994.

Trimingham, J. Spencer. *The Sufi Orders in Islam.* London: Oxford University Press, 1971.

Tucker, Judith E. *In the House of the Law: Gender and Islamic Law in Ottoman Syria and Palestine.* Berkeley: University of California Press, 1998.

Turner, Bryan S. *Weber and Islam: A critical study.* London: Routledge and Kegan Paul, 1974.

Tyan, Emile. *Histoire de l'organisation judiciaire en pays d'Islam.* 2nd rev. edn, Leiden: E.J. Brill, 1960.

——. "Judicial Organization." In *Law in the Middle East.* Ed. by Majid Khadduri and Herbert J. Liebesny. Washington DC: The Middle East Institute, 1955, 236–78.

Van Staëvel, Jean-Pierre. "Savoir voir et le faire savoir: des relations entre qāḍī/s et experts en construction, d'apres un auteur tunisois du VIIIeme siècle." Paper presented at the II Joseph Schacht Conference on Islamic Law, Granada, December 1997.

Varisco, Daniel M. "Water Sources and Traditional Irrigation in Yemen." *New Arabian Studies*, 3 (1996), 238–57.

——. "*Sayl* and *Ghayl*: The Ecology of Water Allocation in Yemen." *Human Ecology*, 11 (1983), 365–83.

Vidal Castro, Francisco. "Aḥmad al-Wanšarīsī (m. 914/1508). Principales Aspectos de su Vida." *al-Qanṭara*, XII (1991), 315–52.

——. "Las obras de Aḥmad al-Wanšarīsī (m. 914/1508). Inventario analítico." *Anaquel de Estudios Árabes*, III (1992), 73–112.

——. "El *Mi*ʿ*yār* de al-Wanšarīsī (m. 914/1508). I: Fuentes, manuscritos, ediciones, traducciones." *Miscelánea de Estudio Árabes y Hebráicos*, XLII-XLIII (1993–94), 317–61.

——. "El *Mi*ʿ*yār* de al-Wanšarīsī (m. 914/1508). II: Contenido." *Miscelánea de Estudio Árabes y Hebráicos*, 44 (1995), 213–46.

——. "El Agua en el Derecho Islámico: Introducción a sus orígenes, propriedad y uso." In *El Agua en la Agricultura de al-Andalus*. Granada: El legado Andalusi, 1995, 99–117.

Wakin, Jeanette. *The Function of Documents in Islamic Law*. Albany: State University of New York Press, 1972.

Weber, Max. *Wirtschaft und Gesellschaft*. 2nd edn, 1925. Tr. by Edward Shils as *Max Weber on Law in Economy and Society*. Cambridge MA: Harvard University Press, 1959–69.

Weiss, Bernard. "Language and Law: The Linguistic Premises of Islamic Legal Science." In *In Quest of Islamic Humanism: Arabic and Islamic Studies in Memory of Mohamed al-Nowaihi*. Ed. by Arnold Green. Cairo: American University Press, 1984, 15–21.

——. "Exotericism and Objectivity in Islamic Jurisprudence." In *Islamic Law and Jurisprudence: Studies in Honor of Farhat J. Ziadeh*. Ed. by Nicholas Heer. Seattle and London: University of Washington Press, 1990, 53–72.

——. *The Search for God's Law: Islamic Jurisprudence in the Writings of Sayf al-Dīn al-Āmidī*. Salt Lake City: University of Utah Press, 1992.

Wensinck, A. J. *Concordance et indices de la tradition musulmane*. 8 vols, Leiden: E.J. Brill, 1936–88.

Wheeler, Brannon. "From Dar al-Hijra to Dar al-Islam: The Islamic Utopia." In *The Concept of Territory in Islamic Law and Thought*. Ed. by Hiroyuki Yanagihashi. London: Kegan Paul International, 2000, 3–36.

White, James Boyd. *Justice as Translation: An Essay in Cultural and Legal Criticism*. Chicago: University of Chicago Press, 1990.

Wiederhold, Lutz. "Legal Doctrines in Conflict: The Relevance of *Madhhab* Boundaries to Legal Reasoning in the Light of an Unpublished Treatise on *Taqlīd* and *Ijtihād*." *Islamic Law and Society*, 3:2 (1996), 234–304.

——. "Blasphemy against the Prophet Muḥammad and his Companions (*sabb al-rasūl, sabb al-saḥābah*): The Introduction of the Topic into the Shāfiʿī Legal Literature and its Relevance for Legal Practice under Mamluk Rule." *Journal of Semitic Studies*, 42:1 (1997), 39–70.

Wolf, Eric. *Europe and the People without History*. Berkeley: University of California Press, 1982.

Wright, W. *A Grammar of the Arabic Language*. 2 vols, 3rd edn, Cambridge: Cambridge University Press, 1955.

Yanagihashi, Hiroyuki. "The Judicial Functions of the *Sulṭān* in Civil Cases according to the Mālikīs up to the Sixth/Twelfth Century." *Islamic Law and Society*, 3 (1996), 41–74.

——. "Doctrinal Development of *Maraḍ al-Mawt* in the Formative Period of Islamic Law." *Islamic Law and Society*, 5:3 (1998), 326–58.

Ziadeh, Farhat J. "Compelling Defendant's Appearance at Court in Islamic Law." *Islamic Law and Society*, 3:3 (1996), 305–15.

Zomeño, Amalia. "Transferencias matrimoniales en el Occidente islamico medieval: las joyas como regalo de boda." *Revista de Dialectologia y Tradiciones Populaires*, LI (1996), 79–95.

——. "Donaciones matrimoniales y transmissión de propriedades inmuebles: estudio del contenido de la *siyāqa* y la *niḥla* en al-Andalus." In *Urbanisme musulman*, ed. P. Cressier, M. Fierro et J.-P Van Staëvel. Madrid: Consejo Superior de Investigaciones científicas, 2000, 75–99.

——. *Dote y matrimonio en al-Andalus y el norte de África: Estudio sobre la jurisprudencia islámica medieval*. Madrid: Consejo Superior de Investigaciones científicas, 2000.

Index of Qur'ānic Verses

Index of Prophetic Ḥadith

Index of Names

Subject index

Acknowledgement (*iqrār*), 18, 32–3, 84, 92, 209–10, 215, 220, 222–8
by a "stranger", 222–3, 225, 227
by *walī*, on behalf of minor wards, 222–4
of debt, 208, 220, 224–8
of fictitious transaction, 210
of gift, 209
of paternity, 31–3, 43 n. 80
of sale, 212, 215
of *zinā*, 62, 76, 84, 92
ʿĀda (local custom), 107–8, 119, 129, 134, 156
ʿAdāla. *See* Witnesses
ʿĀdil. *See* Witnesses
Advice for rulers (*naṣīḥat al-mulūk*), 83
Agency, appointment of, 30, 158
See also Wakīl
Analogy. See *Qiyās*
Arbitration. *See Sulḥ*
ʿĀriyya (loan). *See* Water law
Aṣl (initial claim), 66, 75–7, 220
See also Ghālib

Bāʾin. *See* Divorce
Barāʾa (quittance), 218–20
issued in place of a fatwā, 40, 46, 48, 50
Baraka (saintly power), 174, 183, 201
Berbers, 96–7, 101–3, 117, 164, 180 n. 40, 201
and meso-scale irrigation systems, 117
and *sharīf*s, 201
customary law of, 103, 118
compared to Islamic law, 117–18
in Wadi Zgane, 96–7
Black Death, 10, 141–3, 147, 164, 170
impact of, 141–2, 170
mortality rates, 141
origin and spread of, 141
recurrences, 142, 151–2, 164, 177

Canals. *See* Irrigation systems
Castle/Village complex. *See* Irrigation systems
Commanding good and forbidding evil, 84
Concubine, 7–8, 27–8, 44, 49, 73 n. 83, 74 n. 83,
See also Slaves, female; *Umm al-walad*
Curses, 169, 176, 191–5, 197–8, 231. *See also* Legal doctrine, Mālikī, on *sabb al-nabī*
Custom, linguistic, 174, 195
Custom, local. *See ʿĀda*

Denial
of paternity, 28, 31–3, 43, 45, 50
of fornication, 75–6, 81, 84
of rumor, 40
Dhurriyya (descendants), 182, 184–5, 193
in connection with *sharaf*, 185, 193
See also Language, legal significance of; *Sharīf*
Dīnārs, ʿUthmānī, 217–20
Dispute resolution
Alternative means of, 95, 137
Diversion dams. *See* Irrigation systems; Mills
Divorce
Bāʾin (irrevocable), 56–7, 61–2, 69–70
Faskh (annulment), 58, 61, 63, 66, 69–70
ʿIdda (waiting period) after, 56–8
Khulʿ, 56–8, 63, 66, 69–71
treated as annulment, 66
Rajʿī (revocable), 56–8, 61
Taḥlīl (a device to remove an impediment to marriage), 56–7, 70, 72, 91, 93 n. 153
Tamlīk (delegated), 56–8
Dīwān. *See* Qāḍī court
Document specialist (*muwaththiq*), 147–9, 153, 158
Documents, 19, 35–6, 47, 55, 76, 88, 98, 107, 119, 121–2, 128, 130, 133, 160, 176, 187–8, 218, 220, 225, 229

Lightning Source UK Ltd.
Milton Keynes UK
30 October 2010

162126UK00002B/136/P

9 780521 120593